Ethnic Cookbooks and Food Marketplace

Ethnic Cookbooks and Food Marketplace

A Complete Bibliographic Guide & Directory
to Armenian, Iranian, Afghan, Israeli
Middle Eastern, North African and Greek
Foods
in the U.S.A. & Canada

Third Edition

Hamo B. Vassilian, Editor

1992

Ethnic Cookbooks and Food Marketplace
Published by
Armenian Reference Books Co.
P.O. Box 231
Glendale, California 91209
(818) 504-2550

Third Edition

Copyright © 1992 by Hamo B. Vassilian

All rights reserved. No part of this publication may be reproduced or transmitted in any form or by any means, electronic or mechanical, including photocopy, recording, xerography, or any information storage and retrieval system, without permission in writing from the publisher.

No payment is either solicited or accepted for the inclusion of entries in this publication. Every possible precaution has been made to avoid errors. However, the publisher does not assume and hereby disclaims any liability to any party for any loss or damage caused by errors or omissions in the Ethnic Cookbook and Food Marketplace, whether such errors or omissions result from negligence, accident, or any cause.

Library of Congress Cataloging-in-Publication Data

Vassilian, Hamo B.
  Ethnic cookbooks and food marketplace: a complete bibliographic guide & directory to Armenian, Iranian, Afghan, Israeli, Middle Eastern, North African, and Greek foods in the U.S.A. & Canada / Hamo B. Vassilian--3rd ed.

   144 p. cm.
   Includes bibliographical references and index.
   ISBN: 0-931539-06-4 : $ 29.95
   1. Cookery, Middle Eastern--Bibliography. 2. Grocery trade--United States--Directories.
 3. Grocery trade--Canada--Directories. I. Title: Ethnic cookbooks and food marketplace.

TX725.M628V37 1992
 380.1'456415956'025--dc20   92-16356
                                                                          CIP

ISBN: 0-931539-06-4

Manufactured in the United States of America

This book is dedicated with deep affection
to my parents and sisters

ARMENIAN REFERENCE BOOKS CO.
P.O. Box 231 Glendale, California 91209 (818) 504-2550

Table of Contents

Introduction 9

Bibliographies 11

Food Marketplace by Category 64

Food Marketplace by Business Name 114

Food Marketplace (Geographical Index) 129

Book Order Form 144

Introduction

With great pride we are introducing our third edition of the Ethnic Cookbooks and Food Marketplace. In this edition you will find more bibliographies, more names and addresses, and more pictures in bibliography section. Plus we updated addresses and phone numbers too.

This reference book covers all Armenian, Persian, Middle Eastern, Israeli, Afghan and Greek food marketplace in the U.S. & Canada, and cookbook bibliographies in the English language.

Ethnic Cookbooks and Food Marketplace is designed to help you find the most current and accurate information on ethnic food industry. This book is also prepared to serve as a useful reference book for those who are interested in finding recipe sources related to these particular ethnic groups.

Preparing such a book is very expensive, time consuming, and requires much effort and patience. However, I am very happy to have conducted this research, and I am certain that it is a very useful reference book for ethnic food lovers, as well as reference librarians and cookbook collectors.

This guide has been arranged in four parts. Each part is broken down into several sections with more specific categories. The first part includes information about 275 published cookbooks in the English language related to these ethnic groups. It is arranged by author, title and subject. Part two is a guide to food marketplace in the U.S. & Canada with categories, address, name and phone number of more than 2,300 places. In part three, food marketplace is arranged by business name, city, state and phone numbers. Finally, in part four, you will find geographical index of ethnic food marketplace arranged by name of state and business name.

For those who are interested in complete mailing list of ethnic food marketplace, or some of those cookbooks may contact our office for more information. Also if you are cookbook publisher I am very interested in receiving an examination copy of your book to consider for inclusion in our forthcoming cookbook catalog. Your publication's bibliographic information will be included in next edition of this book at no charge.

I wish to thank all of those who helped to improve this publication, without which this guide would have never been completed. Also, special thanks to Dalia Carmel, wellknown cookbook collector and freelance source and Mary Seybold, Director of Cultural Program at Middle East Institute in Washington D.C., whose assistance made this book a challenge but a possible experience for me.

To make the Ethnic Cookbooks and Food Marketplace a much more valuable source of information, your assistance will be greatly appreciated. Since this publication is planned to be revised periodically, I encourage those businesses that are not included in this edition, to contact us for inclusion of their information in the next edition. Please send your correspondence to Armenian Reference Books Co., P. O. Box 231, Glendale, California 91209. If you wish to contact me personally, you may reach me at (818) 504-2550.

Hamo B. Vassilian, Editor
May 1992

ARMENIAN REFERENCE BOOKS CO.
P.O. Box 231 Glendale, California 91209 (818) 504-2550

Bibliographies
(Author, Title and Subject Index)

101 ARABIAN DELIGHTS: A BOOK OF ARABIC COOKERY

1. Philippou, Margaret Joy. 101 Arabian delights: a book of Arabic Cookery. Brighton: Clifton Books; 1969. 99 p.; ISBN: 90125505X.

101 GREEK WAYS

2. 101 Greek Ways. Denver, CO: Greek Orthodox Church of Denver; 1972.

101 PARSI RECIPES

3. Mehta, Jeroo. 101 Parsi Recipes. Bombay, India: Vakils, Feffer & Simon; c1973. 146 p.

ABDENNOUR, SAMIA

4. Abdennour, Samia. Egyptian cooking: a practical guide. Cairo, Egypt: American University in Cairo Press; c1964. 160 p.; ISBN: 977424026X.

ACCENT ON GREEK COOKING

5. Accent on Greek Cooking. Olathe, Kanzas: Cookbook Publishers; c1987. A-D, 178 p., viii p.

ADVENTURES IN ARMENIAN COOKING

6. Adventures in Armenian Cooking. Armenian Church. Indian Orchard, MA: St. Gregory's Armenian Apostolic Church; 1973. 150 p.

ADVENTURES IN GREEK COOKERY

7. Kopulos, Stella. Adventures in Greek Cookery. Dorothy P. Jones, Co-author. Rev. Edition ed. James Stewart, Illustrator. New York, NY: The World Publishing Co.; 1972. xiii, 337 p.; ISBN: 0529045516.

AFGHAN COOKERY

8. Amini, Rahima. A Pinch of salt. Classic Afghan Cookery. London, England: Quartet; 1991. 275 p.; ISBN: 0704327694.

9. Husain, S.A. Muslim Cooking of Pakistan. Lahore, Pakestan: Sh. Muhammad Ashraf; c1974.

10. McKellar, Doris, Compiler. Afghan Cookery. an Afghan recipe book: 2nd ed. Kabul, Afghanistan: Afghan Book Publisher; 1971 90 p.

11. Parenti, Cathy. A Taste of Afghanistan: The Cuisine of the Crossroads of the World. Phoenix, AZ: Author; c1987. 84 p.

12. Saberi, Helen. Noshe Djan: Afghan Food and Cookery. with the help of Najiba Zaka and Shaima Breshna and drawings by Abdullah Breshna. London, England: Prospect Books; c1986. 160 p.; ISBN: 0-907325-32-7.

13. Weidenweber, Sigrid, Compiler. Best of Afghan Cookery, an Afghan Recipe Book. Portland, OR: American Aid for Afghans; c1980.

AGIA, EMELIE

14. Agia, Emelie, Editor. Cookin' good with Sitto. Compiled by Our Lady of Perpetual Help Society of St. Ann's Melkite Catholic Church. 2nd ed. West Paterson, NJ: St. Ann's Melkite Catholic Church; 1982 ix, 95 p.

AH! COOKING THE MIDDLE EASTERN WAY

15. Farah, Nadia, 1940-. Ah! Cooking the Middle Eastern Way. Ottawa, Canada: Deneau Publishers; 1982? 118 p.; ISBN: 0-88879-061-9.

ALCHEMIST'S COOKBOOK: MOROCCAN SCIENTIFIC CUISINE.

16. Yacoubi, Ahmed. Alchemist's Cookbook: Moroccan Scientific Cuisine. Tucson, AZ: Omen Press; 1972. X, 142.

ALEXANDRA'S LEBANESE COOKING

17. Mansour, Valerie, 1957-. Alexandra's Lebanese Cooking. authentic recipes from a Nova Scotia home: Halifax, Nova Scotia, Canada: V. Mansour; 1983. 86 p.; ISBN: 0969159803.

ALPHA AND OMEGA OF GREEK COOKING

18. Krieg, Saul. The Alpha and Omega of Greek Cooking. New York, NY: Macmillan; 1973. xii, 266 p.

12-Bibliographies

Ethnic Cookbooks

AMARI, SUAD

19. Amari, Suad. Cooking the Lebanese way. Robert L. & Diane Wolfe, Photographers. Minneapolis: Lerner Publications Co.; 1986. 47 p.; ISBN: 082250913X.

AMERICAN BELLY DANCER'S SECRETS OF A BEAUTIFUL BODY

20. Lebwa, , 1938-. An American belly dancer's secrets of a beautiful body. West Nyack, NY: Parker Publishing Co.; 1981.; c1979. 202 p.; ISBN: 01302239526.

AMINI, RAHIMA

21. Amini, Rahima. A Pinch of salt. Classic Afghan Cookery. London, England: Quartet; 1991. 275 p.; ISBN: 0704327694.

ANATOLIA COLLEGE COOKBOOK

22. Anatolia College Cookbook. Boston, MA: Anatolia College Graduates 95 p.

ANCIENT HERITAGE LIVES ON

23. An Ancient heritage lives on. Las Vegas, NV: St. John Greek Orthodox Church; 1984 ? 104 p.

AND THE GREEKS

24. MacDougall, Allan Ross, 1893-. And the Greeks. a book of Hellenic recipes and culinary lore,: New York, NY: Near East Foundation; c1942. 109 p.

ANDREWS, JASMINE PANOS

25. Andrews, Jasmine Panos. My Greek heritage cookbook. Paul A. Andrews, Photographer; Thalia L. Bredakis, Illustrator. Coolierville, TN: Fundcraft Pub.; c1989. A-I, 162, A-D p.

ANTHONY, DAWN

26. Anthony, Dawn. Lebanese Cookbook. Elaine & Selwa Anthoney, Co-authors. Sydney, Australia; New York, NY: Lansdowne Press; 1978 109 p.; ISBN: 0701817534.

ANTREASSIAN, ALICE, 1922-

27. Antreassian, Alice, 1922-. Armenian Cooking Today. Adrina Zanazanian, Illustrator. New York, NY: St. Vartan Press; c1975. 189, xxviii p.

28. Antreassian, Alice, 1922-. Armenian Cooking Today. Fifth ed. New York, NY: St. Vartan Press; 1989.; c1975. 189, XXIX p.; ISBN: 0-934728-20-8.

29. Antreassian, Alice, 1922-. Classic Armenian Recipes: Cooking Without Meat. Mariam Jebejian, Co-author. 2nd ed. Adrina Zanazanian, Illustrator. New York, NY: Ashod Press; 1983.; c1981. 308, xxxip.; ISBN: 0-935102-05-1.

30. Antreassian, Alice, 1922-. The Forty Days of Lent: Selected Armenian Recipes. New York, NY: Ashod Press; c1985. 130 p.; ISBN: 0-935102-16-7.

APHRODITE'S COOKBOOK

31. Pourounas, Andreas. Aphrodite's Cookbook. Grosvenor, Helene, Co-author.: Spearman; 1977. 174 p.

APHRODITE'S KITCHEN: HOMESTYLE GREEK COOKING

32. Polemis, Aphrodite. Aphrodite's Kitchen: homestyle Greek cooking. New York, NY: Golden Press; c1978. 96 p.; ISBN: 0-307-49426-8.

ARAB WORLD COOKBOOK

33. Shasheer, Jameela. Arab World Cookbook. Dubai: International Bookshop; 1973.

ARAB WORLD COOKBOOK : THE BOOK OF ONE THOUSAND AND ONE DELIGHTS

34. Salah, Nahda S. Arab World Cookbook : the book of one thousand and one delights. Basem S. Salah, Photographer. Dhahran, Saudi Arabia: Said Salah International Publications Agencies; 1977.; c1973. 345 p.

ARABIAN CUISINE

35. Weiss-Armush, Anne Marie. Arabian Cuisine. John Berry, Illus. Beirut, Lebanon; 1984

ARMENIAN REFERENCE BOOKS CO.
P.O. Box 231 Glendale, California 91209 (818) 504-2550

Ethnic Cookbooks

Bibliographies-13

ARMENIAN AMERICAN CUISINE

36. Armenian American Cuisine. Evanston, IL: St. James Armenian Church 124 p.
Note: Title on cover: a Taste of Armenia.

ARMENIAN AND ORIENTAL COOKING

37. Doniguian, Mireille H. Armenian and Oriental Cooking. Beirut, Lebanon: G. Doniguian & Sons; 1987? 233 p.

ARMENIAN AND SELECTED FAVORITE RECIPES

38. Armenian and selected favorite recipes. 3rd ed. Fresno, CA: Holy Trinity Armenian Church; c1971. 156 p.
Note: Introduction by Kricor Naccachian.

ARMENIAN COOKBOOK

39. Hogrogian, Rachel. The Armenian Cookbook. Nonny Hogrogian, Illustrator. 1st ed. New York, NY: Atheneum; 1971. xxi, 152 p.

ARMENIAN COOKERY

40. Adventures in Armenian Cooking. Armenian Church. Indian Orchard, MA: St. Gregory's Armenian Apostolic Church; 1973. 150 p.

41. Antreassian, Alice, 1922-. Armenian Cooking Today. Adrina Zanazanian, Illustrator. New York, NY: St. Vartan Press; c1975. 189, xxviii p.

42. Antreassian, Alice, 1922-. Armenian Cooking Today. Fifth ed. New York, NY: St. Vartan Press; 1989.; c1975. 189, XXIX p.; ISBN: 0-934728-20-8.

43. Antreassian, Alice, 1922-. Classic Armenian Recipes: Cooking Without Meat. Mariam Jebejian, Co-author. 2nd ed. Adrina Zanazanian, Illustrator. New York, NY: Ashod Press; 1983.; c1981. 308, xxxip.; ISBN: 0-935102-05-1.

44. Antreassian, Alice, 1922-. The Forty Days of Lent: Selected Armenian Recipes. New York, NY: Ashod Press; c1985. 130 p.; ISBN: 0-935102-16-7.

45. Armenian American Cuisine. Evanston, IL: St. James Armenian Church 124 p.
Note: Title on cover: a Taste of Armenia.

46. Armenian and selected favorite recipes. 3rd ed. Fresno, CA: Holy Trinity Armenian Church; c1971. 156 p.
Note: Introduction by Kricor Naccachian.

14-Bibliographies   Ethnic Cookbooks

47. Armenian Cooking. Kansas, KS: Armenian Society of Greater Kansas City; 1990. ? 90 p.

48. Azarian, Tomas. Recipes from Armenia. Plainfield, VA: Farmhouse Press; c1985. 65 p.

49. Baboian, Rose. The Art of Armenian Cooking. 1st ed. Garden City, NY: Doubleday; 1971; c1971 xviii, 264 p.

50. Baboian, Rose. Baboian's Armenian American Cookbook. Boston ?: Baboian; 1964; c1964.

51. Bedrosian, Sirvart, Editor. Armenian Heritage Recipes. Montvale, NJ: Heritage Kitchens; 1966; c1966.

52. Bezjian, Alice. The Complete Armenian Cookbook Including Favorite International Recipes. Fair Lawn, NJ: Rosekeer Press; c1983. 278 p.; ISBN: 0-915033-00-03.

53. A Book of Favorite Recipes. compiled by Daughters of Vartan: : Daughters of Vartan, Los Angeles; 1981; c1968. 196 p.

54. A Book of Favorite Recipes. Watertown, MA: St. James Armenian Apostolic Church; 1984. 178 p.

55. The California Courier Cookbook. Berkeley, CA: George Mason; c1968. 128 p.

56. Chirinian, Linda. Secrets of Cooking. Armenian/Lebanese/Persian: Rene Chirinian, Photographer. New Canaan, CT: Lionhart Inc./Publishers; c1987. 264 p.; ISBN: 0-9617033-0-X.

57. Creative Cooking. Kansas City, KS: St. Peter Armenian Church; c1973. 120 p.

58. Doniguian, Mireille H. Armenian and Oriental Cooking. Beirut, Lebanon: G. Doniguian & Sons; 1987? 233 p.

59. Favorite Armenian Recipes. 2nd ed. Racine, WI: St. Mesrob Armenian Church; 1988. 102 p.

ARMENIAN REFERENCE BOOKS CO.
P.O. Box 231 Glendale, California 91209 (818) 504-2550

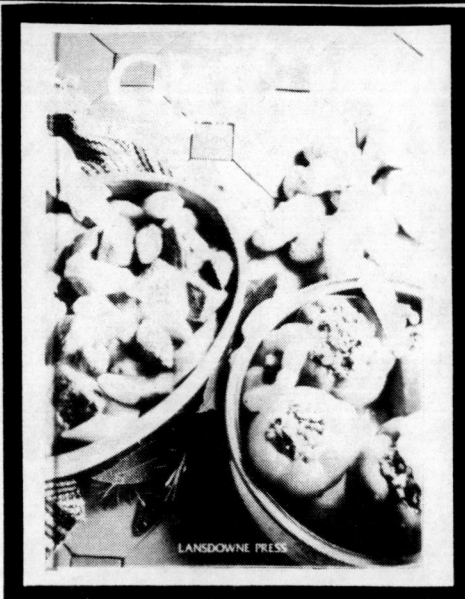

60. Favorite Recipes of Armenian Memorial Church. 2nd ed. Watertown, MA: Armenian Memorial Church; 1967.

61. Garabedian, Z. M. Fifty Famous Armenian Recipes. Michael Nacashian, Introduction. Fresno, CA: Z. M. Enterprises; 1979.

62. Getsoian, Anne. Favorite Armenian and Syrian recipes of Anne Getsoian. San Diego, CA: Getsoian; c1979. 89 p.

63. Hogrogian, Rachel. The Armenian Cookbook. Nonny Hogrogian, Illustrator. 1st ed. New York, NY: Atheneum; 1971. xxi, 152 p.

64. Keoleian, Ardashes H. The Oriental Cookbook. Wholesome, Dainty and Economical Dishes of the Orient, Specially Adapted to American Tastes and Methods of Preparation.: New York, NY: Sully & Kleinteich; 1913. 346 p.
Note: Possibly the first Armenian Cookbook to be published in this country.

65. Mardikian, George. Dinner at Omar Khayyam's. Salt Lake City: Viking Press; 1969, 13th printing; c1944. 150 p.

66. Mcqueen-Williams, Morvyth, 1911-1976. A Diet for 100 healthy, happy years. Barbara Apisson, Co-author; Norman Ober, Editor. Englewood Cliffs, NJ: Prentice-Hall; c1977. vi, 220 p.; ISBN: 0-13-211185-3.

67. Merjanian-Piranian, Louise. The Pleasure of Cooking. Beirut, Lebanon: Donigian & Sons; 1974. 304 p.

68. The New Gourmet. Holy Trinity Armenian Apostolic Church of Greater Boston. Cambridge, MA: 1974 178 p.

69. Our Culinary Treasures. Compiled by Kirikian Armenian School of St. Thomas Armenian Church. Tenafly, New Jersey: St. Thomas Armenian Church; 1989. 203, viii p.

70. Paree Josh! Good Eating. A collection of favorite Armenian American Recipes: St. Mary Armenian Apostolic Church. Livingston, NJ: St. Mary Armenian Apostolic Church; 1984, third printing; c1968 253 p.

71. Poetry in Portions. An Armenian American Cookbook: Chevy Chase, MD: Soorp Khatch Armenian Apostolic Church; c1981. 349 p.

72. Tootelian, Elizabeth D. Please Pass the Pilaf: a Collection of Armenian Recipes. 1st ed. Richmond, VA; c1975. 98 p.

73. Torunian, Armen, Editor. Tasty Armenian Dishes. Pailig Hanenian & George Guzelimian, Illustrators. Montreal, Quebec Canada: The First Armenian Evangelical Church; 1979.; c1972. 131 p.

74. Treasured Armenian recipes. 1st ed. Detroit, MI: A.G.B.U., Detroit; 1989, 29th printing; c1944. 126 p.

75. Uvezian, Sonia. The Cuisine of Armenia. Dickran Palulian, Illustrator. New York, NY: Harper & Row; 1974; c1974. xiii, 412 p.; ISBN: 0-06-014472-06.

76. Uvezian, Sonia. The Cuisine of Armenia. Dickran Palulian, Illustrator. Harper Colophon Books ed. New York, NY: Harper & Row; c1985. xiii, 400 p.; ISBN: 0609912294.

77. Varjabedian, Ida P. Exotic, Light & Easy Cookbook of Middle Eastern Cuisine. Great Neck, NY: Todd & Honeywell, Inc.; c1985.; ISBN: 0-89962-410-3.

ARMENIAN COOKING

78. Armenian Cooking. Kansas, KS: Armenian Society of Greater Kansas City; 1990. ? 90 p.

ARMENIAN COOKING TODAY

79. Antreassian, Alice, 1922-. Armenian Cooking Today. Adrina Zanazanian, Illustrator. New York, NY: St. Vartan Press; c1975. 189, xxviii p.

80. Antreassian, Alice, 1922-. Armenian Cooking Today. Fifth ed. New York, NY: St. Vartan Press; 1989.; c1975. 189, XXIX p.; ISBN: 0-934728-20-8.

ARMENIAN HERITAGE RECIPES

81. Bedrosian, Sirvart, Editor. Armenian Heritage Recipes. Montvale, NJ: Heritage Kitchens; 1966; c1966.

ART OF ARMENIAN COOKING

82. Baboian, Rose. The Art of Armenian Cooking. 1st ed. Garden City, NY: Doubleday; 1971; c1971 xviii, 264 p.

ART OF FILO COOKBOOK: INTERNATIONAL ENTREES, APPETIZERS & DESSERTS WRAPPED IN FLAKY PASTRY.

83. Sousanis, Mart, 1943-. The Art of filo cookbook: International entrees, appetizers & desserts wrapped in flaky pastry.. Masayo Suzuki, Illustrator. Berkeley, CA: Aris Books; 1988, 3rd printing; c1983. 143 p.; ISBN: 0943186064.

16-Bibliographies — Ethnic Cookbooks

ART OF GREEK COOKERY, BASED ON THE GRECIAN GOURMET

84. Art of Greek Cookery, based on the Grecian Gourmet. Garden City, NY: St. Paul's Greek Orthodox Church; 1963 234 p.

ART OF GREEK COOKING

85. The Art of Greek Cooking. Elkins Park, PA: Evangelismos Greek Orthodox Community of Philadelphia; 1973.

ART OF ISRAELI COOKING; ORIGINAL ISRAELI RECIPES NEVER BEFORE PUBLISHED, AS WELL AS FAVORITE TRADITIONAL DISHES, ALL KOS

86. Nahoum, Aldo. The Art of Israeli Cooking; original Israeli recipes never before published, as well as favorite traditional dishes, all kosher. 1st ed. New York, NY: Holt, Rinehart and Winston; 1971.; c1970. 152 p.; ISBN: 0-03-085176-9.

ART OF PERSIAN COOKING

87. Hekmat, Forough-es-Saltaneh. The Art of Persian Cooking. Garden City, NY: Doubleday; 1961. 190 p.

ART OF SYRIAN COOKERY

88. Corey, Helen. The Art of Syrian cookery. A culinary trip to the land of Bible history: Syria and Lebanon: 1st ed. Garden City, NY: Doubleday; 1962. 186 p.

ASHKHAIN'S SAUDI COOKING OF TODAY

89. Skipwith, Ashkhain. Ashkhain's Saudi Cooking of Today. London, England: Stacey International; c1986. 160 p.; ISBN: 0905743-42-3.

AT THE TABLE OF ISRAEL: A UNIQUE COLLECTION OF THREE HUNDRED TRADITIONAL AND MODERN ISRAELI RECIPES.

90. Lesberg, Sandy. At the table of Israel: a unique collection of three hundred traditional and modern Israeli recipes. Indianapolis; New York: Bobbs-Merrill; Peebles Press.; c1973,.

ATHENIAN CUISINE: OVER 600 RECIPES

91. Terzi, Popi. Athenian cuisine: over 600 recipes. Joe Nadziejko, Drawer. Tarrytown, NY: Pilgrimage Pub.; 1987. xii, 183 p.; ISBN: 0935819037.

ATHENS A LA CARTE, THE BEST OF GREEK COOKING

92. Marketos, Olympia. Athens a la carte, the best of Greek cooking. Chicago, IL: Rand McNally; 1963. 119 p.

ATIYEH, WADEEHA

93. Atiyeh, Wadeeha. Scheherazade Cooks. John Alcorn, Illustrator. Great Neck, NY: Channel Press; c1960. 189 p.

AUTHENTIC GREEK RECIPES

94. Authentic Greek Recipes. Memphis, TN: Annunciation Greek Orthodox Community; 1963.

95. Authentic Greek Recipes. Tarpon Springs, FL: St. Nicholas Greek Orthodox Church; 1974.

AVADANIAN, ROSE

96. Avadanian, Rose. Kitchen Kapers Featuring Mideastern Cuisine. Leawood, KS: Circulation Service; 1991. 358, 38, p.

AZARIAN, TOMAS

97. Azarian, Tomas. Recipes from Armenia. Plainfield, VA: Farmhouse Press; c1985. 65 p.

Ethnic Cookbooks
Bibliographies-17

BABOIAN'S ARMENIAN AMERICAN COOKBOOK

98. Baboian, Rose. Baboian's Armenian American Cookbook. Boston ?: Baboian; 1964; c1964.

BABOIAN, ROSE

99. Baboian, Rose. The Art of Armenian Cooking. 1st ed. Garden City, NY: Doubleday; 1971; c1971 xviii, 264 p.

100. Baboian, Rose. Baboian's Armenian American Cookbook. Boston ?: Baboian; 1964; c1964.

BABYLONIAN CUISINE: CHALDEAN COOKBOOK FROM THE MIDDLE EAST

101. Najor, Julia, 1941-. Babylonian Cuisine: Chaldean cookbook from the Middle East. Nobil Kirma, Photographer. New York, NY: Vantage Press; 1981 xxiii, 213 p.; ISBN: 0533046289.

BACON, JOSEPHINE, 1942-

102. Bacon, Josephine, 1942-. Cooking the Israeli Way. Robert L.; Diane Wolfe, Photographers. Minneapolis, MN: Lerner Publications; 1986.
Note: Juvenile literature.

BANAI, MARGALIT, 1928-

103. Banai, Margalit, 1928-. What's Cooking in Israel. New York, NY: Crowell; 1972. 181 p.; ISBN: 0-690-87825-7.

BARBECUE COOKBOOK

104. der Haroutunian, Arto, 1940-1987. Barbecue Cookbook. London, England.

BARBECUE COOKERY

105. der Haroutunian, Arto, 1940-1987. Barbecue Cookbook. London, England.

BARRON, ROSEMARY

106. Barron, Rosemary. Flavors of Greece. New York, NY: W. Morrow; 1991; ISBN: 0688070876.

18-Bibliographies — Ethnic Cookbooks

BATMANGLIJ, NAJMIEH, 1947-

107. Batmanglij, Najmieh, 1947-. Food of Life. A book of ancient Persian and modern Iranian cooking and ceremonies: 1st ed. Washington, D.C.: Mage Publishers, Inc.; c1986. 245 p.; ISBN: 0-934211-00-0.
Note: Rev. translation of Ma cusine d'Iran.

108. Batmanglij, Najmieh, 1947-. Food of Life. A book of ancient Persian and modern Iranian cooking and ceremonies.: 2nd ed. Washington, D.C.: Mage Publishers; c1990. 248 p.; ISBN: 0934211000.

BEATTIE, MAY H.

109. Beattie, May H., Editor. Recipes from Baghdad. With contributions from more than a hundred ladies.: Baghdad, Iraq: Indian Red Cross; 1946.

BEDROSIAN, SIRVART

110. Bedrosian, Sirvart, Editor. Armenian Heritage Recipes. Montvale, NJ: Heritage Kitchens; 1966; c1966.

BENGHIAT, SUZY

111. Benghiat, Suzy. Middle Eastern Cooking. New York, NY: Harmony Books; 1985.; c1984. 144 p.; ISBN: 0-517-55608-1.

BEST BOOK OF GREEK COOKERY

112. Paradisis, Chrissa. The Best Book of Greek Cookery. New York, NY: International Publications Service; 1981.

BEST OF AFGHAN COOKERY, AN AFGHAN RECIPE BOOK

113. Weidenweber, Sigrid, Compiler. Best of Afghan Cookery, an Afghan Recipe Book. Portland, OR: American Aid for Afghans; c1980.

BEST OF BAGHDAD COOKING, WITH TREATS FROM TEHRAN

114. Iny, Daisy. The Best of Baghdad cooking, with treats from Tehran. New York, NY: Saturday Review Press/E.P. Dutton & Co.; 1976. 187 p.; ISBN: 0-8415-0400-8.

BEST OF GREEK COOKERY

115. Paradissis, Chrissa. The Best of Greek Cookery. 5th ed. Athens, Greece: Efstathiadis Group; New York, NY.; 1983.; c1976. 192 p.

BEST OF GREEK COOKERY: BASED ON THE AMBROSIA AND NECTAR COOKBOOK.

116. The Best of Greek Cookery: based on the Ambrosia and Nectar Cookbook. Baltimore, MD: Annunciation Greek Orthodox Community; 1972. 210 p.

BEST OF NEAR EASTERN COOKERY

117. Seranne, Ann. The Best of Near Eastern Cookery. Favorite Dishes from the Balkans, Turkey, Israel, Jordan, Saudi Arabia & other Countries of the Arabian Peninsula: Eileen Gaden, Photographic Illustrator. Garden City, NY: Doubleday & Co., Inc.; 1964; c1964. 158 p.

BETAR, YASMINE

118. Betar, Yasmine. Finest Recipes from the Middle East. Over one Hundred Recipes simplified with Suggested Menus their uses Origin and History, also spices and herbs some stories of folklore origin: Washington, D.C.; 1971; c1957. Over 145 p.

BEZJIAN, ALICE

119. Bezjian, Alice. The Complete Armenian Cookbook Including Favorite International Recipes. Fair Lawn, NJ: Rosekeer Press; c1983. 278 p.; ISBN: 0-915033-00-03.

BIBLIOGRAPHIES-MIDDLE EASTERN COOKERY

120. Vassilian, Hamo, 1952-. Ethnic Cookbooks & Food Marketplace: A Complete Bibliographic Guide & Directory to Armenian, Iranian, Afghan, Middle Eastern, North African and Greek Foods in the U.S.A. & Canada. Glendale, CA: Armenian Reference Books Co.; 1991.; c1991. 124 p. 1st ed.
Note: The most complete reference book for Middle Eastern foods.

BITAR, NOHA

121. Bitar, Noha. Lebanese cuisine and Middle Eastern Recipes: Exclusive Recipes. Montreal, Canada: Trait d'union; 1985. 150 p.

BOND, JULES JEROME

122. Bond, Jules Jerome. The Mid-Eastern Cuisine I love. New York, NY: Leon Amiel; 1977; c1977. 160 p.; ISBN: 0-8148-0693-7.

BOOK OF FAVORITE RECIPES

123. A Book of Favorite Recipes. compiled by Daughters of Vartan: : Daughters of Vartan, Los Angeles; 1981; c1968. 196 p.

124. A Book of Favorite Recipes. Watertown, MA: St. James Armenian Apostolic Church; 1984. 178 p.

BOOK OF MIDDLE EASTERN FOOD

125. Roden, Claudia. A Book of Middle Eastern Food. Edward Bawden, Illustrator; Bruce Pinkard, Photographer. London, England: Nelson; 1968. 320 p.

126. Roden, Claudia. A Book of Middle Eastern Food. Alta Ann Parkins, Illustrator. New York, NY: Alfred A. Knopf; 1985. 453, xiv, p.; ISBN: 0-394-47181-4.

BUNCH OF GREEK DISHES

127. Triantafyllidis, Alexandra. A Bunch of Greek Dishes 95 p.

BUTTROSS, WADDAD HABEEB

128. Buttross, Waddad Habeeb. Waddad's Kitchen, Lebanese zest and southern best. Natchez, Miss.: W. H. Buttross; c1982. 150 p.; ISBN: 0-939114-36-4.

CALIFORNIA COURIER COOKBOOK

129. The California Courier Cookbook. Berkeley, CA: George Mason; c1968. 128 p.

CAMEL LAND COOKERY

130. Short, Dorothy. Camel Land Cookery. Beirut, Lebanon; 1965.

CAN THE GREEKS COOK

131. Venos, Fannie, 1914-. Can the Greeks Cook. Lillian Prichard, Co-author. Richmond, VA: Dietz Press; 1950. xiii, 121 p.

CARPOU, MARY

132. Carpou, Mary, Editor. Greek cookery-Marin/by the Philoptochos Society of Nativity of Christ Greek Orthodox Church, Ignacio, California.. Catherine Banks, Co-editor. Novato, CA: The Society; 1981. ix, 183 p.; ISBN: 0961116404.

CAUCASIAN COOKERY

133. Uvezian, Sonia. Cooking from the Caucasus: First Harvest Press/HBJ edition 1978; c1976. 280 p.; ISBN: 0-15-622594-8.
Note: Originally published as The Best Foods of Russia. Armenian, Azerbaidzhani and Georgian recipies.

CHAITOW, ALKMINI

134. Chaitow, Alkmini. Greek Vegetarian Cooking. colorful dishes from the eastern shores of the Mediterranean: Clive Birch, Illustrator. 1st U.S. ed. New York, NY: Thorsons; 1991. 160 p.; ISBN: 072252496X.

CHANTILES, VILMA LIACOURAS

135. Chantiles, Vilma Liacouras. The Food of Greece. New York, NY: Dod, Mead; 1985; c1975. xvii, 364 p.; ISBN: 0396086136.

CHAPMAN, PAT, 1940-

136. Chapman, Pat, 1940-. The Curry Club Middle Eastern cookbook: Piatkus; 1989. 192 p.; ISBN: 0861888936.

CHATTO, JAMES

137. Chatto, James. A Kitchen in Corfu. W. L. Martin, Co-author. New American Edition ed. Joy Fitz Simmons, Illustrator. New York, NY: New Amsterdam Books; 1988.; c1987. vi, 199 p.; ISBN: 0941533174.

CHIRINIAN, LINDA

138. Chirinian, Linda. Secrets of Cooking. Armenian/Lebanese/Persian: Rene Chirinian, Photographer. New Canaan, CT: Lionhart Inc./Publishers; c1987. 264 p.; ISBN: 0-9617033-0-X.

CHRISTOU, BARBARA

139. Christou, Barbara, Editor. Key to Greek Cooking. Seattle, WA: Church of the Assumption; 1960 122 p.

CLASSIC ARMENIAN RECIPES: COOKING WITHOUT MEAT

140. Antreassian, Alice, 1922-. Classic Armenian Recipes: Cooking Without Meat. Mariam Jebejian, Co-author. 2nd ed. Adrina Zanazanian, Illustrator. New York, NY: Ashod Press; 1983.; c1981. 308, xxxip.; ISBN: 0-935102-05-1.

CLASSIC GREEK COOKING

141. Hartwing, Daphne Metaxas. Classic Greek cooking. Mike Nelson, Illustrator. Concord, CA: Nitty Gritty Productions; 1974. 179 p.; ISBN: 0911954317.

142. Metaxas, Daphne. Classic Greek Cooking. Concord, CA: Nitty Gritty Productions; 1974. 179 p.; ISBN: 0-911954-31-7.

CLASSIC VEGETABLE COOKING

143. der Haroutunian, Arto, 1940-1987. Classic Vegetable Cooking. London, England.

COME COOK WITH US; A TREASURY OF GREEK COOKING

144. Come cook with us; a treasury of Greek cooking. Norfolk, VA: Hellenic Woman's Club; c1967. 322 p.

COME WITH ME TO THE KASBAH: A COOK'S TOUR OF MOROCCO

145. Morse, Kitty. Come with Me to the Kasbah: A Cook's Tour of Morocco. 1st ed. Casablanca, Morocco: Editions SERAR; 1989. 237 p.

COMMONSENSE GREEK COOKERY BOOK

146. Kapsaskis, Angeline. The Commonsense Greek Cookery Book. London, England: Angus and Robertson; 1977. viii, 112 p.; ISBN: 0207135029.

COMPLETE ARMENIAN COOKBOOK INCLUDING FAVORITE INTERNATIONAL RECIPES

147. Bezjian, Alice. The Complete Armenian Cookbook Including Favorite International Recipes. Fair Lawn, NJ: Rosekeer Press; c1983. 278 p.; ISBN: 0-915033-00-03.

COMPLETE BOOK OF GREEK COOKING

148. The Complete book of Greek cooking. the Recipe Club of St. Pauls Greek Orhtodox Cathedral: Manny Malhado, Drawer. 1st. ed. New York, NY: Harper & Row; c1990. x, 336 p.; ISBN: 0060162597.

COMPLETE GREEK COOKBOOK: THE BEST FROM THREE THOUSAND YEARS OF GREEK COOKING.

149. Yianilos, Theresa Karas. The Complete Greek Cookbook: the Best from Three Thousand Years of Greek Cooking. New York, NY: Funk & Wagnalls; c1970. xiii, 254 p.; ISBN: 0517128780.

Note: Revised edition, 1986. La Jolla, CA.

COMPLETE MEZE TABLE

150. Man, Rosamond. The Complete Meze Table. Veronica Sperling & Caroline Schuck, Editors. London, England: Ebury Press; 1986. 111 p.; ISBN: 0852235461.

COMPLETE MIDDLE EAST COOKBOOK

151. Mallos, Tess. The Complete Middle East Cookbook. Reg Morrison, Photographer; Sue Wagner, Editor. New York, NY: McGraw-Hill; c1979. 400 p.; ISBN: 0-07-039810-0.

CONSTANTINE COOKS THE GREEK WAY

152. Hassalevris, Constantine, 1913-. Constantine Cooks the Greek Way. Los Angeles, CA: Ward Ritchie Press; 1962. 125 p.

COOKERY, MIDDLE EASTERN-BIBLIOGRAPHY

153. Vassilian, Hamo, 1952-. Ethnic Cookbooks & Food Marketplace: A Complete Bibliographic Guide & Directory to Armenian, Iranian, Afghan, Middle Eastern, North African and Greek Foods in the U.S.A. & Canada. Glendale, CA: Armenian Reference Books Co.; 1991.; 1st ed.,c1991. 124 p. Note: The most complete reference book for Middle Eastern foods.

COOKIN' GOOD WITH SITTO

154. Agia, Emelie, Editor. Cookin' good with Sitto. Compiled by Our Lady of Perpetual Help Society of St. Ann's Melkite Catholic Church. 2nd ed. West Paterson, NJ: St. Ann's Melkite Catholic Church; 1982 ix, 95 p.

COOKING AND BAKING THE GREEK WAY

155. Theoharous, Anne. Cooking and Baking the Greek Way. New York, NY: Holt, Rinehart & Winston; 1977. xi, 257 p.; ISBN: 0-03-017521-6.

COOKING FROM CYPRUS, THE ISLAND OF APHRODITE

156. Nicalaou, Nearchos. Cooking from Cyprus, the Island of Aphrodite. Nicosia, Cyprus: Published by author; 1979.

COOKING FROM THE CAUCASUS

157. Uvezian, Sonia. Cooking from the Caucasus: First Harvest Press/HBJ edition 1978; c1976. 280 p.; ISBN: 0-15-622594-8.

Note: Originally published as The Best Foods of Russia. Armenian, Azerbaidzhani and Georgian recipies.

COOKING OF GREECE

158. Schmaeling, Tony. The Cooking of Greece. Secaucus, NJ: Chartwell Books; c1983. 144 p.; ISBN: 0890096694.

COOKING THE GREEK WAY

159. Duncan, Maro. Cooking the Greek Way. London, England: Spring Books; 1964.

160. Smith, Viola. Cooking the Greek way. L.A. "Andy" Anderson, Art Work. Pensacola, FL: Foote Printing Co.; 1980. 221 p.

161. Theoharous, Anne. Cooking the Greek Way. London, England: Methuen; 1982.; c1979. 252 p.; ISBN: 0417038402.

162. Villios, Lynne W. Cooking the Greek way. Robert L. & Diane Wolfe, Photographers; Jeanette Swofford, Illustrator. Minneapolis: Lerner Publications; c1984. 51 p.; ISBN: 0822509105.

COOKING THE ISRAELI WAY

163. Bacon, Josephine, 1942-. Cooking the Israeli Way. Robert L.; Diane Wolfe, Photographers. Minneapolis, MN: Lerner Publications; 1986.
Note: Juvenile literature.

COOKING THE LEBANESE WAY

164. Amari, Suad. Cooking the Lebanese way. Robert L. & Diane Wolfe, Photographers. Minneapolis: Lerner Publications Co.; 1986. 47 p.; ISBN: 082250913X.

COOKING THE MIDDLE EAST WAY

165. Orga, Irfan. Cooking the Middle East Way. London, England: Spring Books; c1962. 256 p.

COOKING THE MIDDLE EASTERN WAY

166. Osborne, Christine. Cooking the Middle Eastern Way. Secaucus, NJ: Chartwell Books, Inc.; c1985. 152 p.; ISBN: 0-89009-838-7.

COOKING WITH GREECE

167. Cooking with Greece. Phoenix, AZ: Trinity Greek Orthodox Church; 1973.

COREY, HELEN

168. Corey, Helen. The Art of Syrian cookery. A culinary trip to the land of Bible history: Syria and Lebanon: 1st ed. Garden City, NY: Doubleday; 1962. 186 p.

169. Corey, Helen. Food from biblical lands: a culinary trip to the land of Bible history. Terre Haute, IN: H. Corey; c1989. xx, 154 p.

CORNFELD, LILIAN

170. Cornfeld, Lilian. Israeli Cookery. Westport, CT: Avi Pub. Co.; 1962. 356 p.

COUSCOUS AND OTHER GOOD FOOD FROM MOROCCO

171. Wolfert, Paula. Couscous and other Good Food from Morocco. Bill Bayer, Photographer; Sidonie Coryn, Illustrator. New York, NY: Harper & Row; 1973 xv, 351 p.; ISBN: 0-06-014721-0.

CREATIVE COOKING

172. Creative Cooking. Kansas City, KS: St. Peter Armenian Church; c1973. 120 p.

CUISINE OF ARMENIA

173. Uvezian, Sonia. The Cuisine of Armenia. Dickran Palulian, Illustrator. New York, NY: Harper & Row; 1974; c1974. xiii, 412 p.; ISBN: 0-06-014472-06.

174. Uvezian, Sonia. The Cuisine of Armenia. Dickran Palulian, Illustrator. Harper Colophon Books ed. New York, NY: Harper & Row; c1985. xiii, 400 p.; ISBN: 0609912294.

CUISINES OF THE EASTERN WORLD

175. Laas, W. Cuisines of the Eastern World. New York, NY: Golden Press; 1967.

CULINARY TOUR OF THE MIDDLE EAST

176. Langton. A Culinary Tour of the Middle East.

CULTURES IN COMMON: RECIPES FROM THE CUISINES OF TURKEY, GREECE AND THE BALKANS.

177. Rocca-Butler, Suzanne, 1946-. Cultures in common: recipes from the cuisines of Turkey, Greece and the Balkans. Menlo Park, CA: Folkloric Studies TGB Press; c1985. 144 p.; ISBN: 096157450X.

22-Bibliographies

Ethnic Cookbooks

CURRY CLUB MIDDLE EASTERN COOKBOOK

178. Chapman, Pat, 1940-. The Curry Club Middle Eastern cookbook: Piatkus; 1989. 192 p.; ISBN: 0861888936.

CYPRIOT COOKERY

179. Mourdjis, Marios, 1942-. The Cypriots at table. Nicosia, Cyprus: C.A.L. Graphics 220 p.

180. Nicalaou, Nearchos. Cooking from Cyprus, the Island of Aphrodite. Nicosia, Cyprus: Published by author; 1979.

181. Pourounas, Andreas. Aphrodite's Cookbook. Grosvenor, Helene, Co-author.: Spearman; 1977. 174 p.

CYPRIOTS AT TABLE

182. Mourdjis, Marios, 1942-. The Cypriots at table. Nicosia, Cyprus: C.A.L. Graphics 220 p.

DAVID, ISABELLE

183. David, Isabelle. Lebanese Cookery: an easy way.: Laughing Sams Press; 1982. 160 p.

DAY, IRENE F.

184. Day, Irene F. The Moroccan Cookbook. New York, NY: Putnam Publishing Group; 1982.; c1975, by Andre Deutsch. 155 p.; ISBN: 0-399-5-704-3.
Note: Original title of the is Kitchen in the Kasbah.

DEBASQUE, ROGER

185. Debasque, Roger. Eastern Mediterranean Cooking, Exotic delicacies from Greece, Turkey, Israel, Lebanon and Iran. New York, NY: Galahad Books; 1973.

DELIGANIS, CHRISTINA

186. Deliganis, Christina. Greek pastries: easy step by step instructions. Bruce Terami, Photographer. Seattle, WA: Kandylas Press; 1977 41 p.; ISBN: 0-930694-01-5.

DELIGHTS OF JERUSALEM: A TREASURY OF COOKING AND FOLKLORE

187. Valero, Rina. Delights of Jerusalem: a Treasury of Cooking and Folklore. Shlesinger, Miriam, Translator.: Nahar Publishing; Steimatzky; 1985 ?

DER HAROUTUNIAN, ARTO, 1940-1987.

188. der Haroutunian, Arto, 1940-1987. Barbecue Cookbook. London, England.

189. der Haroutunian, Arto, 1940-1987. Classic Vegetable Cooking. London, England.

190. der Haroutunian, Arto, 1940-1987. Middle Eastern Cookery. London, England: Century Publishing Co.; 1982 Over 369 p.; ISBN: 0-330-26783-3.

191. der Haroutunian, Arto, 1940-1987. North African Cookery. London, England: Century Publishing Co.; 1985; c1985.; ISBN: 0-7126-0925-3.

192. der Haroutunian, Arto, 1940-1987. Patisserie of the Eastern Mediterranean.: McGraw-Hill Book; 1989.; c1988. 128 p.; ISBN: 0-07-026665-4.

193. der Haroutunian, Arto, 1940-1987. Sweets & Desserts from the Middle East. London, England: Century Publishing; 1984. 224 p.; ISBN: 0712602925.

194. der Haroutunian, Arto, 1940-1987. Vegetarian Dishes from the Middle East. London, England: Century Publishing; 1987.; c1983. 224 p.; ISBN: 0-7126-0120-1.

195. der Haroutunian, Arto, 1940-1987. Whole Grain Cookbook. London, England.

196. der Haroutunian, Arto, 1940-1987. The Yoghurt Book. Food of the Gods: London, England: Penguin Books; 1983. Over 200 p.

DESSERTS-MIDDLE EASTERN

197. der Haroutunian, Arto, 1940-1987. Sweets & Desserts from the Middle East. London, England: Century Publishing; 1984. 224 p.; ISBN: 0712602925.

DIET FOR 100 HEALTHY, HAPPY YEARS

198. Mcqueen-Williams, Morvyth, 1911-1976. A Diet for 100 healthy, happy years. Barbara Apisson, Co-author; Norman Ober, Editor. Englewood Cliffs, NJ: Prentice-Hall; c1977. vi, 220 p.; ISBN: 0-13-211185-3.

DINNER AT OMAR KHAYYAM'S

199. Mardikian, George. Dinner at Omar Khayyam's. Salt Lake City: Viking Press; 1969, 13th printing; c1944. 150 p.

Ethnic Cookbooks

Bibliographies-23

DONIGUIAN, MIREILLE H.

200. Doniguian, Mireille H. Armenian and Oriental Cooking. Beirut, Lebanon: G. Doniguian & Sons; 1987? 233 p.

DOSTI, ROSE

201. Dosti, Rose. Middle Eastern Cooking. Tucson, AZ: HP Books, Inc.; c1982. 192 p.; ISBN: 0-89586-184-4.

DUNCAN, MARO

202. Duncan, Maro. Cooking the Greek Way. London, England: Spring Books; 1964.

EASTERN MEDITERRANEAN COOKING, EXOTIC DELICACIES FROM GREECE, TURKEY, ISRAEL, LEBANON AND IRAN

203. Debasque, Roger. Eastern Mediterranean Cooking, Exotic delicacies from Greece, Turkey, Israel, Lebanon and Iran. New York, NY: Galahad Books; 1973.

EGYPTIAN COOKERY

204. Abdennour, Samia. Egyptian cooking: a practical guide. Cairo, Egypt: American University in Cairo Press; c1964. 160 p.; ISBN: 977424026X.

205. Gadalla, Maher. Original Egyptian recipes. Rockford, IL: Nile Publications; c1981. 48 p.

206. Khalil, Nagwa E. Egyptian Cuisine: over 500 contemporary recipes from various Middle Eastern and Egyptian cooks. Washington, D.C.: Three Continents; c1980. 406 p.

207. Wilson, Hilary. Egyptian food and drink. Aylesbury, Bucks [England]: Shire; 1988. 64 p.

EGYPTIAN COOKING: A PRACTICAL GUIDE

208. Abdennour, Samia. Egyptian cooking: a practical guide. Cairo, Egypt: American University in Cairo Press; c1964. 160 p.; ISBN: 977424026X.

EGYPTIAN CUISINE: OVER 500 CONTEMPORARY RECIPES FROM VARIOUS MIDDLE EASTERN AND EGYPTIAN COOKS

209. Khalil, Nagwa E. Egyptian Cuisine: over 500 contemporary recipes from various Middle Eastern and Egyptian cooks. Washington, D.C.: Three Continents; c1980. 406 p.

EGYPTIAN FOOD AND DRINK

210. Wilson, Hilary. Egyptian food and drink. Aylesbury, Bucks [England]: Shire; 1988. 64 p.

ENGLISH ARABIC COOKERY BOOK

211. Joly, E. Gertrude. The English Arabic Cookery book. Beirut, Lebanon; 1950. 239 p.

ENTERTAINING THE PERSIAN WAY

212. Simmons, Shirin. Entertaining the Persian Way. London, England: Lennard Publishing; c1988. 156 p.; ISBN: 1-85291-0267.

ETHNIC COOKBOOKS & FOOD MARKETPLACE: A COMPLETE BIBLIOGRAPHIC GUIDE & DIRECTORY TO ARMENIAN, IRANIAN, AFGHAN, MIDDLE EA

213. Vassilian, Hamo, 1952-. Ethnic Cookbooks & Food Marketplace: A Complete Bibliographic Guide & Directory to Armenian, Iranian, Afghan, Middle Eastern, North African and Greek Foods in the U.S.A. & Canada. Glendale, CA: Armenian Reference Books Co.; 1991.; 1st ed.,c1991. 124 p. Note: The most complete reference book for Middle Eastern foods.

EVERYDAY DELIGHTS OF LEBANESE-SYRIAN COOKERY

214. Isaac, Barbara Thomas. Everyday delights of Lebanese-Syrian Cookery. Kathryn Arwady, Co-author; Cal Matle, Illustrator. Harper Woods, MI: Author; 1977. xviii, 280 p.

EXCITING GREEK DISHES

215. Sklavunu, Maria N. Exciting Greek Dishes, Athens, Greece. Artemis: 1976. 104 p.

EXOTIC, LIGHT & EASY COOKBOOK OF MIDDLE EASTERN CUISINE

216. Varjabedian, Ida P. Exotic, Light & Easy Cookbook of Middle Eastern Cuisine. Great Neck, NY: Todd & Honeywell, Inc.; c1985.; ISBN: 0-89962-410-3.

FABULOUS GREEK FOODS

217. Reynolds, Helne, 1921-. Fabulous Greek foods. Eilen Tomlinson, Drawer. Fallbrook, CA: Aero Publishers; c1977. 126 p.

FAMOUS GREEK RECIPES

218. Famous Greek Recipes. Oakland, CA: Ascension Greek Orthodox Church; 1972.

FARAH, MADELAIN

219. Farah, Madelain. Lebanese Cuisine: Over two hundred authentic recipes designed for the gourmet, the vegetarian, the healthfood enthusiast. 4th ed. Portland, OR: Madelain Farah; 1979; c1974 159 p.

220. Farah, Madelain. Pocket Bread Potpourri, Meals in Minutes. Leila Habib, Co-author. Memphis, TN: Wimmer Brothers Books; c1984. 108 p.

FARAH, NADIA, 1940-

221. Farah, Nadia, 1940-. Ah! Cooking the Middle Eastern Way. Ottawa, Canada: Deneau Publishers; 1982? 118 p.; ISBN: 0-88879-061-9.

FAVORITE ARMENIAN AND SYRIAN RECIPES OF ANNE GETSOIAN

222. Getsoian, Anne. Favorite Armenian and Syrian recipes of Anne Getsoian. San Diego, CA: Getsoian; c1979. 89 p.

FAVORITE ARMENIAN RECIPES

223. Favorite Armenian Recipes. 2nd ed. Racine, WI: St. Mesrob Armenian Church; 1988. 102 p.

Ethnic Cookbooks

FAVORITE GREEK RECIPES

224. Favorite Greek Recipes. Manchester, NH: Daughters of Penelope; 1955.

FAVORITE RECIPES OF ARMENIAN MEMORIAL CHURCH

225. Favorite Recipes of Armenian Memorial Church. 2nd ed. Watertown, MA: Armenian Memorial Church; 1967.

FIFTY FAMOUS ARMENIAN RECIPES

226. Garabedian, Z. M. Fifty Famous Armenian Recipes. Michael Nacashian, Introduction. Fresno, CA: Z. M. Enterprises; 1979.

FILLO PASTRY COOKBOOK: AND INTRODUCING KATAIFI PASTRY

227. Mallos, Tess. Fillo Pastry Cookbook: And Introducing Kataifi Pastry. Andrew Warn, Photographer; Suzanne Mallos, Illustrator. London, England: Merehurst Press; 1987.; c1983 96 p.; ISBN: 0-948075-47-3.

FILO

228. Nix, Jan. Filo: Crossing Press; 1991. 139 p.

FINEST RECIPES FROM THE MIDDLE EAST

229. Betar, Yasmine. Finest Recipes from the Middle East. Over one Hundred Recipes simplified with Suggested Menus their uses Origin and History, also spices and herbs some stories of folklore origin: Washington, D.C.; 1971; c1957. Over 145 p.

FINEST RECIPES FROM THE MIDDLE EAST; OVER ONE HUNDRED RECIPES SIMPLIFIED WITH SUGGESTED MENUS, THEIR USES, ORIGIN, AND H

230. Powell, Jessie (Johns) 1914-. Finest recipes from the Middle East; over one hundred recipes simplified with suggested menus, their uses, origin, and history; also , spicelore and herbs, some stories of folklore origin. Silver Spring, MD; 1968; c1957. 150 p.

FLAVOR OF JERUSALEM

231. Nathan, Joan. The Flavor of Jerusalem. Goldman, Judy Stacey, Co-author. Boston, MA: Little, Brown; 1975. 242 p.

FLAVORS OF GREECE

232. Barron, Rosemary. Flavors of Greece. New York, NY: W. Morrow; 1991; ISBN: 0688070876.

FLAVORS OF THE MIDDLE EAST

233. Flavors of the Middle East. Washington, D.C.: Aramco; 1988. 40 p.

FOOD AND WINE OF GREECE

234. Kochilas, Diane. The Food and Wine of Greece. Vassilis Stenos, Illustrator. New York, NY: St. Martin's Press; 1990. xiii, 354 p.; ISBN: 0312050887.

FOOD FOR THE VEGETARIAN

235. Karaoglan, Aida. Food for the Vegetarian. Brooklyn, NY: Interlink Publishing Group; c1988. 167 p.; ISBN: 0-940793-15-6.

FOOD FROM BIBLICAL LANDS: A CULINARY TRIP TO THE LAND OF BIBLE HISTORY.

236. Corey, Helen. Food from biblical lands: a culinary trip to the land of Bible history. Terre Haute, IN: H. Corey; c1989. xx, 154 p.

FOOD FROM THE ARAB WORLD

237. Khayat, Marie Karam. Food from the Arab world. Margaret Clark Keatinge. 3nd ed. Beirut, Lebanon; 1965. x, 163 p.
Note: 1st edition published in 1959.

FOOD OF GREECE

238. Chantiles, Vilma Liacouras. The Food of Greece. New York, NY: Dod, Mead; 1985; c1975. xvii, 364 p.; ISBN: 0396086136.

FOOD OF LIFE

239. Batmanglij, Najmieh, 1947-. Food of Life. A book of ancient Persian and modern Iranian cooking and ceremonies: 1st ed. Washington, D.C.: Mage Publishers, Inc.; c1986. 245 p.; ISBN: 0-934211-00-0.

Note: Rev. translation of Ma cusine d'Iran.

240. Batmanglij, Najmieh, 1947-. Food of Life. A book of ancient Persian and modern Iranian cooking and ceremonies.: 2nd ed. Washington, D.C.: Mage Publishers; c1990. 248 p.; ISBN: 0934211000.

FORTY DAYS OF LENT: SELECTED ARMENIAN RECIPES

241. Antreassian, Alice, 1922-. The Forty Days of Lent: Selected Armenian Recipes. New York, NY: Ashod Press; c1985. 130 p.; ISBN: 0-935102-16-7.

FRANK, BERYL, 1927-

242. Frank, Beryl, 1927-. Middle Eastern cooking. New York, NY: Weathervane Books; 1980. 64 p.; ISBN: 0517318350.

FRANKLIN, RENA

243. Franklin, Rena. Soups of Hakafri Restaurant: Kosher Edition. Florida: Triad Pub.; 1981. 144 p.; ISBN: 0-937404-13-6.

FRUGAL GOURMET COOKS THREE ANCIENT CUISINES: CHINA, GREECE, AND ROME

244. Smith, Jeff. The Frugal Gourmet cooks three ancient cuisines: China, Greece, and Rome. Craig Wollam, Culinary Consultant. 1st. ed. Terrin Haley, Research Assistant; Chris Cart, Illustrator. New York, NY: W. Morrow; c1989. 525 p.; ISBN: 0688075894.

FRUGAL GOURMET ON OUR IMMIGRANT ANCESTORS

245. Smith, Jeff. The Frugal Gourmet on Our Immigrant Ancestors [Recipes You Should Have Gotten from Your Grandmother.]. New York, NY: William Morrow & Co.; 1990. 539 p.; ISBN: 0-688-07590-8.
Note: Has Middle Eastern Recipes.

FURGIS, ELLEN VIDALAKIS

246. Furgis, Ellen Vidalakis. Greek cooking at its American best. D. Eugene Valentine. Westport, CT: Wildcat Pub. Co.; c1979. x, 118 p.; ISBN: 0941968014.

GADALLA, MAHER

247. Gadalla, Maher. Original Egyptian recipes. Rockford, IL: Nile Publications; c1981. 48 p.

Ethnic Cookbooks

Bibliographies-27

GARABEDIAN, Z. M.

248. Garabedian, Z. M. Fifty Famous Armenian Recipes. Michael Nacashian, Introduction. Fresno, CA: Z. M. Enterprises; 1979.

GETSOIAN, ANNE

249. Getsoian, Anne. Favorite Armenian and Syrian recipes of Anne Getsoian. San Diego, CA: Getsoian; c1979. 89 p.

GHANOONPARVAR, MOHAMMAD R.

250. Ghanoonparvar, Mohammad R. Persian Cuisine. Jill Lieber and Claudia Kane, Illustrators. 1st ed. Lexington, KY: Mazda Publisher; c1982; 2 Vol.; ISBN: 0939214105.
Note: Vol 1. = Traditional foods. Vol 2. Regional and modern foods. English & Persian. 5th printing, 1990.

GIANNOUL-E, ANNA

251. Giannoul-e, Anna. Greek Calendar Cookbook. a seasonal guide to cooking in Greece: Abigail Camp, Illustrator. Athens, Greece: Lycabettus Press; c1989. ix, 209 p.; ISBN: 9607269322.

GOOD FOOD FROM THE NEAR EAST; FIVE HUNDRED FAVORITE RECIPES FROM TWELVE COUNTRIES

252. Rowland, Joan. Good food from the Near East; five hundred favorite recipes from twelve countries. New York, NY: M. Barrow & Co., Inc.; 1950. 274 p.

GOURMET COOKING, PERSIAN STYLE

253. Motamen Reid, Mehry. Gourmet Cooking, Persian Style. Ceresville, MD: c1989. 197 p.

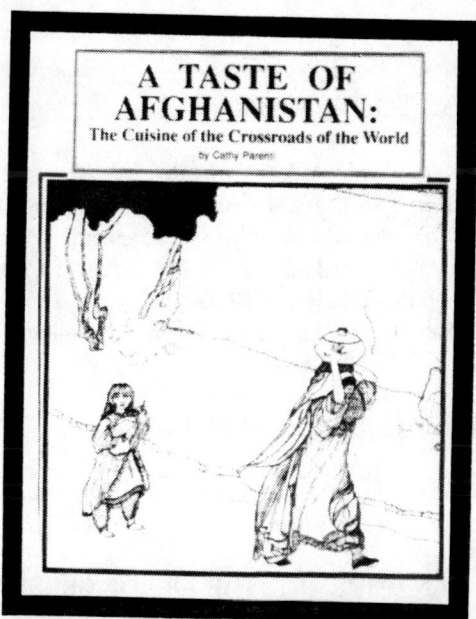

GOURMET'S DELIGHT

254. Karaoglan, Aida, Compiler. A Gourmet's delight. Selected recipes from the haute cuisine of the Arab world: Illustrations by Mouna Bassili Sehanaoui. Photographs by George Abdini. 2nd ed. Delmar, New York: Caravan Books; c1976. 160 p.; ISBN: 0-882206-007-4.
Note: Reprint of the 1969 edition published 1969 by Dar An-Nahar, Beirut, Lebanon.

GRECIAN GOURMET WITH LAMB

255. Papas, Mary. Grecian Gourmet with Lamb. 4th ed. Loma, CO: Woolgrowers Auxiliary; 1976.

GRECIAN GOURMET, THE ART OF GREEK COOKERY

256. Grecian Gourmet, The art of Greek Cookery. based on the Grecian gourmet. By the women of St.: Paul's Greek Orthodox Church, Art Seiden. Drawer. Garden City, NY: Doubleday; c1963. 234 p.

GRECIAN PLATE/ COMPILED BY THE HELLENIC LADIES SOCIETY, ST. BARBARA GREEK ORTHODOX CHURCH

257. The Grecian plate/ compiled by the Hellenic Ladies Society, St. Barbara Greek Orthodox Church. Durham, NC: The Society; c1984. 256 p.; ISBN: 096138560X.

GREECE

258. Loewen, Nancy, 1964-. Greece. Vero Beach, FL: Rourke Publications; 1991.; ISBN: 0866253483.

GREEK CALENDAR COOKBOOK

259. Giannoul-e, Anna. Greek Calendar Cookbook. a seasonal guide to cooking in Greece: Abigail Camp, Illustrator. Athens, Greece: Lycabettus Press; c1989. ix, 209 p.; ISBN: 9607269322.

GREEK COOKBOOK

260. Mallos, Tess. Greek Cookbook. Howard Joes, Photographer. Sydney, Australia: Books for Pleasure; 1976 128 p.; ISBN: 0-7271-0038-6.

261. Philips, Margot Kopsidas. Greek cookbook. Sherrill Weary, Editor; Joy Taylor, Assistant editor. New York, NY: The Culinary Arts Institute; c1980. 96 p.; ISBN: 0832606111.

262. Skoura, Sophia. The Greek Cookbook. Helen Georges, Translator & adaptor. New York, NY: Crow Publishers; 1967. xiii, 230 p.

263. Wason, Elizabeth Betty, 1912-. Greek Cookbook. Giulio Maestro, Illustrator. New York, NY: Macmillan; 1969. 216 p.

GREEK COOKERY

264. 101 Greek Ways. Denver, CO: Greek Orthodox Church of Denver; 1972.

265. Accent on Greek Cooking. Olathe, Kanzas: Cookbook Publishers; c1987. A-D, 178 p., viii p.

266. Anatolia College Cookbook. Boston, MA: Anatolia College Graduates 95 p.

267. An Ancient heritage lives on. Las Vegas, NV: St. John Greek Orthodox Church; 1984 ? 104 p.

268. Andrews, Jasmine Panos. My Greek heritage cookbook. Paul A. Andrews, Photographer; Thalia L. Bredakis, Illustrator. Coolierville, TN: Fundcraft Pub.; c1989. A-I, 162, A-D p.

269. Art of Greek Cookery, based on the Grecian Gourmet. Garden City, NY: St. Paul's Greek Orthodox Church; 1963 234 p.

270. The Art of Greek Cooking. Elkins Park, PA: Evangelismos Greek Orthodox Community of Philadelphia; 1973.

271. Authentic Greek Recipes. Memphis, TN: Annunciation Greek Orthodox Community; 1963.

272. Authentic Greek Recipes. Tarpon Springs, FL: St. Nicholas Greek Orthodox Church; 1974.

273. Barron, Rosemary. Flavors of Greece. New York, NY: W. Morrow; 1991; ISBN: 0688070876.

274. The Best of Greek Cookery: based on the Ambrosia and Nectar Cookbook. Baltimore, MD: Annunciation Greek Orthodox Community; 1972. 210 p.

275. Carpou, Mary, Editor. Greek cookery-Marin/by the Philoptochos Society of Nativity of Christ Greek Orthodox Church, Ignacio, California.. Catherine Banks, Co-editor. Novato, CA: The Society; 1981. ix, 183 p.; ISBN: 0961116404.

Ethnic Cookbooks

276. Chaitow, Alkmini. Greek Vegetarian Cooking. colorful dishes from the eastern shores of the Mediterranean: Clive Birch, Illustrator. 1st U.S. ed. New York, NY: Thorsons; 1991. 160 p.; ISBN: 072252496X.

277. Chantiles, Vilma Liacouras. The Food of Greece. New York, NY: Dod, Mead; 1985; c1975. xvii, 364 p.; ISBN: 0396086136.

278. Chatto, James. A Kitchen in Corfu. W. L. Martin, Co-author. New American Edition ed. Joy Fitz Simmons, Illustrator. New York, NY: New Amsterdam Books; 1988.; c1987. vi, 199 p.; ISBN: 0941533174.

279. Christou, Barbara, Editor. Key to Greek Cooking. Seattle, WA: Church of the Assumption; 1960 122 p.

280. Come cook with us; a treasury of Greek cooking. Norfolk, VA: Hellenic Woman's Club; c1967. 322 p.

281. The Complete book of Greek cooking. the Recipe Club of St. Pauls Greek Orhtodox Cathedral: Manny Malhado, Drawer. 1st. ed. New York, NY: Harper & Row; c1990. x, 336 p.; ISBN: 0060162597.

282. Cooking with Greece. Phoenix, AZ: Trinity Greek Orthodox Church; 1973.

283. Duncan, Maro. Cooking the Greek Way. London, England: Spring Books; 1964.

284. Famous Greek Recipes. Oakland, CA: Ascension Greek Orthodox Church; 1972.

285. Favorite Greek Recipes. Manchester, NH: Daughters of Penelope; 1955.

286. Furgis, Ellen Vidalakis. Greek cooking at its American best. D. Eugene Valentine. Westport, CT: Wildcat Pub. Co.; c1979. x, 118 p.; ISBN: 0941968014.

287. Giannoul-e, Anna. Greek Calendar Cookbook. a seasonal guide to cooking in Greece: Abigail Camp, Illustrator. Athens, Greece: Lycabettus Press; c1989. ix, 209 p.; ISBN: 9607269322.

288. Grecian Gourmet, The art of Greek Cookery. based on the Grecian gourmet. By the women of St.: Paul's Greek Orthodox Church, Art Seiden. Drawer. Garden City, NY: Doubleday; c1963. 234 p.

289. The Grecian plate/ compiled by the Hellenic Ladies Society, St. Barbara Greek Orthodox Church. Durham, NC: The Society; c1984. 256 p.; ISBN: 096138560X.

290. Greek Cooking in an American Kitchen. Seattle, WA: St. Demetrios Church; c1982. 264 p.

291. Gregory, Penelope D. Sketching in the Greek Kitchen: A Family Cookbook. Ann Wiseman: Co-author: Ansayre Press; 1989. 87 p.; ISBN: 0937369039.

292. Hartwing, Daphne Metaxas. Classic Greek cooking. Mike Nelson, Illustrator. Concord, CA: Nitty Gritty Productions; 1974. 179 p.; ISBN: 0911954317.

293. Hassalevris, Constantine, 1913-. Constantine Cooks the Greek Way. Los Angeles, CA: Ward Ritchie Press; 1962. 125 p.

294. Hassalevris, Constantine, 1913-. Moussaka, baklava, and love; cooking the Greek way. Los Angeles, CA: Ward Ritchie Press; 1973. 141 p.; ISBN: 0378010824.

295. Hellenic Cookery of Hollywood. 4th ed. Daughters of Penelope: Hollywood, CA; 1959.

296. Hellenic Cuisine: a Collection of Greek Recipes. Detroit, MI: St. Helen's Philoptochos Society; 1957.

297. Howe, Robin. Greek Cooking. London, England; 1960 282 p.

298. International Hellenic Cuisine. Daughters of Penelope. Montgomery, AL: Favorite Recipes Press; c1975. 198 p.; ISBN: 0-87197-096-1.

299. Kapsaskis, Angeline. The Commonsense Greek Cookery Book. London, England: Angus and Robertson; 1977. viii, 112 p.; ISBN: 0207135029.

30-Bibliographies — Ethnic Cookbooks

300. Karay, Mary Pyrros, Editor. Hellenic cuisine. a collection of Greek recipes: Fannie C. Nome, Co-editor; Cleonike Stathes Bradley, Illustrator. Detroit, MI: St. Helen's Philoptochos Society; 1957. Vii, 180 p.

301. Kaufman, William I. Greek Dinner Party. Anaheim, CA: Buzza Books; 1971.

302. Kershner, Ruth. Greek Cooking: Weathervane Books; c1977. 64 p.; ISBN: 0-517-23932-9.

303. The Key to Good Cooking. Wauwatosa, WI: Sts. Constantine and Helen Greek Orthodox Church; 1972.

304. The Key to Greek Cooking. Seattle, Washington: Greek Orthodox Church; 1960.

305. The Key to Greek Cooking. Atlanta, GA: Greek Orthodox Cathedral of the Annunciation; 1974.

306. Kochilas, Diane. The Food and Wine of Greece. Vassilis Stenos, Illustrator. New York, NY: St. Martin's Press; 1990. xiii, 354 p.; ISBN: 0312050887.

307. Kopulos, Stella. Adventures in Greek Cookery. Dorothy P. Jones, Co-author. Rev. Edition ed. James Stewart, Illustrator. New York, NY: The World Publishing Co.; 1972. xiii, 337 p.; ISBN: 0529045516.

308. Krieg, Saul. The Alpha and Omega of Greek Cooking. New York, NY: Macmillan; 1973. xii, 266 p.

309. Kyriacopoulis, Florica. Self-catering in Greece: mainland and island. making the most of local food and drink: Tim Salmon, Co-author. New York, NY: Hippocrene Books; 1986. 155 p.

310. A Lenten Cookbook for Orthodox. Seattle, WA: St. Nectarios American Orthodox Church; 1972.

311. Loewen, Nancy, 1964-. Greece. Vero Beach, FL: Rourke Publications; 1991.; ISBN: 0866253483.

312. MacDougall, Allan Ross, 1893-. And the Greeks. a book of Hellenic recipes and culinary lore,: New York, NY: Near East Foundation; c1942. 109 p.

313. Mallos, Tess. Greek Cookbook. Howard Joes, Photographer. Sydney, Australia: Books for Pleasure; 1976 128 p.; ISBN: 0-7271-0038-6.

Ethnic Cookbooks

Bibliographies-31

314. Mallos, Tess. Greek Cooking for Pleasure. Howard Jones, Photographer. Secaucus, NJ: Chartwell Books; 1978. 112 p.; ISBN: 0890092516.

315. Mark, Theonie. Greek Islands Cooking. Maris Platais, Illustrator. Boston, MA: Little, Brown & Co.; 1974 xvi, 303 p.; ISBN: 0-316-54623-2.
Note: Also published by Bastsford, in London in 1978.

316. Marketos, Olympia. Athens a la carte, the best of Greek cooking. Chicago, IL: Rand McNally; 1963. 119 p.

317. Metaxas, Daphne. Classic Greek Cooking. Concord, CA: Nitty Gritty Productions; 1974. 179 p.; ISBN: 0-911954-31-7.

318. Monroe, Elvira. Greek moods and menus. Theoni Pappas, Co-author. San Carlos, CA: Wide World; c1980. 119 p.; ISBN: 0933174055.

319. The New festival of Greek Cooking. Santa Barbara, CA: St. Barbara Greek Orthodox Church; c1981. 160 p.

320. Odyssey of Greek cooking. Annapolis, MD: Greek Orthodox Ladies Philoptochos Society; c1980. 175 p.

321. Our Collection of Secret Greek Recipes. 4th ed. Milwaukee, WI: Assumption Greek Orhtodox Church; 1968.

322. Papas, Mary. Grecian Gourmet with Lamb. 4th ed. Loma, CO: Woolgrowers Auxiliary; 1976.

323. Pappas, Lou Seibert. Greek Cooking. New York, NY: Harper & Row; 1973 xx, 196 p.; ISBN: 0060132736.

324. Pappas, Theoni. Greek cooking for everyone. Elvira Monrose, Co-author. 2nd ed. San Carlos, CA: Wide World Pub./Tetra; 1986.; c1989. 167 p.; ISBN: 0933174616.

325. Paradisis, Chrissa. The Best Book of Greek Cookery. New York, NY: International Publications Service; 1981.

32-Bibliographies

Ethnic Cookbooks

326. Paradissis, Chrissa. The Best of Greek Cookery. 5th ed. Athens, Greece: Efstathiadis Group; New York, NY.; 1983.; c1976. 192 p.

327. Philips, Margot Kopsidas. Greek cookbook. Sherrill Weary, Editor; Joy Taylor, Assistant editor. New York, NY: The Culinary Arts Institute; c1980. 96 p.; ISBN: 0832606111.

328. Polemis, Aphrodite. Aphrodite's Kitchen: homestyle Greek cooking. New York, NY: Golden Press; c1978. 96 p.; ISBN: 0-307-49426-8.

329. Popular Greek Recipes. The Ladies of the Philoptochos Society, Holy Trinity Greek Orthodox Church. Charleston, S. Carolina: Holy Trinity Greek Orthodox Church; 1976. 222 p.

330. Precope, Kathleen. Secrets of Greek Cooking. London, England: New Europe Publishing Co.; 1944. 28 p.

331. The Regional Cuisines of Greece: St. Paul's Greek Orthodox Church; 1981. 256 p.

332. Reynolds, Helne, 1921-. Fabulous Greek foods. Eilen Tomlinson, Drawer. Fallbrook, CA: Aero Publishers; c1977. 126 p.

333. Rocca-Butler, Suzanne, 1946-. Cultures in common: recipes from the cuisines of Turkey, Greece and the Balkans. Menlo Park, CA: Folkloric Studies TGB Press; c1985. 144 p.; ISBN: 096157450X.

334. Roukes, Nicholas. Greek with gusto. Greek cuisine, easy & delicious: Calgary, Canada: Juniro Arts Pub.; 1990. 170 p.; ISBN: 0919845800.

335. Salaman, Rena. Greek Food. London, England: Fontana; 1983.

336. Salaman, Rena. Greek Island Cookery: an evocation in words and watercolors. Linda Smith, Co-author. London, England: Ebury Press; c1987. 128 p.; ISBN: 08522236212.

337. Salaman, Rena. A little Greek Cookbook. San Francisco, CA: Chronicle Books; 1990. 60 p.; ISBN: 0877017956.

338. Santa Maria, Jack. Greek Vegetarian Cookery. Kate Simunek, Illustrator. Boston, MA: Shambhala Publishers, Inc.; c1984. 160 p.; ISBN: 0877733325.

339. Schmaeling, Tony. The Cooking of Greece. Secaucus, NJ: Chartwell Books; c1983. 144 p.; ISBN: 0890096694.

340. Semos, Evelyn, 1915-. More than baklava: a Greek cookbook. Ann Pearle, Illustrator. Dallas, TX: Neiman Marcus; 1982. x, 87 p.; ISBN: 0960666818.

341. Sklavunu, Maria N. Exciting Greek Dishes, Athens, Greece. Artemis: 1976. 104 p.

342. Skoura, Sophia. The Greek Cookbook. Helen Georges, Translator & adaptor. New York, NY: Crow Publishers; 1967. xiii, 230 p.

343. Smith, Jeff. The Frugal Gourmet cooks three ancient cuisines: China, Greece, and Rome. Craig Wollam, Culinary Consultant. 1st. ed. Terrin Haley, Research Assistant; Chris Cart, Illustrator. New York, NY: W. Morrow; c1989. 525 p.; ISBN: 0688075894.

344. Smith, Viola. Cooking the Greek way. L.A. "Andy" Anderson, Art Work. Pensacola, FL: Foote Printing Co.; 1980. 221 p.

345. Spanos, Anna Z., 1899-. The Simple art of Greek Cooking. John Spanos, Co-author. New York, NY: Perigee Books; 1976.; c1990. 204 p.; ISBN: 0399516182.
Note: Title: also published under Pure Greek Cooking.

346. Spoerri, Daniel, 1930-. Mythology and Meatballs: a Greek Island Diary Cookbook. Emmett Williams, Translator; Jeanne Jambo, Illustrator. Berkeley, CA: Aris; 1982. 238 p.; ISBN: 0943196013.

347. Step-By-Step Greek Cooking: Smith Publishers; 1989.; ISBN: 08317-8006.

348. Stubbs, Joyce M. The Home Book of Greek Cookery. a selection of traditional Greek recipes.: London, England: Faber and Faber; 1963. 159 p.

349. Tagas, Louis. Hellenic Cuisine: cooking Greek style. New York, NY: Vantage Press; c1984. xi, 51 p.; ISBN: 0533058988.

350. Tambakeras, Rena. Greek Cooking. Per Ericson, Photographer. Mississauga, Ontario: Cupress; 1987. viii, 160 p.; ISBN: 0920691358.

351. A Taste for it: Greek and other Recipes for the Discriminating Palate. Seattle, Washington: St. Demetrios Greek Orthodox Church; 1964.

352. Tavlarios, Irene. Greek food and drink. New York, NY: Bookwright Press; 1988.; c1987. 48 p.; ISBN: 0531181723.
Note: Juvenile Literature.

Ethnic Cookbooks   Bibliographies-33

353. Tender loving cooking: favorite recipes by the women of Holy Apostles Greek Church. Holy Apostles Philoptohos Society. Westchester, IL: The Society; c1984. 223 p.

354. Terzi, Popi. Athenian cuisine: over 600 recipes. Joe Nadziejko, Drawer. Tarrytown, NY: Pilgrimage Pub.; 1987. xii, 183 p.; ISBN: 0935819037.

355. Theoharous, Anne. Cooking and Baking the Greek Way. New York, NY: Holt, Rinehart & Winston; 1977. xi, 257 p.; ISBN: 0-03-017521-6.

356. Theoharous, Anne. Cooking the Greek Way. London, England: Methuen; 1982.; c1979. 252 p.; ISBN: 0417038402.

357. Treasured Greek recipes. Compiled by the Greek Ladies Philoptochos Society, St. Sophia Greek Orthodox Chruch. Albany, NY: St. Sophia Greek Orthodox Church; 1981. xx, 264 p.

358. Treasures of Greek and International Cooking. Miami, FL: St. Andrew Greek Orthodox Church of Kendall; c1988. 246 p.

359. Triantafyllidis, Alexandra. A Bunch of Greek Dishes 95 p.

360. Tselementes, Nicholas, 1880-. Greek Cookery. 3rd ed. New York, NY: D.C. Divry; 1956. 239 p.; ISBN: 0685090353.

361. Venos, Fannie, 1914-. Can the Greeks Cook. Lillian Prichard, Co-author. Richmond, VA: Dietz Press; 1950. xiii, 121 p.

362. Villios, Lynne W. Cooking the Greek way. Robert L. & Diane Wolfe, Photographers; Jeanette Swofford, Illustrator. Minneapolis: Lerner Publications; c1984. 51 p.; ISBN: 0822509105.

363. Wason, Elizabeth Betty, 1912-. Greek Cookbook. Giulio Maestro, Illustrator. New York, NY: Macmillan; 1969. 216 p.

364. Westland, Pamela. Greek Cooking. London, England: Ward Lock; 1987. 96 p.; ISBN: 0706365720.

365. Yianilos, Theresa Karas. The Complete Greek Cookbook: the Best from Three Thousand Years of Greek Cooking. New York, NY: Funk & Wagnalls; c1970. xiii, 254 p.; ISBN: 0517128780.
Note: Revised edition, 1986. La Jolla, CA.

366. Zane, Eva. Greek Cooking for the Gods. W. Busser Howel and the author, Illustrators. San Ramon, CA: 101 Productions; 1970; c1989. 192 p.

GREEK COOKERY-MARIN/BY THE PHILOPTOCHOS SOCIETY OF NATIVITY OF CHRIST GREEK ORTHODOX CHURCH, IGNACIO, CALIFORNIA.

367. Carpou, Mary, Editor. Greek cookery-Marin/by the Philoptochos Society of Nativity of Christ Greek Orthodox Church, Ignacio, California.. Catherine Banks, Co-editor. Novato, CA: The Society; 1981. ix, 183 p.; ISBN: 0961116404.

GREEK COOKING

368. Howe, Robin. Greek Cooking. London, England; 1960 282 p.

369. Kershner, Ruth. Greek Cooking: Weathervane Books; c1977. 64 p.; ISBN: 0-517-23932-9.

370. Pappas, Lou Seibert. Greek Cooking. New York, NY: Harper & Row; 1973 xx, 196 p.; ISBN: 0060132736.

371. Tambakeras, Rena. Greek Cooking. Per Ericson, Photographer. Mississauga, Ontario: Cupress; 1987. viii, 160 p.; ISBN: 0920691358.

372. Westland, Pamela. Greek Cooking. London, England: Ward Lock; 1987. 96 p.; ISBN: 0706365720.

GREEK COOKING AT ITS AMERICAN BEST

373. Furgis, Ellen Vidalakis. Greek cooking at its American best. D. Eugene Valentine. Westport, CT: Wildcat Pub. Co.; c1979. x, 118 p.; ISBN: 0941968014.

GREEK COOKING FOR EVERYONE

374. Pappas, Theoni. Greek cooking for everyone. Elvira Monrose, Co-author. 2nd ed. San Carlos, CA: Wide World Pub./Tetra; 1986.; c1989. 167 p.; ISBN: 0933174616.

GREEK COOKING FOR PLEASURE

375. Mallos, Tess. Greek Cooking for Pleasure. Howard Jones, Photographer. Secaucus, NJ: Chartwell Books; 1978. 112 p.; ISBN: 0890092516.

GREEK COOKING FOR THE GODS

376. Zane, Eva. Greek Cooking for the Gods. W. Busser Howel and the author, Illustrators. San Ramon, CA: 101 Productions; 1970; c1989. 192 p.

GREEK COOKING IN AN AMERICAN KITCHEN

377. Greek Cooking in an American Kitchen. Seattle, WA: St. Demetrios Church; c1982. 264 p.

GREEK DINNER PARTY

378. Kaufman, William I. Greek Dinner Party. Anaheim, CA: Buzza Books; 1971.

GREEK FOOD

379. Salaman, Rena. Greek Food. London, England: Fontana; 1983.

GREEK FOOD AND DRINK

380. Tavlarios, Irene. Greek food and drink. New York, NY: Bookwright Press; 1988.; c1987. 48 p.; ISBN: 0531181723.
Note: Juvenile Literature.

GREEK ISLAND COOKERY: AN EVOCATION IN WORDS AND WATERCOLORS

381. Salaman, Rena. Greek Island Cookery: an evocation in words and watercolors. Linda Smith, Co-author. London, England: Ebury Press; c1987. 128 p.; ISBN: 08522236212.

Ethnic Cookbooks

Bibliographies-35

GREEK ISLANDS COOKING

382. Mark, Theonie. Greek Islands Cooking. Maris Platais, Illustrator. Boston, MA: Little, Brown & Co.; 1974 xvi, 303 p.; ISBN: 0-316-54623-2.
Note: Also published by Bastsford, in London in 1978.

GREEK MOODS AND MENUS

383. Monroe, Elvira. Greek moods and menus. Theoni Pappas, Co-author. San Carlos, CA: Wide World; c1980. 119 p.; ISBN: 0933174055.

GREEK PASTRIES: EASY STEP BY STEP INSTRUCTIONS

384. Deliganis, Christina. Greek pastries: easy step by step instructions. Bruce Terami, Photographer. Seattle, WA: Kandylas Press; 1977 41 p.; ISBN: 0-930694-01-5.

GREEK VEGETARIAN COOKERY

385. Santa Maria, Jack. Greek Vegetarian Cookery. Kate Simunek, Illustrator. Boston, MA: Shambhala Publishers, Inc.; c1984. 160 p.; ISBN: 0877733325.

GREEK VEGETARIAN COOKING

386. Chaitow, Alkmini. Greek Vegetarian Cooking. colorful dishes from the eastern shores of the Mediterranean: Clive Birch, Illustrator. 1st U.S. ed. New York, NY: Thorsons; 1991. 160 p.; ISBN: 072252496X.

GREEK WITH GUSTO

387. Roukes, Nicholas. Greek with gusto. Greek cuisine, easy & delicious: Calgary, Canada: Juniro Arts Pub.; 1990. 170 p.; ISBN: 0919845800.

GREGORY, PENELOPE D.

388. Gregory, Penelope D. Sketching in the Greek Kitchen: A Family Cookbook. Ann Wiseman: Co-author: Ansayre Press; 1989. 87 p.; ISBN: 0937369039.

HABEEB, VIRGINIA

389. Habeeb, Virginia. Pita the Great. New York, NY: Workman; 1986; ISBN: 0-89480-039-6.

HARTWING, DAPHNE METAXAS

390. Hartwing, Daphne Metaxas. Classic Greek cooking. Mike Nelson, Illustrator. Concord, CA: Nitty Gritty Productions; 1974. 179 p.; ISBN: 0911954317.

HASSALEVRIS, CONSTANTINE, 1913-

391. Hassalevris, Constantine, 1913-. Constantine Cooks the Greek Way. Los Angeles, CA: Ward Ritchie Press; 1962. 125 p.

392. Hassalevris, Constantine, 1913-. Moussaka, baklava, and love; cooking the Greek way. Los Angeles, CA: Ward Ritchie Press; 1973. 141 p.; ISBN: 0378010824.

HATTON, D.

393. Hatton, D. Oriental Cookery. London, England: William Collins Sons & Co.; 1969.
Note: Includes Armenian Recipes.

HEKMAT, FOROUGH-ES-SALTANEH

394. Hekmat, Forough-es-Saltaneh. The Art of Persian Cooking. Garden City, NY: Doubleday; 1961. 190 p.

HELLENIC COOKERY OF HOLLYWOOD

395. Hellenic Cookery of Hollywood. 4th ed. Daughters of Penelope: Hollywood, CA; 1959.

HELLENIC CUISINE

396. Karay, Mary Pyrros, Editor. Hellenic cuisine. a collection of Greek recipes: Fannie C. Nome, Co-editor; Cleonike Stathes Bradley, Illustrator. Detroit, MI: St. Helen's Philoptochos Society; 1957. Vii, 180 p.

HELLENIC CUISINE: A COLLECTION OF GREEK RECIPES.

397. Hellenic Cuisine: a Collection of Greek Recipes. Detroit, MI: St. Helen's Philoptochos Society; 1957.

HELLENIC CUISINE: COOKING GREEK STYLE

398. Tagas, Louis. Hellenic Cuisine: cooking Greek style. New York, NY: Vantage Press; c1984. xi, 51 p.; ISBN: 0533058988.

HOGROGIAN, RACHEL

399. Hogrogian, Rachel. The Armenian Cookbook. Nonny Hogrogian, Illustrator. 1st ed. New York, NY: Atheneum; 1971. xxi, 152 p.

HOME BOOK OF GREEK COOKERY

400. Stubbs, Joyce M. The Home Book of Greek Cookery. a selection of traditional Greek recipes.: London, England: Faber and Faber; 1963. 159 p.

HOWE, ROBIN

401. Howe, Robin. Greek Cooking. London, England; 1960 282 p.

402. Howe, Robin. Middle Eastern Cookery. Tony Streek, Illustrator. London, England: Eyre Mehtuen; 1978 189 p.; ISBN: 0413382206.

HUSAIN, S.A.

403. Husain, S.A. Muslim Cooking of Pakistan. Lahore, Pakestan: Sh. Muhammad Ashraf; c1974.

IN A CALIPH'S KITCHEN

404. Waines, David, Compiler. In a Caliph's Kitchen: Riad El-Rayyes; 1989. 119 p.

IN A PERSIAN KITCHEN

405. Mazda, Maideh. In a Persian Kitchen. Favorite Recipes from the Near East: M. Kuwata, Illustrator. Rutland, Vermont: Charles E. Tuttle Co.; c1960. 175 p.

INTERNATIONAL HELLENIC CUISINE

406. International Hellenic Cuisine. Daughters of Penelope. Montgomery, AL: Favorite Recipes Press; c1975. 198 p.; ISBN: 0-87197-096-1.

INY, DAISY

407. Iny, Daisy. The Best of Baghdad cooking, with treats from Tehran. New York, NY: Saturday Review Press/E.P. Dutton & Co.; 1976. 187 p.; ISBN: 0-8415-0400-8.

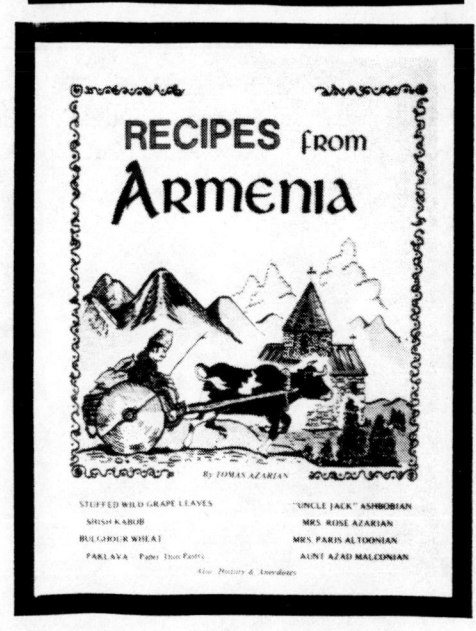

Ethnic Cookbooks

IRAQI COOKERY

408. Beattie, May H., Editor. Recipes from Baghdad. With contributions from more than a hundred ladies.: Baghdad, Iraq: Indian Red Cross; 1946.

409. Iny, Daisy. The Best of Baghdad cooking, with treats from Tehran. New York, NY: Saturday Review Press/E.P. Dutton & Co.; 1976. 187 p.; ISBN: 0-8415-0400-8.

ISAAC, BARBARA THOMAS

410. Isaac, Barbara Thomas. Everyday delights of Lebanese-Syrian Cookery. Kathryn Arwady, Co-author; Cal Matle, Illustrator. Harper Woods, MI: Author; 1977. xviii, 280 p.

ISRAELI COOKERY

411. Bacon, Josephine, 1942-. Cooking the Israeli Way. Robert L.; Diane Wolfe, Photographers. Minneapolis, MN: Lerner Publications; 1986.
Note: Juvenile literature.

412. Banai, Margalit, 1928-. What's Cooking in Israel. New York, NY: Crowell; 1972. 181 p.; ISBN: 0-690-87825-7.

413. Cornfeld, Lilian. Israeli Cookery. Westport, CT: Avi Pub. Co.; 1962. 356 p.

414. Franklin, Rena. Soups of Hakafri Restaurant: Kosher Edition. Florida: Triad Pub.; 1981. 144 p.; ISBN: 0-937404-13-6.

415. Lesberg, Sandy. At the table of Israel: a unique collection of three hundred traditional and modern Israeli recipes. Indianapolis; New York: Bobbs-Merrill; Peebles Press.; c1973,.

416. Maiberg, Ron. A Taste of Israel. New York, NY: Rizoli International; 1990. 240 p.; ISBN: 0847811956.

417. Nahoum, Aldo. The Art of Israeli Cooking; original Israeli recipes never before published, as well as favorite traditional dishes, all kosher. 1st ed. New York, NY: Holt, Rinehart and Winston; 1971.; c1970. 152 p.; ISBN: 0-03-085176-9.

418. Nathan, Joan. The Flavor of Jerusalem. Goldman, Judy Stacey, Co-author. Boston, MA: Little, Brown; 1975. 242 p.

JOHNS, AGGIE, 1911-

419. Johns, Aggie, 1911-. The Original Lebanese & Middle East Cookbook. Kent Thompson, Illustrator. Portland, OR: A. Johns; 1983. iii, 112 p.; ISBN: 0961214805.

JOLY, E. GERTRUDE

420. Joly, E. Gertrude. The English Arabic Cookery book. Beirut, Lebanon; 1950. 239 p.

KAPSASKIS, ANGELINE

421. Kapsaskis, Angeline. The Commonsense Greek Cookery Book. London, England: Angus and Robertson; 1977. viii, 112 p.; ISBN: 0207135029.

KARAOGLAN, AIDA

422. Karaoglan, Aida. Food for the Vegetarian. Brooklyn, NY: Interlink Publishing Group; c1988. 167 p.; ISBN: 0-940793-15-6.

423. Karaoglan, Aida, Compiler. A Gourmet's delight. Selected recipes from the haute cuisine of the Arab world: Illustrations by Mouna Bassili Sehanaoui. Photographs by George Abdini. 2nd ed. Delmar, New York: Caravan Books; c1976. 160 p.; ISBN: 0-882206-007-4.
Note: Reprint of the 1969 edition published 1969 by Dar An-Nahar, Beirut, Lebanon.

KARAY, MARY PYRROS

424. Karay, Mary Pyrros, Editor. Hellenic cuisine. a collection of Greek recipes: Fannie C. Nome, Co-editor; Cleonike Stathes Bradley, Illustrator. Detroit, MI: St. Helen's Philoptochos Society; 1957. Vii, 180 p.

KAUFMAN, WILLIAM I

425. Kaufman, William I. Greek Dinner Party. Anaheim, CA: Buzza Books; 1971.

KEOLEIAN, ARDASHES H.

426. Keoleian, Ardashes H. The Oriental Cookbook. Wholesome, Dainty and Economical Dishes of the Orient, Specially Adapted to American Tastes and Methods of Preparation.: New York, NY: Sully & Kleinteich; 1913. 346 p.
Note: Possibly the first Armenian Cookbook to be published in this country.

KERSHNER, RUTH

427. Kershner, Ruth. Greek Cooking: Weathervane Books; c1977. 64 p.; ISBN: 0-517-23932-9.

KEY TO GOOD COOKING

428. The Key to Good Cooking. Wauwatosa, WI: Sts. Constantine and Helen Greek Orthodox Church; 1972.

KEY TO GREEK COOKING

429. Christou, Barbara, Editor. Key to Greek Cooking. Seattle, WA: Church of the Assumption; 1960 122 p.

430. The Key to Greek Cooking. Seattle, Washington: Greek Orthodox Church; 1960.

431. The Key to Greek Cooking. Atlanta, GA: Greek Orthodox Cathedral of the Annunciation; 1974.

KHALIL, NAGWA E.

432. Khalil, Nagwa E. Egyptian Cuisine: over 500 contemporary recipes from various Middle Eastern and Egyptian cooks. Washington, D.C.: Three Continents; c1980. 406 p.

KHAYAT, MARIE KARAM

433. Khayat, Marie Karam. Food from the Arab world. Margaret Clark Keatinge. 3nd ed. Beirut, Lebanon; 1965. x, 163 p.
Note: 1st edition published in 1959.

KITCHEN IN CORFU

434. Chatto, James. A Kitchen in Corfu. W. L. Martin, Co-author. New American Edition ed. Joy Fitz Simmons, Illustrator. New York, NY: New Amsterdam Books; 1988.; c1987. vi, 199 p.; ISBN: 0941533174.

KITCHEN KAPERS FEATURING MIDEASTERN CUISINE.

435. Avadanian, Rose. Kitchen Kapers Featuring Mideastern Cuisine. Leawood, KS: Circulation Service; 1991. 358, 38, p.

KOCHILAS, DIANE

436. Kochilas, Diane. The Food and Wine of Greece. Vassilis Stenos, Illustrator. New York, NY: St. Martin's Press; 1990. xiii, 354 p.; ISBN: 0312050887.

KOPULOS, STELLA

437. Kopulos, Stella. Adventures in Greek Cookery. Dorothy P. Jones, Co-author. Rev. Edition ed. James Stewart, Illustrator. New York, NY: The World Publishing Co.; 1972. xiii, 337 p.; ISBN: 0529045516.

KOSHER SYRIAN COOKING

438. Sasson, Grace. Kosher Syrian Cooking. Rev. & enlarged ed. Brooklyn, NY: Grace Sasson; 1988. xvi, 202 p. Note: Rev. edition of Syrian Cooking, 1970.

KRIEG, SAUL

439. Krieg, Saul. The Alpha and Omega of Greek Cooking. New York, NY: Macmillan; 1973. xii, 266 p.

KYRIACOPOULIS, FLORICA

440. Kyriacopoulis, Florica. Self-catering in Greece: mainland and island. making the most of local food and drink: Tim Salmon, Co-author. New York, NY: Hippocrene Books; 1986. 155 p.

LAAS, W.

441. Laas, W. Cuisines of the Eastern World. New York, NY: Golden Press; 1967.

LAIRD HAMADY, MARY, 1948-

442. Laird Hamady, Mary, 1948-. Lebanese Mountain Cookery. Jana Fothergill, Illustrator. Boston, MA: D. R. Godine; 1987. 278 p.; ISBN: 0879236183.

LANGTON

443. Langton. A Culinary Tour of the Middle East.

LEBANESE COOKBOOK

444. Anthony, Dawn. Lebanese Cookbook. Elaine & Selwa Anthoney, Co-authors. Sydney, Australia; New York, NY: Lansdowne Press; 1978 109 p.; ISBN: 0701817534.

445. Lebanese Cookbook. St. Mary's Sunday School Church Guild.: New York, NY: Carlton Press; 1967. 63 p.

LEBANESE COOKERY

446. Amari, Suad. Cooking the Lebanese way. Robert L. & Diane Wolfe, Photographers. Minneapolis: Lerner Publications Co.; 1986. 47 p.; ISBN: 082250913X.

447. Anthony, Dawn. Lebanese Cookbook. Elaine & Selwa Anthoney, Co-authors. Sydney, Australia; New York, NY: Lansdowne Press; 1978 109 p.; ISBN: 0701817534.

448. Bitar, Noha. Lebanese cuisine and Middle Eastern Recipes: Exclusive Recipes. Montreal, Canada: Trait d'union; 1985. 150 p.

449. Buttross, Waddad Habeeb. Waddad's Kitchen, Lebanese zest and southern best. Natchez, Miss.: W. H. Buttross; c1982. 150 p.; ISBN: 0-939114-36-4.

450. Chirinian, Linda. Secrets of Cooking. Armenian/Lebanese/Persian: Rene Chirinian, Photographer. New Canaan, CT: Lionhart Inc./Publishers; c1987. 264 p.; ISBN: 0-9617033-0-X.

451. Corey, Helen. The Art of Syrian cookery. A culinary trip to the land of Bible history: Syria and Lebanon: 1st ed. Garden City, NY: Doubleday; 1962. 186 p.

452. David, Isabelle. Lebanese Cookery: an easy way.: Laughing Sams Press; 1982. 160 p.

453. Farah, Madelain. Lebanese Cuisine: Over two hundred authentic recipes designed for the gourmet, the vegetarian, the healthfood enthusiast. 4th ed. Portland, OR: Madelain Farah; 1979; c1974 159 p.

454. Isaac, Barbara Thomas. Everyday delights of Lebanese-Syrian Cookery. Kathryn Arwady, Co-author; Cal Matle, Illustrator. Harper Woods, MI: Author; 1977. xviii, 280 p.

455. Johns, Aggie, 1911-. The Original Lebanese & Middle East Cookbook. Kent Thompson, Illustrator. Portland, OR: A. Johns; 1983. iii, 112 p.; ISBN: 0961214805.

456. Karaoglan, Aida. Food for the Vegetarian. Brooklyn, NY: Interlink Publishing Group; c1988. 167 p.; ISBN: 0-940793-15-6.

457. Laird Hamady, Mary, 1948-. Lebanese Mountain Cookery. Jana Fothergill, Illustrator. Boston, MA: D. R. Godine; 1987. 278 p.; ISBN: 0879236183.

458. The Lebanese Kitchen: Recipes for evry occasion. Ladies Society of St. Elijah's Church.: Carp, Ontario, Canada: Gai-Garet Design; 1990.; ISBN: 0921165145.

459. Lovell, Emily Kalled. Lebanese Cooking, Streamlined. Virginia Harrison, Illustrator. San Antonio, TX: Naylor Co.; 1972. vii, 90 p.; ISBN: 0-8111-0459-1.

460. Mansour, Valerie, 1957-. Alexandra's Lebanese Cooking. authentic recipes from a Nova Scotia home: Halifax, Nova Scotia, Canada: V. Mansour; 1983. 86 p.; ISBN: 0969159803.

461. Mouzannar, Ibrahim. Lebanese Cooking: International Book Center.; 1981.

462. Rayess, George N. Rayess' Art of Lebanese Cooking. Translated from Arabic by Najla Showker: Beirut, Lebanon: Librairie du Liban; 1966. 244 p.

463. Rayess, George N. Rayess' Art of Lebanese Cooking. Translated from Arabic by Najla Showker: 2nd ed. Beirut, Lebanon: Librairie Du Liban; c1991 xxvi, 276 p.

464. Sahtein, Foods from the Middle East Mainly Lebanon, Palestine, and Syria. Southfield, MI: Arab Women Union; c1976. 312 p.

465. Salloum, Mary. A Taste of Lebanon. Brooklyn, NY: Interlink Books; c1988. 190 p.; ISBN: 0-940793-08-3.

Ethnic Cookbooks and Food Marketplace

First Edition

Hamo Vassilian, Editor

Ethnic Cookbooks

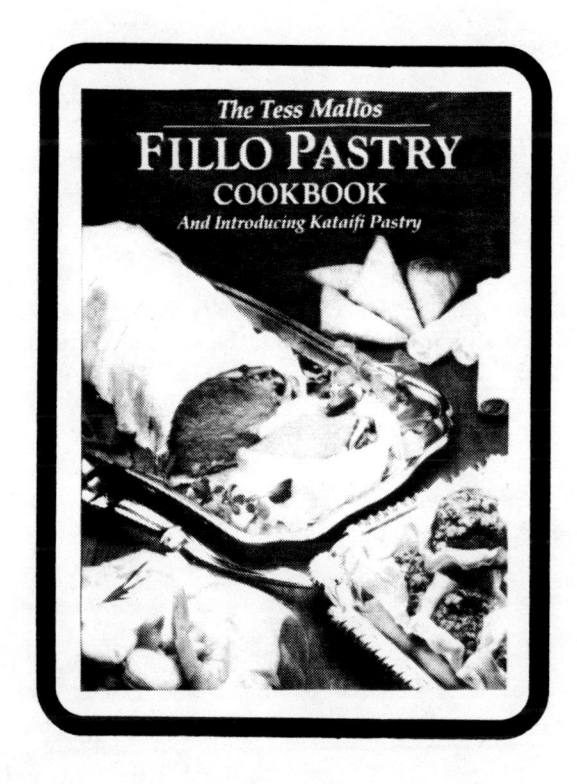

Bibliographies-41

466. Stephan, Lily. Lebanese dishes made delicious. Sidon, Lebanon: Modern Library; 1975. 85 p.

LEBANESE COOKERY: AN EASY WAY.

467. David, Isabelle. Lebanese Cookery: an easy way.: Laughing Sams Press; 1982. 160 p.

LEBANESE COOKING

468. Mouzannar, Ibrahim. Lebanese Cooking: International Book Center.; 1981.

LEBANESE COOKING, STREAMLINED

469. Lovell, Emily Kalled. Lebanese Cooking, Streamlined. Virginia Harrison, Illustrator. San Antonio, TX: Naylor Co.; 1972. vii, 90 p.; ISBN: 0-8111-0459-1.

LEBANESE CUISINE AND MIDDLE EASTERN RECIPES: EXCLUSIVE RECIPES

470. Bitar, Noha. Lebanese cuisine and Middle Eastern Recipes: Exclusive Recipes. Montreal, Canada: Trait d'union; 1985. 150 p.

LEBANESE CUISINE: OVER TWO HUNDRED AUTHENTIC RECIPES DESIGNED FOR THE GOURMET, THE VEGETARIAN, THE HEALTHFOOD ENTHUSIAST

471. Farah, Madelain. Lebanese Cuisine: Over two hundred authentic recipes designed for the gourmet, the vegetarian, the healthfood enthusiast. 4th ed. Portland, OR: Madelain Farah; 1979; c1974 159 p.

LEBANESE DISHES MADE DELICIOUS.

472. Stephan, Lily. Lebanese dishes made delicious. Sidon, Lebanon: Modern Library; 1975. 85 p.

LEBANESE KITCHEN: RECIPES FOR EVRY OCCASION

473. The Lebanese Kitchen: Recipes for evry occasion. Ladies Society of St. Elijah's Church.: Carp, Ontario, Canada: Gai-Garet Design; 1990.; ISBN: 0921165145.

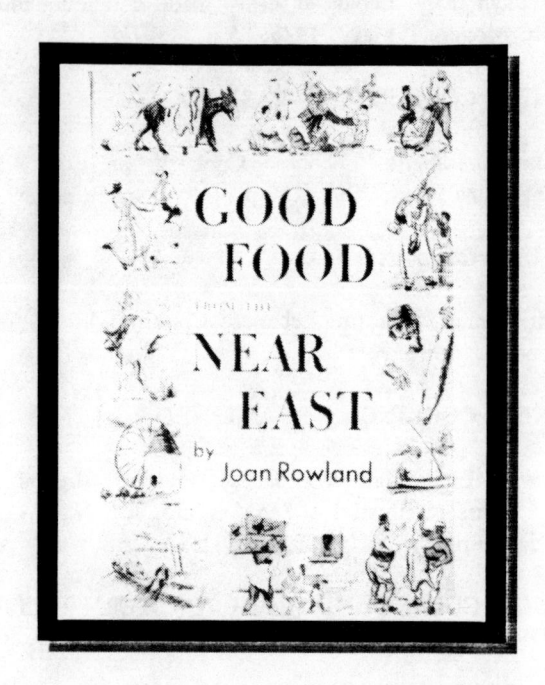

LEBANESE MOUNTAIN COOKERY

474. Laird Hamady, Mary, 1948-. Lebanese Mountain Cookery. Jana Fothergill, Illustrator. Boston, MA: D. R. Godine; 1987. 278 p.; ISBN: 0879236183.

LEBWA, , 1938-

475. Lebwa, , 1938-. An American belly dancer's secrets of a beautiful body. West Nyack, NY: Parker Publishing Co.; 1981.; c1979. 202 p.; ISBN: 01302239526.

LENTEN COOKBOOK FOR ORTHODOX

476. A Lenten Cookbook for Orthodox. Seattle, WA: St. Nectarios American Orthodox Church; 1972.

LESBERG, SANDY

477. Lesberg, Sandy. At the table of Israel: a unique collection of three hundred traditional and modern Israeli recipes. Indianapolis; New York: Bobbs-Merrill; Peebles Press.; c1973,.

LITTLE GREEK COOKBOOK

478. Salaman, Rena. A little Greek Cookbook. San Francisco, CA: Chronicle Books; 1990. 60 p.; ISBN: 0877017956.

LOEWEN, NANCY, 1964-

479. Loewen, Nancy, 1964-. Greece. Vero Beach, FL: Rourke Publications; 1991.; ISBN: 0866253483.

LOVELL, EMILY KALLED

480. Lovell, Emily Kalled. Lebanese Cooking, Streamlined. Virginia Harrison, Illustrator. San Antonio, TX: Naylor Co.; 1972. vii, 90 p.; ISBN: 0-8111-0459-1.

MACDOUGALL, ALLAN ROSS, 1893-

481. MacDougall, Allan Ross, 1893-. And the Greeks. a book of Hellenic recipes and culinary lore,: New York, NY: Near East Foundation; c1942. 109 p.

MAGIC COOKERY.

482. St. Nicholas Orthodox Cathedral Ladies' Society. Magic Cookery. Los Angeles, CA: St. Nicholas; 1987. 309 p.

Ethnic Cookbooks

MAIBERG, RON

483. Maiberg, Ron. A Taste of Israel. New York, NY: Rizoli International; 1990. 240 p.; ISBN: 0847811956.

MALLOS, TESS

484. Mallos, Tess. The Complete Middle East Cookbook. Reg Morrison, Photographer; Sue Wagner, Editor. New York, NY: McGraw-Hill; c1979. 400 p.; ISBN: 0-07-039810-0.

485. Mallos, Tess. Fillo Pastry Cookbook: And Introducing Kataifi Pastry. Andrew Warn, Photographer; Suzanne Mallos, Illustrator. London, England: Merehurst Press; 1987.; c1983 96 p.; ISBN: 0-948075-47-3.

486. Mallos, Tess. Greek Cookbook. Howard Joes, Photographer. Sydney, Australia: Books for Pleasure; 1976 128 p.; ISBN: 0-7271-0038-6.

487. Mallos, Tess. Greek Cooking for Pleasure. Howard Jones, Photographer. Secaucus, NJ: Chartwell Books; 1978. 112 p.; ISBN: 0890092516.

MAN, ROSAMOND

488. Man, Rosamond. The Complete Meze Table. Veronica Sperling & Caroline Schuck, Editors. London, England: Ebury Press; 1986. 111 p.; ISBN: 0852235461.

MANSOUR, VALERIE, 1957-

489. Mansour, Valerie, 1957-. Alexandra's Lebanese Cooking. authentic recipes from a Nova Scotia home: Halifax, Nova Scotia, Canada: V. Mansour; 1983. 86 p.; ISBN: 0969159803.

MARDIKIAN, GEORGE

490. Mardikian, George. Dinner at Omar Khayyam's. Salt Lake City: Viking Press; 1969, 13th printing; c1944. 150 p.

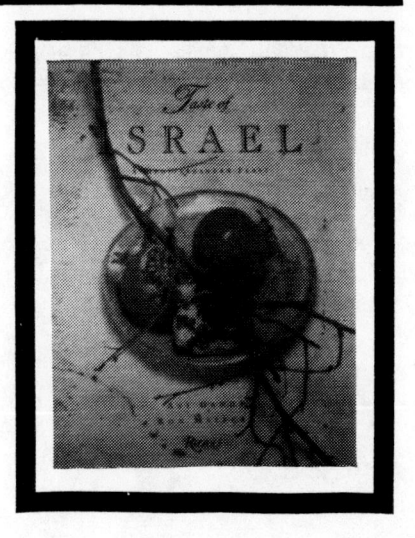

MARK, THEONIE

491. Mark, Theonie. Greek Islands Cooking. Maris Platais, Illustrator. Boston, MA: Little, Brown & Co.; 1974 xvi, 303 p.; ISBN: 0-316-54623-2.
Note: Also published by Bastsford, in London in 1978.

MARKETOS, OLYMPIA

492. Marketos, Olympia. Athens a la carte, the best of Greek cooking. Chicago, IL: Rand McNally; 1963. 119 p.

MAZDA, MAIDEH

493. Mazda, Maideh. In a Persian Kitchen. Favorite Recipes from the Near East: M. Kuwata, Illustrator. Rutland, Vermont: Charles E. Tuttle Co.; c1960. 175 p.

MCKELLAR, DORIS

494. McKellar, Doris, Compiler. Afghan Cookery. an Afghan recipe book: 2nd ed. Kabul, Afghanistan: Afghan Book Publisher; 1971 90 p.

MCQUEEN-WILLIAMS, MORVYTH, 1911-1976.

495. Mcqueen-Williams, Morvyth, 1911-1976. A Diet for 100 healthy, happy years. Barbara Apisson, Co-author; Norman Ober, Editor. Englewood Cliffs, NJ: Prentice-Hall; c1977. vi, 220 p.; ISBN: 0-13-211185-3.

MEHTA, JEROO

496. Mehta, Jeroo. 101 Parsi Recipes. Bombay, India: Vakils, Feffer & Simon; c1973. 146 p.

MERJANIAN-PIRANIAN, LOUISE

497. Merjanian-Piranian, Louise. The Pleasure of Cooking. Beirut, Lebanon: Donigian & Sons; 1974. 304 p.

METAXAS, DAPHNE

498. Metaxas, Daphne. Classic Greek Cooking. Concord, CA: Nitty Gritty Productions; 1974. 179 p.; ISBN: 0-911954-31-7.

MID-EASTERN CUISINE I LOVE

499. Bond, Jules Jerome. The Mid-Eastern Cuisine I love. New York, NY: Leon Amiel; 1977; c1977. 160 p.; ISBN: 0-8148-0693-7.

MIDDLE EAST COOK: PURE AND SIMPLE

500. Sayegh, Lily. Middle East Cook: Pure and Simple; 1992. 52 p.

MIDDLE EASTERN COOKERY

501. Agia, Emelie, Editor. Cookin' good with Sitto. Compiled by Our Lady of Perpetual Help Society of St. Ann's Melkite Catholic Church. 2nd ed. West Paterson, NJ: St. Ann's Melkite Catholic Church; 1982 ix, 95 p.

502. Atiyeh, Wadeeha. Scheherazade Cooks. John Alcorn, Illustrator. Great Neck, NY: Channel Press; c1960. 189 p.

503. Avadanian, Rose. Kitchen Kapers Featuring Mideastern Cuisine. Leawood, KS: Circulation Service; 1991. 358, 38, p.

504. Benghiat, Suzy. Middle Eastern Cooking. New York, NY: Harmony Books; 1985.; c1984. 144 p.; ISBN: 0-517-55608-1.

505. Betar, Yasmine. Finest Recipes from the Middle East. Over one Hundred Recipes simplified with Suggested Menus their uses Origin and History, also spices and herbs some stories of folklore origin: Washington, D.C.; 1971; c1957. Over 145 p.

506. Bezjian, Alice. The Complete Armenian Cookbook Including Favorite International Recipes. Fair Lawn, NJ: Rosekeer Press; c1983. 278 p.; ISBN: 0-915033-00-03.

507. Bitar, Noha. Lebanese cuisine and Middle Eastern Recipes: Exclusive Recipes. Montreal, Canada: Trait d'union; 1985. 150 p.

508. Bond, Jules Jerome. The Mid-Eastern Cuisine I love. New York, NY: Leon Amiel; 1977; c1977. 160 p.; ISBN: 0-8148-0693-7.

509. Chapman, Pat, 1940-. The Curry Club Middle Eastern cookbook: Piatkus; 1989. 192 p.; ISBN: 0861888936.

510. Corey, Helen. Food from biblical lands: a culinary trip to the land of Bible history. Terre Haute, IN: H. Corey; c1989. xx, 154 p.

511. Debasque, Roger. Eastern Mediterranean Cooking, Exotic delicacies from Greece, Turkey, Israel, Lebanon and Iran. New York, NY: Galahad Books; 1973.

512. der Haroutunian, Arto, 1940-1987. Barbecue Cookbook. London, England.

513. der Haroutunian, Arto, 1940-1987. Middle Eastern Cookery. London, England: Century Publishing Co.; 1982 Over 369 p.; ISBN: 0-330-26783-3.

514. der Haroutunian, Arto, 1940-1987. Vegetarian Dishes from the Middle East. London, England: Century Publishing; 1987.; c1983. 224 p.; ISBN: 0-7126-0120-1.

515. der Haroutunian, Arto, 1940-1987. Whole Grain Cookbook. London, England.

516. der Haroutunian, Arto, 1940-1987. The Yoghurt Book. Food of the Gods: London, England: Penguin Books; 1983. Over 200 p.

517. Doniguian, Mireille H. Armenian and Oriental Cooking. Beirut, Lebanon: G. Doniguian & Sons; 1987? 233 p.

518. Dosti, Rose. Middle Eastern Cooking. Tucson, AZ: HP Books, Inc.; c1982. 192 p.; ISBN: 0-89586-184-4.

519. Farah, Madelain. Pocket Bread Potpourri, Meals in Minutes. Leila Habib, Co-author. Memphis, TN: Wimmer Brothers Books; c1984. 108 p.

520. Farah, Nadia, 1940-. Ah! Cooking the Middle Eastern Way. Ottawa, Canada: Deneau Publishers; 1982? 118 p.; ISBN: 0-88879-061-9.

521. Flavors of the Middle East. Washington, D.C.: Aramco; 1988. 40 p.

522. Frank, Beryl, 1927-. Middle Eastern cooking. New York, NY: Weathervane Books; 1980. 64 p.; ISBN: 0517318350.

523. Habeeb, Virginia. Pita the Great. New York, NY: Workman; 1986; ISBN: 0-89480-039-6.

524. Hatton, D. Oriental Cookery. London, England: William Collins Sons & Co.; 1969.
Note: Includes Armenian Recipes.

46-Bibliographies — Ethnic Cookbooks

525. Howe, Robin. Middle Eastern Cookery. Tony Streek, Illustrator. London, England: Eyre Mehtuen; 1978 189 p.; ISBN: 0413382206.

526. Johns, Aggie, 1911-. The Original Lebanese & Middle East Cookbook. Kent Thompson, Illustrator. Portland, OR: A. Johns; 1983. iii, 112 p.; ISBN: 0961214805.

527. Joly, E. Gertrude. The English Arabic Cookery book. Beirut, Lebanon; 1950. 239 p.

528. Karaoglan, Aida, Compiler. A Gourmet's delight. Selected recipes from the haute cuisine of the Arab world: Illustrations by Mouna Bassili Sehanaoui. Photographs by George Abdini. 2nd ed. Delmar, New York: Caravan Books; c1976. 160 p.; ISBN: 0-882206-007-4.
Note: Reprint of the 1969 edition published 1969 by Dar An-Nahar, Beirut, Lebanon.

529. Khalil, Nagwa E. Egyptian Cuisine: over 500 contemporary recipes from various Middle Eastern and Egyptian cooks. Washington, D.C.: Three Continents; c1980. 406 p.

530. Khayat, Marie Karam. Food from the Arab world. Margaret Clark Keatinge. 3nd ed. Beirut, Lebanon; 1965. x, 163 p.
Note: 1st edition published in 1959.

531. Laas, W. Cuisines of the Eastern World. New York, NY: Golden Press; 1967.

532. Langton. A Culinary Tour of the Middle East.

533. Lebwa, , 1938-. An American belly dancer's secrets of a beautiful body. West Nyack, NY: Parker Publishing Co.; 1981.; c1979. 202 p.; ISBN: 01302239526.

534. Mallos, Tess. The Complete Middle East Cookbook. Reg Morrison, Photographer; Sue Wagner, Editor. New York, NY: McGraw-Hill; c1979. 400 p.; ISBN: 0-07-039810-0.

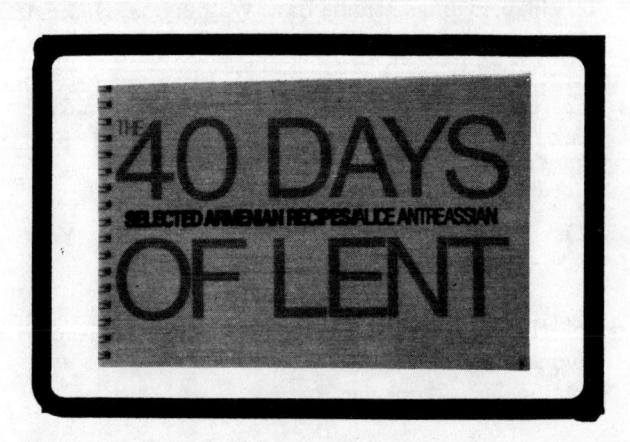

535. Man, Rosamond. The Complete Meze Table. Veronica Sperling & Caroline Schuck, Editors. London, England: Ebury Press; 1986. 111 p.; ISBN: 0852235461.

536. Merjanian-Piranian, Louise. The Pleasure of Cooking. Beirut, Lebanon: Donigian & Sons; 1974. 304 p.

537. Moorish recipes/ collected and compiled by John. Edinburgh, England: Oliver & Boyd; c1955. xxiv, 80 p.

538. Najor, Julia, 1941-. Babylonian Cuisine: Chaldean cookbook from the Middle East. Nobil Kirma, Photographer. New York, NY: Vantage Press; 1981 xxiii, 213 p.; ISBN: 0533046289.

539. Nickles, Harry G. Middle Eastern Cooking. and the editors of Time-Life Books: David Lees and Richard Jeffery, Photographers. New York, NY: Time-Life Books; 1969. 206 p.

540. Orga, Irfan. Cooking the Middle East Way. London, England: Spring Books; c1962. 256 p.

541. Osborne, Christine. Cooking the Middle Eastern Way. Secaucus, NJ: Chartwell Books, Inc.; c1985. 152 p.; ISBN: 0-89009-838-7.

542. Osborne, Christine. Middle Eastern food and drink. New York, NY: Bookwright Press; c1988. 48 p.; ISBN: 0531182002.
Note: Juvenile Literature.

543. Perl, Lila. Rice, Spice and Bitter Oranges. Mediterranean Foods and Festivals: Stanislao Dino Rigolo, Illustrator. Cleveland, Ohio: World Publishing Co.; 1967.; c1967. 272 p.

544. Philippou, Margaret Joy. 101 Arabian delights: a book of Arabic Cookery. Brighton: Clifton Books; 1969. 99 p.; ISBN: 90125505X.

545. Powell, Jessie (Johns) 1914-. Finest recipes from the Middle East; over one hundred recipes simplified with suggested menus, their uses, origin, and history; also , spicelore and herbs, some stories of folklore origin. Silver Spring, MD; 1968; c1957. 150 p.

546. Ridgwell, Jenny. Middle Eastern Cooking. New York, NY: Crescent Books; 1987; c1986 by Ward Lock Limited 96 p.; ISBN: 0-517-62452-4.

547. Roden, Claudia. A Book of Middle Eastern Food. Edward Bawden, Illustrator; Bruce Pinkard, Photographer. London, England: Nelson; 1968. 320 p.

548. Roden, Claudia. A Book of Middle Eastern Food. Alta Ann Parkins, Illustrator. New York, NY: Alfred A. Knopf; 1985. 453, xiv, p.; ISBN: 0-394-47181-4.

549. Roden, Claudia. A New Book of Middle Eastern Food. Revised ed. Penguin Books: New York; c1985.

550. Rowland, Joan. Good food from the Near East; five hundred favorite recipes from twelve countries. New York, NY: M. Barrow & Co., Inc.; 1950. 274 p.

551. Sahtein, Foods from the Middle East Mainly Lebanon, Palestine, and Syria. Southfield, MI: Arab Women Union; c1976. 312 p.

552. Salah, Nahda S. Arab World Cookbook : the book of one thousand and one delights. Basem S. Salah, Photographer. Dhahran, Saudi Arabia: Said Salah International Publications Agencies; 1977.; c1973. 345 p.

553. Salah, Nahda. One Thousand and One Delights: Authentic Home Cooking of the Middle East.. Saleh, Basem S., Photographer: ?; ? 396 p.

554. Sayegh, Lily. Middle East Cook: Pure and Simple; 1992. 52 p.

555. Scott, David, 1944-. Middle Eastern Vegetarian Cookery. London, England: Hutchinson Group; 1983; c1981. 176 p.; ISBN: 0-09-145341-0.

556. Scott, David, 1944-. Recipes for an Arabian night. 1st American ed. New York, NY: Pantheon Books, a division of Random House, Inc.; 1983; c1983; ISBN: 0-394-72292-2.
Note: Originally published in Great Britain as Traditional Arabic Cookery by Hutchinson Publishing Group.

557. Scott, David, 1944-. Traditional Arab Cookery. Steve Hardstaff, Illustrator. London, England: Rider; 1983. 160 p.; ISBN: 0091533317.

558. Seranne, Ann. The Best of Near Eastern Cookery. Favorite Dishes from the Balkans, Turkey, Israel, Jordan, Saudi Arabia & other Countries of the Arabian Peninsula: Eileen Gaden, Photographic Illustrator. Garden City, NY: Doubleday & Co., Inc.; 1964; c1964. 158 p.

559. Shasheer, Jameela. Arab World Cookbook. Dubai: International Bookshop; 1973.

560. Shepard, Sigrid M. Natural Food Feasts from the Eastern World. New York, NY: Arco Publishing, Inc.; 1979.

561. Short, Dorothy. Camel Land Cookery. Beirut, Lebanon; 1965.

562. Smouha, Patricia. Middle Eastern Cooking. London, England: Andre Deutsch; 1955. 133 p.
Note: 1st American Edition 1957 published by Citadel Press, NY.

563. St. Nicholas Orthodox Cathedral Ladies' Society. Magic Cookery. Los Angeles, CA: St. Nicholas; 1987. 309 p.

564. Valero, Rina. Delights of Jerusalem: a Treasury of Cooking and Folklore. Shlesinger, Miriam, Translator.: Nahar Publishing; Steimatzky; 1985 ?

565. Waines, David, Compiler. In a Caliph's Kitchen: Riad El-Rayyes; 1989. 119 p.

566. Weiss-Armush, Anne Marie. Arabian Cuisine. John Berry, Illustrator. Beirut, Lebanon; 1984. 402 p.

567. Wells, Troth. The New International Food Book. Oxford, England: New Internationalist Publications; 1990. 182 p.

568. Yassine, Sima Osman. Middle Eastern Cuisine; 1984. 120 p.

569. Zane, Eva. Middle Eastern Cookery, Drawings & Annotations by Keith Halonen. San Francisco: 101 Productions; 1974; c1974 144 p.

MIDDLE EASTERN COOKING

570. Benghiat, Suzy. Middle Eastern Cooking. New York, NY: Harmony Books; 1985.; c1984. 144 p.; ISBN: 0-517-55608-1.

571. Dosti, Rose. Middle Eastern Cooking. Tucson, AZ: HP Books, Inc.; c1982. 192 p.; ISBN: 0-89586-184-4.

572. Frank, Beryl, 1927-. Middle Eastern cooking. New York, NY: Weathervane Books; 1980. 64 p.; ISBN: 0517318350.

573. Nickles, Harry G. Middle Eastern Cooking. and the editors of Time-Life Books: David Lees and Richard Jeffery, Photographers. New York, NY: Time-Life Books; 1969. 206 p.

574. Ridgwell, Jenny. Middle Eastern Cooking. New York, NY: Crescent Books; 1987; c1986 by Ward Lock Limited 96 p.; ISBN: 0-517-62452-4.

575. Smouha, Patricia. Middle Eastern Cooking. London, England: Andre Deutsch; 1955. 133 p.
Note: 1st American Edition 1957 published by Citadel Press, NY.

MIDDLE EASTERN CUISINE

576. Yassine, Sima Osman. Middle Eastern Cuisine; 1984. 120 p.

MIDDLE EASTERN FOOD AND DRINK

577. Osborne, Christine. Middle Eastern food and drink. New York, NY: Bookwright Press; c1988. 48 p.; ISBN: 0531182002.
Note: Juvenile Literature.

MIDDLE EASTERN VEGETARIAN COOKERY

578. Scott, David, 1944-. Middle Eastern Vegetarian Cookery. London, England: Hutchinson Group; 1983; c1981. 176 p.; ISBN: 0-09-145341-0.

MONROE, ELVIRA

579. Monroe, Elvira. Greek moods and menus. Theoni Pappas, Co-author. San Carlos, CA: Wide World; c1980. 119 p.; ISBN: 0933174055.

Ethnic Cookbooks — Bibliographies-49

MOORISH RECIPES/ COLLECTED AND COMPILED BY JOHN

580. Moorish recipes/ collected and compiled by John. Edinburgh, England: Oliver & Boyd; c1955. xxiv, 80 p.

MORE THAN BAKLAVA: A GREEK COOKBOOK
581. Semos, Evelyn, 1915-. More than baklava: a Greek cookbook. Ann Pearle, Illustrator. Dallas, TX: Neiman Marcus; 1982. x, 87 p.; ISBN: 0960666818.

MOROCCAN COOKBOOK

582. Day, Irene F. The Moroccan Cookbook. New York, NY: Putnam Publishing Group; 1982.; c1975, by Andre Deutsch. 155 p.; ISBN: 0-399-5-704-3.
Note: Original title of the is Kitchen in the Kasbah.

MOROCCAN COOKERY

583. Day, Irene F. The Moroccan Cookbook. New York, NY: Putnam Publishing Group; 1982.; c1975, by Andre Deutsch. 155 p.; ISBN: 0-399-5-704-3.
Note: Original title of the is Kitchen in the Kasbah.

584. Morse, Kitty. Come with Me to the Kasbah: A Cook's Tour of Morocco. 1st ed. Casablanca, Morocco: Editions SERAR; 1989. 237 p.

585. Neitzert, Evelyn A. Moroccan Cookery; fifty recipes compiled and adapted to American Cooking methods. Casablanca, Morocco; 1954. 46 p.

586. Wolfert, Paula. Couscous and other Good Food from Morocco. Bill Bayer, Photographer; Sidonie Coryn, Illustrator. New York, NY: Harper & Row; 1973 xv, 351 p.; ISBN: 0-06-014721-0.

587. Yacoubi, Ahmed. Alchemist's Cookbook: Moroccan Scientific Cuisine. Tucson, AZ: Omen Press; 1972. X, 142.

MOROCCAN COOKERY; FIFTY RECIPES COMPILED AND ADAPTED TO AMERICAN COOKING METHODS.

588. Neitzert, Evelyn A. Moroccan Cookery; fifty recipes compiled and adapted to American Cooking methods. Casablanca, Morocco; 1954. 46 p.

MORSE, KITTY

589. Morse, Kitty. Come with Me to the Kasbah: A Cook's Tour of Morocco. 1st ed. Casablanca, Morocco: Editions SERAR; 1989. 237 p.

MOTAMEN REID, MEHRY

590. Motamen Reid, Mehry. Gourmet Cooking, Persian Style. Ceresville, MD: Author; c1989. 197 p.

MOURDJIS, MARIOS, 1942-

591. Mourdjis, Marios, 1942-. The Cypriots at table. Nicosia, Cyprus: C.A.L. Graphics 220 p.

MOUSSAKA, BAKLAVA, AND LOVE; COOKING THE GREEK WAY.

592. Hassalevris, Constantine, 1913-. Moussaka, baklava, and love; cooking the Greek way. Los Angeles, CA: Ward Ritchie Press; 1973. 141 p.; ISBN: 0378010824.

MOUZANNAR, IBRAHIM

593. Mouzannar, Ibrahim. Lebanese Cooking: International Book Center.; 1981.

MUSLIM COOKING OF PAKISTAN

594. Husain, S.A. Muslim Cooking of Pakistan. Lahore, Pakestan: Sh. Muhammad Ashraf; c1974.

MY GREEK HERITAGE COOKBOOK

595. Andrews, Jasmine Panos. My Greek heritage cookbook. Paul A. Andrews, Photographer; Thalia L. Bredakis, Illustrator. Coolierville, TN: Fundcraft Pub.; c1989. A-I, 162, A-D p.

MYTHOLOGY AND MEATBALLS: A GREEK ISLAND DIARY COOKBOOK

596. Spoerri, Daniel, 1930-. Mythology and Meatballs: a Greek Island Diary Cookbook. Emmett Williams, Translator; Jeanne Jambo, Illustrator. Berkeley, CA: Aris; 1982. 238 p.; ISBN: 0943196013.

Ethnic Cookbooks

NAHOUM, ALDO

597. Nahoum, Aldo. The Art of Israeli Cooking; original Israeli recipes never before published, as well as favorite traditional dishes, all kosher. 1st ed. New York, NY: Holt, Rinehart and Winston; 1971.; c1970. 152 p.; ISBN: 0-03-085176-9.

NAJOR, JULIA, 1941-

598. Najor, Julia, 1941-. Babylonian Cuisine: Chaldean cookbook from the Middle East. Nobil Kirma, Photographer. New York, NY: Vantage Press; 1981 xxiii, 213 p.; ISBN: 0533046289.

NATHAN, JOAN

599. Nathan, Joan. The Flavor of Jerusalem. Goldman, Judy Stacey, Co-author. Boston, MA: Little, Brown; 1975. 242 p.

NATURAL FOOD FEASTS FROM THE EASTERN WORLD

600. Shepard, Sigrid M. Natural Food Feasts from the Eastern World. New York, NY: Arco Publishing, Inc.; 1979.

NEITZERT, EVELYN A.

601. Neitzert, Evelyn A. Moroccan Cookery; fifty recipes compiled and adapted to American Cooking methods. Casablanca, Morocco; 1954. 46 p.

NEW BOOK OF MIDDLE EASTERN FOOD

602. Roden, Claudia. A New Book of Middle Eastern Food. Revised ed. Penguin Books: New York; c1985.

NEW FESTIVAL OF GREEK COOKING

603. The New festival of Greek Cooking. Santa Barbara, CA: St. Barbara Greek Orthodox Church; c1981. 160 p.

NEW GOURMET

604. The New Gourmet. Holy Trinity Armenian Apostolic Church of Greater Boston. Cambridge, MA: 1974 178 p.

NEW INTERNATIONAL FOOD BOOK

605. Wells, Troth. The New International Food Book. Oxford, England: New Internationalist Publications; 1990. 182 p.

NICALAOU, NEARCHOS

606. Nicalaou, Nearchos. Cooking from Cyprus, the Island of Aphrodite. Nicosia, Cyprus; 1979.

NICKLES, HARRY G.

607. Nickles, Harry G. Middle Eastern Cooking. and the editors of Time-Life Books: David Lees and Richard Jeffery, Photographers. New York, NY: Time-Life Books; 1969. 206 p.

NIX, JAN

608. Nix, Jan. Filo: Crossing Press; 1991. 139 p.

NORTH AFRICAN COOKERY

609. der Haroutunian, Arto, 1940-1987. North African Cookery. London, England: Century Publishing Co.; 1985; c1985.; ISBN: 0-7126-0925-3.

610. Perl, Lila. Rice, Spice and Bitter Oranges. Mediterranean Foods and Festivals: Stanislao Dino Rigolo, Illustrator. Cleveland, Ohio: World Publishing Co.; 1967.; c1967. 272 p.

NOSHE DJAN: AFGHAN FOOD AND COOKERY

611. Saberi, Helen. Noshe Djan: Afghan Food and Cookery. with the help of Najiba Zaka and Shaima Breshna and drawings by Abdullah Breshna. London, England: Prospect Books; c1986. 160 p.; ISBN: 0-907325-32-7.

ODYSSEY OF GREEK COOKING

612. Odyssey of Greek cooking. Annapolis, MD: Greek Orthodox Ladies Philoptochos Society; c1980. 175 p.

ONE THOUSAND AND ONE DELIGHTS: AUTHENTIC HOME COOKING OF THE MIDDLE EAST.

613. Salah, Nahda. One Thousand and One Delights: Authentic Home Cooking of the Middle East.. Saleh, Basem S., Photographer: ?; ? 396 p.

ORGA, IRFAN

614. Orga, Irfan. Cooking the Middle East Way. London, England: Spring Books; c1962. 256 p.

ORIENTAL COOKBOOK

615. Keoleian, Ardashes H. The Oriental Cookbook. Wholesome, Dainty and Economical Dishes of the Orient,

Specially Adapted to American Tastes and Methods of Preparation.: New York, NY: Sully & Kleinteich; 1913. 346 p.
Note: Possibly the first Armenian Cookbook to be published in this country.

ORIENTAL COOKERY

616. Hatton, D. Oriental Cookery. London, England: William Collins Sons & Co.; 1969.
Note: Includes Armenian Recipes.

ORIGINAL EGYPTIAN RECIPES

617. Gadalla, Maher. Original Egyptian recipes. Rockford, IL: Nile Publications; c1981. 48 p.

ORIGINAL LEBANESE & MIDDLE EAST COOKBOOK

618. Johns, Aggie, 1911-. The Original Lebanese & Middle East Cookbook. Kent Thompson, Illustrator. Portland, OR: A. Johns; 1983. iii, 112 p.; ISBN: 0961214805.

OSBORNE, CHRISTINE

619. Osborne, Christine. Cooking the Middle Eastern Way. Secaucus, NJ: Chartwell Books, Inc.; c1985. 152 p.; ISBN: 0-89009-838-7.

620. Osborne, Christine. Middle Eastern food and drink. New York, NY: Bookwright Press; c1988. 48 p.; ISBN: 0531182002.
Note: Juvenile Literature.

OUR COLLECTION OF SECRET GREEK RECIPES

621. Our Collection of Secret Greek Recipes. 4th ed. Milwaukee, WI: Assumption Greek Orhtodox Church; 1968.

OUR CULINARY TREASURES

622. Our Culinary Treasures. Compiled by Kirikian Armenian School of St. Thomas Armenian Church. Tenafly, New Jersey: St. Thomas Armenian Church; 1989. 203, viii p.

PALESTINE COOKERY

623. Sahtein, Foods from the Middle East Mainly Lebanon, Palestine, and Syria. Southfield, MI: Arab Women Union; c1976. 312 p.

PAPAS, MARY

624. Papas, Mary. Grecian Gourmet with Lamb. 4th ed. Loma, CO: Woolgrowers Auxiliary; 1976.

PAPPAS, LOU SEIBERT

625. Pappas, Lou Seibert. Greek Cooking. New York, NY: Harper & Row; 1973 xx, 196 p.; ISBN: 0060132736.

PAPPAS, THEONI

626. Pappas, Theoni. Greek cooking for everyone. Elvira Monrose, Co-author. 2nd ed. San Carlos, CA: Wide World Pub./Tetra; 1986.; c1989. 167 p.; ISBN: 0933174616.

PARADISIS, CHRISSA

627. Paradisis, Chrissa. The Best Book of Greek Cookery. New York, NY: International Publications Service; 1981.

PARADISSIS, CHRISSA

628. Paradissis, Chrissa. The Best of Greek Cookery. 5th ed. Athens, Greece: Efstathiadis Group; New York, NY.; 1983.; c1976. 192 p.

PAREE JOSH! GOOD EATING

629. Paree Josh! Good Eating. A collection of favorite Armenian American Recipes: St. Mary Armenian Apostolic Church. Livingston, NJ: St. Mary Armenian Apostolic Church; 1984, third printing; c1968 253 p.

Ethnic Cookbooks

Bibliographies-53

PARENTI, CATHY

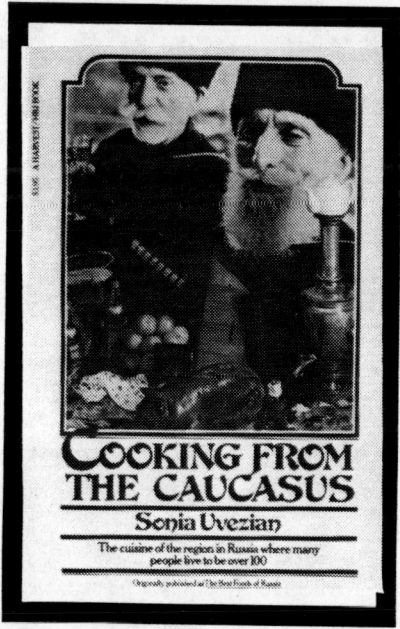

630. Parenti, Cathy. A Taste of Afghanistan: The Cuisine of the Crossroads of the World. Phoenix, AZ: Author; c1987. 84 p.

PASTRY-GREEK

631. Deliganis, Christina. Greek pastries: easy step by step instructions. Bruce Terami, Photographer. Seattle, WA: Kandylas Press; 1977 41 p.; ISBN: 0-930694-01-5.

PASTRY-MIDDLE EASTERN

632. der Haroutunian, Arto, 1940-1987. Patisserie of the Eastern Mediterranean.: McGraw-Hill Book; 1989.; c1988. 128 p.; ISBN: 0-07-026665-4.

633. der Haroutunian, Arto, 1940-1987. Sweets & Desserts from the Middle East. London, England: Century Publishing; 1984. 224 p.; ISBN: 0712602925.

634. Mallos, Tess. Fillo Pastry Cookbook: And Introducing Kataifi Pastry. Andrew Warn, Photographer; Suzanne Mallos, Illustrator. London, England: Merehurst Press; 1987.; c1983 96 p.; ISBN: 0-948075-47-3.

635. Nix, Jan. Filo: Crossing Press; 1991. 139 p.

636. Sousanis, Mart, 1943-. The Art of filo cookbook: International entrees, appetizers & desserts wrapped in flaky pastry.. Masayo Suzuki, Illustrator. Berkeley, CA: Aris Books; 1988, 3rd printing; c1983. 143 p.; ISBN: 0943186064.

PATISSERIE OF THE EASTERN MEDITERRANEAN.

637. der Haroutunian, Arto, 1940-1987. Patisserie of the Eastern Mediterranean.: McGraw-Hill Book; 1989.; c1988. 128 p.; ISBN: 0-07-026665-4.

PERL, LILA

638. Perl, Lila. Rice, Spice and Bitter Oranges. Mediterranean Foods and Festivals: Stanislao Dino Rigolo, Illustrator. Cleveland, Ohio: World Publishing Co.; 1967.; c1967. 272 p.

PERSIAN COOKERY

639. Batmanglij, Najmieh, 1947-. Food of Life. A book of ancient Persian and modern Iranian cooking and ceremonies: 1st ed. Washington, D.C.: Mage Publishers, Inc.; c1986. 245 p.; ISBN: 0-934211-00-0.
Note: Rev. translation of Ma cuisine d'Iran.

54-Bibliographies

Ethnic Cookbooks

640. Batmanglij, Najmieh, 1947-. Food of Life. A book of ancient Persian and modern Iranian cooking and ceremonies.: 2nd ed. Washington, D.C.: Mage Publishers; c1990. 248 p.; ISBN: 0934211000.

641. Chirinian, Linda. Secrets of Cooking. Armenian/Lebanese/Persian: Rene Chirinian, Photographer. New Canaan, CT: Lionhart Inc./Publishers; c1987. 264 p.; ISBN: 0-9617033-0-X.

642. Ghanoonparvar, Mohammad R. Persian Cuisine. Jill Lieber and Claudia Kane, Illustrators. 1st ed. Lexington, KY: Mazda Publisher; c1982; 2 Vol.; ISBN: 0939214105. Note: Vol 1. = Traditional foods. Vol 2. Regional and modern foods. English & Persian. 5th printing, 1990.

643. Hekmat, Forough-es-Saltaneh. The Art of Persian Cooking. Garden City, NY: Doubleday; 1961. 190 p.

644. Mazda, Maideh. In a Persian Kitchen. Favorite Recipes from the Near East: M. Kuwata, Illustrator. Rutland, Vermont: Charles E. Tuttle Co.; c1960. 175 p.

645. Mehta, Jeroo. 101 Parsi Recipes. Bombay, India: Vakils, Feffer & Simon; c1973. 146 p.

646. Motamen Reid, Mehry. Gourmet Cooking, Persian Style. Ceresville, MD: Author; c1989. 197 p.

647. Ramazani, Nesta, 1932-. Persian Cooking. A Table of Exotic Delights: New York, NY: Quadrangle; 1984, Second printing; c1974. xx, 296 p.; ISBN: 0-8139-0962-7.

648. Simmons, Shirin. Entertaining the Persian Way. London, England: Lennard Publishing; c1988. 156 p.; ISBN: 1-85291-0267.

649. Varjabedian, Ida P. Exotic, Light & Easy Cookbook of Middle Eastern Cuisine. Great Neck, NY: Todd & Honeywell, Inc.; c1985.; ISBN: 0-89962-410-3.

PERSIAN COOKING

650. Ramazani, Nesta, 1932-. Persian Cooking. A Table of Exotic Delights: New York, NY: Quadrangle; 1984, Second printing; c1974. xx, 296 p.; ISBN: 0-8139-0962-7.

PERSIAN CUISINE

651. Ghanoonparvar, Mohammad R. Persian Cuisine. Jill Lieber and Claudia Kane, Illustrators. 1st ed. Lexington, KY: Mazda Publisher; c1982; 2 Vol.; ISBN: 0939214105. Note: Vol 1. = Traditional foods. Vol 2. Regional and modern foods. English & Persian. 5th printing, 1990.

PHILIPPOU, MARGARET JOY

652. Philippou, Margaret Joy. 101 Arabian delights: a book of Arabic Cookery. Brighton: Clifton Books; 1969. 99 p.; ISBN: 90125505X.

PHILIPS, MARGOT KOPSIDAS

653. Philips, Margot Kopsidas. Greek cookbook. Sherrill Weary, Editor; Joy Taylor, Assistant editor. New York, NY: The Culinary Arts Institute; c1980. 96 p.; ISBN: 0832606111.

PINCH OF SALT. CLASSIC AFGHAN COOKERY.

654. Amini, Rahima. A Pinch of salt. Classic Afghan Cookery. London, England: Quartet; 1991. 275 p.; ISBN: 0704327694.

PITA THE GREAT

655. Habeeb, Virginia. Pita the Great. New York, NY: Workman; 1986; ISBN: 0-89480-039-6.

PLEASE PASS THE PILAF: A COLLECTION OF ARMENIAN RECIPES

656. Tootelian, Elizabeth D. Please Pass the Pilaf: a Collection of Armenian Recipes. 1st ed. Richmond, VA; c1975. 98 p.

PLEASURE OF COOKING

657. Merjanian-Piranian, Louise. The Pleasure of Cooking. Beirut, Lebanon: Donigian & Sons; 1974. 304 p.

POCKET BREAD POTPOURRI, MEALS IN MINUTES

658. Farah, Madelain. Pocket Bread Potpourri, Meals in Minutes. Leila Habib, Co-author. Memphis, TN: Wimmer Brothers Books; c1984. 108 p.

POETRY IN PORTIONS

659. Poetry in Portions. An Armenian American Cookbook: Chevy Chase, MD: Soorp Khatch Armenian Apostolic Church; c1981. 349 p.

POLEMIS, APHRODITE

660. Polemis, Aphrodite. Aphrodite's Kitchen: homestyle Greek cooking. New York, NY: Golden Press; c1978. 96 p.; ISBN: 0-307-49426-8.

POPULAR GREEK RECIPES

661. Popular Greek Recipes. The Ladies of the Philoptochos Society, Holy Trinity Greek Orthodox Church. Charleston, S. Carolina: Holy Trinity Greek Orthodox Church; 1976. 222 p.

POUROUNAS, ANDREAS

662. Pourounas, Andreas. Aphrodite's Cookbook. Grosvenor, Helene, Co-author.: Spearman; 1977. 174 p.

POWELL, JESSIE (JOHNS) 1914-

663. Powell, Jessie (Johns) 1914-. Finest recipes from the Middle East; over one hundred recipes simplified with suggested menus, their uses, origin, and history; also , spicelore and herbs, some stories of folklore origin. Silver Spring, MD; 1968; c1957. 150 p.

PRECOPE, KATHLEEN

664. Precope, Kathleen. Secrets of Greek Cooking. London, England: New Europe Publishing Co.; 1944. 28 p.

RAMAZANI, NESTA, 1932-

665. Ramazani, Nesta, 1932-. Persian Cooking. A Table of Exotic Delights: New York, NY: Quadrangle; 1984, Second printing; c1974. xx, 296 p.; ISBN: 0-8139-0962-7.

RAYESS' ART OF LEBANESE COOKING

666. Rayess, George N. Rayess' Art of Lebanese Cooking. Translated from Arabic by Najla Showker: Beirut, Lebanon: Librairie du Liban; 1966. 244 p.

667. Rayess, George N. Rayess' Art of Lebanese Cooking. Translated from Arabic by Najla Showker: 2nd ed. Beirut, Lebanon: Librairie Du Liban; c1991 xxvi, 276 p.

RAYESS, GEORGE N.

668. Rayess, George N. Rayess' Art of Lebanese Cooking. Translated from Arabic by Najla Showker: Beirut, Lebanon: Librairie du Liban; 1966. 244 p.

669. Rayess, George N. Rayess' Art of Lebanese Cooking. Translated from Arabic by Najla Showker: 2nd ed. Beirut, Lebanon: Librairie Du Liban; c1991 xxvi, 276 p.

RECIPES FOR AN ARABIAN NIGHT

670. Scott, David, 1944-. Recipes for an Arabian night. 1st American ed. New York, NY: Pantheon Books, a division of Random House, Inc.; 1983; c1983; ISBN: 0-394-72292-2. Note: Originally published in Great Britain as Traditional Arabic Cookery by Hutchinson Publishing Group.

RECIPES FROM ARMENIA

671. Azarian, Tomas. Recipes from Armenia. Plainfield, VA: Farmhouse Press; c1985. 65 p.

RECIPES FROM BAGHDAD

672. Beattie, May H., Editor. Recipes from Baghdad. With contributions from more than a hundred ladies.: Baghdad, Iraq: Indian Red Cross; 1946.

REGIONAL CUISINES OF GREECE

673. The Regional Cuisines of Greece: St. Paul's Greek Orthodox Church; 1981. 256 p.

REYNOLDS, HELNE, 1921-

674. Reynolds, Helne, 1921-. Fabulous Greek foods. Eilen Tomlinson, Drawer. Fallbrook, CA: Aero Publishers; c1977. 126 p.

RICE, SPICE AND BITTER ORANGES

675. Perl, Lila. Rice, Spice and Bitter Oranges. Mediterranean Foods and Festivals: Stanislao Dino Rigolo, Illustrator. Cleveland, Ohio: World Publishing Co.; 1967.; c1967. 272 p.

RIDGWELL, JENNY

676. Ridgwell, Jenny. Middle Eastern Cooking. New York, NY: Crescent Books; 1987; c1986 by Ward Lock Limited 96 p.; ISBN: 0-517-62452-4.

ROCCA-BUTLER, SUZANNE, 1946-

677. Rocca-Butler, Suzanne, 1946-. Cultures in common: recipes from the cuisines of Turkey, Greece and the Balkans. Menlo Park, CA: Folkloric Studies TGB Press; c1985. 144 p.; ISBN: 096157450X.

RODEN, CLAUDIA

678. Roden, Claudia. A Book of Middle Eastern Food. Edward Bawden, Illustrator; Bruce Pinkard, Photographer. London, England: Nelson; 1968. 320 p.

679. Roden, Claudia. A Book of Middle Eastern Food. Alta Ann Parkins, Illustrator. New York, NY: Alfred A. Knopf; 1985. 453, xiv, p.; ISBN: 0-394-47181-4.

680. Roden, Claudia. A New Book of Middle Eastern Food. Revised ed. Penguin Books: New York; c1985.

ROUKES, NICHOLAS

681. Roukes, Nicholas. Greek with gusto. Greek cuisine, easy & delicious: Calgary, Canada: Juniro Arts Pub.; 1990. 170 p.; ISBN: 0919845800.

ROWLAND, JOAN

682. Rowland, Joan. Good food from the Near East; five hundred favorite recipes from twelve countries. New York, NY: M. Barrow & Co., Inc.; 1950. 274 p.

SABERI, HELEN

683. Saberi, Helen. Noshe Djan: Afghan Food and Cookery. with the help of Najiba Zaka and Shaima Breshna and drawings by Abdullah Breshna. London, England: Prospect Books; c1986. 160 p.; ISBN: 0-907325-32-7.

SAHTEIN, FOODS FROM THE MIDDLE EAST MAINLY LEBANON, PALESTINE, AND SYRIA

684. Sahtein, Foods from the Middle East Mainly Lebanon, Palestine, and Syria. Southfield, MI: Arab Women Union; c1976. 312 p.

SALADS-MIDDLE EASTERN

685. Man, Rosamond. The Complete Meze Table. Veronica Sperling & Caroline Schuck, Editors. London, England: Ebury Press; 1986. 111 p.; ISBN: 0852235461.

SALAH, NAHDA

686. Salah, Nahda. One Thousand and One Delights: Authentic Home Cooking of the Middle East.. Saleh, Basem S., Photographer: ?; ? 396 p.

SALAH, NAHDA S.

687. Salah, Nahda S. Arab World Cookbook : the book of one thousand and one delights. Basem S. Salah, Photographer. Dhahran, Saudi Arabia: Said Salah International Publications Agencies; 1977.; c1973. 345 p.

SALAMAN, RENA

688. Salaman, Rena. Greek Food. London, England: Fontana; 1983.

689. Salaman, Rena. Greek Island Cookery: an evocation in words and watercolors. Linda Smith, Co-author. London, England: Ebury Press; c1987. 128 p.; ISBN: 08522236212.

690. Salaman, Rena. A little Greek Cookbook. San Francisco, CA: Chronicle Books; 1990. 60 p.; ISBN: 0877017956.

SALLOUM, MARY

691. Salloum, Mary. A Taste of Lebanon. Brooklyn, NY: Interlink Books; c1988. 190 p.; ISBN: 0-940793-08-3.

SANTA MARIA, JACK

692. Santa Maria, Jack. Greek Vegetarian Cookery. Kate Simunek, Illustrator. Boston, MA: Shambhala Publishers, Inc.; c1984. 160 p.; ISBN: 0877733325.

SASSON, GRACE

693. Sasson, Grace. Kosher Syrian Cooking. Rev. & enlarged ed. Brooklyn, NY: Grace Sasson; 1988. xvi, 202 p. Note: Rev. edition of Syrian Cooking, 1970.

694. Sasson, Grace. Syrian Cooking: RDG Publishing; 1970.; c1958. xvi, 174 p.

SAUDI ARABI COOKERY

695. Skipwith, Ashkhain. Ashkhain's Saudi Cooking of Today. London, England: Stacey International; c1986. 160 p.; ISBN: 0905743-42-3.

SAYEGH, LILY

696. Sayegh, Lily. Middle East Cook: Pure and Simple; 1992. 52 p.

SCHEHERAZADE COOKS

697. Atiyeh, Wadeeha. Scheherazade Cooks. John Alcorn, Illustrator. Great Neck, NY: Channel Press; c1960. 189 p.

Ethnic Cookbooks

SCHMAELING, TONY

698. Schmaeling, Tony. The Cooking of Greece. Secaucus, NJ: Chartwell Books; c1983. 144 p.; ISBN: 0890096694.

SCOTT, DAVID, 1944-

699. Scott, David, 1944-. Middle Eastern Vegetarian Cookery. London, England: Hutchinson Group; 1983; c1981. 176 p.; ISBN: 0-09-145341-0.

700. Scott, David, 1944-. Recipes for an Arabian night. 1st American ed. New York, NY: Pantheon Books, a division of Random House, Inc.; 1983; c1983; ISBN: 0-394-72292-2. Note: Originally published in Great Britain as Traditional Arabic Cookery by Hutchinson Publishing Group.

701. Scott, David, 1944-. Traditional Arab Cookery. Steve Hardstaff, Illustrator. London, England: Rider; 1983. 160 p.; ISBN: 0091533317.

SECRETS OF COOKING

702. Chirinian, Linda. Secrets of Cooking. Armenian/Lebanese/Persian: Rene Chirinian, Photographer. New Canaan, CT: Lionhart Inc./Publishers; c1987. 264 p.; ISBN: 0-9617033-0-X.

SECRETS OF GREEK COOKING

703. Precope, Kathleen. Secrets of Greek Cooking. London, England: New Europe Publishing Co.; 1944. 28 p.

SELF-CATERING IN GREECE: MAINLAND AND ISLAND

704. Kyriacopoulis, Florica. Self-catering in Greece: mainland and island. making the most of local food and drink: Tim Salmon, Co-author. New York, NY: Hippocrene Books; 1986. 155 p.

SEMOS, EVELYN, 1915-

705. Semos, Evelyn, 1915-. More than baklava: a Greek cookbook. Ann Pearle, Illustrator. Dallas, TX: Neiman Marcus; 1982. x, 87 p.; ISBN: 0960666818.

SERANNE, ANN

706. Seranne, Ann. The Best of Near Eastern Cookery. Favorite Dishes from the Balkans, Turkey, Israel, Jordan, Saudi Arabia & other Countries of the Arabian Peninsula: Eileen Gaden, Photographic Illustrator. Garden City, NY: Doubleday & Co., Inc.; 1964; c1964. 158 p.

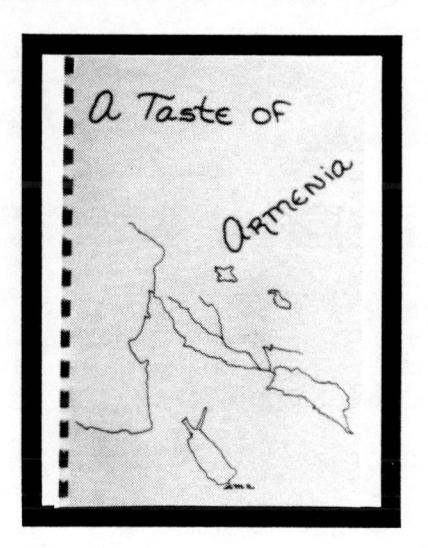

SHASHEER, JAMEELA

707. Shasheer, Jameela. Arab World Cookbook. Dubai: International Bookshop; 1973.

SHEPARD, SIGRID M.

708. Shepard, Sigrid M. Natural Food Feasts from the Eastern World. New York, NY: Arco Publishing, Inc.; 1979.

SHORT, DOROTHY

709. Short, Dorothy. Camel Land Cookery. Beirut, Lebanon; 1965.

SIMMONS, SHIRIN

710. Simmons, Shirin. Entertaining the Persian Way. London, England: Lennard Publishing; c1988. 156 p.; ISBN: 1-85291-0267.

SIMPLE ART OF GREEK COOKING

711. Spanos, Anna Z., 1899-. The Simple art of Greek Cooking. John Spanos, Co-author. New York, NY: Perigee Books; 1976.; c1990. 204 p.; ISBN: 0399516182.
Note: Title: also published under Pure Greek Cooking.

SKETCHING IN THE GREEK KITCHEN: A FAMILY COOKBOOK

712. Gregory, Penelope D. Sketching in the Greek Kitchen: A Family Cookbook. Ann Wiseman: Co-author: Ansayre Press; 1989. 87 p.; ISBN: 0937369039.

SKIPWITH, ASHKHAIN

713. Skipwith, Ashkhain. Ashkhain's Saudi Cooking of Today. London, England: Stacey International; c1986. 160 p.; ISBN: 0905743-42-3.

SKLAVUNU, MARIA N.

714. Sklavunu, Maria N. Exciting Greek Dishes, Athens, Greece. Artemis: 1976. 104 p.

SKOURA, SOPHIA

715. Skoura, Sophia. The Greek Cookbook. Helen Georges, Translator & adaptor. New York, NY: Crow Publishers; 1967. xiii, 230 p.

SMITH, JEFF

716. Smith, Jeff. The Frugal Gourmet cooks three ancient cuisines: China, Greece, and Rome. Craig Wollam, Culinary Consultant. 1st. ed. Terrin Haley, Research Assistant; Chris Cart, Illustrator. New York, NY: W. Morrow; c1989. 525 p.; ISBN: 0688075894.

717. Smith, Jeff. The Frugal Gourmet on Our Immigrant Ancestors [Recipes You Should Have Gotten from Your Grandmother.]. New York, NY: William Morrow & Co.; 1990. 539 p.; ISBN: 0-688-07590-8.
Note: Has Middle Eastern Recipes.

SMITH, VIOLA

718. Smith, Viola. Cooking the Greek way. L.A. "Andy" Anderson, Art Work. Pensacola, FL: Foote Printing Co.; 1980. 221 p.

SMOUHA, PATRICIA

719. Smouha, Patricia. Middle Eastern Cooking. London, England: Andre Deutsch; 1955. 133 p.
Note: 1st American Edition 1957 published by Citadel Press, NY.

SOUPS OF HAKAFRI RESTAURANT: KOSHER EDITION

720. Franklin, Rena. Soups of Hakafri Restaurant: Kosher Edition. Florida: Triad Pub.; 1981. 144 p.; ISBN: 0-937404-13-6.

SOUSANIS, MART, 1943-

721. Sousanis, Mart, 1943-. The Art of filo cookbook: International entrees, appetizers & desserts wrapped in flaky pastry.. Masayo Suzuki, Illustrator. Berkeley, CA: Aris Books; 1988, 3rd printing; c1983. 143 p.; ISBN: 0943186064.

SPANOS, ANNA Z., 1899-

722. Spanos, Anna Z., 1899-. The Simple art of Greek Cooking. John Spanos, Co-author. New York, NY: Perigee Books; 1976.; c1990. 204 p.; ISBN: 0399516182.
Note: Title: also published under Pure Greek Cooking.

SPOERRI, DANIEL, 1930-

723. Spoerri, Daniel, 1930-. Mythology and Meatballs: a Greek Island Diary Cookbook. Emmett Williams, Translator; Jeanne Jambo, Illustrator. Berkeley, CA: Aris; 1982. 238 p.; ISBN: 0943196013.

ST. NICHOLAS ORTHODOX CATHEDRAL LADIES' SOCIETY

724. St. Nicholas Orthodox Cathedral Ladies' Society. Magic Cookery. Los Angeles, CA: St. Nicholas; 1987. 309 p.

STEP-BY-STEP GREEK COOKING

725. Step-By-Step Greek Cooking: Smith Publishers; 1989.; ISBN: 08317-8006.

STEPHAN, LILY

726. Stephan, Lily. Lebanese dishes made delicious. Sidon, Lebanon: Modern Library; 1975. 85 p.

STUBBS, JOYCE M.

727. Stubbs, Joyce M. The Home Book of Greek Cookery. a selection of traditional Greek recipes.: London, England: Faber and Faber; 1963. 159 p.

SWEETS & DESSERTS FROM THE MIDDLE EAST

728. der Haroutunian, Arto, 1940-1987. Sweets & Desserts from the Middle East. London, England: Century Publishing; 1984. 224 p.; ISBN: 0712602925.

SYRIAN COOKERY

729. Corey, Helen. The Art of Syrian cookery. A culinary trip to the land of Bible history: Syria and Lebanon: 1st ed. Garden City, NY: Doubleday; 1962. 186 p.

730. Getsoian, Anne. Favorite Armenian and Syrian recipes of Anne Getsoian. San Diego, CA: Getsoian; c1979. 89 p.

731. Isaac, Barbara Thomas. Everyday delights of Lebanese-Syrian Cookery. Kathryn Arwady, Co-author; Cal Matle, Illustrator. Harper Woods, MI: Author; 1977. xviii, 280 p.

732. Sahtein, Foods from the Middle East Mainly Lebanon, Palestine, and Syria. Southfield, MI: Arab Women Union; c1976. 312 p.

733. Sasson, Grace. Kosher Syrian Cooking. Rev. & enlarged ed. Brooklyn, NY: Grace Sasson; 1988. xvi, 202 p.
Note: Rev. edition of Syrian Cooking, 1970.

734. Sasson, Grace. Syrian Cooking: RDG Publishing; 1970.; c1958. xvi, 174 p.

SYRIAN COOKING

735. Sasson, Grace. Syrian Cooking: RDG Publishing; 1970.; c1958. xvi, 174 p.

TAGAS, LOUIS

736. Tagas, Louis. Hellenic Cuisine: cooking Greek style. New York, NY: Vantage Press; c1984. xi, 51 p.; ISBN: 0533058988.

TAMBAKERAS, RENA

737. Tambakeras, Rena. Greek Cooking. Per Ericson, Photographer. Mississauga, Ontario: Cupress; 1987. viii, 160 p.; ISBN: 0920691358.

TASTE FOR IT: GREEK AND OTHER RECIPES FOR THE DISCRIMINATING PALATE.

738. A Taste for it: Greek and other Recipes for the Discriminating Palate. Seattle, Washington: St. Demetrios Greek Orthodox Church; 1964.

TASTE OF AFGHANISTAN: THE CUISINE OF THE CROSSROADS OF THE WORLD

739. Parenti, Cathy. A Taste of Afghanistan: The Cuisine of the Crossroads of the World. Phoenix, AZ: Author; c1987. 84 p.

TASTE OF ISRAEL

740. Maiberg, Ron. A Taste of Israel. New York, NY: Rizoli International; 1990. 240 p.; ISBN: 0847811956.

TASTE OF LEBANON

741. Salloum, Mary. A Taste of Lebanon. Brooklyn, NY: Interlink Books; c1988. 190 p.; ISBN: 0-940793-08-3.

TASTY ARMENIAN DISHES

742. Torunian, Armen, Editor. Tasty Armenian Dishes. Pailig Hanenian & George Guzelimian, Illustrators. Montreal, Quebec Canada: The First Armenian Evangelical Church; 1979.; c1972. 131 p.

TAVLARIOS, IRENE

743. Tavlarios, Irene. Greek food and drink. New York, NY: Bookwright Press; 1988.; c1987. 48 p.; ISBN: 0531181723. Note: Juvenile Literature.

TENDER LOVING COOKING: FAVORITE RECIPES BY THE WOMEN OF HOLY APOSTLES GREEK CHURCH

744. Tender loving cooking: favorite recipes by the women of Holy Apostles Greek Church. Holy Apostles Philoptohos Society. Westchester, IL: The Society; c1984. 223 p.

TERZI, POPI

745. Terzi, Popi. Athenian cuisine: over 600 recipes. Joe Nadziejko, Drawer. Tarrytown, NY: Pilgrimage Pub.; 1987. xii, 183 p.; ISBN: 0935819037.

THEOHAROUS, ANNE

746. Theoharous, Anne. Cooking and Baking the Greek Way. New York, NY: Holt, Rinehart & Winston; 1977. xi, 257 p.; ISBN: 0-03-017521-6.

747. Theoharous, Anne. Cooking the Greek Way. London, England: Methuen; 1982.; c1979. 252 p.; ISBN: 0417038402.

TOOTELIAN, ELIZABETH D.

748. Tootelian, Elizabeth D. Please Pass the Pilaf: a Collection of Armenian Recipes. 1st ed. Richmond, VA; c1975. 98 p.

TORUNIAN, ARMEN

749. Torunian, Armen, Editor. Tasty Armenian Dishes. Pailig Hanenian & George Guzelimian, Illustrators. Montreal, Quebec Canada: The First Armenian Evangelical Church; 1979.; c1972. 131 p.

TRADITIONAL ARAB COOKERY

750. Scott, David, 1944-. Traditional Arab Cookery. Steve Hardstaff, Illustrator. London, England: Rider; 1983. 160 p.; ISBN: 0091533317.

TREASURED ARMENIAN RECIPES.

751. Treasured Armenian recipes. 1st ed. Detroit, MI: A.G.B.U., Detroit; 1989, 29th printing; c1944. 126 p.

TREASURED GREEK RECIPES

752. Treasured Greek recipes. Compiled by the Greek Ladies Philoptochos Society, St. Sophia Greek Orthodox Chruch. Albany, NY: St. Sophia Greek Orthodox Church; 1981. xx, 264 p.

TREASURES OF GREEK AND INTERNATIONAL COOKING

753. Treasures of Greek and International Cooking. Miami, FL: St. Andrew Greek Orthodox Church of Kendall; c1988. 246 p.

TRIANTAFYLLIDIS, ALEXANDRA

754. Triantafyllidis, Alexandra. A Bunch of Greek Dishes 95 p.

TSELEMENTES, NICHOLAS, 1880-

755. Tselementes, Nicholas, 1880-. Greek Cookery. 3rd ed. New York, NY: D.C. Divry; 1956. 239 p.; ISBN: 0685090353.

UVEZIAN, SONIA

756. Uvezian, Sonia. Cooking from the Caucasus: First Harvest Press/HBJ edition 1978; c1976. 280 p.; ISBN: 0-15-622594-8.
Note: Originally published as The Best Foods of Russia. Armenian, Azerbaidzhani and Georgian recipies.

757. Uvezian, Sonia. The Cuisine of Armenia. Dickran Palulian, Illustrator. New York, NY: Harper & Row; 1974; c1974. xiii, 412 p.; ISBN: 0-06-014472-06.

758. Uvezian, Sonia. The Cuisine of Armenia. Dickran Palulian, Illustrator. Harper Colophon Books ed. New York, NY: Harper & Row; c1985. xiii, 400 p.; ISBN: 0609912294.

VALERO, RINA

759. Valero, Rina. Delights of Jerusalem: a Treasury of Cooking and Folklore. Shlesinger, Miriam, Translator.: Nahar Publishing; Steimatzky; 1985 ?

VARJABEDIAN, IDA P.

760. Varjabedian, Ida P. Exotic, Light & Easy Cookbook of Middle Eastern Cuisine. Great Neck, NY: Todd & Honeywell, Inc.; c1985.; ISBN: 0-89962-410-3.

VASSILIAN, HAMO, 1952-

761. Vassilian, Hamo, 1952-. Ethnic Cookbooks & Food Marketplace: A Complete Bibliographic Guide & Directory to Armenian, Iranian, Afghan, Middle Eastern, North African and Greek Foods in the U.S.A. & Canada. Glendale, CA: Armenian Reference Books Co.; 1991.; 1st ed., c1991. 124 p.
Note: The most complete reference book for Middle Eastern foods.

VEGETARIAN COOKERY

762. Antreassian, Alice, 1922-. Classic Armenian Recipes: Cooking Without Meat. Mariam Jebejian, Co-author. 2nd ed. Adrina Zanazanian, Illustrator. New York, NY: Ashod Press; 1983.; c1981. 308, xxxip.; ISBN: 0-935102-05-1.

763. Chaitow, Alkmini. Greek Vegetarian Cooking. colorful dishes from the eastern shores of the Mediterranean: Clive Birch, Illustrator. 1st U.S. ed. New York, NY: Thorsons; 1991. 160 p.; ISBN: 072252496X.

764. der Haroutunian, Arto, 1940-1987. Classic Vegetable Cooking. London, England.

765. der Haroutunian, Arto, 1940-1987. Vegetarian Dishes from the Middle East. London, England: Century Publishing; 1987.; c1983. 224 p.; ISBN: 0-7126-0120-1.

766. Karaoglan, Aida. Food for the Vegetarian. Brooklyn, NY: Interlink Publishing Group; c1988. 167 p.; ISBN: 0-940793-15-6.

767. Santa Maria, Jack. Greek Vegetarian Cookery. Kate Simunek, Illustrator. Boston, MA: Shambhala Publishers, Inc.; c1984. 160 p.; ISBN: 0877733325.

768. Scott, David, 1944-. Middle Eastern Vegetarian Cookery. London, England: Hutchinson Group; 1983; c1981. 176 p.; ISBN: 0-09-145341-0.

VEGETARIAN DISHES FROM THE MIDDLE EAST

769. der Haroutunian, Arto, 1940-1987. Vegetarian Dishes from the Middle East. London, England: Century Publishing; 1987.; c1983. 224 p.; ISBN: 0-7126-0120-1.

VENOS, FANNIE, 1914-

770. Venos, Fannie, 1914-. Can the Greeks Cook. Lillian Prichard, Co-author. Richmond, VA: Dietz Press; 1950. xiii, 121 p.

VILLIOS, LYNNE W.

771. Villios, Lynne W. Cooking the Greek way. Robert L. & Diane Wolfe, Photographers; Jeanette Swofford, Illustrator. Minneapolis: Lerner Publications; c1984. 51 p.; ISBN: 0822509105.

WADDAD'S KITCHEN, LEBANESE ZEST AND SOUTHERN BEST

772. Buttross, Waddad Habeeb. Waddad's Kitchen, Lebanese zest and southern best. Natchez, Miss.: W. H. Buttross; c1982. 150 p.; ISBN: 0-939114-36-4.

WAINES, DAVID

773. Waines, David, Compiler. In a Caliph's Kitchen: Riad El-Rayyes; 1989. 119 p.

WASON, ELIZABETH BETTY, 1912-

774. Wason, Elizabeth Betty, 1912-. Greek Cookbook. Giulio Maestro, Illustrator. New York, NY: Macmillan; 1969. 216 p.

WEIDENWEBER, SIGRID

775. Weidenweber, Sigrid, Compiler. Best of Afghan Cookery, an Afghan Recipe Book. Portland, OR: American Aid for Afghans; c1980.

WEISS-ARMUSH, ANNE MARIE

776. Weiss-Armush, Anne Marie. Arabian Cuisine. John Berry, Illustrator. Beirut, Lebanon; 1984. 402 p.

WELLS, TROTH

777. Wells, Troth. The New International Food Book. Oxford, England: New Internationalist Publications; 1990. 182 p.

WESTLAND, PAMELA

778. Westland, Pamela. Greek Cooking. London, England: Ward Lock; 1987. 96 p.; ISBN: 0706365720.

Ethnic Cookbooks

Bibliographies-63

WHAT'S COOKING IN ISRAEL

779. Banai, Margalit, 1928-. What's Cooking in Israel. New York, NY: Crowell; 1972. 181 p.; ISBN: 0-690-87825-7.

WHOLE GRAIN COOKBOOK

780. der Haroutunian, Arto, 1940-1987. Whole Grain Cookbook. London, England.

WILSON, HILARY

781. Wilson, Hilary. Egyptian food and drink. Aylesbury, Bucks [England]: Shire; 1988. 64 p.

WOLFERT, PAULA

782. Wolfert, Paula. Couscous and other Good Food from Morocco. Bill Bayer, Photographer; Sidonie Coryn, Illustrator. New York, NY: Harper & Row; 1973 xv, 351 p.; ISBN: 0-06-014721-0.

YACOUBI, AHMED

783. Yacoubi, Ahmed. Alchemist's Cookbook: Moroccan Scientific Cuisine. Tucson, AZ: Omen Press; 1972. X, 142.

YASSINE, SIMA OSMAN

784. Yassine, Sima Osman. Middle Eastern Cuisine; 1984. 120 p.

YIANILOS, THERESA KARAS

785. Yianilos, Theresa Karas. The Complete Greek Cookbook: the Best from Three Thousand Years of Greek Cooking. New York, NY: Funk & Wagnalls; c1970. xiii, 254 p.; ISBN: 0517128780.
Note: Revised edition, 1986. La Jolla, CA.

YOGHURT

786. der Haroutunian, Arto, 1940-1987. The Yoghurt Book. Food of the Gods: London, England: Penguin Books; 1983. Over 200 p.

YOGHURT BOOK

787. der Haroutunian, Arto, 1940-1987. The Yoghurt Book. Food of the Gods: London, England: Penguin Books; 1983. Over 200 p.

ZANE, EVA

788. Zane, Eva. Greek Cooking for the Gods. W. Busser Howel and the author, Illustrators. San Ramon, CA: 101 Productions; 1970; c1989. 192 p.

789. Zane, Eva. Middle Eastern Cookery, Drawings & Annotations by Keith Halonen. San Francisco: 101 Productions; 1974; c1974 144 p.

64-Food Marketplace — Ethnic Cookbooks

Ethnic Food Marketplaces in the U.S. and Canada

BAKERS

Ace Baking Co.
1803 E. 58th Ave.
Denver, CO — (303) 296-7482

Afghan Bakery
134 West Jefferson St.
Falls Church, VA — (703) 241-7855

Aladdin's Middle East Bakery
1301 Carnegie Ave.
Cleveland, OH — (216) 861-0317

Alexander Bakery Corp
878 W. 8th St.
Miami, FL — (305) 858-4218

Ali Baba Bakery
2507 Central Ave. N.E.
Minneapolis, MN

Alwan Pastry Shop
183 Atlantic Ave.
Brooklyn, NY

Amir's Bakery
949 Main St.
Paterson, NJ — (201) 345-5030

Ara's Pastry
4945 Hollywood Blvd.
Hollywood, CA — (213) 661-1116

Ararat Bakery
220 Horace Harding Exp. Hwy.
Bayside, NY — (718) 225-3478

Arax Bakery
4871 Santa Monica Blvd.
Hollywood, CA — (213) 666-7313

Araz Bakery
5637 1/2 Lankershim Blvd.
N. Hollywood, CA — (818) 753-0839

Armand's Bake Shop, Inc.
18962 Bonanza Way
Gaithersburg, MD

Armenian Bakery
1646 Victoria Park Ave.
Scarborough, — (416) 757-1559

Atlas Oriental Pastry Shop
419 Elm Street
Buffalo, NY

Avo's Bakery
6740 Reseda Blvd.
Reseda, CA — (818) 774-1032

Afghan Bakery
134 W. Jefferson St.
Falls Church, VA — (703) 241-7855

Bakery Panos
1649 E. Washington Blvd.
Pasadena, CA — (818) 791-1311

Bijan Bakery & Cafe
441 Saratoga Ave.
San Jose, CA — (408) 247-4888

Burbank Bakery
1213 W. Magnolia Blvd.
Burbank, CA — (818) 841-7209

Byblo's Bakery, Inc.
73 Northern Blvd.
Jackson Heights, NY — (718) 779-6909

Cake Castle
4261 Mayfield Road
Cleveland, OH — (216) 381-5782

Cedar's Bakery
953 Teaneck Road
Teaneck, NJ — (201) 837-4330

Daily Bread Bakery
1691 Cristal Square 5
Arlington, VA — (703) 920-2525

Damascus Bakery
195 Atlantic Ave.
Brooklyn, NY — (718) 855-1456

Danaian's Bakery
1108 N. Kenmore Ave.
Hollywood, CA — (213) 664-8842

Danielle's Bakery & Imported
123 Jamacha Road
El Cajon, CA — (619) 579-1999

Droubi's Bakery & Grocery
7333 Hillcroft
Houston, TX — (713) 988-5897

Droubi's Bakery & Grocery
3223 Hillcroft
Houston, TX — (713) 782-6160

Droubi's Bakery & Grocery
7807 Kirby Dr.
Houston, TX — (713) 790-0101

Eastern Lamejun Bakers
145 Belmont St.
Belmont, MA — (617) 484-5239

Eastern Star Bakery
440 S.W. 8th St.
Miami, FL — (305) 854-6381

Farin Co.
6411 Sepulveda Blvd.
Van Nuys, CA — (818) 376-0188

Fattal's Syrian Bakery
977 Main St.
Paterson, NJ — (201) 742-7125

Flor de Cafe Bakery
801 S. Glendale Ave.
Glendale, CA — (818) 543-1401

Garni Bakery
508 McNicoll Ave.
Willowdale, — (416) 492-7200

Goglanian Bakeries Inc.
2052 Placentia Ave.
Costa Mesa, CA — (714) 642-3570

Golden French Bakers
6521 Van Nuys Blvd.
Van Nuys, CA — (818) 785-1184

Golden State Bakery
5158 Hollywood Blvd.
Hollywood, CA — (213) 666-6713

Haddad Bakery
4612 Dufferin St.
Downsview,

Hakeems's Bakery & Grocery
5854 Osuna, N.E.
Albuquerque, NM — (505) 881-4019

Heller's Baking Co.
1776 E. Washington Blvd.
Pasadena, CA — (818) 794-5422

Holy Land Bakery & Grocery
4809 Kedzie Ave.
Chicago, IL — (312) 588-3306

Hye Bakery
314 W. Beverly Blvd.
Montebello, CA — (213) 722-8706

Hye Quality Bakery
2222 Santa Clara
Fresno, CA — (209) 445-1511

Ethnic Cookbooks

Food Marketplace-65

International Bakery
5216 W. Sunset Blvd.
Hollywood, CA   (213) 953-1724

Jerusalem Bakery & Grocery
4070 N. Beltline
Irving, TX   (214) 257-0447

Jim's Family Catering & Bakery
Millbury St.
Worcester, MA   (508) 752-1731

Joseph Assi Bakery & Deli
3316 Beach Blvd.
Jacksonville, FL   (904) 398-5167

Katina Ice Gream & Bakery
621 E. Glenoaks Blvd.
Glendale, CA   (818) 247-4068

Kermanig Bakery
1371 E. Colorado St.
Glendale, CA   (818) 246-2750

King of Pita Bakery, Inc.
6460 General Greenway Dr.
Alexandria, VA   (703) 941-8999

La Belle Epooue
2128 Hillhurst Ave.
Los Angeles, CA   (213) 669-7640

La Miche
1107 W. El Camino Real
Sunnyvale, CA   (408) 730-5518

La Miche
10487 De Anza Blvd.
Cupertino, CA   (408) 725-1131

La Miche
39104 Argonaut Way
Fremont, CA   (415) 795-1105

Marash Bakery
51 Dexter Ave.
Watertown, MA   (617) 924-0098

Marcel's Bakery
12908 Sherman Way
N. Hollywood, CA   (818) 765-3844

Masis Bakery
4959 Sunset Blvd.
Hollywood, CA   (213) 667-3001

Massis Bakery
569 Mount Auburn St.
Watertown, MA   (617) 924-0537

Mediterranean Bakery
374 S. Pickett St.
Alexandria, VA   (703) 751-1702

Mediterranean Bakery
6516 Horsepan Rd.
Richmond, VA   (804) 285-1488

Mediterranean Bakery
174 Fenmar Dr.
Weston,   (416) 743-2267

Middle East Bakery
7006 Carroll Ave.
Takoma Park, MD

Middle East Bakery
11400 Old Balto Pike
Beltsville, MD

Middle East Baking Co.
4000 Pleasantdale Road N.E.
Atlanta, GA

Middle East Lamejun
355 Anderson Ave.
Fairview, NJ   (201) 941-5662

Middle Eastern Bakery
513 Ortiz Dr. S.E.
Albuquerque, NM   (505) 255-2939

Mignon Bakery
452 W. Stocker St.
Glendale, CA   (818) 246-2217

Movses Golden Pastry
321 E. Alameda
Burbank, CA   (818) 559-5200

Near East Bakery
878 S.W. 8th St.
Miami, FL

Near East Baking Co.
5268 Washington St.
West Roxbury, MA   (617) 327-0217

Norik Bakery
2889 "C" Street Clair Ave. E
Toronto,   (416) 757-8314

Northridge Bakery
8968 Corbin Ave.
Northridge, CA   (818) 993-7469

Nouri's Syrian Bakery & Grocer
983 Main St.
Paterson, NJ

Old Sasoun Bakery
1132 N. Allen Ave.
Pasadena, CA   (818) 791-3280

Omar's Pastry
14282 Brookhurst
Garden Grove, CA   (714) 531-3551

Oriental Pastry & Grocery
170 Atlantic Ave.
Brooklyn, NY   (718) 875-7687

Oven Fresh Bakery
3600 Ocean View Blvd.
Glendale, CA   (818) 249-3587

Palestine Bakery
2639 W. 63rd St.
Chicago, IL   (312) 925-5978

Pan Hellenic Pastry Shop
322 S. Halsted St.
Chicago, IL   (312) 454-1886

Panos Pastry Shop # 1
5150 Hollywood Blvd.
Hollywood, CA   (213) 661-0335

Panos Pastry Shop # 2
418 S. Central Ave.
Glendale, CA   (818) 502-0549

Paradise Pastry
1815 W. Glenoaks Blvd.
Glendale, CA   (818) 545-4000

Partamian Armenian Bakery
5410 W. Adams Blvd.
Los Angeles, CA   (213) 937-2870

Paterson Syrian Bakery
983 Main St.
Paterson, NJ   (201) 279-2388

Patisserie Armenia
414 Fleury Ouest
Montreal,   (516) 389-4696

Pizzajoun
Montreal,   (514) 383-5588

Poseidon Greek Bakery
629 Ninth Ave.
New York, NY   (212) 757-6173

Pouri Bakery
109 S. Adams St.
Glendale, CA   (818) 244-4064

Sako's Bakery
1321 E. Colorado St.
Glendale, CA   (818) 247-3333

Sam's Armenian Bakery
400 Raliegh St.
Glendale, CA   (818) 247-6281

Sam's Pastry
620 S. Glendale Ave.
Glendale, CA   (818) 246-3811

66-Food Marketplace

Ethnic Cookbooks

Santa Teresa Bakery
7064 Santa Teresa Blvd.
San Jose, CA   (408) 578-1520

Sasoun Bakery
5114 Santa Monica Blvd.
Hollywood, CA   (213) 661-1868

Sassoon Bakery & Grocery
72 Shaw Ave.
Clovis, CA   (209) 323-1185

Sevan Bakery
598 Mount Auburn St.
Watertown, MA   (617) 924-9843

Sevan Bakery & Grocery
17743 Saticoy St.
Reseda, CA   (818) 343-0486

Shad Zee Bakery
1510 Westwood Blvd.
Los Angeles, CA   (213) 474-7907

Shalom Market & Bakery
2307 University Blvd. W.
Silver Spring, MD

St. Georges Bakery & Grocery
231 S. Orlando Ave.
Winter Park, FL   (407) 647-1423

Steve-Vin Bake-A-Deli, Inc.
741 Mount Auburn St.
Watertown, MA   (617) 924-3666

Tabrizi Bakery
56 Mt. Auburn St.
Watertown, MA   (617) 926-0880

Taslakian's Pastry
4906 Santa Monica Blvd.
Hollywood, CA   (213) 662-5588

Taste It, House of Cookies
2451 E. Washington Blvd.
Pasadena, CA   (818) 794-4280

Tiffany's Bakery
1163 Glendale Galleria
Glendale, CA   (818) 242-3470

Toufayan Bakery
9255 Kennedy Blvd.
North Bergen, NJ   (201) 861-4131

Village Pastry Shop
1414 W. Kenneth Road
Glendale, CA   (818) 241-2521

Wheatly Bake Shop
190 Wheatly Plaza
Greenvale, NY   (516) 621-7575

Yas Bakery & Confectionery
785 Rockville Pike
Rockville, MD   (301) 762-5416

Yassin Royal Bakery
10609 W. Warren
Dearborn, MI   (313) 945-1550

BAKERS-WHOLESALE

American Pita Corporation
Houston, TX   (713) 776-3976

Anoush Bakery
11142 Burbank Blvd.
N. Hollywood, CA   (818) 766-2998

Ararat Bakeries
Kings Canyon
Sanger, CA   (209) 875-7579

Armani Bakery, Inc.
3658 San Fernando Road
Glendale, CA   (213) 662-7479

Avo's Bakery
6740 Reseda Blvd.
Reseda, CA   (818) 774-1032

Babylon Bakery
119 4th St.
Turlock, CA   (209) 634-8061

Babylon Bakery
11693 Sheldon Ave.
Sun Valley, CA   (818) 767-6076

Bread & Pizz
3330 Hillcroft
Houston, TX   (713) 783-9898

Georgig's Bakery, Inc.
3421 Rowena Ave
Hollywood, CA

Glendale Bakery
4722 San Fernando Road
Glendale, CA   (818) 247-2966

Global Bakeries, Inc.
13336 Paxton St.
Pacoima, CA   (818) 896-0525

International Bread and Crois.
2537 San Fernando Road
Los Angeles, CA

Lavash Corporation of America
2835 Newell St.
Los Angeles, CA   (213) 663-5249

Marcel's Bakery
12908 Sherman Way
N. Hollywood, CA   (818) 765-3844

Maxim's Nutricare, Inc.
3685 S. 900 E. Victoria Park
Salt Lake City, UT   (801) 262-6767

Rubic's Bakery
12616-18 Asborn St.
Pacoima, CA   (818) 890-7299

Soojian, Inc.
89 Academy
Sanger, CA   (209) 875-7579

Sunrise Bakery
2610 Geer Road
Turlock, CA   (209) 632-3228

Turlock Bakery
11908 Balboa Blvd.
Granada Hills, CA   (818) 360-7223

Yerevan Bakery, Inc.
42 43rd Ave.
New York, NY   (718) 729-5400

BEVERAGE PRODUCERS

Carlo Beverage Enterprises
P. O. Box 5476
Glendale, CA

Margosian Beverage Co.
2377 S. Oragne Ave.
Fresno, CA   (209) 264-2823

Sun Beverage Co. (Abali)
5471 San Fernando Road
Los Angeles, CA   (818) 409-0117

CANDY MAKERS

Amoretti
10021 Canoga Ave.
Chatsworth, CA   (818) 346-1454

Angel Candies, Inc.
16716 Johnson Drive
City of Commerce, CA   (818) 961-4171

Ethnic Cookbooks

Food Marketplace-67

Fard Candies
2517 W. 237th St.
Torrance, CA   (310) 326-6012

Imperial Gaz Co.
P. O. Box 2851
Santa Fe Springs, CA   (213) 693-8423

Nory
Winnetka, CA

Yasha's
6149 Vineland
N. Hollywood, CA   (818) 508-0905

CATERERS

Aivazian Super Catering & Hall
119 S. Kenwood
Glendale, CA   (818) 241-8829

Al-Mimas Catering
Burbank, CA   (818) 845-5765

Alpha Catering
1505 Mountain View
Oxnard, CA   (805) 486-4554

Angel's Catering
Glendale, CA   (818) 507-8518

Ara's Catering
Toronto,   (416) 495-9549

Ararat Catering
1719 Glenwood Road
Glendale, CA   (818) 243-7468

Armitage Restaurant
1767 N. Vermont Ave.
Hollywood, CA   (213) 664-5467

Azar Kamarei Catering
San Jose, CA   (408) 245-6141

Badry's Catering
San Jose, CA   (408) 274-0738

Caspian Catering Service
San Francisco, CA   (415) 581-7253

Catering By Arut
5074 Franklin Ave.
Hollywood, CA   (213) 668-9115

Catering by Herach & Ara
Montebello, CA   (213) 724-5622

Chef Diko Catering
6470 Foothill Blvd.
Tujunga, CA   (818) 951-3799

Classy Catering
7782 San Fernando Road
Sun Valley, CA   (213) 875-1030

Culinary Creations
, MA   (617) 893-6865

Glenoaks Deli & Grocery
621 E. Glenoaks Blvd.
Glendale, CA   (818) 247-4021

Golden Dream
Pasadena, CA   (818) 798-7952

Gourmet Affair
2080 S. Occasions
Cleveland, OH   (216) 397-1414

Gyro Time Restaurant
5547 W. Manchester Ave.
Westchester, CA   (310) 337-1728

Jaleh Catering
San Jose, CA   (408) 277-0506

Janet's Catering
Glendale, CA   (818) 248-8907

Jonelle's Restaurants & Cater.
108 Horace Harding Exp.
Flushing, NY   (718) 699-0500

Karo's Catering
N. Hollywood, CA   (818) 509-3952

Krivaar Cafe
475 Pine St.
San Francisco, CA   (415) 781-0894

La Mediterranee
843 E. Orange Grove
Pasadena, CA   (818) 797-1558

La Mediterranee
857 4th St.
San Rafael, CA   (415) 258-9123

La Mediterranee
2936 College Ave.
Berkeley, CA   (415) 540-7730

La Mediterranee
2210 Fillmore St.
San Francisco, CA   (415) 921-2956

La Mediterranee
288 Noe Street
San Francisco, CA   (415) 431-7210

Le Gourmet Caterers
New York, NY   (718) 778-6666

Le Gourmet Elegance
1249 W. Glenoaks Blvd.
Glendale, CA   (818) 956-5079

Le Papillon Restaurant
460 S. Myrtle Ave.
Monrovia, CA   (818) 357-7211

Loft Catering
1361 S. Winchester Blvd.
San Jose, CA   (408) 866-2200

M & A Kebab King Catering
P. O. Box   117
Montebello, CA   (213) 725-1395

Marash Catering
463 N. Martelo Ave.
Pasadena, CA   (213) 629-2802

Middle Eastern & Armenian Cat.
65 N. Craig St.
Pasadena, CA   (818) 792-7663

Mike's Catering
701 S. Central Ave.
Glendale, CA   (818) 241-1463

Minoo Khosher Restaurant
11550 Santa Monica Blvd.
Los Angeles, CA   (310) 478-0072

Mona Lisa Catering
18901 Kingsbury St.
Northridge, CA   (818) 887-2424

Mukuch Aintab Catering
Sun Valley, CA   (818) 768-4929

Nob Hill Banquet Center
8229 Van Nuys Blvd.
Panorama City, CA   (818) 989-2222

Orient Express
1 Market St.
San Francisco, CA   (415) 957-1795

Randy's M.E. Market & Catering
430 N. Harbor Blvd.
La Habra, CA   (714) 738-1337

Robert's Catering Service
435 Main St.
Burbank, CA   (818) 848-8337

Royal Events
5250 Santa Monica Blvd.
Hollywood, CA   (213) 667-9141

S & D Caterers
1255 Hewlett Plaza
Hewlett, NY   (516) 374-6300

S.E.A. Catering
Montebello, CA   (213) 724-3782

Silver Platter Catering
112 E. Lime Ave.
Monrovia, CA   (818) 791-8248

68-Food Marketplace

Ethnic Cookbooks

Smorgasbord Restaurant & Cater
2423 Honolulu Ave.
Montrose, CA   (818) 248-9536

Susan's Catering
, VA   (703) 369-1413

Temple Torah
54 Little Neck Pkwy
Little Neck, NY   (718) 423-2100

Yafa Restaurant
637 S. Fairfax Ave.
Los Angeles, CA   (213) 934-7255

CHEESE PRODUCERS

King Cheese & Deli
2487 E. Washington Blvd.
Pasadena, CA   (818) 791-2254

Victor's Cheese Corp.
476 Broad Ave.
Palisades Park, NJ   (201) 947-3677

COFFEE & TEA DEALERS

Alvin's Scrumptious Coffee Tea
2165 Irving St.
San Francisco, CA   (415) 661-2888

Coffee Najjar, Inc.
1440 Third St.
Riverside, CA   (714) 276-4966

Mt. Ararat Coffee Traders
P.O. Box 2218
Los Banos, CA   (209) 826-1961

Royal Coffee & Tea Co.
715 N. Main St.
Oklahoma City, OK   (405) 848-2002

Top Star Co.
P.O. Box 784 Station B
Willowdale,   (416) 477-1877

COFFEE & TEA DEALERS-WHOLESALE

Mediterranean Coffee
P.O. Box 821192
Houston, TX   (713) 827-7799

COFFEE PRODUCERS

Jamai Coffee Co.
820 Thompson Ave.
Glendale, CA   (818) 241-8156

Temco, Inc.
4551 San Fernando Road
Glendale, CA   (818) 241-2333

DATE GARDENS

Oasis Date Gardens
P.O. Box 111 Hwy.
Thermal, CA   (619) 399-5665

DELIS

Al's Italian American Deli
2332 Honolulu Ave.
Montrose, CA   (818) 249-3031

Andre Mini Kabob
1321 E. Colorado St.
Glendale, CA   (818) 247-1772

Andre's Cafe
105 S. Maryland Ave.
Glendale, CA   (818) 549-9590

Ararat Sandwich
655 S. Spring
Los Angeles, CA   (213) 488-1499

Armenian Delight
2591 W. Chester Pike
Broomall, PA   (215) 353-1981

Arsen's Liquor and Deli
1801 Polk St.
San Francisco, CA   (415) 673-4900

Bianca's Deli
1506 N. Vermont Ave.
Hollywood, CA   (213) 669-1829

Big Bite Sandwiches
334 N. Central Ave.
Glendale, CA   (818) 241-0687

Big Bite Sandwiches
2418 Honolulu Ave.
Montrose, CA   (818) 957-5162

Brashov Restaurant
1301 N. Vermont Ave.
Hollywood, CA   (213) 660-0309

Burger Time
7747 N. First St.
Fresno, CA   (209) 432-4178

Byblos Deli & Sandwiches
129 W. Chapman
Orange, CA   (714) 538-7180

Cafe Paris
1415 E. Colorado St.
Glendale, CA   (818) 247-5787

Caravansary Restaurants & Deli
2263 Chestnut St.
San Francisco, CA   (415) 921-3466

Central Deli
4325 N. Blackstone Ave.
Fresno, CA   (209) 222-9327

Crest Delicatessen Ltd.
607 Central Ave.
East Orange, NJ

Dairy Fair Delicatessen
31 Station Plaza
Hempstead, NY

Dan's Super Subs
22446 Ventura Blvd.
Woodland Hills, CA   (818) 702-8880

Dana Point Liquor & Deli
34320 Coast Highway
Dana Point, CA   (714) 861-6455

Delphi Deli & Cheese Shop
2151 Lemoine Ave.
Fort Lee, NJ   (201) 592-1697

Dick's Liquor & Deli.
737 Pearl St.
La Jolla, CA

Ethnic Cookbooks

Food Marketplace-69

Ella Wendy
77 Lexington Ave.
New York, NY   (212) 686-2349

Falafel Arax
5101 Santa Monica Blvd.
Hollywood, CA   (213) 663-9687

Falafel Roxy # 1
629 S. Hill St.
Los Angeles, CA   (818) 781-0805

Falafel Roxy # 2
6407 Sepulveda Blvd.
Van Nuys, CA   (818) 781-0805

Father Nature's Cafe
19535 Ventura Blvd.
Tarzana, CA   (818) 344-7758

Fresno Deli
4627 Fresno St.
Fresno, CA   (209) 225-7906

Garden of Delights
1192 Lexington Ave.
New York, NY

Gary's Submarine Sandwich
12507 Victory Blvd.
N. Hollywood, CA   (818) 763-0886

Haig's Delicacies
642 Clement St.
San Francisco, CA   (415) 752-6283

Hollywood Deli & Jr. Market
1243 N. Vine St.
Hollywood, CA   (213) 460-4373

Hye Deli
3083 W. Bullard
Fresno, CA   (209) 431-7798

IZI Deli
4821 E. Bullard Ave.
Fresno, CA   (209) 251-6599

International Deli
4810 Fulton Ave.
Sherman Oaks, CA   (818) 990-4916

International Deli
795 The Alameda
San Jose, CA   (408) 286-2036

Italian American Delicatessen
52 W. Merrik Road
Freeport, NY

J & T Greek-Italian Deli
31 Ditmars Blvd.
New York, NY   (212) 545-7920

Jack's Cold Cuts
Street & Hulmeville Roads
Cornwells, PA   (215) 639-2346

Jack's Deli & Ice Cream
110 E. 7th St.
Los Angeles, CA   (213) 627-9997

Jimmy's Deli
4080 Bay Street
Fremont, CA   (415) 490-2056

Joelle's Kabobland Deli
208 S. Central Ave.
Glendale, CA   (818) 500-3962

John's Delicatessen
9 Washington St.
Morristown, NJ

K & S Deli
1168 San Gabriel Blvd.
Rosemead, CA   (818) 288-2333

Kafe Katz
4860 Boiling Brook Parkway
Rockville, MD

King Falafel
7408 3rd Ave.
New York, NY   (718) 745-4188

Kupelian Foods, Inc.
146 Bergen Pike
Ridgefield Park, NJ   (201) 440-8055

Leo's Sandwiches
139 S. Verdugo Rd.
Glendale, CA   (818) 247-2050

Leonardo's Italian & Greek Del
1406 S. Pacific Coast Highway
Redondo Beach, CA   (310) 316-4433

M & M International Deli
12120 Sylvan St.
N. Hollywood, CA   (818) 980-0608

Mac's Deli
526 W. Huntington Dr.
Monrovia, CA   (818) 303-3016

Market Express & Liquor
5658 Sepulveda Blvd.
Van Nuys, CA   (818) 781-0325

Massis Armenian Sandwich
411 7th St.
Los Angeles, CA   (213) 623-8302

Mediterranean Deli
4629 41st St., N.W.
Washington, DC

Mediterranean Deli
81 N. Glebe Road
Arlington, VA

Mid-Eastern Pastries & Grocery
2354 University Ave.
San Diego, CA   (619) 295-2311

Mini Kabob
313 W. Vine St.
Glendale, CA   (818) 244-1343

N & K Groceries & Deli
1183 E. Main St.
El Cajon, CA   (619) 447-9471

Ohanyan's Int. Delicatessen
1335 W. Shields Ave.
Fresno, CA   (209) 225-4290

One & One Pizza & Deli
5940 San Fernando Road
Glendale, CA   (818) 246-9496

Papa Joe's Liqour Deli
2745 W. Lincoln Ave.
Anaheim, CA   (714) 826-0981

Paradise Health Juice
312 W. Sixth St.
Los Angeles, CA   (213) 628-4530

Pick-A-Deli
1200 S. Brand Blvd.
Glendale, CA   (818) 244-4190

Ponzo's Deli
2495 E. Washington Blvd.
Pasadena, CA   (818) 794-5682

Raffi's Place # 1
452 W. Stocker St.
Glendale, CA   (818) 241-9960

Raffi's Place # 2
211 E. Broadway
Glendale, CA   (818) 247-0575

Rodeo Deli & Grocery
205 S. Glendale Ave.
Glendale, CA   (818) 244-6969

Sahag's Basturma
5183 Sunset Blvd.
Hollywood, CA   (213) 661-5311

Sam's International Deli
354 N. La Brea Ave.
Hollywood, CA   (213) 935-7212

Sandwich Construction Co.
1723 W. Verdugo
Burbank, CA   (818) 842-0715

70-Food Marketplace

Ethnic Cookbooks

Sandwich Shop
25530 W. Ave. Stanford
Valencia, CA

Sandwiches By Connal
1505 E. Washington Blvd.
Pasadena, CA (818) 798-0751

Serge's Deli
12801 Sherman Way
N. Hollywood, CA (818) 765-1200

Sevan Deli & Imported Foods
1012 W. Beverly Blvd.
Montebello, CA (213) 721-3804

Sevan Falafel
7605 White Oak Ave.
Reseda, CA (818) 881-3909

Siham's Deli & Sandwiches
550 N. State College Blvd.
Fullerton, CA (714) 871-0131

Sparta Greek Deli
429 W. 8th St.
Los Angeles, CA (213) 622-5950

Subway Sandwiches
110 N. Brand Blvd.
Glendale, CA (818) 244-0411

Subway Sandwiches
730 S. Central Ave.
Glendale, CA (818) 243-9692

Sunrise Deli
2115 Irving St.
San Francisco, CA (415) 664-8210

Tasty Hamburger
628 S. Hill St.
Los Angeles, CA (213) 623-4798

Tip-Top Deli
8108 W. 3rd St.
Los Angeles, CA (213) 653-6222

Uptown Deli
28948 Orchard Lake Rd
Farmington Hills, MI (313) 626-3715

Van Nuys Cafe
7211 Van Nuys Blvd.
Van Nuys, CA (818) 994-9948

FOOD PRODUCERS

Assan Caltex Foods
9045 Eton Ave.
Canoga Park, CA (818) 700-8657

Barmaki's Pastry Shop
1151 N. Euclid St.
Anaheim, CA (714) 776-2621

Del-Pack Foods Abjad Corporat.
20620 Superior St.
Chatsworth, CA (818) 407-0887

E. Demakis & Co. Inc.
37 Waterhill St.
Lynn, MA (617) 595-1557

Erivan Dairy
105 Allison Road
Oreland, PA

Golchin Overseas Corp.
12381 Foothill Blvd.
Sylmar, CA (818) 896-6127

Jamai Coffee Co.
820 Thompson Ave.
Glendale, CA (818) 241-8156

Khooban Foods Inc.
1715 W. 130th St.
Gardena, CA (310) 719-2390

Krinos Foods, Inc.
47-00 Northern Blvd.
Long Island City, NY (718) 729-9000

Near East Food Products, Inc.
Leominster, MA

Nick's Produce
401 W. Marshall St.
Richmond, VA (804) 644-0683

Pak Dairy, Inc.
658 W. Hawthorne
Glendale, CA (818) 244-9435

Rooster Brand Products Corp.
2856 E. 54th St.
Los Angeles, CA (213) 582-5000

Roses International Trade, Inc
170 S. Beverly Dr.
Los Angeles, CA

Sahara Natural Foods, Inc.
Berkeley, CA

Shemshad Food, Inc.
3630 Foothill Blvd.
La Crescenta, CA (818) 249-9066

Shoosh International
195 Channal Ave.
San Francisco, CA (415) 626-1847

Soghomonian Farms
10179 E. Belmont
Sanger, CA (209) 252-7848

Soofer Co., Inc. Sadaf
2828 S. Alameda St.
Los Angeles, CA (213) 234-6666

South Gate Frozen Food
3211 Independence Ave.
South Gate, CA (213) 567-1359

Sun-Ni Armenian String Cheese
8738 W. Chester Pike
Upper Darby, PA (215) 853-3449

FRESH PRODUCE- RETAIL

4 Seasons Produce
1315 W. Glenoaks Blvd.
Glendale, CA (818) 244-9698

Amo's Produce & Grocery
15711 Vanowen St.
Van Nuys, CA (818) 904-9938

Ayoub's Fruits & Vegetable
322 Somerset East
Ottawa, (613) 233-6417

California Fruit and Produce
637 Mount Auburn St.
Watertown, MA

Carlo Washington Produce
1458 E. Washington Blvd.
Pasadena, CA (818) 797-0017

Cerritos Produce
9055 Cerritos Ave.
Anaheim, CA (714) 995-1407

Da Giovanni Fruit Store
12251 Boul. Laurentien
Montreal, (514) 332-2550

Danny's Fresh Meat & Produce
17648 Vanowen St.
Van Nuys, CA (818) 708-9775

Discount Produce Market
8741 Laurel Canyon Blvd.
Sun Valley, CA (818) 768-0091

Family Meat Market & Produce
3452 79th St.
Chicago, IL (312) 434-0095

Family Produce & Market
926 S. Magnolia Ave.
Anaheim, CA (714) 821-7102

Ethnic Cookbooks

Food Marketplace-71

Farmer's Ranch
1801 W. Whittier Blvd.
Montebello, CA   (213) 728-2615

Fresh " N" Green
15430 E. Francisquito Ave.
La Puente, CA   (818) 917-6189

Garden Produce
Glendale, CA   (818) 240-4821

Garny Fruits & Nuts
1416 W. Glenoaks Blvd.
Glendale, CA   (818) 242-9240

Glendale 1st Produce
726 S. Glendale Ave.
Glendale, CA   (818) 247-3730

Glendale Farmer's Market
620 S. Glendale Ave.
Glendale, CA   (818) 507-8041

Italian Deli & Produce
12932 Sherman Way
N. Hollywood, CA   (818) 982-5781

Olympic Produce Market
1717 E. Washington Blvd.
Pasadena, CA   (818) 797-7437

Panjoyan Produce
2016 Newport Blvd.
Costa Mesa, CA   (714) 646-5718

Prime Produce
Van Nuys, CA   (818) 905-9538

Quality Produce
13732 E. Amar Road
La Puente, CA   (818) 918-1225

Rainbow Produce & Grocery
490 Taraval St.
San Francisco, CA   (415) 731-8715

Robert's Fresh Produce
7100 Foothill Blvd.
Tujunga, CA   (818) 352-7787

Sunland Produce
8255 Sunland Blvd.
Sun Valley, CA   (818) 504-6629

Yerevan Ranch Market
1501 W. Beverly Blvd.
Montebello, CA   (213) 722-3780

FRESH PRODUCE-WHOLESALE

Antoyan Wholesale Produce
12500 E. Slauson Ave.
Santa Fe Springs, CA   (213) 693-6966

Bakker Produce, Inc.
211 W. Main St. Box249
Griffith, IN   (219) 924-8950

Girazian Fruit Co.
39400 Clarkson Dr.
Kingsburg, CA   (209) 888-2255

GROCERS

1 Stop Market
19801 Vanowen St.
Canoga Park, CA   (818) 713-9165

4 Seasons Produce
1315 W. Glenoaks Blvd.
Glendale, CA   (818) 244-9698

7 Star Deli & Market
10128 Balboa Blvd.
Granada Hills, CA   (818) 363-8577

7 to 7 Market
3964 Redondo Beach Blvd.
Torrance, CA   (213) 370-5707

A & A Food Market Inc.
14 Central Square
Cambridge, MA

A & A Foods
266 Elgin St.
Ottawa, Canada   (613) 737-2144

A & P Market
410 W. Colorado St.
Glendale, CA   (818) 243-2709

A-1 Liquor & Jr. Mart
1145 E. Colorado St.
Glendale, CA   (818) 500-8471

A-Z Food Market
703 Middle Neck Road
Great Neck, NY   (516) 829-3525

A. Marino Grocery
1716 S. 13th St.
Omaha, NB

Abadan Bazar
7350 Reseda Blvd.
Reseda, CA   (818) 345-7602

Abner's Broasted Chicken
22757 Ventura Blvd.
Woodland Hills, CA   (818) 340-9466

Acacia Grocery
402 E. Acacia Ave.
Glendale, CA   (818) 956-5341

Acropolis Delicatessen Store
1004 Main St.
Asbury Park, NJ   (201) 988-3030

Acropolis Food Market
1206 Underwood St. N.W.
Washington, DC   (202) 829-1414

Acropolis Market
8441 Joy Road
Detroit, MI

Adelphia Delicatessen
19 E. Market St.
Wilkes-Barre, PA

Afghan Grocery
42-34 Collage Point Blvd.
Flushing, NY   (718) 461-7975

Afghan Market
5709 Edsel Road
Alexandria, VA   (703) 212-9529

Agaty's Groceries
148 Sabin St.
Pawtucket, RI   (401) 728-1660

Agop's Market
1020 E. Broadway
Glendale, CA   (818) 502-0924

Ahwaz International Groceries
2133 W. Lincoln Ave.
Anaheim, CA   (714) 772-4492

Akoubian's Deli Grocery
16535 Brookhurts St.
Fountain Valley, CA   (714) 775-7977

Akropol Pastry Shop
2601 W. Lawrence Ave.
Chicago, IL

Al-Ahram Supermarket
2424 W. Ball Road
Anaheim, CA   (714) 527-9190

Al-Hilal Market
3025 S. Vermont Ave.
Los Angeles, CA   (213) 731-0868

72-Food Marketplace — Ethnic Cookbooks

Al-Khayam
7723 Bergenline Ave.
N. Bergen, NJ

Al-Madinah
14282 Brookhurst St.
Garden Grove, CA   (714) 531-0321

Al-Madinah
1807 Pacific Coast Hwy.
Lomita, CA   (310) 325-4778

Al-Manar Market
6331 Mission St.
Daly City, CA   (415) 756-1133

Al-Nogoom Grocery & Meat
2805 W. 63rd St.
Chicago, IL   (312) 918-1700

Al-Noor Market
14328 Brookhurst St.
Garden Grove, CA   (714) 839-5123

Al-Rasheed Grocery
3255 W. 63rd St.
Chicago, IL   (312) 925-4711

Al-Tayebat Market
1217 S. Brookhurst St.
Anaheim, CA   (714) 520-4723

Aleksan Narliyan Grocery
1530 St. Nicholas Ave.
Detroit, MI

Aleman Meat & Grocery
5413 W. 79th St.
Burbank, IL   (312) 425-2711

Alexander Bakery Corp
878 W. 8th St.
Miami, FL   (305) 858-4218

Alexander's Market
30745 Pacific Coast Hwy
Malibu, CA   (310) 457-9776

Alexis Deli & Grocery
4050 La Crescenta Ave.
Montrose, CA   (818) 957-5687

Ali Baba Market
100 S. Brookhurst
Anaheim, CA   (714) 774-5064

Ali's Market
1915 W. Redlands Blvd.
Redlands, CA   (714) 798-7454

Aljibani Halal Market
23385 Golden Springs Dr.
Diamond Bar, CA   (714) 861-3865

Almaden Bazar
6065 Meridian Ave.
San Jose, CA   (408) 268-6867

Aloonak Market
11628 Santa Monica Blvd.
Los Angeles, CA   (310) 820-1844

Aloupis Company
916 Ninth St. N.W.
Washington, DC

Alvand Market
3033 S. Bristol
Costa Mesa, CA   (714) 545-7177

Amamchyan Market
1273 N. Wilton
Hollywood, CA   (213) 462-8675

American Armenian Grocery
1442 E. Washington Blvd.
Pasadena, CA   (818) 794-9220

American Oriental Grocery
20736 Lahser Rd.
Southfield, MI   (313) 352-5733

Amo's Produce & Grocery
15711 Vanowen St.
Van Nuys, CA   (818) 904-9938

Anahit Market
7908 Foothill Blvd.
Sunland, CA   (818) 353-1968

Andre Market
625 E. Colorado Blvd.
Glendale, CA   (818) 548-5884

Andre' Market
1478 W. Spring Valley
Richardson, TX   (214) 644-7644

Andrew's Delicatessen
305 Sewell Ave.
Asbury Park, NJ

Angel's Market
455 Athens St.
Tarpon Springs, FL   (813) 937-6731

Angelo Merlina & Sons
816 6th Ave., St.
Seattle, WA

Ani Grocery & Deli
1500 W. Glenoaks Blvd.
Glendale, CA   (818) 241-7229

Anoush Deli & Grocery
1468 N. Tamarid
Hollywood, CA   (213) 465-4062

Anthony Lazieh
182 Washington St.
Central Falls, RI

Antone's Import Co.
807 Taft St.
Houston, TX   (713) 526-1046

Antonio Sofo & Son Import. Co.
3253 Monroe St.
Toledo, OH

Apadana Market & Deli.
2971 Agoura Road
Westlake Village, CA   (818) 991-1268

Aphrodite Greek Imports
5886 Leesburg Pike
Falls Church, VA   (703) 931-5055

Apollo Greek Imports
4782 Lee Highway
Arlington, VA

Apollo Market
11853 Ingelwood Ave.
Hawthorne, CA   (213) 644-8956

Ara Deli & Grocery
1021 E. Broadway
Glendale, CA   (818) 241-2390

Arabic Grocery & Bakery
123 S.W. 27th Ave.
Miami, FL

Arabic Town
16511 Woodward
Highland Park, MI

Ararat Bakery & Deli
1800 Ave. Road
Toronto,   (416) 782-5722

Ararat Deli & Grocery
1340 E. Colorado St.
Glendale, CA   (818) 243-0918

Ararat Fruit Market
Hollywood, CA

Ararat International Grocery
11960 E. Carson
Hawaiian Gardens, CA   (310) 420-2022

Arax Deli
316 W. Beverly Blvd.
Montebello, CA   (213) 721-1986

Arax Groceries & Deli
17644 Vanowen St.
Van Nuys, CA   (818) 705-0395

Ethnic Cookbooks

Food Marketplace-73

Arax Market
502 "L" Street
Fresno, CA   (209) 237-5048

Arax Market
603 Mount Auburn St.
Watertown, MA   (617) 924-3399

Araz International Grocery
10668 Zelzah Ave.
Granada Hills, CA   (818) 368-8442

Ardem Grocery
5102 Fountain Ave.
Hollywood, CA   (213) 665-6984

Aremia Imported Foods
S. Saginaw St.
Grand Blanc, MI

Aresh Grocery
2159 Parker
Denver, CO   (303) 752-9272

Aresh Meat & Grocery
3305 W. Magnolia Blvd.
Burbank, CA   (818) 569-7405

Arian Del Mart
9663 Folsom Blvd.
Sacramento, CA   (916) 363-6982

Arimes Market
218 Walton Ave.
Lexington, KY

Arka Grocery & Record
4855 Santa Monica Blvd.
Hollywood, CA   (213) 666-6949

Armen Foods
42 43rd Steeet
New York, NY   (718) 729-3749

Armenia International Market
12452 Oxanard
N. Hollywood, CA   (818) 760-4848

Armenian Delight
2591 W. Chester Pike
Broomall, PA   (215) 353-1981

Armenian Pizza
6204 Woodbine Ave.
Philadelphia, PA

Arsham's Deli & Grocery
5051 Hollywood Blvd.
Hollywood, CA   (213) 660-7508

Artesia Market
2322 Artesia Blvd.
Redondo Beach, CA   (310) 379-6995

Arya Food Imports
5061 Clark
Chicago, IL   (312) 878-2092

Arya International Market
2710 Garnet Ave.
San Diego, CA   (619) 274-9632

Arzan Market
14311 Newport Ave.
Tustin, CA   (714) 544-6706

Asadur's Market
5558 Randolph Road
Rockville, MD   (301) 770-5558

Asia Center & Grocery
303 W. Broad St.
Falls Church, VA   (703) 533-2112

Assal Supermarket I
118 W. Maple Ave.
Vienna, VA   (703) 578-3232

Assal Supermarket II
6039 Leesburg Pike
Falls Church, VA   (703) 281-2248

Astoria Superette
29 23rd Ave.
Astoria, NY   (212) 728-8928

Athenian Market
17024 Devonshire St.
Northridge, CA   (818) 363-1160

Athens Bakery & Grocery Co.
527 Monroe Ave.
Detroit, MI

Athens Greek & Italian Deli
616 Five Oaks Ave.
Dayton, OH

Athens Grocery
324 S. Halsted St.
Chicago, IL   (312) 454-0940

Athens Imported Food
222 E. Market St.
Indianapolis, IN   (317) 632-0269

Athens West
111 N. Dale Ave.
Anaheim, CA   (714) 826-2560

Athina Supermrche
4919 Note-Dame
Chomedey,   (514) 682-8010

Atlas Foods
1818 W. Waters Ave.
Tampa, FL   (813) 933-5581

Atlas Market
15030 Ventura Blvd.
Sherman Oaks, CA   (818) 784-2763

Attari
1386 Westwood Blvd.
Los Angeles, CA   (310) 470-1003

Attari Food- Deli and Spices
156 W. El Camino Real
Sunnyvale, CA   (408) 773-0290

Avakian's Grocery
1100 S. Glendale Ave.
Glendale, CA   (818) 242-3222

B & E. Masion d'Aliments
6929 Sherbrooke West
N.D.G., Quebec,   (514) 482-0262

Baggal Market
1067 Rockville Pike
Rockville, MD   (301) 424-5522

Bahar Market
595 Middle Neck Road
Great Neck, NY   (516) 466-2222

Bahar Market
2432 Dafrin
Toranto, Ontario,   (416) 256-1268

Bahnan's Bakery & Market
369 Pleasant St.
Worcester, MA   (508) 791-8566

Balian Markets
5469 W. Adams Blvd.
Los Angeles, CA   (213) 870-9219

Balian's Grocery
2219 Irving St.
San Francisco, CA   (415) 664-1870

Balji's Deli
369 E. 17th St.
Costa Mesa, CA   (714) 631-0855

Balkan Bakery
1590 St. Nicholas Ave.
New York, NY

Barsamian Grocery
1030 Massachusetts Ave.
Cambridge, MA   (617) 661-9300

Baruir's Oriental-American Gro
40 Queens Blvd
Sunnyside, NY   (212) 784-0842

Barzizza Brothers, Inc.
2216 Dunn Ave.
Memphis, TN   (901) 744-0054

74-Food Marketplace   Ethnic Cookbooks

Bazaar Market
22 154th St.
Whitestone, NY   (718) 762-4222

Bazaar Pars
3377 Stevens Creek Blvd.
San Jose, CA   (408) 985-8545

Bazaarak Persian/M.E. Grocer
28293 Mission Blvd.
Hayward, CA   (510) 581-7253

Bazar
303 Spanish Villge
Dallas, TX   (214) 702-9505

Bazar Market # 1
451 N. Fairfax
Los Angeles, CA   (213) 852-1981

Bazar Market # 2
1410 Livonia
Los Angeles, CA   (213) 274-9077

Bazarak (Victorian Liquor)
28293 Mission Blvd.
Hayward, CA   (415) 581-7253

Beijing Islamic Restaurant
2809 Via Campo
Montebello, CA   (213) 728-8021

Bell-Bates Co.,Inc
107 W. Broadway
New York, NY   (212) 267-4300

Ben Disalvo & Sons,
802 Regent St.
Madison, WI

Best Buy Market
736 S. Adams St.
Glendale, CA   (818) 244-3892

Betar's Market
703 Broad St.
Bridgeport, CT

Better Life
2380 N. Tustin Ave.
Santa Ana, CA   (714) 547-0613

Beverly Hills Meats
303 N. Crescent Dr.
Beverly Hills, CA

Beverly Hills Pita House
127 N. La Cienega Blvd.
Beverly Hills, CA   (213) 659-8347

Beverly Market
9238 W. Pico Blvd.
Los Angeles, CA   (213) 278-6329

Bezjian's Grocery, Inc.
4725 Santa Monica Blvd.
Hollywood, CA   (213) 663-1503

Bharat Bazar
565 S. Azusa Way
La Puente, CA   (818) 912-2014

Biblos International Foods
1984 Foxworthy Ave.
San Jose, CA   (408) 371-4829

Big Apple Market
15417 E. Fairgrove
La Puente, CA   (818) 918-2335

Bijan Market
806 W. Pico Blvd.
Santa Monica, CA   (213) 395-8979

Bijan Specialty Food
1369 Marine Dr.
Ambleside, Vancouver,   (604) 925-1055

Bit of Lebanon
637 Laurel St.
San Carlos, CA

Bitar's
947 Federal St.
Philadelphia, PA

Bob Corey's Flaming
1719 S. 13th St.
Terre Haute, IN

Boucouralas Brothers Super M.
 Common & Middle St.
Saco, ME   (207) 284-4314

Brentwood Village Market
11725 Barrington
Brentwood, CA

Broadway Mart & Deli
508 W. Broadway
Glendale, CA   (818) 243-3332

Broiler
6051 Hollywood Blvd.
Hollywood, CA   (213) 462-5101

Bruno Foods
4970 Glenway Ave.
Cincinnati, OH

Bruno's Food Store
2620 13th Ave.W.
Birmingham, AL

Bucharest Grocery
5235 Hollywood Blvd.
Hollywood, CA   (213) 462-8407

Buy Direct Food Warehouse
2220 Business Circle
San Jose, CA   (408) 292-2211

C & K Importing Co.
2771 W. Pico Blvd.
Los Angeles, CA   (213) 737-2970

Cafe De Leon
28 W. Portal Ave.
San Francisco, CA   (415) 664-1050

Cahalan Groceries
5754 Cahalan Shopping Center
San Jose, CA   (408) 226-5992

Calamata Groceries
27 E. Northampton St.
Wilkes Barre, PA   (717) 823-7761

California Market & Deli
1803 W. Glenoaks Blvd.
Glendale, CA   (818) 244-9541

Calvert Delicatessen
2418 Wisconsin Ave. N.W.
Washington, DC

Campus Eastern Foods
408 Locust St.
Columbia, MO

Canton Importing Co.
1136 Wertz Ave. N.W.
Canton, OH

Capello's Import. & American
5328 Lemmon Ave.
Dallas, TX

Capitol Italian Grocery
32 S. 4th St.
Harrisburg, PA

Caras Greek Product Co.
2002 Main St.
Columbia, SC

Caravan Market
615 S. Frederick Ave.
Gaithersburg, MD   (301) 258-8380

Cardoos Int. Food Corp.
 Weybossett St.
Providence, RI   (401) 272-9373

Cardoos Inter. Food Corp.
 Corner of North & Steven St
Hyannis, MA   (617) 775-7702

Cardullo's Gourmet Shop
6 Brattle St.
Cambridge, MA   (617) 491-8888

Ethnic Cookbooks

Food Marketplace-75

Carmel Grocery
9888 Carmel Mountain Road
San Diego, CA   (619) 538-1069

Carmel Kohsher Market
11777 Santa Monica Blvd.
Los Angeles, CA   (310) 479-4030

Carmen's Pastries
701 E. Broadway
Glendale, CA   (818) 243-8761

Cash Produce Co.
2216 Morris Ave.
Birmingham, AL

Cater-Maid Bake Shop
1135 E. Glendale Ave.
Phoenix, AZ

Cedar Foods
4610 Dufferin St.
Downsview,   (416) 661-8999

Cedar Market
413 S. Main St.
Royal Oak, MI   (313) 547-7856

Central Food Stores Inc.
63 Main St.
Hackensack, NJ

Central Grocery Company
923 Decatur St.
New Orleans, LA   (504) 523-1620

Central Market
730 S. Central Ave.
Glendale, CA   (818) 240-3450

Century Market
11901 Santa Monica Blvd.
Los Angeles, CA   (310) 473-1568

Cerritos Produce
9055 Cerritos Ave.
Anaheim, CA   (714) 995-1407

Charlie's Market
3960 Irving St.
San Francisco, CA   (415) 681-9569

Cheese Market, the
503 Clinch Ave. S.W.
Knoxville, TN   (615) 525-3352

Cheese N Coffee
2679 Louisiana Blvd.
Albuquerque, NM   (505) 883-1226

Chef Bijan
210 Live Oaks Center
Casselberry, FL   (407) 260-8855

City Market
4948 El Cajon Blvd.
San Diego, CA   (619) 583-5811

Clover Leaf Market, Inc.
28905 Telegraph
Southfield, MI   (313) 357-0400

Columbia Delicatessen
17th St & Columbia
Washington, DC

Connemara Food Mart
462 Troy Schenectady Rd.
Latham, NY   (518) 785-7555

Constantine's Delicatessen
205 48th Ave.
Bayside, NY

Consumer's Market
141 E. Florida Ave.
Youngstown, OH

Continental Pastry Shop
4549 University Wayd N.E.
Seattle, WA

Cordoos International Food Cor
Dedham Plaza Route 1
Dedham, MA   (617) 329-3230

Cottage Market
785 Mount Auburn St.
Watertown, MA   (617) 924-9718

Crown Market
818 N. Pacific Ave.
Glendale, CA   (818) 956-0113

Daglian's Grocery
13305 Victory Blvd.
Van Nuys, CA   (818) 786-5595

Damascus Imported Grocery
5721 Hollywood Blvd.
Hollywood, FL   (305) 962-4552

Damavand Market
37013 Powers Way
Fremont, CA   (510) 793-2606

Daniel's Bakery
395 Washington St.
Brighton Center, MA   (617) 254-7718

Danielle's Bakery & Imported
123 Jamacha Road
El Cajon, CA   (619) 579-1999

Danny's Foods
7905 Hartford Road
Parkville, MD

Day Mart Market
5554 Reseda Blvd.
Tarzana, CA   (818) 996-8805

Ddroubi's Bakery & Imports
7333 Hillcroft
Houston, TX   (713) 988-5897

Del Mar & Co., Inc.
501 Monroe Ave.
Detroit, MI   (313) 961-5504

Delaurenti's Italian Market
Lower Pike Place Market
Seattle, WA

Delicacies, Inc.
12 Rolfe Square
Cranston, RI   (401) 461-4774

Demoulas Super Market No.1
321 Main St.
Andover, MA

Demoulas Super Market No.10
10 Main St.
Twieksbury, MA

Demoulas Super Market No.11
240 Main St.
Wilmington, MA

Demoulas Super Market No.2
288 Chelmsford St.
Chelmsford, MA

Demoulas Super Market No.3
25 Lowell St.
Haverhill, MA

Demoulas Super Market No.4
700 Essex St.
Lawrence, MA

Demoulas Super Market No.5
80 Dummer St.
Lowell, MA

Demoulas Super Market No.6
1200 Bridge St.
Lowell, MA

Demoulas Super Market No.7
164 Haverhill St.
Methuen, MA

Demoulas Super Market No.8
350 Winthrop Ave.
N. Andover, MA

Demoulas Super Market No.9
700 Boston Road
Pinehurst, MA

76-Food Marketplace

Ethnic Cookbooks

Demoulas Super Market, Inc.
Route 28
Salem, NH   (603) 898-5161

Dimyan's Market
116 Elm Street
Danbury, CT

Diran International Grocery
13655 Vanowen St.
Van Nuys, CA   (818) 988-2882

Discount Produce Market
8741 Laurel Canyon Blvd.
Sun Valley, CA   (818) 768-0091

Discount Produce Market
6800 Reseda Blvd.
Reseda, CA   (818) 344-2959

Ditmars & 35th St. Market
28 Ditmars Blvd.
Astoria, NY

Do Do Inc.
2409 Central Ave.
Union City, NJ   (201) 863-3350

Dokan Market, Inc.
7921 Old Georgetown Road
Bethesda, MD   (301) 657-2361

Domestic Foods
595 Gladstone
Ontario,   (613) 236-6421

Donikian's Market
1138 Chula Vista Ave.
Burlingame, CA   (415) 348-9297

Downtown Delicatessen
345 S.W. Yamhill St.
Portland, OR

Droubi's Bakery & Grocery
7333 Hillcroft
Houston, TX   (713) 988-5897

Droubi's Bakery & Grocery
3223 Hillcroft
Houston, TX   (713) 782-6160

Droubi's Bakery & Grocery
7807 Kirby Dr.
Houston, TX   (713) 790-0101

Dudemaine Groceteria
1570 Dudemaine
Montreal,   (514) 334-8267

Dvin Market
17757 Sherman Way
Reseda, CA   (818) 344-0408

Dvin Market
1418 W. Beverly Blvd.
Montebello, CA   (213) 725-7250

East Trade Company
402 E. Trade St.
Charlotte, NC

Eastern Market
2400 Coffee Road
Modesto, CA   (209) 575-0344

Easy Shop
250 Allen St.
New Britain, CT   (203) 225-7810

Economy Greek Market
973 Broadway
Denver, CO   (303) 623-9682

Eden Market
16411 E. 14th St.
San Leandro, CA   (510) 276-0212

Edna's Coffee & Grocery
420 S. Glendale Ave.
Glendale, CA   (818) 243-0445

Eema's Market
21925 Ventura Blvd.
Woodland Hills, CA   (818) 702-9272

Elat Market
8730 W. Pico Blvd.
Los Angeles, CA   (310) 659-0576

Elias Kosher Market
8829 W. Pico Blvd.
Los Angeles, CA   (213) 278-7503

Elliniki Agora Market
32 30th Ave.
New York, NY   (212) 728-9122

Ellis Bakery
577 Grant St.
Akron, OH

Emil's Grocery
27737 Bouquet Cyn Road
Saugus, CA   (805) 297-3184

Emir Grocery
135 Roosevelt Ave.
Flushing, NY

Empire Coffee and Tea Co.
486 Ninth Ave.
New York, NY   (212) 564-1460

Encino Market
17977 Ventura Blvd.
Encino, CA   (818) 343-7900

Erebuni Grocery
4900 Fountain Ave.
Hollywood, CA   (213) 664-1700

Ernest Grocery Inc.
501 S. Newkirk St.
Baltimore, MD

Euphrates Bakery Inc.
10 Mt. Auburn St.
Watertown, MA

Euphrates Grocery
101 Shawmut Ave.
Boston, MA

European Deli Middle East
1500 Monument Blvd.
Concord, CA   (510) 689-1011

European Gourmet Deli
5427 El Cajon Blvd.
San Diego, CA   (619) 582-0444

European Grocery Store
520 Court Pl.
Pittsburgh, PA

European Importing Co.
910 Preston Ave.
Houston, TX

Excel Market
3230 Tidewater Dr.
Norfolk, VA

Fairfax Family Market
451 N. Fairfax
Los Angeles, CA   (213) 852-1981

Fairuz M.E. Grocery & Deli
3306 N. Garey
Pomona, CA   (714) 596-2932

Faisal International Market
1450 University Ave.
Riverside, CA   (714) 784-7111

Fakhr El Din
2620 S. Figueroa
Los Angeles, CA   (213) 747-7839

Family Grocery
1515 E. Washington Blvd.
Pasadena, CA   (818) 791-1086

Family Market
8515 Reseda Blvd.
Northridge, CA   (818) 349-2222

Family Produce & Market
926 S. Magnolia Ave.
Anaheim, CA   (714) 821-7102

Ethnic Cookbooks

Food Marketplace-77

Farah's Imported Foods
705 McDuff Ave. S.
Jacksonville, FL   (904) 388-0691

Farmer's Ranch
1801 W. Whittier Blvd.
Montebello, CA   (213) 728-2615

Fernando's Int. Food Mkt.
3045 N. Federal Highway
Miami, FL   (305) 566-3104

Fertitta's Delicatessens
1124 6301 Line Ave.
Shreveport, LA

Filippo's Italian Groc.& Liqu.
3435 E. McDowell Road
Phoenix, AZ

Fish Town
414 Brighton Beach Ave.
Brooklyn, NY

Five Stars Corp. Market
6347 Columbia Pike
Falls Church, VA   (703) 256-6000

Five Ten Mini Market
25845 San Fernando Road
Santa Clarita, CA   (805) 259-2680

Flamingo Grocery Inc.
630 S. Federal Highway
Fort Lauderdale, FL

Food Mart
3848 E. Chapman
Orange, CA   (714) 538-9428

Food Stop Market
3800 San Pablo Dam Road
El Sobrante, CA   (510) 223-1111

Food of All Nations
130 W. Stocker St.
Glendale, CA   (818) 956-5572

Foothill Market
547 E. Foothill Blvd.
Monrovia, CA   (818) 301-0089

Foothill Village Market
1404 W. Kenneth Road
Glendale, CA   (818) 242-1257

Foxies Delicatessen
659 Peachtree St.
Atlanta, GA

Franklin Int. Grocery
5825 Franklin Ave.
Hollywood, CA   (213) 465-0214

Fred Bridge and Co.
212 E. 52nd St.
New York, NY

Freddie's Market
930 Ontario Ave.
Niagara Falls, NY   (716) 285-8344

Freeport Italian American Deli
52 W. Merrick Road
Freeport, NY

Freeway Market
4121 Pennsylvania Ave.
La Crescenta, CA   (818) 249-6701

Fresh " N" Green
15430 E. Francisquito Ave.
La Puente, CA   (818) 917-6189

Fresh Market
321 E. Alameda Ave.
Burbank, CA   (818) 848-4742

Fresno Deli
4627 Fresno St.
Fresno, CA   (209) 225-7906

Friendly Grocery Company
1420 St. Nicholas Ave
New York, NY   (212) 923-2654

Fruits and Things
1125 Lexington Ave.
New York, NY

G & A Grocery
640 Holmdel Rd.
Hazlet, NJ   (201) 264-0176

G & M Deli
4605 Gary Blvd.
San Francisco, CA

G.B. Ratto & Co.Int. Grocers
821 Washington St.
Oakland, CA   (415) 832-6503

Gabriel Importing Co.
2461 Russell St.
Detroit, MI   (313) 961-2890

Galanides, Inc.
902 Cooke Ave.
Norfolk, VA

Galanides-Raleigh Inc.
Wicker & Campbell St.
Raleigh, NC

Galina's Deli
2226 W. Devon Ave.
Chicago, IL

Gardullo's Gourmet Shop
6 Brattle St.
Cambridge, MA

Garine Deli & Grocery
7213 Balboa Blvd.
Van Nuys, CA   (818) 786-0946

Garny Fruits & Nuts
1416 W. Glenoaks Blvd.
Glendale, CA   (818) 242-9240

Garny Grocery
402 S. Glenoaks Blvd.
Burbank, CA   (818) 841-7965

Garo's Basturma
1088 N. Allen Ave.
Pasadena, CA   (818) 794-0460

Genoosi's Imported Foods
4016 E. Broad St.
Columbus, OH

George A. Nassaur
909 Cherry St.
Vicksburg, MS   (601) 636-4443

George A. Skaff & Sons
801 Court St.
Sioux City, IA

George Malko
185 Atlantic Ave.
Brooklyn, NY

George's Delicatessen
1041 N. Highland Ave. N.E
Atlanta, GA

George's Food Market
428 Montana Ave.
S. Milwaukee, WI   (414) 762-1232

George's Middle East Market
368 Getty Ave.
Paterson, NJ   (201) 278-1771

Giavis Market
351 Market St.
Lowell, MA   (617) 458-4721

Ginger Grocer
29 Valley Road
Montclair, NJ   (201) 744-1012

Gino's World Food Mart
126 N. Washington St.
Spokane, WA

Gira Market Int. Grocery
3250 Duke St.
Alexandria, VA   (703) 370-3632

78-Food Marketplace

Ethnic Cookbooks

Glen Elk Market
400 S. Glendale Ave.
Glendale, CA   (818) 545-0325

Glendale 1st Produce
726 S. Glendale Ave.
Glendale, CA   (818) 247-3730

Glendale Farmer's Market
620 S. Glendale Ave.
Glendale, CA   (818) 507-8041

Glendale House of Liquore
420 S. Glendale Ave.
Glendale, CA   (818) 243-5855

Glendale Market
513 W. Glenoaks Blvd.
Glendale, CA   (818) 243-2554

Glenoaks Deli & Grocery
621 E. Glenoaks Blvd.
Glendale, CA   (818) 247-4021

Glenoaks Market
401 S. Glenoaks Blvd.
Burbank, CA   (818) 559-7508

Golden State Bakery
5158 Hollywood Blvd.
Hollywood, CA   (213) 666-6713

Good Fellow Produce
1010 E. Broadway
Glendale, CA   (818) 243-3745

Good Foods Market
1864 E. Washington Blvd.
Pasadena, CA   (818) 794-5367

Gourmet Basket
6829 Tennyson Road
McLean, VA

Gourmet Bazaar
   International Market Place
Honolulu, HI   (808) 923-7658

Gourmet Food & Beverage Dist.
195 Channel St.
San Francisco, CA   (415) 626-1847

Gourmet International Market
585 Grove St.
Herndon, VA   (703) 478-6393

Gourmet Market, Inc.
2737 Devonshire Place, NW
Washington, DC

Grecian Phoenix Pastries
5530 W. Harrison St.
Chicago, IL

Greek Agora and Deli
5437 Hollywood Blvd.
Hollywood, CA   (213) 462-3766

Greek American Grocery Co.
2690 Coral Way
Miami, FL

Greek American Grocery Store
2961 Coral Way
Miami, FL

Greek American Importing Co.
518 E. Marshall St.
Richmond, VA

Greek Armenian Deli
9984 S. Lakewood Blvd.
Downey, CA   (310) 862-4566

Greek House Importing Co.
7856 E. Firestone Blvd.
Doweny, CA   (310) 862-1220

Greek Market & Restaurants
9034 Tampa Ave.
Northridge, CA   (818) 349-9689

Greek Pastries by Despine's
4715 W. Lisbon Ave.& W.Center St

Milwaukee, WI

Greek Store Liberty Market
612 Boulevard
Kennilworth, NJ   (201) 272-2550

Green Field Market
5567 N. Azusa Ave.
Azusa, CA   (818) 969-4232

Green Market # 1
1388 Westwood Blvd.
Los Angeles, CA   (213) 470-3808

Green Market # 2
8842 W. Pico Blvd.
Los Angeles, CA   (310) 276-9336

Grocery House Market
N. Hollywood, CA   (818) 503-1222

H. & H. Grocers
901 Beneat Placae
Baltimore, MD   (301) 728-0022

H. Roth & Son
1577 1st Ave
New York, NY

HHH Distributors
7006 Carrolln Ave.
Takoma Park, MD

Haddy's Food Market
1503 Washington St.
Charleston, WV

Haddy's Prime Meats
1422 E. Washington St.
Charleston, WV

Haig's Delicacies
642 Clement St.
San Francisco, CA   (415) 752-6283

Haji Baba Middle Eastern Food
1513 E. Apache
Tempe, AZ   (602) 894-1905

Hakeems's Bakery & Grocery
5854 Osuna, N.E.
Albuquerque, NM   (505) 881-4019

Halal Meats Deli & Grocery
1538 Saratoga
San Jose, CA   (408) 865-1222

Halalco
108 E. Fairfax St.
Falls Church, VA

Hanoian's Market
1439 S. Cedar Ave.
Fresno, CA   (209) 233-7301

Harbor Liquor
1417 W. Pacific Coast Hwy
Harbor City, CA   (310) 326-9554

Harry's Deli
2072 S. Taylor Road
Cleveland Heights, OH

Hassey Grocery Store
234 Hampshire St.
Lawrence, MA   (617) 686-6096

Hawthorne Market
24202 Hawthorne Blvd.
Torrance, CA   (310) 373-4448

Heidi's Around the World Food
1149 S. Brentwood Blvd.
St. Louis, MO

Hellas Baking Co.
6 Porter St.
Somerville, MA

Hellas Greek Imports
1245 20th St. N.W.
Washington, DC

Hellas Grocery Store & Pastry
2621 W. Lawrence Ave.
Chicago, IL

Ethnic Cookbooks

Food Marketplace-79

Hellenic-American Im.Fd.&Past.
2308 Market St.
San Francisco, CA

Henry's Delicatessen Inc.
41 Warwick Ave.
Cranston, RI

Hi "Hye" Market
684 Central Ave.
Pawtucket, RI   (401) 728-1596

Hi Ho Market
824 E. Lincoln Ave.
Orange, CA   (714) 637-9525

Hinkley Market
37466 Hinkley Road
Hinkley, CA   (619) 253-2315

Hollywood Deli & Jr. Market
1243 N. Vine St.
Hollywood, CA   (213) 460-4373

Hollywood Mart
5638 Hollywood Blvd.
Hollywood, CA   (213) 464-3566

Holy Land Bakery & Grocery
4809 Kedzie Ave.
Chicago, IL   (312) 588-3306

Holy Land Mini Market
15639 Brookhurst St.
Westminster, CA   (714) 839-9865

Homa International Market
10900 Los Alamitos Blvd.
Los Alamitos, CA   (213) 596-9999

Homs'y Groceries
224 Providence Highway
Dedham, MA   (617) 326-9659

Honolulu Jr. Market and Deli
2529 Honolulu Ave.
Montrose, CA   (818) 249-2532

Hons Market
17261 Vanowen St.
Van Nuys, CA   (818) 996-5553

House of Yemen
370 Third Ave.
New York, NY   (212) 532-3430

Hun-I-Nut Co.
789 The Alameda
San Jose, CA

Hy Mart Deli
4762 Lankershim Blvd.
N. Hollywood, CA   (818) 506-7264

Hye Center Market
7543 Tampa Ave.
Reseda, CA   (818) 701-7784

Hye Deli
3083 W. Bullard
Fresno, CA   (209) 431-7798

Hye Market & Deli
1900 W. Glenoaks Blvd.
Glendale, CA   (818) 566-9942

Hye Neighbor Market
14524 Lanark St.
Panorama City, CA   (818) 994-4592

Impero Import Co.Inc
121 S. Main St.
Waterbury, CT

Import Liquor & Food Stores
910 Preston Ave.
Houston, TX

International Fine Foods
845 388 Jefferson Road
Detroit, MI

International Food
7754 Santa Monica
Hollywood, CA

International Food Bazar
915 9th St.
Portland, OR   (503) 228-1960

International Food Bazar
2052 Curtner Ave.
San Jose, CA   (408) 559-3397

International Food Bazar
5491 Snell Ave.
San Jose, CA   (408) 365-1922

International Food Center
305 S. Brookhurst
Anaheim, CA   (714) 533-7730

International Food Market
212 Mineola Ave.
Roslyn Heights, NY   (516) 625-5800

International Food Mart
5122 Nolensville Road
Nashville, TN   (615) 333-9651

International Food Mart
347 Broad Ave.
Leonia, NJ   (201) 947-4449

International Foods
142 Front St.
Rochester, NY   (716) 288-3686

International Gift Corner
181 Union Ave.
Memphis, TN

International Grocery
1428 Huntington Dr.
Duarte, CA   (818) 301-0270

International Grocery Store
529 Ninth Ave.
New York, NY   (212) 279-5514

International Grocery of S.D.
3548 Ashford St.
San Diego, CA   (619) 569-0362

International House
765 Rockville Pike # H
Rockville, MD   (301) 279-2121

International Market
1112 N. Brookhurst St.
Anaheim, CA   (714) 774-9191

International Market
1226 Wisconsin Ave. N.W.
Washington, DC

International Market
15375 Inkster Rd.
Livonia, MI   (313) 522-2220

International Market
1381 E. Las Tunas Dr.
San Gabriel, CA   (818) 286-4077

International Market
5676 La Jolla Blvd.
La Jolla, CA   (619) 454-5835

International Market & Deli
2010 "P" Street, N.W.
Washington, DC   (202) 293-0499

International Market Place
21755 Michigan Ave.
Dearborn, MI   (313) 274-6100

International Mini Market
10185 Verree Road
Philadelphia, PA

International Super Market
13460 Hawthorne Blvd.
Hawthorne, CA   (310) 676-1482

International Super Market
1905 W. Mississippi Ave.
Denver, CO   (303) 934-3337

Iran Market
5621 Hillcroft
Houston, TX   (713) 789-5943

80-Food Marketplace

Ethnic Cookbooks

Iran Market
6114 Reseda Blvd.
Reseda, CA   (818) 342-9753

Iransara
3080 Magliocco Dr.
San Jose, CA   (408) 241-3912

Islam Grocery International
2630 Columbia Pike
Arlington, VA

Islamic Food Mart
690 S. Vermont Ave.
Los Angeles, CA   (213) 383-2583

Italian Deli & Produce
12932 Sherman Way
N. Hollywood, CA   (818) 982-5781

Italian Imported Super Market
2412 N. Armenia Ave.
Tampa, FL

Italian Importing Co.
316 3rd St.
Des Moines, IA

Italian Middle East Market
13246 Riverside Dr.
Sherman Oaks, CA   (818) 995-6944

Italo-American Importing
581 Elizabeth Ave.
St. Louis, MO   (314) 645-9781

J & K Grocers
324 W. Highland Ave.
San Bernardino, CA   (714) 882-1700

J. B.'s Grocery
3350 N. Verdugo Rd.
Glendale, CA   (818) 249-8224

Jabourian's Grocery
8415 Reseda Blvd.
Northridge, CA   (818) 349-5746

Jack's International Deli
1008 E. Colorado St.
Glendale, CA   (818) 242-3054

Jacob's Grocery & Deli
14105 Burbank Blvd.
Van Nuys, CA   (818) 782-0536

James Heonis Co.
218 S. Blount St.
Raleigh, NC

Jerusalem Bakery & Grocery
4070 N. Beltline
Irving, TX   (214) 257-0447

Jim Dandy Fried Chicken
3831 Beverly Blvd.
Los Angeles, CA   (213) 666-8627

Jimmy's Deli
4080 Bay Street
Fremont, CA   (415) 490-2056

Joey Kay's Market
879 Main St.
Paterson, NJ   (201) 523-9809

John's Fruit Market
31-27 Ditmas Blvd.
New York, NY   (718) 278-0705

John's Market
62 Orchard St.
Elizabeth, NJ

Johnny's Italian & Greek Deli
636 State St.
Santa Barbara, CA

Jons Supermarket
6655 Van Nuys Blvd.
Van Nuys, CA   (818) 781-1772

Jons Supermarket
1717 W. Glenoaks Blvd.
Glendale, CA   (818) 244-8206

Jons Supermarket
5311 Santa Monica Blvd.
Hollywood, CA   (213) 461-9382

Jonson's Market
Culver City, CA   (213) 390-9639

Jose's Delicatessen
422 Cambridge Ave.
Palo Alto, CA

Joseph Baratta
2503 S.W. 8th St.
Miami, FL

Joseph's Brothers Market
196 Lake Ave.
Manchester, NH   (603) 623-0302

K. Barishian
75 Messer St.
Providence, RI

Kal's Market
620 S. Glendale Ave.
Glendale, CA   (818) 507-7810

Kalamata Food Imports, Inc.
38-01 Ditmars Blvd.
New York, NY   (718) 626-1250

Kalunian Grocery
57 Dix Street
Dorchester, MA

Kam Shing Co.
2246 S. Wentworth Ave
Chicago, IL

Kandes Liquor & Imports
1202 N. Main
Victoria, TX

Kandoo Grocery
Chicago, IL   (312) 275-0006

Karo's Importing Deli
1225 N. Vine St.
Hollywood, CA   (213) 465-6486

Karoun Market
1201 N. Vermont Ave.
Hollywood, CA   (213) 665-7237

Kassos Brothers
32 30th Ave.
New York, NY   (212) 932-5479

Katz Kosher Supermarket
4860 Boiling Brook Parkway
Rockville, MD

Kebab Bakery & Delicatessen
2703 E. 3rd Ave.
Denver, CO

Kelly's Food Mart
1132 Broadway
Rockford, IL

Khatib Butcher Shop
3817 George Mason Dr.
Falls Church, VA   (703) 845-9388

Khayber International
37070 Fremont Blvd.
Fremont, CA   (510) 795-9549

Khayyam International Market
608 E. Gate St.
Saint Louis, MO   (314) 727-8993

Khazar Markets
357 N. Fairfax
Los Angeles, CA   (213) 655-8674

Khorak Market
6125 Young Ave.
Toronto, Ontario,   (416) 221-7558

Khyber Halal Market
5216 Wilson Blvd.
Arlington, VA   (703) 525-8323

Ethnic Cookbooks

Food Marketplace-81

King Cheese & Deli
2487 E. Washington Blvd.
Pasadena, CA   (818) 791-2254

King Deli
1702 S. Robertson Blvd.
Los Angeles, CA   (310) 204-1149

King Market
1117 S. Glendale Ave.
Glendale, CA   (818) 246-4015

Kiryakos Grocery
29-29 23rd Ave.
New York, NY   (718) 545-3931

Kismet Grocery
1212 Broadway
Burlingame, CA   (415) 343-8919

Kismet Oriental Pastries Co.
27 Ditmars Blvd.
Astoria, NY

Kizmet Fancy Grocery
240 Main St.
Hempstead, NY

Koko's Grocery
12523 1/2 Victory Blvd.
N. Hollywood, CA   (818) 763-6731

Kozanian Grocery
4920 Santa Monica Blvd.
Hollywood, CA   (213) 668-2514

Kozanian Grocery
12001 Victory Blvd.
N. Hollywood, CA   (818) 952-9030

Kozanian Grocery
1248 S. Glendale Ave.
Glendale, CA   (818) 502-1013

Kupelian Foods, Inc.
146 Bergen Pike
Ridgefield Park, NJ   (201) 440-8055

L & H Superette
508 Monroe Ave.
Detroit, MI

L. Paletta's
425 N. Santa Rosa
San Antonio, TX

La Cresta Market & Liquor
3904 Foothill Blvd.
La Crescenta, CA   (818) 248-0098

La Mesa Market
6062 Lake Murray Blvd.
La Mesa, CA   (619) 589-6789

Laconia Grocery
908 Washington St.
Boston, MA

Lahmajoon Kitchen
3358 E. Butler
Fresno, CA   (209) 264-5454

Lake Forest Mini Market
22722 Lambert
Lake Forest, CA   (714) 859-9132

Lake Murray Liquor & Market
6001 Lake Murray Blvd.
La Mesa, CA   (619) 464-8477

Le Capitaine
5839 Sherbrooke West
Montreal,   (514) 489-2642

Le Petit Gourmet
44 Douglaston Parkway
Douglaston, NY   (718) 224-9665

Lebanese Delicatessen
4163 Salem Ave.
Dayton, OH

Lebanese Grocery
4640 Washington St.
Roslindale, MA   (617) 469-2900

Lebanese-Syrian Bakery
3246 S. Grand Blvd.
St. Louis, MO

Leon's Food Mart
Winthrop & Ryons St.
Lincoln, NB

Leon's Grocery & Deli
14102 Victory Blvd.
Van Nuys, CA   (818) 787-8910

Lev's Armenian Market
400 W. Washington Blvd.
Montebello, CA   (213) 721-2391

Levant International Food
9421 Alondra Blvd.
Bellflower, CA   (310) 920-0623

Liamos Market
176 W. Pearl St.
Nashua, NH

Lida's Food Center
1842 N. Tustin Ave.
Orange, CA   (714) 998-7760

Lignos Groceries
160 Government St.
Mobile, AL   (205) 432-9870

Lingos Grocery
126 W. & South St.
Salt Lake City, UT

Little Rose Armenian Grocery
2379 E. Washington Blvd.
Pasadena, CA   (818) 797-9022

Los Feliz European Deli
1748 N. Vermont Ave.
Hollywood, CA   (213) 660-9412

Lucky Boy Market
22 Ditmars Blvd.
New York, NY

Lucy's Mini Mart
1734 E. Washington Blvd.
Pasadena, CA   (818) 791-1177

M & J Market & Deli
12924 Vanowen St.
N. Hollywood, CA   (818) 765-7671

M & M International Deli
12120 Sylvan St.
N. Hollywood, CA   (818) 980-0608

M & M Liquor & Market
1951 W. Glenoaks Blvd.
Glendale, CA   (818) 848-7470

M & M Market
5721 Lincoln Ave.
Cypress, CA   (310) 220-2207

Maha Imports and Groceries
3087 El Camino Real
Santa Clara, CA   (408) 248-5025

Mahtab Market
29505 S. Western Ave.
Rancho Palos Vrd., CA (310) 833-6026

Mainly Cheese Inc.
898 Prospect St.
Glen Rock, NJ   (201) 447-4141

Majestic Market
25877 Lahser
Southfield, MI   (313) 352-8556

Makhoul Corner Store
448 N. 2nd St.
Allentown, PA

Manigian Grocery
Central & Southern N.J.
, NJ   (201) 531-6810

Manley Produce
1101 Grant Ave.
San Francisco, CA

82-Food Marketplace   Ethnic Cookbooks

Marche Adonis
9590 L'Acadie
Montreal, Canada   (514) 382-8606

Marhaba Market
10932 E. Imperial Hwy
Norwalk, CA   (310) 864-2665

Market Express & Liquor
5658 Sepulveda Blvd.
Van Nuys, CA   (818) 781-0325

Mary's Greek Grocery
7037 Caster Ave.
Philadelphia, PA   (215) 722-2845

Mashti Ice Cream
1525 N. La Brea Ave.
Hollywood, CA   (213) 874-0144

Masis Grocery
4110 S. Maryland
Las Vegas, NV   (702) 369-0090

Masis Market
2735 N. Blackstone Ave.
Fresno, CA   (209) 224-1228

Massis Grocery & Deli
22330 Sherman Way
Canoga Park, CA   (818) 888-6664

Max's Market
2603 Broadway
New York, NY

Mc Allister Grocery
136 McAllister St.
San Francisco, CA   (415) 861-5315

Mediterranean
Fresno, CA   (209) 229-6347

Mediterranean Food Store
8457 Baltimore National Pike
Ellicott City, MD   (301) 465-8555

Mediterranean Gourmet
73 Hillside Ave.
Williston Park, NY   (516) 741-3664

Mediterranean Groceries & Deli
25381 Alicia Pkwy
Laguna Hills, CA   (714) 770-2007

Mediterranean Imports
316 N. Genesee St.
Waukegan, IL   (312) 244-4040

Mediterranean Imports
36 N. MacArthur
Oklahoma City, OK

Mediterranean Imports
170 Spring St.
West Roxbury, MA   (617) 323-4341

Mediterranean Marketplace
Park Ave.
Worcester, MA   (508) 755-0258

Mediterranean Store
81 N. Glebe Road
Arlington, VA   (703) 527-0423

Menora Market
8664 W. Pico Blvd.
Los Angeles, CA   (310) 854-0447

Metropolitan Coffee Co.
451 Cuyahoga Falls
Akron, OH

Michael Nafash & Sons
2717 Bergenline Ave.
Union City, NJ

Michael's Deli & Grocery
5001 Hollywood Blvd.
Hollywood, CA   (213) 662-6311

Michell's Grocery
137 N. Dargan St.
Florence, SC

Mid-Eastern Pastries & Grocery
2354 University Ave.
San Diego, CA   (619) 295-2311

Middle East Bakery
316 Hazle St.
Wilkes-Barre, PA

Middle East Bakery
1529 S. "B" Street
San Mateo, CA

Middle East Foods
19 W. 25th St.
Cleveland, OH

Middle East Foods
26 Washington St.
Santa Clara, CA   (408) 248-5112

Middle East Grocery
2238 S. Colorado Blvd.
Denver, CO   (303) 756-4580

Middle East Market
529 E. Live Oaks Ave.
Arcadia, CA   (818) 574-1971

Middle East Market
7006 Carroll Ave.
Takoma Park, MD

Middle East Trading
2636 W. Devon Ave.
Chicago, IL   (312) 262-2848

Middle Eastern Bakery
5405 Hollywood Blvd.
Hollywood, CA

Middle Eastern Bakery & Grocer
1512 W. Foster Ave.
Chicago, IL   (312) 561-2224

Middle Eastern Bazar
4149 S. Maryland Pky.
Las Vegas, NV   (702) 731-6030

Middle Eastern Groceries
22 Cobb Parkway
Smyrna, GA

Middle Eastern Grocery
2954 W. Ball Road
Anaheim, CA   (714) 826-8700

Middle Eastern Market
2054 San Pablo Ave.
Berkeley, CA   (510) 548-2213

Middle Eastern Market & Deli
1775 E. Tropicana Liberace Pl.
Las Vegas, NV   (702) 736-8887

Mideast Specialty
2055 Boston Ave.
Bridgeport, CT   (203) 878-8337

Mikaelyan Food Market
109 N. Cedar St.
Glendale, CA   (818) 548-8045

Milano Super Market Inc.
870 Dixwell Ave.
Hamden, CT

Miller's Market
18248 Sherman Way
Reseda, CA   (818) 345-9222

Minoo Market
18582 Beach Blvd.
Huntington Beach, CA   (714) 962-0305

Model Food Importers & Distri.
115 Middle St.
Portland, ME   (207) 774-3671

Morgan's Grocery
736 S. Robert St.
St. Paul, MN

Moulasadra Grocery
1438 Westwood Blvd.
Los Angeles, CA   (213) 470-4646

Ethnic Cookbooks

Mount of Olives Market
3405 Payne St.
Falls Church, VA   (703) 379-1156

Mourad Grocery
13847 Hamilton St.
Highland Park, MI

Mr. Deli
3440 Foothill Blvd.
La Crescenta, CA   (818) 957-7018

N & K Groceries & Deli
1183 E. Main St.
El Cajon, CA   (619) 447-9471

Nablus Grocery
456 S. Broadway
Yonkers, NY

Nader Grocery
1 E. 28th St.
New York, NY   (212) 686-5793

Nafash & Sons
2717 Bergenline Ave.
Union City, NJ

Nagilah Market
63-69 108th St.
Forest Hills, NY   (718) 268-2626

Nasr Mini Market
1996 Lawrence Ave. E.
Scarborough,   (416) 757-1611

Nassim Grocery
Pomona, CA   (714) 593-8244

National Foods
1905 W. Mississippi
Denver, CO

Naz Market
Anaheim, CA   (714) 956-8926

Near East Bakery
183 Atlantic Ave.
New York, NY   (718) 875-0016

Near East Foods
4595 El Cajon Blvd.
San Diego, CA   (619) 284-6361

Near East Market
602 Reservoir Ave.
Cranston, RI   (401) 941-9763

Near East Market
41 Cranston St.
Providence, RI

Neda's Market
1934 Harbor Blvd.
Costa Mesa, CA   (714) 650-5424

Nemouneh (Unique Market)
2031 E. First St.
Santa Ana, CA   (714) 836-8674

Nettuno Italian Delicacies
129 E. Court St.
Cincinnati, OH

New Deal Grocery
2604 W. Lawrence Ave.
Chicago, IL

New Santa Clara Market
799 Haight St.
San Francisco, CA

New World Market
2051 Balboa St.
San Francisco, CA   (415) 751-8810

New Yorker Delicatessen
2602 Williamson Road N.W.
Roanoke, VA

Next Door Deli
2113 N. Glenoaks Blvd.
Burbank, CA   (818) 842-2383

Nick's Importing Co.
2416 N. Western Ave.
Oklahoma City, OK

Nick's Produce & Import. Co.
504 E. Marshall St.
Richmond, VA

Nissan Market
6007 Lankershime Blvd.
N. Hollywood, CA   (818) 763-3424

Norooz Bazar
1378 S. Bascon Ave.
Berkeley, CA   (408) 295-2323

Norooz Grocery & Deli
6801 Old Springfield Plaza
Springfield, VA   (703) 866-4444

North Street Market
96 N. Street
New Britain, CT   (203) 229-5481

Nouri's Syrian Bakery & Grocer
983 Main St.
Paterson, NJ

Nur, Inc.
223 Avent Ferry Road
Raleigh, NC

Nuts Bazaar
4252 Piedmont Ave.
Oakland, CA   (510) 601-1997

O'Neil's Department Store Food
226 S. Main St.
Akron, OH

O.K. Fairbank's Sugar Market
84 Marlboro St.
Keene, NH

Oasis Mart
4270 Woodward Ave.
Royal Oak, MI   (313) 549-0001

Oasis Mart Importing Co.
4130 Rochester Rd
Royal Oak, MI   (313) 588-2210

Old Fashion Deli
1225 N. Pacific Ave.
Glendale, CA   (818) 244-9300

Old World Market
8125 Wisconsin Ave.
Bethesda, MD   (301) 654-4880

Olson's Grocery
5608 Blondo St.
Omaha, NB

Olympia Food of all Nations
906 Kinderkamack Road
River Edge, NJ   (201) 261-3703

Olympia Grocery
4303 W. Vliet St.& W.Center St.
Milwaukee, WI

Olympia Market
617 Main St.
Worcester, MA

Omid Market
27230 E. La Paz Road
Mission Viejo, CA   (714) 458-7343

Orchard Market
8815 Orchard Tree Lane
Towson, MD   (301) 339-7700

Orchid Market
11856 Balboa Blvd.
Granada Hills, CA   (818) 366-6969

Oriental Import-Export Co.
2009 Polk St.
Houston, TX

Oriental Pastry & Grocery
170 Atlantic Ave.
Brooklyn, NY   (718) 875-7687

P & S Importing Co.
36 Canal St.
Waterbury, CT

84-Food Marketplace — Ethnic Cookbooks

Paak International Gourmet
1614 S. E. Camino Real
San Mateo, CA   (415) 574-3536

Pacific Food Bazar
469 W. Broadway
Glendale, CA   (818) 956-1021

Pacific Food Mart
1008 N. Pacific Ave.
Glendale, CA   (818) 242-8352

Palestine Bakery
2639 W. 63rd St.
Chicago, IL   (312) 925-5978

Palmer Market
1017 E. Palmer Ave.
Glendale, CA   (818) 243-4879

Pamir Food Market
37422 Fremont Blvd.
Fremont, CA   (510) 790-7015

Papa Joe's Deli
5940 Cerritos Ave.
Cypress, CA   (714) 527-2350

Paparian's Food Market
205 2nd Ave.
Albany, NY

Pari's Deli
842 Geary St.
San Francisco, CA   (415) 771-2219

Pars International Market
1801 Lonsdale Ave.
N. Vancouver,   (604) 988-3515

Pars Market
9373 Mira Mesa Blvd.
San Diego, CA   (619) 566-7277

Pars Market
5911 Balboa Ave.
San Diego, CA

Pars Market
2010 N. Farwell Ave.
Milwaukee, WI   (414) 278-7175

Pars Market
9016 W. Pico Blvd.
Los Angeles, CA   (310) 859-8125

Pars Market
13433 N.E. 20th ST.
Bellevue, WA   (206) 641-5265

Patrik's Quick Market
1143 E. Broadway
Glendale, CA   (818) 247-7329

Pavo Co., Inc.
7041 Boone Ave. N.
Minneapolis, MN   (612) 533-4525

Persian Center Bazaar
398 Saratoga Ave.
San Jose, CA   (408) 241-3700

Peter Pan Superette
2 Park Ave.
Arlington, MA   (617) 648-9771

Pharaoh's Market
1843 E. Chapman
Orange, CA   (714) 633-2360

Phoenicia Bakery & Deli
2912 S. Lamar
Austin, TX   (512) 447-4444

Phoenicia Imports & Deli
12116 Westheimer
Houston, TX   (713) 558-0416

Pieri's Delicacies Inc
3824 S.E. Powell Blvd.
Portland, OR

Piggly Wiggly
445 Meeting St.
Charlestown, SC

Pittsburgh Grocery Store
520 Courth Place
Pittsburgh, PA

Polsano's Deli & Gourmet Food
2410 N. May Ave.
Oklahoma City, OK

Pondfield Produce Market
57 Pondfield Rd. West
Yonkers, NY   (914) 961-9566

Pop's Restaurant and Grocery
8385 Leesburg Pike
Vienna, VA

Progress Grocery Co.
915 Decatur St.
New Orleans, LA

Purity Importing Co.
4507 Swiss Ave.
Dallas, TX

Pyramid Bakery
43 43rd Street
New York, NY   (718) 392-2702

Pyramid Market
4721 Telegraph Ave.
Oakland, CA   (415) 428-1833

Quik Pik Market
14108 Magnolia Blvd.
Sherman Oaks, CA   (818) 501-6094

Quincy Syrian Baking Co.
723 Washington St.
Quincy, MA

R. A. Medonic
2201 Market St.
Wheeling, WV

R. H. Macy & Co.
151 34th St.
Herald Square, NY   (212) 695-4400

Rahal & Sons, Inc.
1615 S.W. 8th St.
Miami, FL

Rainbow Produce & Grocery
490 Taraval St.
San Francisco, CA   (415) 731-8715

Rainbow Stores
12326 Venice Blvd.
Los Angeles, CA   (310) 397-5090

Ramallah Market
10724 S. Harlem Ave.
Worth, IL   (708) 361-5665

Ramsar Maket
433 N. Fairfax Ave.
Los Angeles, CA   (213) 651-1601

Ramses Deli
1981 Lawrence Ave. E.
Toronto,   (416) 755-0244

Rana Food Store
1623 W. Arkansas Lane
Arlington, TX

Rio Deli & Market
20051 Ventura Blvd.
Woodland Hills, CA   (818) 999-9486

Rio's Market
2401 Artesia Blvd.
Redondo Beach, CA   (310) 542-8616

Rodeo Deli & Grocery
205 S. Glendale Ave.
Glendale, CA   (818) 244-6969

Ron's Market
5270 Sunset Blvd.
Hollywood, CA   (213) 465-1164

Rooz Market
14220 Culver Dr.
Irvine, CA   (714) 559-8535

Ethnic Cookbooks

Food Marketplace-85

Rooz Supermarket & Deli
12332 Lake City Way N.E.
Seattle, WA   (206) 363-8639

Rose International Foods
6153 S.W. Murray Blvd.
Beaverton, OR   (503) 646-7673

Rose International Market
1060 Castro St.
Mt. View, CA   (415) 960-1900

Rose Market
1906 Westwood Blvd.
Los Angeles, CA   (213) 470-2121

Rose Market
1028 Castro St.
Mountain View, CA   (415) 960-1900

Royal Coffee & Tea Co.
715 N. Main St.
Oklahoma City, OK   (405) 848-2002

Royal George Grocery
359 Bernars St. W.
Montreal,   (514) 277-4123

Ruben's Market
9406 E. Washington Blvd.
Pico Rivera, CA   (310) 949-1322

Russo's Imported Foods
1935 Eastern Ave. S.E
Grand Rapids, MI

S & J Importing
1770 Pacific Ave.
Long Beach, CA   (310) 599-1341

Saadoun's Cuisine of Bagdad
2136 Placentia Ave.
Costa Mesa, CA   (714) 642-0800

Saba Meat & Market
4605 N. Kedzie
Chicago, IL   (312) 539-0080

Sahadi Importing Co. Inc.
200 Carol Place
Moonachie, NJ

Sahar Meat & Grocery
4508 N. Kedzie
Chicago, IL   (312) 583-7772

Sahar Mini Market
248 W. Foothill Blvd.
Azusa, CA   (818) 969-5010

Sahara II
4914 E. Busch Blvd.
Tampa, FL   (813) 989-3612

Sako's Mini-Mart
270 Babcock St.
Boston, MA   (617) 782-8920

Salamat Market
1718 N. Tustin
Orange, CA   (714) 921-0153

Salim's Middle Eastern Food
47 Central Ave.
Pittsburgh, PA

Salimi Grocery
72-55 Kissena Blvd.
Forest Hills, NY   (718) 793-2984

Sam's Food Market
4356 Sepulveda Blvd.
Culver City, CA   (310) 390-5705

Sam's Market
10099 W. Eleven Mile Road
Huntington Woods, MI (313) 541-8990

Saman Market
6003 Fallbrook
Woodland Hills, CA   (818) 347-8002

Samiramis Imports, Inc.
2990 Mission St.
San Francisco, CA   (415) 824-6555

San Diego Importing Co.
2061 India St.
San Diego, CA

Santa Monica Food House
7416 Santa Monica Blvd.
Santa Monica, CA

Santa Monica Market
12109 Santa Monica Blvd.
Los Angeles, CA   (310) 207-5530

Sarkis Aprozar Grocery
39 Queens Blvd.
New York, NY   (212) 937-4682

Sasoon Meat Market
1359 E. Colorado St.
Glendale, CA   (818) 243-2484

Sasoun Mini Market
201 E. Beverly Blvd.
Montebello, CA   (213) 724-6971

Sassoon Bakery & Grocery
72 Shaw Ave.
Clovis, CA   (209) 323-1185

Sassoon Market
85 Bigelow Ave.
Watertown, MA   (617) 924-1560

Sassoon Supermarche
5025 Rue De Salaberry
Montreal,   (514) 337-7923

Sawaya Delicatessen
1104 S. 10th St.
Birmingham, AL

Sayfy's Groceteria
265 Rue Jean Talon Est
Montreal,   (514) 277-1257

Selin Market
1427 W. Glenoaks Blvd.
Glendale, CA   (818) 502-0403

Sepahan Market
6265 Sepulveda Blvd.
Van Nuys, CA   (818) 988-6278

Setareh Market
12134 Santa Monica Blvd.
Los Angeles, CA   (310) 820-6513

Sevan Bakery & Grocery
17743 Saticoy St.
Reseda, CA   (818) 343-0486

Sevan Deli & Imported Foods
1012 W. Beverly Blvd.
Montebello, CA   (213) 721-3804

Sevan Grocery
1800 1/2 Hillhurst Ave.
Hollywood, CA   (213) 665-6406

Sevan Grocery
630 S. Euclid Ave.
Santa Ana, CA   (714) 775-3776

Sevan Mini Market
1516 N. San Fernando Road
Burbank, CA   (818) 845-3069

Shahrzad International Market
215 Copeland Road
Atlanta, GA   (404) 843-0549

Shahrzad International Market
3338 S. Bristol
Santa Ana, CA   (714) 850-0808

Shalak Market
5640 E. Moreno St.
Montclair, CA   (714) 946-7077

Shalimar Grocery
1665 N. Hacienda Blvd.
La Puente, CA   (818) 918-6227

Shallah's Middle Eastern Imp.
290 White St.
Danbury, CT

86-Food Marketplace / Ethnic Cookbooks

Shalom Market & Bakery
2307 University Blvd. W.
Silver Spring, MD

Shammas Oriental Domestic Food
197 Atlantic Ave.
New York, NY   (212) 855-2455

Shammy's Market
22140 Ventura Blvd.
Woodland Hills, CA   (818) 883-9811

Sharzad Grocery
137 Cove Road
Stamford, CT   (203) 323-5363

Shemiran Market
10610 Pico Blvd.
W. Los Angeles, CA   (213) 836-7286

Sherwood Grocery
790 Garrett Road
Upper Derby, PA

Shiekh Grocery Co.
652 Bolivar Road
Cleveland, OH

Shiraz Food Market
7397 S.W. 40th St.
Miami, FL   (305) 264-8282

Shiraz Market
7319 Fair Oaks Blvd.
Carmichel, CA   (916) 486-1200

Shiraz Market
295 Jentry
Reno, NV   (702) 829-1177

Shireen's Gourmet, Inc.
268 Main St.
Hackensack, NJ   (201) 488-4907

Shirinian Grocery
901 S. Glendale Ave.
Glendale, CA   (818) 243-0611

Shop and Save
1244 Hamilton Ave.
Trenton, NJ

Simon X. Mandros
N. Charlotte & W. Lemon St.
Lancaster, PA

Sinbad Food Imports
2620 N. High St.
Columbus, OH

Sipan Deli & Grocery
7840 Foothill Blvd.
Sunland, CA   (818) 352-3881

Skenderis Greek Imports
1612 20th St. N.W.
Washington, DC   (202) 265-9664

Smiling Fruit
31 Ditmars Blvd.
New York, NY   (212) 932-8006

Sofian Market
10094 Westminster
Garden Grove, CA   (714) 530-7450

Sparta Grocery
6050 W. Diversey Ave.
Chicago, IL

Spiro's Market
65 State Highway 15
Dover, NJ   (201) 361-0884

Spring Market
500 N. Harbor Blvd.
Fullerton, CA   (714) 879-7139

St. Georges Bakery & Grocery
231 S. Orlando Ave.
Winter Park, FL   (407) 647-1423

Stamatelos Grocery
500 E. Blaunt St.
Pensacola, FL   (904) 433-0963

Stamoolis Brotheres Co.
2020 Pennsylvania Ave.
Pittsburgh, PA

Star Market
3349 N. Clark St.
Chicago, IL

Stella Foods Co., Inc.
3815 Eastern Ave.
Baltimore, MD

Stemma Confectionery
514 Monroe Ave.
Detroit, MI

Steve's Superette
1620 W. Garden St.
Pensacola, FL

Stoukas Imports
16401 E. Warren St.
Detroit, MI

Sultan's Delight, Inc.
25 Croton Ave.
Staten Island, NY   (718) 720-1557

Sunflower Grocery
97 Queens Blvd
Rego Park, NY   (718) 275-0479

Sunflower Grocery & Deli
20774 E. Arrow Hwy.
Covina, CA   (818) 339-1141

Sunland Produce
8255 Sunland Blvd.
Sun Valley, CA   (818) 504-6629

Sunnyvale Market (Tajrish)
1512 Sunnyvale Ave.
Walnut Creek, CA   (510) 932-8404

Sunrise Market & Deli
1635 Wisconsin Ave., N.W.
Washington, DC   (202) 333-1972

Sunshine Liquor Market, Inc.
6985 Knott Ave.
Buena Park, CA   (714) 522-3670

Super California
20050 Vanowen St.
Canoga Park, CA   (818) 703-1612

Super Doyar
6228 Rolling Road
Springfield, VA   (703) 866-0222

Super Hero's
509 Mount Auburn St.
Watertown, MA   (617) 924-9507

Super Jordan Market
1449 Westwood Blvd.
Los Angeles, CA   (310) 478-1706

Super Sahel
5627 Hillcroft
Houston, TX   (713) 266-7360

Super Saver Market
3981 Chicago
Riverside, CA   (714) 684-8252

Super Shilan Market
8801 Reseda Blvd.
Northridge, CA   (818) 993-7064

Super Vanak International Food
5692 Hillcroft
Houston, TX   (713) 952-7676

Super Vanak International Food
2319 W. Devon Ave.
Chicago, IL   (312) 465-2424

Supreme International Foods
101 Queens Blvd.
Forest Hills, NY   (718) 897-4700

Sweis International Market
6809 Hazeltine Ave.
Van Nuys, CA   (818) 785-8193

Ethnic Cookbooks

Food Marketplace-87

Syria-Lebanon Baking Co.
716 Bolivar Road
Cleveland, OH

Syrian Grocery Imp.Co.Inc.
270 Shawmut Ave.
Boston, MA (617) 426-1458

Tak Grocery Store
2647 Middle Country Road
Centereach, NY (516) 737-6244

Tampa Deli & Middle East.
8151 Arlington Ave.
Riverside, CA (714) 688-6113

Tarikyan Grocery
1144 N. Vermont Ave.
Hollywood, CA (213) 660-5229

Tarver's Delicacies
1338 S. Mary St.
Sunnyvale, CA

Tarzana Armenian Grocery # 1
18598 Ventura Blvd.
Tarzana, CA (818) 881-6278

Tarzana Armenian Grocery # 2
22776 Ventura Blvd.
Woodland Hills, CA (818) 703-7836

Tarzana Armenian Grocery # 3
500 Broadway Blvd.
Santa Monica, CA (310) 576-6473

Taslakian's Pastry
4906 Santa Monica Blvd.
Hollywood, CA (213) 662-5588

Tavilian Grocery
5100 Santa Monica Blvd.
Hollywood, CA (213) 665-3988

Tehran Market
1417 Wilshire Blvd.
Santa Monica, CA (213) 393-6719

Tehran Pars Market
17620 Ventura Blvd.
Encino, CA (818) 788-6950

Termeh Market & Deli
27221 La Paz Rd
Laguna Niguel, CA (714) 831-4000

Thanos Imported Groceries
424 Pearl St.
Syracuse, NY

Thomas Market
2650 University Blvd. West
Wheaton, MD (301) 942-0839

Three Crown Gourment
18000 Ventura Blvd.
Encino, CA (818) 774-1412

Three Sisters Delicatessen
2854 W. Devon Ave.
Chicago, IL

Tigran's Grocery
1357 E. Colorado St.
Glendale, CA (818) 243-2323

Tochal Market
1418 Westwood Blvd.
Los Angeles, CA (213) 470-6454

Tom's Ravioli Co.
791 S. Orange Ave.
Newark, NJ

Tony's Grocery & Fresh Meat
8221 Woodman Ave.
Panorama City, CA (818) 782-6195

Tony's Market
769 Broad St.
Providence, RI (401) 421-4700

Topping and Co.
5342 N. National
Milwaukee, WI (414) 383-8911

Towne House
3911 Central Ave. N.E.
Albuquerque, NM (505) 255-0057

Tri EZ Foods
1190 Hillside Ave.
San Jose, CA (408) 978-5612

Tru-Valu Market
1001 "E" St.
Sacramento, CA (916) 443-4256

Tu-Tu Halal Meat Market
3811 S. George Mason Dr.
Falls Church, VA (703) 998-5322

Tweeten's Liquor & Deli
190 Golf Club Road
Pleasant Hill, CA (510) 825-2422

UN Market
900 Post St.
San Francisco, CA (415) 563-4726

Unique Market
6635 San Fernando Road
Glendale, CA (818) 247-2633

United Supermarket
84 Mulberry St.
New York, NY

University Market
300 E. Exchange
Akron, OH

University Pantry Deli
7605 University Blvd.
Charlotte, NC (704) 549-9156

V & K Distributing Co.
6108 Hazeltine Ave.
Van Nuys, CA (818) 904-0479

V & K Distributing Co.
3407 Magnolia Blvd.
Burbank, CA (818) 848-1926

V. J. Market
2401 W. Magnolia Blvd.
Burbank, CA (818) 843-3613

Vahe's Grocery
22201 Sherman Way
Canoga Park, CA (818) 702-9092

Valley Bakery
502 M Street
Fresno, CA (209) 485-2700

Valley Food Market
7059 Reseda Blvd.
Reseda, CA (818) 343-0337

Valley Hye Market
14845 Burbank Blvd.
Van Nuys, CA (818) 786-5271

Vardashen Meat & Grocery
12904 Sherman Way
N. Hollywood, CA (818) 765-5725

Variety Food Market
6921 Cerritos Ave.
Stanton, CA (714) 761-5571

Vatan Market
8700 W. Pico Blvd.
Los Angeles, CA (310) 659-4000

Ventura Kosher Meat
18357 Ventura Blvd
Tarzana, CA (818) 881-3777

Verdugo Market & Deli
2519 Canada Blvd.
Glendale, CA (818) 241-5424

Victoria Importing Co.
35 Lafayette St.
New Britain, CT

Victory Meat & Grocery
13258 Victory Blvd.
Van Nuys, CA (818) 787-4081

88-Food Marketplace   Ethnic Cookbooks

Villa Market
1101 W. Glenoaks Blvd.
Glendale, CA   (818) 500-9005

Villa Market
4801 Leland Ave.
Chevy Chase, MD   (301) 951-0062

Village Market
15091 Merrill Ave.
Fontana, CA   (714) 822-5613

Village Super Market Inc.
9 S. Orange Ave.
South Orange, NJ

Washington Dairy Product Co.
625 S. Halsted St.
Chicago, IL

Wayside Market
11790 Cherry Hill Road
Silver Spring, MD

West Meat Market
2549 W. Lawrence Ave.
Chicago, IL   (312) 769-4956

Westwood Grocery
2091 Westwood Blvd.
Los Angeles, CA   (213) 475-9804

Wing Wing Imported Groceries
79 Harrison Ave.
Boston, MA

Worldwide Foods
2203 Greenville Ave.
Dallas, TX   (214) 824-8860

Yaranush Middle Eastern Gourme
322 Central Ave.
New Jersey, NJ   (914) 682-8449

Yekta Middle Eastern Grocery
1488 Rockville Pike
Rockville, MD   (301) 984-1190

Yeraz International Grocery
16207 Parthenia St.
Sepulveda, CA   (818) 895-1838

Yerevan Deli & Bakery
6360 Vineland Ave.
N. Hollywood, CA   (818) 509-0243

Yerevan Ranch Market
1501 W. Beverly Blvd.
Montebello, CA   (213) 722-3780

Yosh Bazaar
346 Lorton Ave.
Burlingame, CA   (415) 343-5833

Youngsville Super Market
1536 Candia Rd.
Manchester, NH   (603) 622-6353

Your Market
3300 Overland Ave.
Los Angeles, CA   (310) 287-0815

Zakarian Family Variety Store
3432 Sheppard Ave. E.
Scarborough,   (416) 298-4118

Zand Market
1021 Solano Ave.
Albany, CA   (510) 528-7027

Zand Market
2671 Thousand Oaks Blvd.
Thousand Oaks, CA   (805) 494-3646

Zangezour Meat Market
1415 E. Colorado St.
Glendale, CA   (818) 545-9988

Zeitoon Grocery
1101 E. Chevy Chase Dr.
Glendale, CA   (818) 247-7093

Zvartnotz Grocery
209 N. Verdugo Rd.
Glendale, CA   (818) 956-0712

GROCERS-WHOLESALE

Ahmad International
P. O. Box 246718
Sacramento, CA   (916) 451-2939

Altira Wholesale, Inc.
2631 W. 63rd St.
Chicago, IL   (312) 476-0511

American International Foods
1310 San Fernando Road
Los Angeles, CA   (213) 225-4151

American Spice Trading Co.
Los Angeles, CA   (213) 664-2232

Antone's Import Co.
807 Taft St.
Houston, TX   (713) 526-1046

Armtex
P. O. Box 90310
Pasadena, CA   (818) 797-0040

Assan Caltex Foods
9045 Eton Ave.
Canoga Park, CA   (818) 700-8657

Athens Imported Foods & Wines
2545 Lorain Road
Cleveland, OH   (216) 861-8149

Aziz Import Co.
9100 N. Central Expressway
Dallas, TX   (214) 369-6982

Basmati Rice Imports, Inc.
19700 Fairchild
Irvine, CA   (714) 474-4220

Basmati Rice of New York, Inc
8000 Cooper Ave.
Glendale, NY   (718) 628-1082

Ciel International, Inc.
29 Grove St.
S. Hackensack, NJ   (201) 807-9329

Commerce International
Miami, FL   (407) 678-6737

Derian Foods
5001 E. Olympic Blvd.
Los Angeles, CA   (213) 263-3447

E & I International, Inc.
5609 Fishers Lane
Rockville, MD   (301) 984-8287

Epicurean International, Inc.
12307 Washington Ave.
Rockville, MD   (301) 231-0700

Five Star Food Distributor
2124 Dunn Road
Hayward, CA   (415) 782-4654

Galil Importing Corp.
8000 Cooper Ave.
Glendale, NY   (718) 894-2030

Geary Wholesale Company
26250 Corporate Ave.
Hayward, CA   (415) 887-6797

Golchin Overseas Corp.
12381 Foothill Blvd.
Sylmar, CA   (818) 896-6127

Gourmet Food & Beverage Dist.
195 Channel St.
San Francisco, CA   (415) 626-1847

Greek House Importing Co.
7856 E. Firestone Blvd.
Doweny, CA   (310) 862-1220

Ethnic Cookbooks

Food Marketplace-89

HHH Distributors
7006 Carrolln Ave.
Takoma Park, MD

Indo Pak Foods
2124 Dunn Road
Haywood, CA   (415) 782-4654

International Food Market
1760 E. 8th St.
Davis, CA   (916) 756-4262

International Golden Foods, Inc
6340 Gross Point Road
Niles, IL   (312) 764-3333

J & J International Import
2534 Seaboard Ave.
San Jose, CA   (408) 428-9221

Kozanian Grocery
12001 Victory Blvd.
N. Hollywood, CA   (818) 952-9030

Kradjian Importing
5018 San Fernando Road
Glendale, CA   (818) 502-1313

Krinos Foods, Inc.
47-00 Northern Blvd.
Long Island City, NY   (718) 729-9000

Main Importing Grocery, Inc.
1188 Blvd. Saint Laurent
Montreal,   (514) 861-5681

Mira International Foods, Inc.
716 Clinton St.
Hoboken, NJ   (201) 963-8289

Nader International
1 E. 28th St.
New York, NY   (212) 481-3117

Nader International Foods
36 E. 31st St.
New York, NY   (212) 889-1752

Near East Importing Co. Inc.
8000 Cooper Ave.
Glendale, NY   (212) 894-3600

Orient Export Trading Co.
123 Lexington Ave.
New York, NY   (212) 685-3451

Pak Dairy, Inc.
658 W. Hawthorne
Glendale, CA   (818) 244-9435

Paletta's Imported Foods
202 Recolleta Rd.
San Antonio, TX   (512) 828-0678

Phoenician Imports
3645 San Fernando Road
Glendale, CA   (818) 247-0500

Roma Importing Co.
886 New Louden Rd.
Latham, NY   (518) 785-7480

Sahadi Importing Co., Co.
187 Atlantic Ave.
Brooklyn, NY   (718) 624-4550

Santos Agency, Inc.
14027 Catalina St.
San Leandro, CA   (510) 357-0277

Shemshad Food, Inc.
3630 Foothill Blvd.
La Crescenta, CA   (818) 249-9066

Shoosh International
195 Channal Ave.
San Francisco, CA   (415) 626-1847

Shtoura Quality
1115 N. Godfrey St.
Allentown, PA   (215) 435-9103

Soofer Co., Inc. Sadaf
2828 S. Alameda St.
Los Angeles, CA   (213) 234-6666

Sunnyland Bulghur Co.
1435 S. Gearhart Ave.
Fresno, CA   (209) 233-4983

Tilda Marketing, Inc.
630 Palisade Ave.
Englewood Cliff, NJ   (201) 569-0909

United Foods & Supply Corp.
1420 Whipple Road
Union City, CA   (510) 471-0984

V & K Distributing Co.
3407 Magnolia Blvd.
Burbank, CA   (818) 848-1926

Yes International Food Co.
165 Church St.
New York, NY   (212) 227-4695

ICE CREAM MAKERS

Ashta Lebanese Ice Cream
7077 Sunset Blvd.
Hollywood, CA   (213) 461-5070

Balian Ice Cream Co.
2916 E. Olympic Blvd.
Los Angeles, CA   (213) 261-6111

Mashti Ice Cream
1525 N. La Brea Ave.
Hollywood, CA   (213) 874-0144

ICE CREAM SHOPS

Carvel Ice Cream Store
633 N. Main St.
Providence, RI   (401) 272-7412

ICE CREAM-DISTRIBUTORS

Valley Ice Cream Distributing
15321 Saticoy St.
Van Nuys, CA   (818) 780-0641

LIQUOR IMPORTERS-WHOLESALE

Constantine International
3713 Clifton Place
Montrose, CA   (818) 249-6574

Saharex Imports, Inc.
5717 Union Pacific Ave.
City of Commerce, CA   (213) 722-0391

LIQUOR STORES

A-1 Liquor & Jr. Mart
1145 E. Colorado St.
Glendale, CA   (818) 500-8471

Arsen's Liquor and Deli
1801 Polk St.
San Francisco, CA   (415) 673-4900

Arthurs Fine Liquors
3407 Central Ave. N.E.
Albuquerque, NM

90-Food Marketplace

Ethnic Cookbooks

Balboa Liquor
16930 Parthenia
Sepulveda, CA   (818) 891-5985

Bootleggers Liquor & Deli
410 N. Brand Blvd.
Glendale, CA   (818) 240-6605

Dana Point Liquor & Deli
34320 Coast Highway
Dana Point, CA   (714) 861-6455

Dorr's Liquor
2408 Artesia Blvd.
Redondo Beach, CA

Euclid Liquors
140 S. Euclid Ave.
Upland, CA

Glendale House of Liquore
420 S. Glendale Ave.
Glendale, CA   (818) 243-5855

Hanoian's Liquors
1439 S. Cedar Ave.
Fresno, CA   (209) 233-7304

J & M Liquor
11306 Santa Monica Blvd.
Los Angeles, CA

J.M. Armelli Liquor Co.
269 S. Lucerne
Los Angeles, CA

La Cresta Market & Liquor
3904 Foothill Blvd.
La Crescenta, CA   (818) 248-0098

Lake Murray Liquor & Market
6001 Lake Murray Blvd.
La Mesa, CA   (619) 464-8477

Lev's Armenian Market
400 W. Washington Blvd.
Montebello, CA   (213) 721-2391

M & M Liquor & Market
1951 W. Glenoaks Blvd.
Glendale, CA   (818) 848-7470

Mission Liquor
1801 E. Washington Blvd.
Pasadena, CA   (818) 794-7026

Papa Joe's Liqour Deli
2745 W. Lincoln Ave.
Anaheim, CA   (714) 826-0981

Player's Liquor
3804 Highland
Manhattan Beach, CA   (310) 545-5664

Sam's Liquor
301 W. Whittier Blvd.
Montebello, CA   (213) 722-1313

Sam's Market
10099 W. Eleven Mile Road
Huntington Woods, MI   (313) 541-8990

Stark Liquor & Jr. Market
14915 Vanowen St.
Van Nuys, CA   (818) 780-3041

Starr Liquor
13656 Victory Blvd.
Van Nuys, CA   (818) 780-1640

Vic & Ray's Liquor
22015 Vanowen St.
Canoga Park, CA   (818) 348-9172

Wiley's Hastings Liquors
3657 E. Foothill Blvd.
Pasadena, CA   (818) 351-9786

MEAT MARKETS

A. Thomas Wholesale Meat Co.
309 E. Jefferson St.
Louisville, KY   (502) 587-6947

Akropolis Meat Market
31 30th Ave.
New York, NY   (212) 728-1760

Al Hilal Halal Meat Shop
7317 Hillcroft
Houston, TX   (713) 988-4330

Al-Hilal Market
3025 S. Vermont Ave.
Los Angeles, CA   (213) 731-0868

Al-Madinah
14282 Brookhurst St.
Garden Grove, CA   (714) 531-0321

Al-Madinah
1807 Pacific Coast Hwy.
Lomita, CA   (310) 325-4778

Al-Nogoom Grocery & Meat
2805 W. 63rd St.
Chicago, IL   (312) 918-1700

Aljibani Halal Market
23385 Golden Springs Dr.
Diamond Bar, CA   (714) 861-3865

Aresh Meat & Grocery
3305 W. Magnolia Blvd.
Burbank, CA   (818) 569-7405

Bismillah Halal Meat Market
1366 Holton Lane
Langley Park, MD   (301) 434-0051

Blikian Brothers Meat Co.
4916 Santa Monica Blvd.
Hollywood, CA   (213) 665-4123

Caspian Meat Market
1854 N. Tustin Ave.
Orange, CA   (714) 998-8440

Danny's Fresh Meat & Produce
17648 Vanowen St.
Van Nuys, CA   (818) 708-9775

Dvin Fresh Meat & Fish Market
107 S. Adams
Glendale, CA   (818) 547-4454

European Sausages
12926 Saticoy St.
N. Hollywood, CA   (818) 982-2325

Family Meat Market & Produce
3452 79th St.
Chicago, IL   (312) 434-0095

Four Star Meat Co., Inc.
934 W. "C" St.
Wilmington, CA   (310) 549-2830

Glendale Fish & Meat Market
1109 S. Glendale Ave.
Glendale, CA   (818) 502-1800

Halal Meat Market
2109 Mt. Vernon Ave.
Alexandria, VA

Halal Meats Deli & Grocery
1538 Saratoga
San Jose, CA   (408) 865-1222

Hanoian's Market
1439 S. Cedar Ave.
Fresno, CA   (209) 233-7301

Hollywood Meat Market
5660 Hollywood Blvd.
Hollywood, CA   (213) 467-7640

Jordan Halal Meat
5636 Hillcroft
Houston, TX   (713) 785-4455

K & S Quality Meat
79 37th Ave.
Jackson Heights, NY

Ethnic Cookbooks

K & T Meat Market
33 Ditmars Blvd.
New York, NY   (212) 728-3810

K.G. Apikoglu, Inc.
New York, NY   (212) 730-2500

Karabagh Armenian Meat Market
5345 Santa Monica Blvd.
Hollywood, CA   (213) 469-5787

Kaysery Food Co.
2555 Victoria Park Ave.
Scarborough,   (416) 498-0547

Khatib Butcher Shop
3817 George Mason Dr.
Falls Church, VA   (703) 845-9388

Lebanese Butcher
113 E. Annandale Road
Falls Church, VA   (703) 533-2903

Lefferts Kosher Meat
81 Lefferts Blvd
Kew Gardens, NY   (718) 441-6887

Mahroukian Meat Market
1864 E. Washington Blvd.
Pasadena, CA   (818) 791-1223

Moulasadra Grocery
1438 Westwood Blvd.
Los Angeles, CA   (213) 470-4646

Princess Meat and Deli
1670 Victoria Park Ave.
Toronto,   (416) 752-4692

Sahag's Basturma
5183 Sunset Blvd.
Hollywood, CA   (213) 661-5311

Santa Monica Khosher
11933 Santa Monica Blvd.
Los Angeles, CA   (213) 473-4435

Shalom Meat Market
18000 Ventura Blvd.
Encino, CA   (818) 345-8612

Shaul's & Hershel's Meatmarket
2503 Ennalls Ave.
Wheaton, MD

Shirak Meat Product Ltd.
1375 Danforth Road
Scarborough,   (416) 266-7519

Shlomo's Meat & Fish Market
607 Reisterstown Road
Baltimore, MD

Shoppers Meat Market
5716 Mayfield Road
Cleveland, OH   (216) 442-8440

Si's BiRite Quality Meats
20884 Royalton Road
Strongsville, OH   (216) 238-8660

Sky Line Butcher Shop
3873 D.S. George Mason Dr.
Falls Church, VA

Souren & Voc's Friendly Hills
14828 E. Whittier Blvd.
Whittier, CA   (213) 693-6116

Tony's Grocery & Fresh Meat
8221 Woodman Ave.
Panorama City, CA   (818) 782-6195

Tu-Tu Halal Meat Market
3811 S. George Mason Dr.
Falls Church, VA   (703) 998-5322

Vardashen Meat & Grocery
12904 Sherman Way
N. Hollywood, CA   (818) 765-5725

Ventura Kosher Meat
18357 Ventura Blvd
Tarzana, CA   (818) 881-3777

Village Deli
846 River Road
New Millford, NJ   (201) 261-3035

West Meat Market
2549 W. Lawrence Ave.
Chicago, IL   (312) 769-4956

Zangezour Meat Market
1415 E. Colorado St.
Glendale, CA   (818) 545-9988

MEAT- WHOLESALE

Blikian Brothers Meat Co.
6835 Tujunga Ave.
N. Hollywood, CA   (818) 985-0201

High Meat Co.
2018 High St.
Delano, CA   (805) 725-1125

Konanyan Meat Co., Inc.
4525 Alger St.
Los Angeles, CA   (818) 242-5603

Mikailian Meat Products
25310 Ave. Stanford
Valencia, CA   (805) 257-1055

Moomjean Meat Co.
466 S. Atlantic
Montebello, CA   (213) 263-7856

Mr. Lamb of California
1908 Doreen Ave.
S. El Monte, CA   (310) 697-6103

NIGHT CLUBS

Aladdin Restaurant
633 W. Alosta Ave.
Glendora, CA   (818) 914-7755

Athenian Gardens
1835 N. Cahuenga Blvd.
Hollywood, CA   (213) 469-7038

Baccarat Night Club
4449 Van Nuys Blvd.
Sherman Oaks, CA   (818) 784-3300

Chelsea's Restaurant
1055 Thomas Jefferson St.
Washington, DC   (202) 298-8222

City Lights Super Night Club
5825 Sunset Blvd.
Hollywood, CA   (213) 489-7571

Club 44 Night Club
811 E. Colorado St.
Glendale, CA   (818) 241-0215

Club Tehran
12229 Ventura Blvd.
Studio City, CA   (818) 985-5800

Colbeh Iran
7240 Reseda Blvd.
Reseda, CA   (818) 344-2300

Crystal Palace
31-01 Broadway
New York, NY   (718) 545-8402

Darvish
23 W. 8th St.
New York, NY   (212) 475-1600

El-Comedor
1161 N. Vermont Ave.
Hollywood, CA   (213) 661-5309

92-Food Marketplace

Ethnic Cookbooks

Grecian Cave
31-11 Broadway
New York, NY　　　　(718) 545-7373

Grecian Village
3707 Cahuenga Blvd.
Studio City, CA　　　(818) 508-0884

Hajji Baba Night Club
824 Camino De La Reina
San Diego, CA　　　(619) 298-2010

Ibis
151 E. 50th St.
New York, NY　　　　(212) 753-3429

Key Club Restaurant
13130 Sherman Way
N. Hollywood, CA　　(818) 765-6600

Kolbeh Restaurant
4501 E. Mission Bay Dr.
San Diego, CA　　　(619) 273-8171

La Strada Restaurant
3000 Los Feliz Blvd.
Los Angeles, CA　　(213) 664-2955

Magic Lamp
2565 E. Colorado Blvd.
Pasadena, CA　　　(818) 795-8701

Microcosmos
21-11 31st St.
New York, NY　　　　(718) 728-7093

Molfetas Restaurants
370 Route 46 West
South Hakensack, NJ　(201) 440-1771

Nite Rock Club Cafe
7179 Foothill Blvd.
Tujunga, CA　　　　(818) 352-1265

Shoumine Restaurant
7271 Harvin
Houston, TX　　　　(713) 266-6677

Stani
290-21 23rd Ave.
New York, NY　　　　(718) 728-4966

Thousand & One Nights
6720 White Oak Ave.
Van Nuys, CA　　　(818) 705-2666

NUTS & DRIED FRUITS

Baba Aroush Nuts
1647 E. Washington Blvd.
Pasadena, CA　　　(818) 798-5338

Kadouri Import Corp.
51 Hester St.
New York, NY　　　　(212) 677-5441

Kharobar Market
875 6th Ave.
New York, NY　　　　(212) 714-9666

Mixed Nuts
630 S. Euclid Ave.
Santa Ana, CA

Mixed Nuts
606 S. Central Ave.
Glendale, CA　　　(818) 240-9282

Mixed Nuts
4779 Santa Monica Blvd.
Hollywood, CA　　　(213) 663-3915

Nut Crackers
818 N. Pacific Ave.
Glendale, CA　　　(818) 545-9730

Shelled Nuts
616 W. Seventh St.
Hanford, CA　　　　(209) 584-1209

Virginia & Spanish Peanut Co.
260 Dexter St.
Providence, RI　　　(401) 421-2543

Yes International Food Co.
165 Church St.
New York, NY　　　　(212) 227-4695

PASTRY SHOPS

A La Mode Ice Cream & Pastry
8064 Rolling Road
Springfield, VA　　　(703) 455-1055

Akropol Pastry Shop
2601 W. Lawrence Ave.
Chicago, IL

Antoine's Pastry Shop
317 Watertown
Newton, MA

Ara's Pastry
4945 Hollywood Blvd.
Hollywood, CA　　　(213) 661-1116

Attari
1386 Westwood Blvd.
Los Angeles, CA　　(310) 470-1003

Bakery Panos
1649 E. Washington Blvd.
Pasadena, CA　　　(818) 791-1311

Barmaki's Pastry Shop
1151 N. Euclid St.
Anaheim, CA　　　(714) 776-2621

Cafe de Jour (French Pastry)
1017 E. Broadway
Glendale, CA　　　(818) 247-9645

Eilat Bakery # 1
513 N. Fairfax Ave.
Los Angeles, CA　　(213) 653-5553

Elysee Pastry Shop
1099 Galey Ave.
Los Angeles, CA　　(310) 208-6505

Etoile French Bakery
21799 Ventura Blvd.
Woodland Hills, CA　(818) 704-8461

Flor de Cafe Bakery
801 S. Glendale Ave.
Glendale, CA　　　(818) 543-1401

French Gourmet
713 Pearl St.
La Jolla, CA　　　(619) 454-6113

Golden French Bakers
1100 S. Central Ave.
Glendale, CA　　　(818) 507-0039

Hansen's Cakes
18432 Ventura Blvd.
Tarzana, CA　　　(818) 708-1208

Hilton Pastry Shop
20 31st St.
New York, NY　　　　(212) 274-6399

La Belle Epooue
2128 Hillhurst Ave.
Los Angeles, CA　　(213) 669-7640

La Galette Pastry # 1
15137 Ventura Blvd.
Sherman Oaks, CA　(818) 905-0726

La Galette Pastry # 2
5301 Sunset Blvd.
Hollywood, CA　　　(213) 467-6606

Le Palais Bakery
8539 Sunset Blvd.
Los Angeles, CA　　(213) 659-8345

Food Marketplace-91

Ethnic Cookbooks

Food Marketplace-93

Mandik's Pastry Shop
4209 Hudson Ave.
Union City, NJ   (201) 866-3827

Mignon Bakery
452 W. Stocker St.
Glendale, CA   (818) 246-2217

Natalie Pastry Shop
1326 Westwood Blvd.
Los Angeles, CA   (213) 470-4811

Nobakht Pastry Shop
7455 Reseda Blvd.
Reseda, CA   (818) 708-2608

Noble Bakery
7875 Santa Monica
Hollywood, CA   (213) 656-7136

Omar's Pastry
14282 Brookhurst
Garden Grove, CA   (714) 531-3551

Oven Fresh Bakery
3600 Ocean View Blvd.
Glendale, CA   (818) 249-3587

Panos Pastry Shop # 1
5150 Hollywood Blvd.
Hollywood, CA   (213) 661-0335

Panos Pastry Shop # 2
418 S. Central Ave.
Glendale, CA   (818) 502-0549

Paradise Pastry
1815 W. Glenoaks Blvd.
Glendale, CA   (818) 545-4000

Petit Cafe
55 Clement St.
San Francisco, CA   (415) 387-5266

Sako's Bakery
1321 E. Colorado St.
Glendale, CA   (818) 247-3333

Sam's Pastry
620 S. Glendale Ave.
Glendale, CA   (818) 246-3811

Samadi Sweets Cafe
5916 Leesburg Pike
Falls Church, VA   (703) 578-0606

Sara's Pastries
951 S. Euclid
Anaheim, CA   (714) 776-4493

Shatila Sweet Trays
6912 Schaefer Road
Dearborn, MI   (313) 582-1952

Smyrna Lowell Confectionary Co
503 Market St.
Lowell, MA   (617) 453-9573

Sweet Stop
1618 Wisconsin Ave. N.W.
Washington, DC   (202) 342-2080

Taste It, House of Cookies
2451 E. Washington Blvd.
Pasadena, CA   (818) 794-4280

Tiffany's Bakery
1163 Glendale Galleria
Glendale, CA   (818) 242-3470

Village Pastry Shop
1414 W. Kenneth Road
Glendale, CA   (818) 241-2521

Wooden Shoe Pastry Shop
11301 Georgia Ave.
Silver Spring, MD

Yas Bakery & Confectionery
785 Rockville Pike
Rockville, MD   (301) 762-5416

Yazdi Pastry Shop
406 Marina Dr.
Seal Beach, CA   (213) 598-9880

RESTAURANTS-AFGHAN

Afghan Kebab House # 1
764 9th Ave.
New York, NY   (212) 307-1612

Afghan Kebab House # 2
1345 2nd Ave.
New York, NY   (212) 517-2776

Afghan Village Restaurant
5 St. Mark Place
New York, NY   (212) 979-6453

Amir Shish Kabob
1629 Hillside Ave.
New Hyde Park, NY   (516) 326-1010

Bobi Keboby
252 W. 38th St.
New York, NY   (212) 840-3700

Caravan Restaurant
741 8th Ave.
New York, NY   (212) 262-2021

Hakim Afghan Restaurant
808 King St.
Alexandria, VA

Kabul Afghani Cuisine
1153 E. Jericho
Huntington, NY   (516) 549-5506

Kabul Caravan
1725 Wilson Blvd.
Arlington, VA   (703) 522-8394

Kabul Kabab House
42 Main St.
Flushing, NY   (718) 461-1919

Kabul West
4871 Cordell Ave.
Bethesda, MD   (301) 986-8566

Khyber Pass
4647 Convoy St.
San Diego, CA   (619) 571-3749

Khyber Pass
3555 Rosecrans St.
San Diego, CA   (619) 224-8200

Khyber Pass
34 St. Mark's Place
New York, NY   (212) 473-0989

Pamir Cuisine of Afghanistan
1437 Second Ave.
New York, NY   (212) 734-3791

Pamir Cuisine of Afghanistan
85 Washington St.
Morristown, NJ   (201) 605-1095

Pasha's Afghan Cuisine
1110 Torrey Pines Road
La Jolla, CA   (619) 454-9229

RESTAURANTS-ARMENIAN

10 to 10 International Cuisine
137 S. Brand Blvd.
Glendale, CA   (818) 545-8506

Akhtamar Armenian Restaurant
16912 Parthenia St.
Sepulveda, CA   (818) 894-5656

Akhtamar Shish Kebab House
644 Anderson St.
Cliffside Park, NJ   (201) 945-9850

Aladdin Kebob House

94-Food Marketplace

Ethnic Cookbooks

1005 Mt. Olive
Duarte, CA (818) 357-0512

Ani Restaurant
4860 1/2 Santa Monica Blvd.
Hollywood, CA (213) 661-6393

Anoush Family Restaurant
5237 Sunset Blvd.
Hollywood, CA (213) 662-5234

Ararat Armenian Restaurant
1076 First Ave.
New York, NY (212) 752-2828

Ararat Middle Eastern Cuisine
1827 W. Katella Ave.
Anaheim, CA (714) 778-5657

Ararat Restaurant
71 Arlington St.
Watertown, MA (617) 924-4100

Arax Restaurant
1979 Lawrence Ave. E.
Scarborough, (416) 288-1485

Araz Restaurant
11717 Moorpark
Studio City, CA (818) 766-1336

Armen & Salpi M. East Cuisine
19014 Ventura Blvd.
Tarzana, CA (818) 343-1301

Armenian Cuisine
742 W. Bullard Ave.
Fresno, CA (209) 435-4892

Armenian Garden Cuisine
15532 Ward St.
Garden Grove, CA (714) 775-4499

Armenian Gourmet
929 E. Duane
Sunnyvale, CA (408) 732-3910

Armenian Kitchen
1646 Victoria Park Ave.
Scarborough, (416) 757-7722

Armitage Restaurant
1767 N. Vermont Ave.
Hollywood, CA (213) 664-5467

Arpa Best Food
801 S. Glendale Ave.
Glendale, CA (818) 507-1626

Arsen's Flaming Shish Kebab
1205 Burlington Mall
Burlington, MA (617) 273-3800

Balkan Armenian Restaurant
129 E. 27th St.
New York, NY (212) 689-7925

Bistro-Metro Restaurant
107-21 Metropolitan Ave.
Forest Hills, NY (718) 263-5444

Cafe Markarian
510 S. Glenoaks Blvd.
Burbank, CA (818) 567-0170

Caroussel Restaurant
5112 Hollywood Blvd.
Hollywood, CA (213) 660-8060

Casbah Armenian Restaurant
514 W. Diversey
Chicago, IL (312) 935-7570

Club 44 Night Club
811 E. Colorado St.
Glendale, CA (818) 241-0215

Elena's Greek Armenian Resta.
1000 S. Glendale Ave.
Glendale, CA (818) 241-5730

George's Shish Kebab
4061 N. Blackstone Ave.
Fresno, CA (209) 228-8556

George's Shish Kebab # 2
2405 Capitol St.
Fresno, CA (209) 264-9433

Hagop Shish Kebab
454 Palisade Ave.
Cliffside Park, NJ (201) 943-9817

Hagop's Restaurant
14228 Ventura Blvd.
Sherman Oaks, CA (818) 995-8254

House of Kabab
2110 W. Whittier Blvd.
Montebello, CA (213) 721-8956

Joseph's Cafe & Restaurants
1775 Ivar Ave.
Hollywood, CA (213) 462-8697

Karoun Armenian Restaurant
839 Washington St.
Newtonville, MA (617) 964-3400

Khaledian Brothers Deli
1014 E. Colorado St.
Glendale, CA (818) 246-5382

Leo's Place
35 J.F.K. St.
Cambridge, MA (617) 354-9192

Marash Coffee Shop
Los Angeles, CA (213) 385-4302

Massis Armenian Food
1148 Glendale Galleria
Glendale, CA (818) 242-2333

Mediterranean Kabob Room
608 S. Myrtle Ave.
Monrovia, CA (818) 358-7177

Middle East Restaurant
1864 N. Allen
Altadena, CA (818) 797-2576

Nazarian's Courtyard
1000 8th Ave.
Watervliet, NY (518) 273-1104

Papa Garo's
1810 S. Catalina Ave.
Redondo Beach, CA (213) 540-7272

Paros Restaurant
1117 N. Hobart Ave.
Hollywood, CA (213) 469-2610

Payton Kabob
145 S. Verdugo Rd.
Glendale, CA (818) 242-8776

Sasoon Restaurant
18970 Ventura Blvd.
Tarzana, CA (818) 708-8986

Sassoon Restaurants
3255 N. Cedar Ave.
Fresno, CA (209) 224-0577

Sayat Nova
157 E. Ohio
Chicago, IL (312) 644-9159

Sayat Nova
20 W. Golf Road
Des Plaines, IL (708) 296-1776

Sears Fine Food
439 Powell St.
San Francisco, CA (415) 986-1160

Sevan Restaurant
415 Third Ave.
New York, NY (212) 545-9538

Shish Kebab at Blvd. Cafe
378 Bergen Blvd.
Fairview, NJ (201) 945-8702

Sibian's Restaurants
13010 E. Bailey
Whittier, CA (310) 698-6808

Ethnic Cookbooks

Uncle Paulie's
2146 Ventura Ave.
Fresno, CA   (209) 233-1111

Ureni Restaurant
4655 Hollywood Blvd.
Hollywood, CA   (213) 666-4686

Vahagen Armenian Cuisine
701 S. Central Ave.
Glendale, CA   (818) 241-1496

Vahe's Armenian Cuisine
356 Arsenal St.
Watertown, MA   (617) 924-9463

Yerevan Lahmadjoun
420 Faillin
Montreal,   (514) 270-1076

Zahle Restaurant
1465 Dudemaiane
Montreal,   (514) 336-3013

Zaven's
260 E. Chestnut
Chicago, IL   (312) 787-8260

Zeytun Restaurant
5125 Sunset Blvd.
Hollywood, CA   (213) 664-3000

Zov's Bistro
17440 E. 17th St.
Tustin, CA   (714) 838-8855

RESTAURANTS-GREEK

Acropolis Greek Restaurant
6760 Hollywood Blvd.
Hollywood, CA   (213) 463-8644

Aegean Isles Restaurant
11919 W. Pico Blvd.
W. Los Angeles, CA (213) 477-7991

Aesop's Tables
8867 Villa La Jolla Dr.
La Jolla, CA   (619) 455-1535

Andros Dinner
628 Trapelo Road
Belmont, MA   (617) 484-7322

Andros Restaurant
8040 E. McDowell Road
Scottsdale, AZ   (602) 945-9573

Athenian Gardens
1835 N. Cahuenga Blvd.
Hollywood, CA   (213) 469-7038

Athenian Gardens Restaurants
3731 India St.
San Diego, CA   (619) 295-0812

Athenian Gyros
241 N. Glendale Ave.
Glendale, CA   (818) 240-3631

Athens Market
109 W. "F" St.
San Diego, CA   (619) 234-1955

Avegerinos
153 E. 53rd St.
New York, NY   (212) 688-8828

Calliope's
3958 Fifth Ave.
San Diego, CA   (619) 291-5588

Dimitri's Greek Cuisine
145 S. Highway
Solana Beach, CA   (619) 259-0733

El Greco's Restaurant
520 N. Park Ave.
Tucson, AZ   (601) 623-2398

Estia
308 E. 86th St.
New York, NY   (212) 628-9100

Fairouz Greek & Lebanese Cuis.
3166 Midway Dr.
San Diego, CA   (619) 225-0308

Galleon & Constandina's Cuisin
540 S. Vermont Ave.
Los Angeles, CA   (213) 388-9478

Georgia's Greek Cuisine
3641 Madison Ave.
San Diego, CA   (619) 284-1007

Grandia Palace
5657 Melrose Ave.
Hollywood, CA   (213) 462-8628

Great Greek Restaurant
13362 Ventura Blvd.
Sherman Oaks, CA   (818) 905-5250

Great Gyros, the
459 La Jolla Village Dr.
La Jolla, CA   (619) 696-0424

Grecian Cuisine
4325 Glencoe Ave.
Marina Del Rey, CA (213) 822-6221

Food Marketplace-95

Grecian Paradise
18928 Ventura Blvd.
Tarzana, CA   (818) 705-0633

Grecian Village
3707 Cahuenga Blvd.
Studio City, CA   (818) 508-0884

Greek American Foods
223 Valencia St.
San Francisco, CA   (415) 864-0978

Greek Connection, The
401 N. La Cienega Blvd.
Los Angeles, CA   (310) 659-2271

Greek Corner Restaurant # 1
5844 Montezuma Road
San Diego, CA   (619) 287-3303

Greek Corner Restaurant # 2
13185 Black Mtn.
San Diego, CA   (619) 484-9197

Greek Island Delights
2218 Fashion Island Blvd.
San Mateo, CA   (415) 341-3383

Greek Islands Restaurants
2930 N. 16th St.
Phoenix, AZ   (602) 274-3515

Greek Place
8445 International Dr.
Orlando, FL   (407) 352-6930

Greek Town Restaurnat
431 "E" Street
San Diego, CA   (619) 232-0461

Greek Village
1016 Lexington Ave.
New York, NY   (212) 288-7378

Jerry G. Bishop's Greek Island
879 W. Harbor Dr.
San Diego, CA   (619) 239-5216

Marathon Restaurant
1070 E. Broadway
Long Beach, CA   (310) 437-6346

Maria's Greek Corner
409 W. Mapel St.
Vienna, VA

Molfetas
307 W. 47th St.
New York, NY   (212) 840-9537

Mumms Restaurant
13075 Victory Blvd.
N. Hollywood, CA   (818) 763-7087

96-Food Marketplace

Ethnic Cookbooks

Nea Hellas
31-15 Ditmars Blvd.
New York, NY   (718) 278-7304

New Parthenon Restaurant
547 Monroe Ave.
Detroit, MI   (313) 963-8888

Old Town Greek Cuisine
2448 San Diego Ave.
San Diego, CA   (619) 291-5770

Panos Char Broiler
16045 Victory
Van Nuys, CA   (818) 780-4041

Papadakis Taverna Restaurant
301 W. 6th St.
San Pedro, CA   (310) 548-1186

Periyali
35 W. 20th St.
New York, NY   (212) 463-7890

Plaka
165 Bleecker St.
New York, NY   (212) 674-9709

Port of Athens Restaurant
12430 Riverside Dr.
N. Hollywood, CA   (818) 508-9486

Shepherd's Cove
11625 Paramount Blvd.
Downey, CA   (310) 862-9441

Sofi Restaurant
8030 W. 3rd St.
Los Angeles, CA   (213) 651-0346

Stoyanof's
1240 Ninth Ave.
San Francisco, CA   (415) 664-3664

Taverna Vraka
23-15 31st St.
New York, NY   (718) 721-3007

Z
117 E. 15th St.
New York, NY   (212) 254-0960

Zorba B.B.Q.
Fashion Fair Shopping Ctr.
Fresno, CA   (209) 225-6774

Zorba's
1612 20th St., N.W.
Washington, DC

Zygos Taverna
22-55 31st St.
New York, NY   (718) 728-7070

RESTAURANTS- LEBANESE

Abou Khodor Restaurant # 1
620 S. Glendale Ave.
Glendale, CA   (818) 241-5562

Abou Khodor Restaurant # 2
7077 Sunset Blvd.
Hollywood, CA   (213) 461-5070

Al-Amir Lebanese Cuisine
1431 Second Ave.
New York, NY   (212) 737-1800

Al-Amir the Prince
5750 Wilshire Blvd.
Los Angeles, CA   (213) 931-8740

Cedars of Lebanon
39 E. 30th St.
New York, NY   (212) 725-9251

George's Townhouse
1205 28th St., N.W.
Washington, DC   (202) 342-2278

Grapeleaf Restaurant, The
4031 Balboa St.
San Francisco, CA   (415) 668-1515

Lebanese Taverna Restaurant
5900 Washington Blvd.
Arlington, VA

Lebanese Taverna Restaurant
2641 Connecticut Ave.
Washington, DC

Sahara Lebanese Cuisine
2401 Artesia Blvd.
Redondo Beach, CA   (310) 371-1533

Yaldzlar Restaurant
566 3rd Ave.
New York, NY   (212) 557-0055

RESTAURANTS- MIDDLE EASTERN

Abou Khodor Restaurant # 1
620 S. Glendale Ave.
Glendale, CA   (818) 241-5562

Abou Khodor Restaurant # 2
7077 Sunset Blvd.
Hollywood, CA   (213) 461-5070

Adnan
129 Atlantic Ave.
New York, NY   (718) 625-2115

Afghan Cuisine Restaurant
2827 Sunset Blvd.
Hollywood, CA   (213) 483-8475

Al-Amir Lebanese Cuisine
1431 Second Ave.
New York, NY   (212) 737-1800

Al-Amir the Prince
5750 Wilshire Blvd.
Los Angeles, CA   (213) 931-8740

Al-Manara Restaurant
2940 W. Lincoln Ave.
Anaheim, CA   (714) 952-3239

Al-Maqha Restaurant
3289 "M" St.
Washington, DC   (202) 342-6140

Al-Rawsha Restaurant
4282 El Cajon Blvd.
San Diego, CA   (619) 281-4259

Al-Salam Restaurant
3292 N. Garey Ave.
Pomona, CA   (714) 593-5225

Al-Sham Restaurant
2424 W. Ball Road
Anaheim, CA   (714) 220-0894

Al-Wazir
1219 S. Glendale Ave.
Glendale, CA   (818) 500-1578

Al-Wazir Restaurant
6051 Hollywood Blvd.
Hollywood, CA   (213) 856-0660

Aladdin Restaurant
633 W. Alosta Ave.
Glendora, CA   (818) 914-7755

Ali Baba Foods
3662 S. Nosales St.
West Covina, CA   (818) 810-5108

Ali Baba Restaurant
100 S. Brookhurst
Anaheim, CA   (714) 774-5632

Antoine's Restaurant
5504 La Jolla Blvd.
La Jolla, CA   (619) 456-1144

Ethnic Cookbooks

Food Marketplace-97

At Our Place
2527 Broadway
New York, NY   (212) 864-1410

Atilla's Restaurant
2705 Columbia Pike
Arlington, VA   (703) 920-4900

Babouch Moroccan Restaurant
810 S. Gaffey St.
San Pedro, CA   (310) 831-0246

Barmaky Restaurant
838 S. Glendale Ave.
Glendale, CA   (818) 240-6133

Bennie's
37 7th Ave.
New York, NY   (212) 633-2044

Black Orchid Restaurant
7410 Little River Turnpike
Annandale, VA   (703) 941-4400

Bourock
172 Atlantic Ave.
New York, NY   (718) 624-9614

Byblos A Lebanese Cuisine
1964 Westwood Blvd.
Los Angeles, CA   (213) 475-9558

Byblos Middle Eastern Cuisine
6887 Orchard Lake Rd
West Bloomfield, MI   (313) 932-3770

Byblos Middle Eastern Cuisine
12967 Woodward
Highland Park, MI   (313) 867-0923

Byblos Restaurant
200 E. 39th Street
New York, NY   (212) 687-0808

Byblos on the Boardwalk
6887 Orchard Lake Road
W. Bloomfield, MI   (313) 932-3770

Cafe Karnak
1608 Mayfair
Orange, CA   (714) 997-8323

Cafe Mediterranean
10151 Riverside Dr.
Burbank, CA   (818) 769-0865

Casa Blanca
1123 N. Vine # 2
Hollywood, CA   (213) 466-3353

Casa d'Mama
7422 Little River Turnpike
Annandale, VA   (703) 256-3780

Casablanca International
1123 N. Vine Street
Hollywood, CA   (213) 467-8230

Cazablanca Restaurant
131 45th St.
New York, NY   (212) 599-0899

Cedars of Lebanon
39 E. 30th St.
New York, NY   (212) 725-9251

Chef's Corner
3430 Foothill Blvd.
La Crescenta, CA   (818) 249-3539

Chez Ali Baba Restaurant
201 Rachel East
Montreal,   (514) 982-9393

Chez Momo
48 MacDougal St.
New York, NY   (212) 979-8588

Chicken Rotissary
5658 Sepulveda Blvd.
Van Nuys, CA   (818) 781-0615

Cuisine on the Green
1000 Las Lomas Road
Duarte, CA   (818) 359-3388

Dar Es Salam
3056 "M" St. N.W.
Georgetown, DC   (202) 342-1925

Dar Maghreb Restaurant
7651 Sunset Blvd.
Hollywood, CA   (213) 876-7651

El Morocco Restaurnat
8222 Santa Monica Blvd.
Hollywood, CA   (213) 654-9550

El-Ajami Restaurant
105 W. Arrow Hwy.
San Demas, CA   (714) 394-0681

El-Manara
7111 3rd Ave.
New York, NY   (718) 745-2284

Falafel Palace
9255 Reseda Blvd.
Northridge, CA   (818) 993-0734

Falafel'N'Stuff
1586 First Ave.
New York, NY   (212) 879-7023

Fettoosh
3277 "M" St., N.W.
Washington, DC   (202) 342-1199

Flaming Pit
18701 N. Frederick Road
Gaithersburg, MD   (301) 977-0700

Food Factory
4221 N. Fairfax
Arlington, VA

Georgetown Cafe
1623 Wisconsin Ave. N.W.
Washington, DC   (202) 333-0215

Gondola Restaurant
2502 W. 63rd St.
Chicago, IL   (312) 737-0386

Gondole Restaurant
2871 W. Lincoln Ave.
Anaheim, CA   (714) 952-1185

Grapeleaf Restaurant, The
4031 Balboa St.
San Francisco, CA   (415) 668-1515

Haji Baba Restaurant
Tempe, AZ   (602) 894-2442

Hassan's Restaurnats
3325 Newport Blvd.
Newport Beach, CA   (714) 675-4668

Jerusalem Restaurant
3815 S. George Mason Dr.
Falls Church, VA   (703) 845-1622

Joseph's Place
1881 Steeles Ave. West
Downsview Ontario,   (416) 739-7221

Just Like Home Restaurant
1924 Irving St.
San Francisco, CA   (415) 681-3337

Kavar Restaurant
4777 Santa Monica Blvd.
Hollywood, CA   (213) 669-1260

Kebob House
2800 Southeast St.
Crystal City, VA

Koutoubia Restaurant
2116 Westwood Blvd.
Los Angeles, CA   (310) 475-0729

Lave Lee Restaurant
12514 Ventura Blvd.
Studio City, CA   (818) 980-8158

Layalina Restaurant
5948 Lankershim Blvd.
N. Hollywood, CA   (818) 766-6575

98-Food Marketplace

Ethnic Cookbooks

Madinah Restaurant Party Hall
401 S. Vermont Ave.
Los Angeles, CA   (213) 383-9976

Mamoun's Middle East Food
2698 E. Garvey Ave. S.
West Covina, CA   (213) 339-3122

Marouch Hollywood
4905 Santa Monica Blvd.
Hollywood, CA   (213) 662-9325

Marrakesh Restaurant # 1
13003 Ventura Blvd.
Studio City, CA   (818) 788-6354

Marrakesh Restaurant # 2
1100 W. Coast Highway
Newport Beach, CA   (714) 645-8384

Marrakesh Restaurant # 3
8240 Parkway Dr.
La Mesa, CA   (619) 462-3663

Marrakesh Restaurant # 4
634 Pearl St.
La Jolla, CA   (619) 454-2500

Mediterranean Feast
19223 Ventura Blvd.
Tarzana, CA   (818) 705-7961

Mesopotamia Restaurant
1467 W. Montrose
Chicago, IL   (312) 348-0654

Metropolis Restaurant
650 N. La Cienega Blvd.
Los Angeles, CA   (310) 659-3333

Middle East Connection
916 W. Burbank Blvd.
Burbank, CA   (818) 843-8339

Middle East Restaurant
472 Massachusetts Ave.
Cambridge, MA   (617) 492-9181

Middle East Restaurant
645 E. Main St.
Alhambra, CA   (818) 576-1048

Middle East Restaurant
2954 W. Ball Road
Anaheim, CA   (714) 826-8700

Middle East Restaurant #2
6749 Greenleaf Ave.
Whittier, CA   (310) 696-2224

Middle Eastern Restaurant
910 E. Main St.
Alhambra, CA   (818) 281-1006

Mihran's Restaurants
19560 Ventura Blvd.
Tarzana, CA   (818) 342-2290

Mitaya Fine Cuisine
4350 Steeles Ave Ave. East
Markham, Ontario,   (416) 940-6296

Moroccan Restaurant
4632 S. Maryland Parkway
Las Vegas, NV   (702) 736-7655

Moroccan Star
205 Atlantic Ave.
New York, NY   (718) 643-0800

Moun of Tunis Restaurant
7445 Sunset Blvd.
Hollywood, CA   (213) 874-3333

Nicol's
17934 Ventura Blvd.
Encino, CA   (818) 881-3099

Noura Restaurant
8479 Melrose Ave.
W. Hollywood, CA   (213) 651-4581

Pasadena Kabob House
2525 E. Foothill Blvd.
Pasadena, CA   (818) 795-3499

Pawinda Restaurnat
1110 Torrey Pines Road
San Diego, CA   (619) 454-9229

Pita Inn
3910 Dempster St.
Skokie, IL   (708) 677-0211

Restaurant Asmar
162 Jean Talon Est.
Montreal,

Royal Morocco
14510 Big Basin Way
Saratoga, CA   (408) 741-0224

Sabrina Middle East Restaurant
4325 S. Sepulveda Blvd.
Culver City, CA   (310) 398-2308

Sahara Lebanese Cuisine
2401 Artesia Blvd.
Redondo Beach, CA   (310) 371-1533

Sahara Restaurnat
13536 Ventura Blvd.
Sherman Oaks, CA   (818) 995-4609

Sahara Room
626 E. Chula Vista
San Diego, CA   (619) 427-8880

Sally's Place
7809 3rd Ave.
Brooklyn, NY   (718) 680-4615

Samira's
6916 4th Ave.
New York, NY   (718) 745-2416

Sheik Cafe
2664 5th Ave.
San Diego, CA   (619) 234-5888

Shish Kabob Express
14357 Victory Blvd.
Van Nuys, CA   (818) 787-6718

Shish Kabob Grill
935 Broxton Ave.
Los Angeles, CA   (213) 824-7739

Sibo, Abu-Salim Restaurant
81 Lexington Ave.
New York, NY   (212) 686-2031

Sphinx
1779 Westwood Blvd.
Los Angeles, CA   (310) 477-2358

Tripoli
6 Atlantic Ave.
New York, NY   (718) 596-5800

Virginia's Mid-East Cafe
2456 Orchard Lake Rd
Sylvan Lake, MI   (313) 681-7170

RESTAURANTS-MOROCCAN

Casablanca
1504 King St.
Alexandria, VA   (703) 549-6464

El Morocco Restaurant
100 Wall St.
Worcester, MA   (508) 756-7117

Marrakesh Restaurant
617 New York Ave., N.W.
Washington, DC

Marrakesh Restaurant # 4
634 Pearl St.
La Jolla, CA   (619) 454-2500

Moroccan Restaurant
4632 S. Maryland Parkway
Las Vegas, NV   (702) 736-7655

Ethnic Cookbooks

Moroccan Star
205 Atlantic Ave.
New York, NY   (718) 643-0800

RESTAURANTS-PERSIAN

1001 Night Restaurant
215 Copeland Road
Atlanta, GA   (404) 851-9566

4 Star General's Kebob
311 S. Boylston St.
Los Angeles, CA   (213) 482-5240

Alex Restaurant
702 Anderson Ave.
Cliffside Park, NJ   (201) 945-4121

Alvie's Restaurant
929 6th Ave.
San Diego, CA   (619) 232-0529

Andre's Restaurant
4743 N. Blackstone
Fresno, CA   (209) 229-6353

Angel Cafe
5990 Pico Blvd.
Los Angeles, CA   (213) 936-3708

Apadana Restaurant
2240 N. Scottsdale Road
Tempe, AZ   (602) 945-5900

B.M.G. Restaurant
2062 Curtner Ave.
San Jose, CA   (408) 559-7330

Baccarat Night Club
4449 Van Nuys Blvd.
Sherman Oaks, CA   (818) 784-3300

Baccarat Restaurant
1092 E. El Camino Road
Sunnyvale, CA   (408) 261-1234

Bahar Restaurant
148 W. Maple Ave.
Vienna, VA   (703) 242-2427

Bay Bistro
43 S. "B" St.
San Mateo, CA   (415) 347-8686

Bazarcheh Restaurant
8849 Beverly Blvd.
Beverly Hills, CA   (310) 273-7420

Beverly Hills Kabab (Firouz)
268 S. La Cienega Blvd.
Beverly Hills, CA   (310) 657-6257

Bisoutoun Restaurant
7545 Reseda Blvd.
Reseda, CA   (818) 434-5115

Bobby Kebobby
54-19 108th St.
Forest Hills, NY   (718) 263-3700

Bobby Kebobby
252 W. 38th St.
New York, NY   (212) 840-3700

Bread & Kabob
3407 Payne St.
Falls Church, VA   (703) 845-2900

Broiler
10800 W. Pico Blvd.
Los Angeles, CA   (310) 470-0525

Cafe Markarian
510 S. Glenoaks Blvd.
Burbank, CA   (818) 567-0170

Cafe Rose
300 W. Broad St.
Falls Church, VA   (703) 532-1700

Caravansary Gourmet Shop & Res
310 Sutter St.
San Francisco, CA   (415) 362-4641

Caspian Persian Cuisine
1063 E. El Camino Real
Sunnyvale, CA   (408) 248-6332

Caspian Regional Cuisine
1063 E. El Camino Road
Sunnyvale, CA   (408) 248-6332

Caspian Restaurant
14130 Culver Dr.
Irvine, CA   (714) 651-8454

Caspian Tea Room
4801 Massachusetts Ave. N.W.
Washington, DC   (202) 244-6363

Chandelier Restaurant
7271 Harwin
Houston, TX   (713) 785-5855

Charlie Kabob
129 Santa Monica Place
Santa Monica, CA   (213) 393-5535

Chatanoga Restaurant
2725 El Camino Real
Santa Clara, CA   (408) 241-1200

Food Marketplace-99

Chelokababi
1236 Wolfe Road
Sunnyvale, CA   (408) 737-1222

Choopan Kabab House
46 Kissena Blvd.
Flushing, NY   (718) 886-0786

Cio-Ce-Pol Restaurant
1773 Westwood Blvd.
Los Angeles, CA   (310) 479-5160

Colbeh Restaurant
75 N. Station Plaza
Great Neck, NY   (516) 466-8181

Culmore Restaurant
6037 Leesburg Pike
Falls Church, VA   (703) 820-7171

Darband Kabobi
5670 Hillcroft
Houston, TX   (713) 975-8350

Darband Restaurant
158 Middle Neck Road
Great Neck, NY   (516) 829-0030

Darband Restaurant
138 S. Beverly Dr.
Beverly Hills, CA   (310) 859-8585

Dariush Restaurant
15651 Hawthorne Blvd.
Lawndale, CA   (310) 644-8672

Darvish Restaurant
980 La Cienega Blvd.
Los Angeles, CA   (310) 659-1112

Darya Restaurant
1840 N. Tustin Ave.
Orange, CA   (714) 921-2773

Darya Restaurant
3316 S. Bristol
Santa Ana, CA   (714) 557-6600

David Restaurant
5151 Stars and Stripes Dr.
Santa Clara, CA   (408) 986-1666

Downtown Kabab
934 S. Los Angeles St.
Los Angeles, CA   (213) 612-0222

Famous Kabob
1290 Fulton Ave.
Sacramento, CA   (916) 483-1700

Farhad Restaurant
801 W. Hamilton Ave.
Campbell, CA   (408) 866-1588

100-Food Marketplace

Ethnic Cookbooks

Farid Restaurant
635 S. Broadway
Los Angeles, CA   (213) 622-0808

Flames Shahrzad Restaurant
1422 Westwood Blvd.
Los Angeles, CA   (213) 470-3242

Garson Restaurant
2926 HillCroft
Houston, TX   (713) 781-0400

Golestan Persian Cuisine
22458 Ventura Blvd.
Woodland Hills, CA   (818) 347-0577

Golestan Restaurant
1398 Westwood Blvd.
Los Angeles, CA   (213) 470-3867

Greek Place
8445 International Dr.
Orlando, FL   (407) 352-6930

Habib Restaurant
1401 S. Las Vegas Blvd.
Las Vegas, NV   (702) 388-9119

Hajji Baba Pasargad Restaurant
8449 40th St.
Miami, FL   (305) 221-7929

Hatam Restaurant
1112 N. Brookhurst
Anaheim, CA   (714) 991-6262

Hatam Restaurant
1115 3rd St.
San Rafael, CA   (415) 454-8888

Hollywood Kabob Restaurant
6056 Hollywood Blvd.
Hollywood, CA   (213) 463-4363

Hollywood Restaurant
99 Queens Blvd.
Forest Hills, NY   (718) 275-5200

House of Shish Kebab
5406 N. Blackstone Ave.
Fresno, CA   (209) 432-0700

Javan Restaurant
11628 Santa Monica Blvd.
Los Angeles, CA   (310) 207-5555

Kabab House (KababKhouneh)
1831 W. Glenoaks Blvd.
Glendale, CA   (818) 243-7001

Kabab Royal
2646 Dupont Dr.
Irvine, CA   (714) 476-9901

Kababi-e-Nader
48 E. 29th St.
New York, NY   (212) 683-4833

Kabob House
2062 Curtner Ave.
San Jose, CA   (408) 559-7330

Kabob House
1300 Galindo
Concord, CA   (510) 671-6969

Kabob No. 1
755 Voltaire St.
San Diego, CA   (619) 222-2656

Kabob's Palace
310 N. Citrus Ave.
Azusa, CA   (818) 334-6759

Kaboby Restaurant #1
1133 Westwood Blvd.
Los Angeles, CA   (310) 208-9208

Kaboby Restaurant #2
15301 Ventura Blvd.
Sherman Oaks, CA   (818) 501-9830

Kanani's Omar Khayyam Rest.
1453 York Ave.
New York, NY   (212) 879-5353

Karoon Restaurant
1608 E. Mayfair
Orange, CA   (714) 997-8323

Karoun Restaurant
375 S. Bacom Ave.
San Jose, CA   (408) 947-1520

Kasra Restaurant
349 Clement St.
San Francisco, CA   (415) 752-1101

Kasra Skeweres
24 Ellis St.
San Francisco, CA   (415) 433-4747

Key Club Restaurant
13130 Sherman Way
N. Hollywood, CA   (818) 765-6600

Khan Baba (House of Kabab)
20050 Vanowen St.
Canoga Park, CA   (818) 887-5450

Khayyam's Chelo Kabab
1373 Solano Ave.
Albany, CA   (510) 526-7200

Kolbeh Restaurant
1645 Wisconsin Ave. N.W.
Washington, DC   (202) 342-2000

Kolbeh Restaurant
4501 E. Mission Bay Dr.
San Diego, CA   (619) 273-8171

Kouche Restaurant
25381 Elisa Parkway
Laguna Hills, CA   (714) 588-8999

Massoud Restaurant
504 E. 12th St.
Los Angeles, CA   (213) 748-1768

Maykadeh Restaurant
470 Green St.
San Francisco, CA   (415) 362-8286

Miami Restaurant
6113 Reseda Blvd.
Reseda, CA   (818) 705-3322

Morae Restaurant
1441 E. Fletcher
La Place Shopping, FL   (813) 977-6018

Mustang Cafe
5005 L.B.J. 150
Dallas, TX   (214) 306-4888

New York New York Restaurant
4251 Burton Dr.
Santa Clara, CA   (408) 727-4420

New York Restaurant
37 Broadway
Astoria, NY   (718) 726-3254

Omar Khayam Restaurant
7360 Center Dr.
Huntington Beach, CA   (714) 373-0810

Orchid Restaurant
3033 S. Bristol
Costa Mesa, CA   (714) 557-8070

Pamchal Restaurant
1389 Westwood Blvd.
Los Angeles, CA   (310) 473-0309

Papa John's Restaurant
765 Rockville Pike
Rockville, MD   (301) 340-6970

Papa's Restaurant
2026 University Ave.
Berkeley, CA   (510) 841-0884

Paradise Restaurant
1350 Grant Road
Mountain View, CA   (415) 968-5949

Paradiso Restaurant
10800 W. Pico Blvd.
Los Angeles, CA   (310) 475-1427

Ethnic Cookbooks

Food Marketplace-101

Pars Restaurant
21008 Hawthorne Blvd.
Torrance, CA   (310) 370-4838

Pars Restaurant
4790 Irvine Blvd.
Irvine, CA   (714) 832-8324

Pars Restaurant
352 El Camino Real
San Bruno, CA   (415) 871-5151

Pars Restaurant
10827 S.W. 40th St.
Miami, FL   (305) 551-1099

Pasha Restaurant
1516 Broadway
San Francisco, CA   (415) 885-4477

Persepolis Restaurant
7141 Wisconsin Ave. N.W.
Bethesda, MD   (301) 656-9339

Perspolis Restaurant
1029 Blossom Hill Road
San Jose, CA   (408) 265-5090

Perspolis Restaurants
130 W. Katella Blvd.
Anaheim, CA   (714) 991-7600

Pollo Clasico
9791 Lincoln Village Dr.
Sacramento, CA   (916) 369-8445

Reza Restaurant
808 S. Brookhurst
Anaheim, CA   (714) 778-2005

Rose's Restaurant
8223 Canoga Ave.
Canoga Park, CA   (818) 716-5222

Royal Kabab
2646 Dupont Dr.
Irvine, CA   (714) 476-9901

Royal Perspolis Restaurant
362 N. Canon Dr.
Beverly Hills, CA   (310) 281-0777

Saam Middle East Restaurant
39 S. Raymond Ave.
Pasadena, CA   (818) 793-8496

Saghi Restaurant
1724 N. Tustin Ave.
Orange, CA   (714) 974-3353

Sahar Restaurant
248 W. Foothill Blvd.
Azusa, CA   (818) 969-9150

Salam International Market
3090 Aloma Ave.
Winter Park, FL   (407) 657-5560

Salar Restaurant
1240 S. Glendale Ave.
Glendale, CA   (818) 500-8661

Salt & Peper (Felfel Namakie)
5621 Hillcroft
Houston, TX   (713) 783-9996

Saray-e Ghalandar
7545 Reseda Blvd.
Reseda, CA   (818) 343-5115

Shahbaz Restaurant
5990 Pico Blvd.
Los Angeles, CA   (213) 936-3708

Shahrzad Restaurant
17547 Ventura Blvd.
Encino, CA   (818) 906-1616

Shahrzad Restaurant
13615 Ventura Blvd.
Sherman Oaks, CA   (818) 905-6363

Shalizar Restaurant
5640 Moreno St.
Montclair, CA   (714) 946-8481

Shalizeh Restaurant
14650 Roscoe Blvd.
Panorama City, CA   (818) 894-7557

Shalton Restaurant
414 W. 6th St.
Los Angeles, CA   (213) 891-1984

Shamshiri Restaurant
1392 S. Bascom Ave.
San Jose, CA   (408) 998-0122

Shamshiri Restaurant # 1
1916 Westwood Blvd.
Los Angeles, CA   (310) 474-1410

Shamshiri Restaurant # 2
5229 Hollywood Blvd.
Hollywood, CA   (213) 469-8434

Shamshiri Restaurant # 3
19249 Roscoe Blvd.
Northridge, CA   (818) 885-7846

Shamshiri Restaurant # 4
122 W. Stocker
Glendale, CA   (818) 246-9541

Shandiz Restaurant
45550 Montgomery Ave.
Bethesda, MD   (301) 961-8989

Shekarchi Kabab # 1
1712 Westwood Blvd.
Los Angeles, CA   (213) 474-6911

Shekarchi Kabab # 2
155 11th St.
Los Angeles, CA   (213) 746-4600

Shiraz Restaurant
15472 Ventura Blvd.
Sherman Oaks, CA   (818) 789-7788

Shish Kabob Cafe
4944 El Cajon Blvd.
San Deigo, CA   (619) 265-7800

Shish Kabob House
639 Pearl St.
La Jolla, CA   (619) 459-4016

Shish Kabob Palace
90 Middle Neck Road
Great Neck, NY   (516) 487-2228

Shish Kebab Restaurant
283 Main St.
Port Washington, NY   (516) 883-9309

Sholeh Restaurant
1440 Westwood Blvd.
Los Angeles, CA   (213) 470-9131

Simon's Kohser Restaurants
8706 W. Pico Blvd.
Los Angeles, CA   (310) 657-5552

Simon's Kosher Restaurants
914 S. Hill St.
Los Angeles, CA   (213) 627-6535

Soultany Restaurant
1535 N. La Brea Ave.
Hollywood, CA   (213) 876-3398

Sports Grill
14130 Culver Dr.
Irvine, CA   (714) 551-6142

Squire
152 Middle Neck Road
Great Neck, NY   (516) 487-4032

Star Kabab
2907 E. 7th St.
Long Beach, CA   (310) 434-4848

Sultan's Kebabs Restaurant
1824 Harrison St.
Hollywood, FL   (305) 927-0002

Sultani Restaurant
1535 N. La Brea
Hollywood, CA   (213) 876-3389

102-Food Marketplace   Ethnic Cookbooks

Sunset House Restaurant
6270 Sunset Blvd.
Hollywood, CA   (213) 464-6555

Tanouri Restaurant
1442 Westwood Blvd.
Los Angeles, CA   (213) 470-7003

Taverna
1401 Old Northern Blvd.
Roslyn, NY   (516) 484-8860

Tavous Restaurant
7125 Columbia Pike
Annandale, VA   (703) 941-1451

Tea Room, Newport Beach
3100 Irvine Ave.
Newport Beach, CA   (714) 756-0121

Tea Sara
1138 Saratoga Ave.
San Jose, CA   (408) 241-5115

Tea Sara # 2
1029 Blossom Hill Road
San Jose, CA   (408) 265-5090

Tehrani Restaurant
18 Hawthorne Blvd.
Redondo Beach, CA   (310) 214-2626

Thousand & One Nights
6720 White Oak Ave.
Van Nuys, CA   (818) 705-2666

University Market Place
2604 Georgia Ave.
Washington, DC   (202) 667-2206

Up All Night
4505 Sepulveda Blvd.
Sherman Oaks, CA   (818) 501-8661

Vanak Kabob Restaurant
18202 Imperial Hwy.
Yorba Linda, CA   (714) 993-0655

Village Persian Restaurant
1722 N. Tustin Ave.
Orange, CA   (714) 282-1010

Wine Gardern Restaurant
30 Jack London Squar
Oakland, CA   (415) 835-4433

Yasaman Restaurant
19047 Bushard St.
Huntington Beach, CA   (714) 968-7333

Your Place # 1
354 N. Beverly Dr.
Beverly Hills, CA   (310) 858-1977

Your Place # 2
17301 Ventura Blvd.
Encino, CA   (818) 501-4646

RESTAURANTS

10 to 10 International Cuisine
137 S. Brand Blvd.
Glendale, CA   (818) 545-8506

1001 Night Restaurant
215 Copeland Road
Atlanta, GA   (404) 851-9566

4 Star General's Kebob
311 S. Boylston St.
Los Angeles, CA   (213) 482-5240

Abou Khodor Restaurant # 1
620 S. Glendale Ave.
Glendale, CA   (818) 241-5562

Abou Khodor Restaurant # 2
7077 Sunset Blvd.
Hollywood, CA   (213) 461-5070

Acropolis Greek Restaurant
6760 Hollywood Blvd.
Hollywood, CA   (213) 463-8644

Aditi Restaurant
3299 "M" St. N.W.
Washington, DC

Adnan
129 Atlantic Ave.
New York, NY   (718) 625-2115

Aegean Isles Restaurant
11919 W. Pico Blvd.
W. Los Angeles, CA   (213) 477-7991

Aesop's Tables
8867 Villa La Jolla Dr.
La Jolla, CA   (619) 455-1535

Afghan Cuisine Restaurant
2827 Sunset Blvd.
Hollywood, CA   (213) 483-8475

Afghan Kebab House # 1
764 9th Ave.
New York, NY   (212) 307-1612

Afghan Kebab House # 2
1345 2nd Ave.
New York, NY   (212) 517-2776

Afghan Village Restaurant
5 St. Mark Place
New York, NY   (212) 979-6453

Akhtamar Armenian Restaurant
16912 Parthenia St.
Sepulveda, CA   (818) 894-5656

Akhtamar Shish Kebab House
644 Anderson St.
Cliffside Park, NJ   (201) 945-9850

Al Nakheel
334 Maple Ave. West
Vienna, VA

Al's Italian American Deli
2332 Honolulu Ave.
Montrose, CA   (818) 249-3031

Al-Amir Lebanese Cuisine
1431 Second Ave.
New York, NY   (212) 737-1800

Al-Amir the Prince
5750 Wilshire Blvd.
Los Angeles, CA   (213) 931-8740

Al-Manara Restaurant
2940 W. Lincoln Ave.
Anaheim, CA   (714) 952-3239

Al-Maqha Restaurant
3289 "M" St.
Washington, DC   (202) 342-6140

Al-Rawsha Restaurant
4282 El Cajon Blvd.
San Diego, CA   (619) 281-4259

Al-Salam Restaurant
3292 N. Garey Ave.
Pomona, CA   (714) 593-5225

Al-Sham Restaurant
2424 W. Ball Road
Anaheim, CA   (714) 220-0894

Al-Wazir
1219 S. Glendale Ave.
Glendale, CA   (818) 500-1578

Al-Wazir Restaurant
6051 Hollywood Blvd.
Hollywood, CA   (213) 856-0660

Aladdin Kebob House
1005 Mt. Olive
Duarte, CA   (818) 357-0512

Aladdin Restaurant
633 W. Alosta Ave.
Glendora, CA   (818) 914-7755

Ethnic Cookbooks

Food Marketplace-103

Alex Restaurant
702 Anderson Ave.
Cliffside Park, NJ   (201) 945-4121

Ali Baba Foods
3662 S. Nosales St.
West Covina, CA   (818) 810-5108

Ali Baba Restaurant
100 S. Brookhurst
Anaheim, CA   (714) 774-5632

Alvie's Restaurant
929 6th Ave.
San Diego, CA   (619) 232-0529

Amir Shish Kabob
1629 Hillside Ave.
New Hyde Park, NY   (516) 326-1010

Andre's Restaurant
4743 N. Blackstone
Fresno, CA   (209) 229-6353

Andrea's House of Pizza
620 Mount Auburn St.
Watertown, MA   (617) 924-1760

Andros Dinner
628 Trapelo Road
Belmont, MA   (617) 484-7322

Andros Restaurant
8040 E. McDowell Road
Scottsdale, AZ   (602) 945-9573

Andy's Burgers
4097 Lankershim Blvd.
N. Hollywood, CA   (818) 985-9855

Angel Cafe
5990 Pico Blvd.
Los Angeles, CA   (213) 936-3708

Ani Restaurant
4860 1/2 Santa Monica Blvd.
Hollywood, CA   (213) 661-6393

Antoine's Restaurant
5504 La Jolla Blvd.
La Jolla, CA   (619) 456-1144

Apadana Restaurant
2240 N. Scottsdale Road
Tempe, AZ   (602) 945-5900

Ararat Armenian Restaurant
1076 First Ave.
New York, NY   (212) 752-2828

Ararat Middle Eastern Cuisine
1827 W. Katella Ave.
Anaheim, CA   (714) 778-5657

Ararat Restaurant
71 Arlington St.
Watertown, MA   (617) 924-4100

Arax Restaurant
1979 Lawrence Ave. E.
Scarborough,   (416) 288-1485

Araz Restaurant
11717 Moorpark
Studio City, CA   (818) 766-1336

Armen & Salpi M. East Cuisine
19014 Ventura Blvd.
Tarzana, CA   (818) 343-1301

Armenian Cuisine
742 W. Bullard Ave.
Fresno, CA   (209) 435-4892

Armenian Garden Cuisine
15532 Ward St.
Garden Grove, CA   (714) 775-4499

Armenian Gourmet
929 E. Duane
Sunnyvale, CA   (408) 732-3910

Armenian Kitchen
1646 Victoria Park Ave.
Scarborough,   (416) 757-7722

Armitage Restaurant
1767 N. Vermont Ave.
Hollywood, CA   (213) 664-5467

Arpa Best Food
801 S. Glendale Ave.
Glendale, CA   (818) 507-1626

Arsen's Flaming Shish Kebab
1205 Burlington Mall
Burlington, MA   (617) 273-3800

Arto's Coffee Shop
645 S. Hill St.
Los Angeles, CA   (213) 627-1970

At Our Place
2527 Broadway
New York, NY   (212) 864-1410

Athenian Gardens
1835 N. Cahuenga Blvd.
Hollywood, CA   (213) 469-7038

Athenian Gardens Restaurants
3731 India St.
San Diego, CA   (619) 295-0812

Athenian Gyros
241 N. Glendale Ave.
Glendale, CA   (818) 240-3631

Athens Market
109 W. "F" St.
San Diego, CA   (619) 234-1955

Atilla's Restaurant
2705 Columbia Pike
Arlington, VA   (703) 920-4900

Avegerinos
153 E. 53rd St.
New York, NY   (212) 688-8828

B.M.G. Restaurant
2062 Curtner Ave.
San Jose, CA   (408) 559-7330

Baba Kabob
5831 Leesburg Pike
Falls Church, VA

Babouch Moroccan Restaurant
810 S. Gaffey St.
San Pedro, CA   (310) 831-0246

Baccarat Night Club
4449 Van Nuys Blvd.
Sherman Oaks, CA   (818) 784-3300

Baccarat Restaurant
1092 E. El Camino Road
Sunnyvale, CA   (408) 261-1234

Bacchus Restaurant
1827 Jefferson Place, N.W.
Washington, DC

Bacchus Restaurant
7945 Norfolk Ave.
Bethesda, MD   (301) 657-1722

Bahar Restaurant
148 W. Maple Ave.
Vienna, VA   (703) 242-2427

Balkan Armenian Restaurant
129 E. 27th St.
New York, NY   (212) 689-7925

Bamian Restaurant
3320 "M" Street N.W.
Washington, DC   (202) 338-1896

Bamiyan Restaurant
3320 "M" St., N.W.
Washington, DC

Bamiyan Restaurant
300 King St.
Alexandria, VA   (703) 548-9006

Barmaky Restaurant
838 S. Glendale Ave.
Glendale, CA   (818) 240-6133

104-Food Marketplace — Ethnic Cookbooks

Bay Bistro
43 S. "B" St.
San Mateo, CA   (415) 347-8686

Bazarcheh Restaurant
8849 Beverly Blvd.
Beverly Hills, CA   (310) 273-7420

Bel Age Restaurant
1020 San Vicente Blvd.
W. Hollywood, CA   (310) 854-6247

Ben's International
18420 Ventura Blvd.
Tarzana, CA   (818) 705-2816

Bennie's
37 7th Ave.
New York, NY   (212) 633-2044

Betty's Place Restaurant
18120 Parthenia
Northridge, CA   (818) 775-1281

Beverly Hills Kabab (Firouz)
268 S. La Cienega Blvd.
Beverly Hills, CA   (310) 657-6257

Bisoutoun Restaurant
7545 Reseda Blvd.
Reseda, CA   (818) 434-5115

Bistro-Metro Restaurant
107-21 Metropolitan Ave.
Forest Hills, NY   (718) 263-5444

Black Orchid Restaurant
7410 Little River Turnpike
Annandale, VA   (703) 941-4400

Black Sea Restaurant
448 N. Fairfax Ave.
Los Angeles, CA   (213) 653-2090

Bob Corey's Flaming
1719 S. 13th St.
Terre Haute, IN

Bobby Kebobby
54-19 108th St.
Forest Hills, NY   (718) 263-3700

Bobby Kebobby
252 W. 38th St.
New York, NY   (212) 840-3700

Bobby Keboby
252 W. 38th St.
New York, NY   (212) 840-3700

Bourock
172 Atlantic Ave.
New York, NY   (718) 624-9614

Brashov Restaurant
1301 N. Vermont Ave.
Hollywood, CA   (213) 660-0309

Bread & Kabob
3407 Payne St.
Falls Church, VA   (703) 845-2900

Broiler
10800 W. Pico Blvd.
Los Angeles, CA   (310) 470-0525

Burger Continental
535 S. Lake Ave.
Pasadena, CA   (818) 792-6634

Byblos A Lebanese Cuisine
1964 Westwood Blvd.
Los Angeles, CA   (213) 475-9558

Byblos Deli & Sandwiches
129 W. Chapman
Orange, CA   (714) 538-7180

Byblos Middle Eastern Cuisine
6887 Orchard Lake Rd
West Bloomfield, MI   (313) 932-3770

Byblos Middle Eastern Cuisine
12967 Woodward
Highland Park, MI   (313) 867-0923

Byblos Restaurant
200 E. 39th Street
New York, NY   (212) 687-0808

Byblos on the Boardwalk
6887 Orchard Lake Road
W. Bloomfield, MI   (313) 932-3770

Cafe Al Dente
485 Sacramento St.
San Francisco, CA   (415) 772-8933

Cafe Karnak
1608 Mayfair
Orange, CA   (714) 997-8323

Cafe Markarian
510 S. Glenoaks Blvd.
Burbank, CA   (818) 567-0170

Cafe Mediterranean
10151 Riverside Dr.
Burbank, CA   (818) 769-0865

Cafe Rose
300 W. Broad St.
Falls Church, VA   (703) 532-1700

Calliope's
3958 Fifth Ave.
San Diego, CA   (619) 291-5588

Caravan Restaurant
741 8th Ave.
New York, NY   (212) 262-2021

Caravansary Gourmet Shop & Res
310 Sutter St.
San Francisco, CA   (415) 362-4641

Caravansary Restaurants & Deli
2263 Chestnut St.
San Francisco, CA   (415) 921-3466

Caroussel Restaurant
5112 Hollywood Blvd.
Hollywood, CA   (213) 660-8060

Casa Blanca
1123 N. Vine # 2
Hollywood, CA   (213) 466-3353

Casa d'Mama
7422 Little River Turnpike
Annandale, VA   (703) 256-3780

Casablanca
1504 King St.
Alexandria, VA   (703) 549-6464

Casablanca International
1123 N. Vine Street
Hollywood, CA   (213) 467-8230

Casablanca Restaurant
979 San Pablo Ave.
Albany, CA   (510) 525-2000

Casbah Armenian Restaurant
514 W. Diversey
Chicago, IL   (312) 935-7570

Caspian Persian Cuisine
1063 E. El Camino Real
Sunnyvale, CA   (408) 248-6332

Caspian Regional Cuisine
1063 E. El Camino Road
Sunnyvale, CA   (408) 248-6332

Caspian Restaurant
14130 Culver Dr.
Irvine, CA   (714) 651-8454

Caspian Tea Room
4801 Massachusetts Ave. N.W.
Washington, DC   (202) 244-6363

Cazablanca Restaurant
131 45th St.
New York, NY   (212) 599-0899

Cedars of Lebanon
39 E. 30th St.
New York, NY   (212) 725-9251

Ethnic Cookbooks

Food Marketplace-105

Chandelier Restaurant
7271 Harwin
Houston, TX   (713) 785-5855

Charleys Famous Hamburger
8213 Broadway
Lemon Grove, CA   (714) 460-2690

Charlie Kabob
129 Santa Monica Place
Santa Monica, CA   (213) 393-5535

Chatanoga Restaurant
2725 El Camino Real
Santa Clara, CA   (408) 241-1200

Chayka Restaurant
4953 Hollywood Blvd.
Hollywood, CA   (213) 660-3739

Chef's Corner
3430 Foothill Blvd.
La Crescenta, CA   (818) 249-3539

Chelokababi
1236 Wolfe Road
Sunnyvale, CA   (408) 737-1222

Chez Ali Baba Restaurant
201 Rachel East
Montreal,   (514) 982-9393

Chez Momo
48 MacDougal St.
New York, NY   (212) 979-8588

Chez Nassons Restaurant
5115 St. Laurent
Montreal,   (514) 276-2719

Choopan Kabab House
46 Kissena Blvd.
Flushing, NY   (718) 886-0786

Cio-Ce-Pol Restaurant
1773 Westwood Blvd.
Los Angeles, CA   (310) 479-5160

Club 44 Night Club
811 E. Colorado St.
Glendale, CA   (818) 241-0215

Club Cafe
Falls Church, VA   (703) 476-8737

Club Tehran
12229 Ventura Blvd.
Studio City, CA   (818) 985-5800

Colbeh Iran
7240 Reseda Blvd.
Reseda, CA   (818) 344-2300

Colbeh Restaurant
75 N. Station Plaza
Great Neck, NY   (516) 466-8181

Country Manor
6975 Promway Ave.
N. Canton, OH   (216) 499-0070

Crystal Restaurant
18509 Victory Blvd.
Van Nuys, CA   (818) 776-9191

Cuisine on the Green
1000 Las Lomas Road
Duarte, CA   (818) 359-3388

Culmore Restaurant
6037 Leesburg Pike
Falls Church, VA   (703) 820-7171

Dar Es Salam
3056 "M" St. N.W.
Georgetown, DC   (202) 342-1925

Dar Maghreb Restaurant
7651 Sunset Blvd.
Hollywood, CA   (213) 876-7651

Darband Kabobi
5670 Hillcroft
Houston, TX   (713) 975-8350

Darband Restaurant
158 Middle Neck Road
Great Neck, NY   (516) 829-0030

Darband Restaurant
138 S. Beverly Dr.
Beverly Hills, CA   (310) 859-8585

Dariush Restaurant
15651 Hawthorne Blvd.
Lawndale, CA   (310) 644-8672

Darvish Restaurant
980 La Cienega Blvd.
Los Angeles, CA   (310) 659-1112

Darvish Restaurants
1549 Bloor St. W.
Toronto,   (416) 535-5530

Darya Restaurant
1840 N. Tustin Ave.
Orange, CA   (714) 921-2773

Darya Restaurant
3316 S. Bristol
Santa Ana, CA   (714) 557-6600

David Restaurant
5151 Stars and Stripes Dr.
Santa Clara, CA   (408) 986-1666

Demmas Shish Kebob
5806 Hampton Ave.
St. Louis, MO

Dimitri's Greek Cuisine
145 S. Highway
Solana Beach, CA   (619) 259-0733

Downtown Kabab
934 S. Los Angeles St.
Los Angeles, CA   (213) 612-0222

Dunes Motel Restaurant
5625 Sunset Blvd.
Hollywood, CA   (213) 467-5171

Eaquire Souvlaki & Steak
2581 Victoria Park Ave.
Scarborough,   (416) 497-0618

El Greco's Restaurant
520 N. Park Ave.
Tucson, AZ   (601) 623-2398

El Morocco Restaurant
100 Wall St.
Worcester, MA   (508) 756-7117

El Morocco Restaurnat
8222 Santa Monica Blvd.
Hollywood, CA   (213) 654-9550

El Nejme Armenian Restaurant
4346 Tujunga
N. Hollywood, CA   (818) 505-8255

El-Ajami Restaurant
105 W. Arrow Hwy.
San Demas, CA   (714) 394-0681

El-Comedor
1161 N. Vermont Ave.
Hollywood, CA   (213) 661-5309

El-Manara
7111 3rd Ave.
New York, NY   (718) 745-2284

Elena's Greek Armenian Resta.
1000 S. Glendale Ave.
Glendale, CA   (818) 241-5730

Estia
308 E. 86th St.
New York, NY   (212) 628-9100

Fairouz Greek & Lebanese Cuis.
3166 Midway Dr.
San Diego, CA   (619) 225-0308

Falafel Arax
5101 Santa Monica Blvd.
Hollywood, CA   (213) 663-9687

106-Food Marketplace

Ethnic Cookbooks

Falafel Palace
9255 Reseda Blvd.
Northridge, CA   (818) 993-0734

Falafel'N'Stuff
1586 First Ave.
New York, NY   (212) 879-7023

Famous Kabob
1290 Fulton Ave.
Sacramento, CA   (916) 483-1700

Fantazia Restaurant
7931 E. Firestone Blvd.
Downey, CA   (310) 869-5733

Farhad Restaurant
801 W. Hamilton Ave.
Campbell, CA   (408) 866-1588

Farid Restaurant
635 S. Broadway
Los Angeles, CA   (213) 622-0808

Father Nature's Cafe
19535 Ventura Blvd.
Tarzana, CA   (818) 344-7758

Fettoosh
3277 "M" St., N.W.
Washington, DC   (202) 342-1199

Fiddler's Coffee Shop
6009 W. Third St.
Los Angeles, CA   (213) 931-8167

Finney's Cafeteria
217 W. Sixth St.
Los Angeles, CA   (213) 688-0995

Flames Shahrzad Restaurant
1422 Westwood Blvd.
Los Angeles, CA   (213) 470-3242

Flaming Pit
18701 N. Frederick Road
Gaithersburg, MD   (301) 977-0700

Food Factory
4221 N. Fairfax
Arlington, VA

Galleon & Constandina's Cuisin
540 S. Vermont Ave.
Los Angeles, CA   (213) 388-9478

Gambino Restaurant
25542 Jeronimo Road
Los Alisos, CA   (714) 458-2249

Garo's Snack Bar
220 W. Fifth St.
Los Angeles, CA   (213) 689-4832

Garson Restaurant
2926 HillCroft
Houston, TX   (713) 781-0400

George's Shish Kebab
4061 N. Blackstone Ave.
Fresno, CA   (209) 228-8556

George's Shish Kebab # 2
2405 Capitol St.
Fresno, CA   (209) 264-9433

George's Townhouse
1205 28th St., N.W.
Washington, DC   (202) 342-2278

Georgetown Cafe
1623 Wisconsin Ave. N.W.
Washington, DC   (202) 333-0215

Georgia's Greek Cuisine
3641 Madison Ave.
San Diego, CA   (619) 284-1007

Golden Steer Steak House
306 W. Sahara Ave.
Las Vegas, NV   (702) 384-4470

Golestan Persian Cuisine
22458 Ventura Blvd.
Woodland Hills, CA   (818) 347-0577

Golestan Restaurant
1398 Westwood Blvd.
Los Angeles, CA   (213) 470-3867

Gondola Restaurant
2502 W. 63rd St.
Chicago, IL   (312) 737-0386

Gondole Restaurant
2871 W. Lincoln Ave.
Anaheim, CA   (714) 952-1185

Good Earth Foods
1336 First Ave.
New York, NY

Gorky's Restaurant
536 E. 8th St.
Los Angeles, CA   (213) 627-4060

Gower Gulch Grill
6124 Sunset Blvd.
Hollywood, CA   (213) 463-5530

Grandia Palace
5657 Melrose Ave.
Hollywood, CA   (213) 462-8628

Grapeleaf Restaurant, The
4031 Balboa St.
San Francisco, CA   (415) 668-1515

Great Greek Restaurant
13362 Ventura Blvd.
Sherman Oaks, CA   (818) 905-5250

Great Gyros, the
459 La Jolla Village Dr.
La Jolla, CA   (619) 696-0424

Grecian Cuisine
4325 Glencoe Ave.
Marina Del Rey, CA   (213) 822-6221

Grecian Paradise
18928 Ventura Blvd.
Tarzana, CA   (818) 705-0633

Grecian Village
3707 Cahuenga Blvd.
Studio City, CA   (818) 508-0884

Greek American Foods
223 Valencia St.
San Francisco, CA   (415) 864-0978

Greek Connection, The
401 N. La Cienega Blvd.
Los Angeles, CA   (310) 659-2271

Greek Corner Restaurant # 1
5844 Montezuma Road
San Diego, CA   (619) 287-3303

Greek Corner Restaurant # 2
13185 Black Mtn.
San Diego, CA   (619) 484-9197

Greek Island Delights
2218 Fashion Island Blvd.
San Mateo, CA   (415) 341-3383

Greek Islands Restaurants
2930 N. 16th St.
Phoenix, AZ   (602) 274-3515

Greek Market & Restaurants
9034 Tampa Ave.
Northridge, CA   (818) 349-9689

Greek Town Restaurnat
431 "E" Street
San Diego, CA   (619) 232-0461

Greek Village
1016 Lexington Ave.
New York, NY   (212) 288-7378

Gyro Time Restaurant
5547 W. Manchester Ave.
Westchester, CA   (310) 337-1728

Habib Restaurant
1401 S. Las Vegas Blvd.
Las Vegas, NV   (702) 388-9119

Ethnic Cookbooks   Food Marketplace-107

Hagop Shish Kebab
454 Palisade Ave.
Cliffside Park, NJ   (201) 943-9817

Hagop's Restaurant
14228 Ventura Blvd.
Sherman Oaks, CA   (818) 995-8254

Haji Baba Restaurant
Tempe, AZ   (602) 894-2442

Hajji Baba Night Club
824 Camino De La Reina
San Diego, CA   (619) 298-2010

Hajji Baba Pasargad Restaurant
8449 40th St.
Miami, FL   (305) 221-7929

Hakim Afghan Restaurant
808 King St.
Alexandria, VA

Hassan's Restaurnats
3325 Newport Blvd.
Newport Beach, CA   (714) 675-4668

Hatam Restaurant
1112 N. Brookhurst
Anaheim, CA   (714) 991-6262

Hatam Restaurant
1115 3rd St.
San Rafael, CA   (415) 454-8888

Hollywood Kabob Restaurant
6056 Hollywood Blvd.
Hollywood, CA   (213) 463-4363

Hollywood Restaurant
99 Queens Blvd.
Forest Hills, NY   (718) 275-5200

Holy Land Restaurants
1801 Lawrence Ave. E.
Scarborough,   (416) 755-0137

House of Kabab
2110 W. Whittier Blvd.
Montebello, CA   (213) 721-8956

House of Shish Kebab
5406 N. Blackstone Ave.
Fresno, CA   (209) 432-0700

IZI Deli
4821 E. Bullard Ave.
Fresno, CA   (209) 251-6599

International Cuisine Caterer
6 Purdue Ct.
Rockville, MD

International Deli
4810 Fulton Ave.
Sherman Oaks, CA   (818) 990-4916

International Foods
4724 N. Kedzie Ave.
Chicago, IL   (312) 478-8643

Islamic Food Restaurant
692 S. Vermont Ave.
Los Angeles, CA   (213) 386-5332

Israeli Accents
11641 Boiling Brook Parkway
Rockville, MD

Javan Restaurant
11628 Santa Monica Blvd.
Los Angeles, CA   (310) 207-5555

Jerry G. Bishop's Greek Island
879 W. Harbor Dr.
San Diego, CA   (619) 239-5216

Jerusalem Restaurant
3815 S. George Mason Dr.
Falls Church, VA   (703) 845-1622

Joelle's Kabobland Deli
208 S. Central Ave.
Glendale, CA   (818) 500-3962

Jonelle's Restaurants & Cater.
108 Horace Harding Exp.
Flushing, NY   (718) 699-0500

Joseph's Cafe & Restaurants
1775 Ivar Ave.
Hollywood, CA   (213) 462-8697

Joseph's Place
1881 Steeles Ave. West
Downsview Ontario,   (416) 739-7221

Just Like Home Restaurant
1924 Irving St.
San Francisco, CA   (415) 681-3337

Kabab House (KababKhouneh)
1831 W. Glenoaks Blvd.
Glendale, CA   (818) 243-7001

Kabab Royal
2646 Dupont Dr.
Irvine, CA   (714) 476-9901

Kababi-e-Nader
48 E. 29th St.
New York, NY   (212) 683-4833

Kabob House
2062 Curtner Ave.
San Jose, CA   (408) 559-7330

Kabob House
1300 Galindo
Concord, CA   (510) 671-6969

Kabob No. 1
755 Voltaire St.
San Diego, CA   (619) 222-2656

Kabob's Palace
310 N. Citrus Ave.
Azusa, CA   (818) 334-6759

Kaboby Restaurant #1
1133 Westwood Blvd.
Los Angeles, CA   (310) 208-9208

Kaboby Restaurant #2
15301 Ventura Blvd.
Sherman Oaks, CA   (818) 501-9830

Kabul Afghani Cuisine
1153 E. Jericho
Huntington, NY   (516) 549-5506

Kabul Caravan
1725 Wilson Blvd.
Arlington, VA   (703) 522-8394

Kabul Kabab House
42 Main St.
Flushing, NY   (718) 461-1919

Kabul West
4871 Cordell Ave.
Bethesda, MD   (301) 986-8566

Kachin's Place
707 S. Broadway
Los Angeles, CA   (213) 622-5621

Kanani's Omar Khayyam Rest.
1453 York Ave.
New York, NY   (212) 879-5353

Karoon Restaurant
1608 E. Mayfair
Orange, CA   (714) 997-8323

Karoun Armenian Restaurant
839 Washington St.
Newtonville, MA   (617) 964-3400

Karoun Restaurant
375 S. Bacom Ave.
San Jose, CA   (408) 947-1520

Kasra Restaurant
349 Clement St.
San Francisco, CA   (415) 752-1101

Kasra Skeweres
24 Ellis St.
San Francisco, CA   (415) 433-4747

108-Food Marketplace — Ethnic Cookbooks

Katmandu
1800 Connecticut Ave., N.W.
Washington, DC

Kavar Restaurant
4777 Santa Monica Blvd.
Hollywood, CA (213) 669-1260

Kazan Restaurant
6813 Redmond Dr.
McLean, VA (703) 734-1960

Kebob House
2800 Southeast St.
Crystal City, VA

Keiv Restaurant
1014 W. Beverly Blvd.
Montebello, CA (213) 722-3321

Key Club Restaurant
13130 Sherman Way
N. Hollywood, CA (818) 765-6600

Khaledian Brothers Deli
1014 E. Colorado St.
Glendale, CA (818) 246-5382

Khan Baba (House of Kabab)
20050 Vanowen St.
Canoga Park, CA (818) 887-5450

Khayyam's Chelo Kabab
1373 Solano Ave.
Albany, CA (510) 526-7200

Khyber Pass
4647 Convoy St.
San Diego, CA (619) 571-3749

Khyber Pass
3555 Rosecrans St.
San Diego, CA (619) 224-8200

Khyber Pass
2309 Calvert St., N.W.
Washington, DC

Khyber Pass
34 St. Mark's Place
New York, NY (212) 473-0989

Kolbeh Restaurant
1645 Wisconsin Ave. N.W.
Washington, DC (202) 342-2000

Kolbeh Restaurant
4501 E. Mission Bay Dr.
San Diego, CA (619) 273-8171

Koo Koo Roo Restaurant
8393 Beverly Blvd.
Los Angeles, CA (213) 655-9045

Koo Koo Roo Restaurant
3450 W. 6th St.
Los Angeles, CA (213) 383-6628

Kouche Restaurant
25381 Elisa Parkway
Laguna Hills, CA (714) 588-8999

Koutoubia Restaurant
2116 Westwood Blvd.
Los Angeles, CA (310) 475-0729

Krivaar Cafe
475 Pine St.
San Francisco, CA (415) 781-0894

La Boheme Greenwich Village
24 Minetta Lane
New York, NY (212) 473-6447

La Mediterranee
857 4th St.
San Rafael, CA (415) 258-9123

La Mediterranee
2936 College Ave.
Berkeley, CA (415) 540-7730

La Mediterranee
2210 Fillmore St.
San Francisco, CA (415) 921-2956

La Mediterranee
288 Noe Street
San Francisco, CA (415) 431-7210

Lave Lee Restaurant
12514 Ventura Blvd.
Studio City, CA (818) 980-8158

Layalina Restaurant
5948 Lankershim Blvd.
N. Hollywood, CA (818) 766-6575

Le Papillon Restaurant
460 S. Myrtle Ave.
Monrovia, CA (818) 357-7211

Lebanese Taverna Restaurant
5900 Washington Blvd.
Arlington, VA

Lebanese Taverna Restaurant
2641 Connecticut Ave.
Washington, DC

Leo's Place
35 J.F.K. St.
Cambridge, MA (617) 354-9192

Little Russia
1132 E. Broadway
Glendale, CA (818) 243-4787

Lucky's Restaurant
209 N. Verdugo Rd.
Glendale, CA (818) 242-8415

Luxe Restaurant
1100 Blair Mill Road
Silver Spring, MD (301) 565-2622

M & R International Cuisine
18525 Burbank Blvd.
Tarzana, CA (818) 705-6630

Madinah Restaurant Party Hall
401 S. Vermont Ave.
Los Angeles, CA (213) 383-9976

Magic Lamp
2565 E. Colorado Blvd.
Pasadena, CA (818) 795-8701

Mama Ayesha's
1967 Calvert St., N.W.
Washington, DC

Mamoun's Middle East Food
2698 E. Garvey Ave. S.
West Covina, CA (213) 339-3122

Manhattan Express
13710 Sherman Way
Van Nuys, CA (818) 997-3663

Marash Coffee Shop
Los Angeles, CA (213) 385-4302

Marathon Restaurant
1070 E. Broadway
Long Beach, CA (310) 437-6346

Maria's Greek Corner
409 W. Mapel St.
Vienna, VA

Marouch Hollywood
4905 Santa Monica Blvd.
Hollywood, CA (213) 662-9325

Marrakesh Restaurant
617 New York Ave., N.W.
Washington, DC

Marrakesh Restaurant # 1
13003 Ventura Blvd.
Studio City, CA (818) 788-6354

Marrakesh Restaurant # 2
1100 W. Coast Highway
Newport Beach, CA (714) 645-8384

Marrakesh Restaurant # 3
8240 Parkway Dr.
La Mesa, CA (619) 462-3663

Ethnic Cookbooks Food Marketplace-109

Marrakesh Restaurant # 4
634 Pearl St.
La Jolla, CA (619) 454-2500

Massis Armenian Food
1148 Glendale Galleria
Glendale, CA (818) 242-2333

Massis Armenian Sandwich
411 7th St.
Los Angeles, CA (213) 623-8302

Massoud Restaurant
504 E. 12th St.
Los Angeles, CA (213) 748-1768

Maykadeh Restaurant
470 Green St.
San Francisco, CA (415) 362-8286

Mediterranean Feast
19223 Ventura Blvd.
Tarzana, CA (818) 705-7961

Mediterranean Kabob Room
608 S. Myrtle Ave.
Monrovia, CA (818) 358-7177

Mediterranean Kitchen
1741 Winchester Road
Bensalem, PA (215) 245-5278

Mere Milia
3005 Boul Cartier O.
Chomedey Laval, (514) 681-8895

Mesopotamia Restaurant
1467 W. Montrose
Chicago, IL (312) 348-0654

Metropolis Restaurant
650 N. La Cienega Blvd.
Los Angeles, CA (310) 659-3333

Miami Restaurant
6113 Reseda Blvd.
Reseda, CA (818) 705-3322

Middle East Connection
916 W. Burbank Blvd.
Burbank, CA (818) 843-8339

Middle East Restaurant
472 Massachusetts Ave.
Cambridge, MA (617) 492-9181

Middle East Restaurant
645 E. Main St.
Alhambra, CA (818) 576-1048

Middle East Restaurant
2954 W. Ball Road
Anaheim, CA (714) 826-8700

Middle East Restaurant
1864 N. Allen
Altadena, CA (818) 797-2576

Middle East Restaurant #2
6749 Greenleaf Ave.
Whittier, CA (310) 696-2224

Middle Eastern Restaurant
910 E. Main St.
Alhambra, CA (818) 281-1006

Mihran's Restaurants
19560 Ventura Blvd.
Tarzana, CA (818) 342-2290

Mitaya Fine Cuisine
4350 Steeles Ave Ave. East
Markham, Ontario, (416) 940-6296

Moby Dick Cafe
7027 Wisconsin Ave.
Bethesda, MD

Molfetas
307 W. 47th St.
New York, NY (212) 840-9537

Molfetas Restaurants
370 Route 46 West
South Hakensack, NJ (201) 440-1771

Morae Restaurant
1441 E. Fletcher
La Place Shopping, FL (813) 977-6018

Moroccan Restaurant
4632 S. Maryland Parkway
Las Vegas, NV (702) 736-7655

Moroccan Star
205 Atlantic Ave.
New York, NY (718) 643-0800

Moscow Nights Restaurant
19655 Sherman Way
Reseda, CA (818) 349-5300

Moun of Tunis Restaurant
7445 Sunset Blvd.
Hollywood, CA (213) 874-3333

Moustache Cafe
8150 Leesburg Pike
Tysons Corner, VA (703) 893-1100

Mr. Big Burger
1516 N. San Fernando
Burbank, CA (818) 846-1406

Mr. Chicken
301 Esplanade Dr.
Oxnard, CA (805) 988-9645

Mr. Chicken
14853 Sherman Way
Van Nuys, CA (818) 786-1055

Mumms Restaurant
13075 Victory Blvd.
N. Hollywood, CA (818) 763-7087

Mustache Cafe
8150 Leesburg Pike
Alexandria, VA (703) 893-1100

Mustang Cafe
5005 L.B.J. 150
Dallas, TX (214) 306-4888

Nakeysa
1564 Wisconsin Ave., N.W.
Washington, DC

Nazarian's Courtyard
1000 8th Ave.
Watervliet, NY (518) 273-1104

Nea Hellas
31-15 Ditmars Blvd.
New York, NY (718) 278-7304

New Parthenon Restaurant
547 Monroe Ave.
Detroit, MI (313) 963-8888

New York Cafe
5519 Leesburg Pike Route 7
Falls Church, VA

New York New York Restaurant
4251 Burton Dr.
Santa Clara, CA (408) 727-4420

New York Restaurant
37 Broadway
Astoria, NY (718) 726-3254

Nicol's
17934 Ventura Blvd.
Encino, CA (818) 881-3099

Nizam's
323 Maple Ave.
W. Vienna, VA

Noura Restaurant
8479 Melrose Ave.
W. Hollywood, CA (213) 651-4581

Old Town Greek Cuisine
2448 San Diego Ave.
San Diego, CA (619) 291-5770

Old Town's Chicken
602 S. Myrtle
Monrovia, CA (818) 303-3393

110-Food Marketplace — Ethnic Cookbooks

Olive Paradis Restaurant
114 E. Fairfax St.
Falls Church, VA   (703) 534-4433

Omar Khayam Restaurant
7360 Center Dr.
Huntington Beach, CA   (714) 373-0810

Orchid Restaurant
3033 S. Bristol
Costa Mesa, CA   (714) 557-8070

Orient Express
1 Market St.
San Francisco, CA   (415) 957-1795

Ozzies Restaurant
7780 E. Slauson Ave.
City of Commerce, CA   (213) 726-0944

Ozzies Restaurant
512 E. Katella Ave.
Orange, CA   (714) 633-3280

Palette Restaurant
8290 Santa Monica Blvd.
Hollywood, CA   (213) 654-8094

Pamchal Restaurant
1389 Westwood Blvd.
Los Angeles, CA   (310) 473-0309

Pamir Cuisine of Afghanistan
1437 Second Ave.
New York, NY   (212) 734-3791

Pamir Cuisine of Afghanistan
85 Washington St.
Morristown, NJ   (201) 605-1095

Panjshir Restaurant
924 W. Broad St.
Falls Church, VA

Panos Char Broiler
16045 Victory
Van Nuys, CA   (818) 780-4041

Papa Garo's
1810 S. Catalina Ave.
Redondo Beach, CA   (213) 540-7272

Papa John's Restaurant
765 Rockville Pike
Rockville, MD   (301) 340-6970

Papa Pooche
8759 N. Glenoaks Blvd.
Sun Valley, CA   (818) 504-9086

Papa's Restaurant
2026 University Ave.
Berkeley, CA   (510) 841-0884

Papadakis Taverna Restaurant
301 W. 6th St.
San Pedro, CA   (310) 548-1186

Paradise Restaurant
1350 Grant Road
Mountain View, CA   (415) 968-5949

Paradise Restaurant
7141 Wisconsin Ave., N.W.
Bethesda, MD

Paradiso Restaurant
10800 W. Pico Blvd.
Los Angeles, CA   (310) 475-1427

Paros Restaurant
1117 N. Hobart Ave.
Hollywood, CA   (213) 469-2610

Pars Restaurant
21008 Hawthorne Blvd.
Torrance, CA   (310) 370-4838

Pars Restaurant
4790 Irvine Blvd.
Irvine, CA   (714) 832-8324

Pars Restaurant
352 El Camino Real
San Bruno, CA   (415) 871-5151

Pars Restaurant
10827 S.W. 40th St.
Miami, FL   (305) 551-1099

Pasadena Kabob House
2525 E. Foothill Blvd.
Pasadena, CA   (818) 795-3499

Pasha Restaurant
1516 Broadway
San Francisco, CA   (415) 885-4477

Pasha's Afghan Cuisine
1110 Torrey Pines Road
La Jolla, CA   (619) 454-9229

Pawinda Restaurnat
1110 Torrey Pines Road
San Diego, CA   (619) 454-9229

Payton Kabob
145 S. Verdugo Rd.
Glendale, CA   (818) 242-8776

Periyali
35 W. 20th St.
New York, NY   (212) 463-7890

Persepolis Restaurant
7141 Wisconsin Ave. N.W.
Bethesda, MD   (301) 656-9339

Perspolis Restaurant
1029 Blossom Hill Road
San Jose, CA   (408) 265-5090

Perspolis Restaurants
130 W. Katella Blvd.
Anaheim, CA   (714) 991-7600

Petit Cafe
55 Clement St.
San Francisco, CA   (415) 387-5266

Petrossian Restaurant
182 W. 58th St.
New York, NY   (212) 245-2214

Phoenicia Restaurant
343 N. Central Ave.
Glendale, CA   (818) 956-7800

Picasso's Restaurants
353 Massachusetts Ave.
Arlington, MA   (617) 648-2800

Pikapita
50 Massachusetts Ave., N.E.
Washington, DC

Pita Inn
3910 Dempster St.
Skokie, IL   (708) 677-0211

Plaka
165 Bleecker St.
New York, NY   (212) 674-9709

Pollo Clasico
9791 Lincoln Village Dr.
Sacramento, CA   (916) 369-8445

Pop's Restaurant and Grocery
8385 Leesburg Pike
Vienna, VA

Port of Athens Restaurant
12430 Riverside Dr.
N. Hollywood, CA   (818) 508-9486

Raffi's Place # 1
452 W. Stocker St.
Glendale, CA   (818) 241-9960

Raffi's Place # 2
211 E. Broadway
Glendale, CA   (818) 247-0575

Restaurant Asmar
162 Jean Talon Est.
Montreal,

Restaurant Georges
4231 Boul Samson
Chomedey,   (514) 681-8189

Ethnic Cookbooks

Food Marketplace-111

Reza Restaurant
808 S. Brookhurst
Anaheim, CA   (714) 778-2005

Ritza Restaurant
5468 Wilshire Blvd.
Los Angeles, CA   (213) 934-2215

Riviera Restaurants
1139 E. Broadway
Glendale, CA   (818) 500-8700

Roastin' Chicken
6255 Foothill Blvd.
Tujunga, CA   (818) 249-7607

Roberto's Restaurant
420 N. Azusa Blvd.
West Covina, CA   (818) 331-0606

Rose's Restaurant
8223 Canoga Ave.
Canoga Park, CA   (818) 716-5222

Rosicler Restaurant
24 W. Colorado Blvd.
Pasadena, CA   (818) 792-9700

Royal Kabab
2646 Dupont Dr.
Irvine, CA   (714) 476-9901

Royal Morocco
14510 Big Basin Way
Saratoga, CA   (408) 741-0224

Royal Perspolis Restaurant
362 N. Canon Dr.
Beverly Hills, CA   (310) 281-0777

Russian House
22864 Ventura Blvd.
Woodland Hills, CA   (818) 348-5112

Saam Middle East Restaurant
39 S. Raymond Ave.
Pasadena, CA   (818) 793-8496

Sabrina Middle East Restaurant
4325 S. Sepulveda Blvd.
Culver City, CA   (310) 398-2308

Saghi Restaurant
1724 N. Tustin Ave.
Orange, CA   (714) 974-3353

Sahar Restaurant
248 W. Foothill Blvd.
Azusa, CA   (818) 969-9150

Sahara Lebanese Cuisine
2401 Artesia Blvd.
Redondo Beach, CA   (310) 371-1533

Sahara Restaurnat
13536 Ventura Blvd.
Sherman Oaks, CA   (818) 995-4609

Sahara Room
626 E. Chula Vista
San Diego, CA   (619) 427-8880

Sako's Sandwich Shop
12000 E. Slauson Ave.
Santa Fe Springs, CA   (310) 693-1138

Salam International Market
3090 Aloma Ave.
Winter Park, FL   (407) 657-5560

Salar Restaurant
1240 S. Glendale Ave.
Glendale, CA   (818) 500-8661

Sally's Place
7809 3rd Ave.
Brooklyn, NY   (718) 680-4615

Salt & Peper (Felfel Namakie)
5621 Hillcroft
Houston, TX   (713) 783-9996

Samira's
6916 4th Ave.
New York, NY   (718) 745-2416

Sandpiper Inn, the
12800 Foxdale Dr.
Desert Hot Springs, CA   (619) 329-6455

Saray-e Ghalandar
7545 Reseda Blvd.
Reseda, CA   (818) 343-5115

Sasoon Restaurant
18970 Ventura Blvd.
Tarzana, CA   (818) 708-8986

Sassoon Restaurants
3255 N. Cedar Ave.
Fresno, CA   (209) 224-0577

Sayat Nova
157 E. Ohio
Chicago, IL   (312) 644-9159

Sayat Nova
20 W. Golf Road
Des Plaines, IL   (708) 296-1776

Sears Fine Food
439 Powell St.
San Francisco, CA   (415) 986-1160

Sevan Falafel
7605 White Oak Ave.
Reseda, CA   (818) 881-3909

Sevan Restaurant
415 Third Ave.
New York, NY   (212) 545-9538

Shahbaz Restaurant
5990 Pico Blvd.
Los Angeles, CA   (213) 936-3708

Shahrzad Restaurant
17547 Ventura Blvd.
Encino, CA   (818) 906-1616

Shahrzad Restaurant
13615 Ventura Blvd.
Sherman Oaks, CA   (818) 905-6363

Shalizar Restaurant
5640 Moreno St.
Montclair, CA   (714) 946-8481

Shalizeh Restaurant
14650 Roscoe Blvd.
Panorama City, CA   (818) 894-7557

Shalton Restaurant
414 W. 6th St.
Los Angeles, CA   (213) 891-1984

Shamshiri Restaurant
1392 S. Bascom Ave.
San Jose, CA   (408) 998-0122

Shamshiri Restaurant # 1
1916 Westwood Blvd.
Los Angeles, CA   (310) 474-1410

Shamshiri Restaurant # 2
5229 Hollywood Blvd.
Hollywood, CA   (213) 469-8434

Shamshiri Restaurant # 3
19249 Roscoe Blvd.
Northridge, CA   (818) 885-7846

Shamshiri Restaurant # 4
122 W. Stocker
Glendale, CA   (818) 246-9541

Shandiz Restaurant
45550 Montgomery Ave.
Bethesda, MD   (301) 961-8989

Shari Ghul-Ghula
512 S. Van Dorn St.
Alexandria, VA

Sheik Cafe
2664 5th Ave.
San Diego, CA   (619) 234-5888

Shekarchi Kabab # 1
1712 Westwood Blvd.
Los Angeles, CA   (213) 474-6911

112-Food Marketplace

Ethnic Cookbooks

Shekarchi Kabab # 2
155 11th St.
Los Angeles, CA   (213) 746-4600

Shepherd's Cove
11625 Paramount Blvd.
Downey, CA   (310) 862-9441

Shiraz Restaurant
15472 Ventura Blvd.
Sherman Oaks, CA   (818) 789-7788

Shish Kabob Cafe
4944 El Cajon Blvd.
San Deigo, CA   (619) 265-7800

Shish Kabob Express
14357 Victory Blvd.
Van Nuys, CA   (818) 787-6718

Shish Kabob Grill
935 Broxton Ave.
Los Angeles, CA   (213) 824-7739

Shish Kabob House
639 Pearl St.
La Jolla, CA   (619) 459-4016

Shish Kabob Palace
90 Middle Neck Road
Great Neck, NY   (516) 487-2228

Shish Kebab Restaurant
283 Main St.
Port Washington, NY   (516) 883-9309

Shish Kebab at Blvd. Cafe
378 Bergen Blvd.
Fairview, NJ   (201) 945-8702

Sholeh Restaurant
1440 Westwood Blvd.
Los Angeles, CA   (213) 470-9131

Shoumine Restaurant
7271 Harvin
Houston, TX   (713) 266-6677

Sibian's Restaurants
13010 E. Bailey
Whittier, CA   (310) 698-6808

Sibo, Abu-Salim Restaurant
81 Lexington Ave.
New York, NY   (212) 686-2031

Simon's Kohser Restaurants
8706 W. Pico Blvd.
Los Angeles, CA   (310) 657-5552

Simon's Kosher Restaurants
914 S. Hill St.
Los Angeles, CA   (213) 627-6535

Skewer's
1633 "P" St., N.W.
Washington, DC

Smorgasbord Restaurant & Cater
2423 Honolulu Ave.
Montrose, CA   (818) 248-9536

Sofi Restaurant
8030 W. 3rd St.
Los Angeles, CA   (213) 651-0346

Soultany Restaurant
1535 N. La Brea Ave.
Hollywood, CA   (213) 876-3398

Sphinx
1779 Westwood Blvd.
Los Angeles, CA   (310) 477-2358

Sports Grill
14130 Culver Dr.
Irvine, CA   (714) 551-6142

Squire
152 Middle Neck Road
Great Neck, NY   (516) 487-4032

Stagecoach Restaurant
44 Montgomery St.
San Francisco, CA   (415) 956-4650

Star Kabab
2907 E. 7th St.
Long Beach, CA   (310) 434-4848

Steak in a Sack
5811 Leesburg Pike
Falls Church, VA

Steven's Steakhouse
City of Commerce, CA   (213) 723-9856

Stoyanof's
1240 Ninth Ave.
San Francisco, CA   (415) 664-3664

Sultan's Kebabs Restaurant
1824 Harrison St.
Hollywood, FL   (305) 927-0002

Sultani Restaurant
1535 N. La Brea
Hollywood, CA   (213) 876-3389

Sunset House Restaurant
6270 Sunset Blvd.
Hollywood, CA   (213) 464-6555

Swedish Inn
19817 Ventura Blvd.
Woodland Hills, CA   (818) 884-7461

Sweety's Cafe
33 N. Station Plaza
Great Neck, NY   (516) 466-6260

Tabeer Restaurant
1401 University Blvd.
Langley Park, MD

Take-5
11555 Ventura Blvd.
Studio City, CA   (818) 509-0084

Tanouri Restaurant
1442 Westwood Blvd.
Los Angeles, CA   (213) 470-7003

Tarabya
613 Middle Neck Road
Great Neck, NY   (516) 482-0760

Tasty Hamburger
628 S. Hill St.
Los Angeles, CA   (213) 623-4798

Taverna
1401 Old Northern Blvd.
Roslyn, NY   (516) 484-8860

Taverna Vraka
23-15 31st St.
New York, NY   (718) 721-3007

Tavous Restaurant
7125 Columbia Pike
Annandale, VA   (703) 941-1451

Tea Room, Newport Beach
3100 Irvine Ave.
Newport Beach, CA   (714) 756-0121

Tea Sara # 2
1029 Blossom Hill Road
San Jose, CA   (408) 265-5090

Tea Sara Restaurant
1138 Saratoga Ave.
San Jose, CA   (408) 241-5115

Tehrani Restaurant
18 Hawthorne Blvd.
Redondo Beach, CA   (310) 214-2626

Thousand & One Nights
6720 White Oak Ave.
Van Nuys, CA   (818) 705-2666

Tip Top Cafe
8108 W. Third St.
Los Angeles, CA   (213) 653-6222

Topkapi Restaurant
3529 Chain Bridge Road
Fairfax, VA

Ethnic Cookbooks

Tripoli
6 Atlantic Ave.
New York, NY   (718) 596-5800

Uncle Paulie's
2146 Ventura Ave.
Fresno, CA   (209) 233-1111

Union Market Station Rest.
17 Nichols Ave.
Watertown, MA   (617) 923-0480

University Market Place
2604 Georgia Ave.
Washington, DC   (202) 667-2206

University Pantry Deli
7605 University Blvd.
Charlotte, NC   (704) 549-9156

Up All Night
4505 Sepulveda Blvd.
Sherman Oaks, CA   (818) 501-8661

Ureni Restaurant
4655 Hollywood Blvd.
Hollywood, CA   (213) 666-4686

Vahagen Armenian Cuisine
701 S. Central Ave.
Glendale, CA   (818) 241-1496

Vahe's Armenian Cuisine
356 Arsenal St.
Watertown, MA   (617) 924-9463

Van's Kabab
7759 Summitrose St.
Tujunga, CA   (818) 353-1239

Vanak Kabob Restaurant
18202 Imperial Hwy.
Yorba Linda, CA   (714) 993-0655

Vic's of San Carlos
1125 San Carlos Ave.
San Carlos, CA   (415) 595-2606

Villa Market
4801 Leland Ave.
Chevy Chase, MD   (301) 951-0062

Village Persian Restaurant
1722 N. Tustin Ave.
Orange, CA   (714) 282-1010

Violet's
1712 Colorado Blvd.
Eagle Rock, CA   (213) 255-4562

Virginia's Mid-East Cafe
2456 Orchard Lake Rd
Sylvan Lake, MI   (313) 681-7170

Wine Gardern Restaurant
30 Jack London Squar
Oakland, CA   (415) 835-4433

Wine Room Restaurant
5925 Franklin Ave.
Hollywood, CA   (213) 462-7672

Yafa Restaurant
637 S. Fairfax Ave.
Los Angeles, CA   (213) 934-7255

Yaldzlar Restaurant
566 3rd Ave.
New York, NY   (212) 557-0055

Yasaman Restaurant
19047 Bushard St.
Huntington Beach, CA (714) 968-7333

Yekta Deli & Grocery
82 Queens Blvd
Elmhurst, NY   (718) 335-6828

Yemeni Cafe
176 Atlantic Ave.
New York, NY   (718) 834-9533

Yerevan Lahmadjoun
420 Faillin
Montreal,   (514) 270-1076

Your Place # 1
354 N. Beverly Dr.
Beverly Hills, CA   (310) 858-1977

Your Place # 2
17301 Ventura Blvd.
Encino, CA   (818) 501-4646

Z
117 E. 15th St.
New York, NY   (212) 254-0960

Zabar's
2245 Broadway
New York, NY   (212) 787-2000

Zahle Restaurant
1465 Dudemaiane
Montreal,   (514) 336-3013

Zankou Chicken
1415 E. Colorado St.
Glendale, CA   (818) 244-2237

Zankou Chicken
5065 Sunset Blvd.
Hollywood, CA   (213) 665-7842

Zaven's
260 E. Chestnut
Chicago, IL   (312) 787-8260

Zeytun Restaurant
5125 Sunset Blvd.
Hollywood, CA   (213) 664-3000

Zorba B.B.Q.
Fashion Fair Shopping Ctr.
Fresno, CA   (209) 225-6774

Zorba's
1612 20th St., N.W.
Washington, DC

Zov's Bistro
17440 E. 17th St.
Tustin, CA   (714) 838-8855

Zygos Taverna
22-55 31st St.
New York, NY   (718) 728-7070

Food Marketplace-113

Ethnic Food Marketplace by Business Name in the U.S. and Canada

1-9

1 Stop Market	Canoga Park,CA	(818) 713-9165
10 to 10 International Cuisine	Glendale,CA	(818) 545-8506
1001 Night Restaurant	Atlanta,GA	(404) 851-9566
4 Seasons Produce	Glendale,CA	(818) 244-9698
4 Star General's Kebob	Los Angeles,CA	(213) 482-5240
7 Star Deli & Market	Granada Hills,CA	(818) 363-8577
7 to 7 Market	Torrance,CA	(213) 370-5707

A

A & A Food Market Inc.	Cambridge,MA	
A & A Foods	Ottawa,	(613) 737-2144
A & P Market	Glendale,CA	(818) 243-2709
A La Mode Ice Cream & Pastry	Springfield,VA	(703) 455-1055
A-1 Liquor & Jr. Mart	Glendale,CA	(818) 500-8471
A-Z Food Market	Great Neck,NY	(516) 829-3525
A. Marino Grocery	Omaha,NB	
A. Thomas Wholesale Meat Co.	Louisville,KY	(502) 587-6947
Abadan Bazar	Reseda,CA	(818) 345-7602
Abner's Broasted Chicken	Woodland Hills,CA	(818) 340-9466
Abou Khodor Restaurant # 1	Glendale,CA	(818) 241-5562
Abou Khodor Restaurant # 2	Hollywood,CA	(213) 461-5070
Acacia Grocery	Glendale,CA	(818) 956-5341
Ace Baking Co.	Denver,CO	(303) 296-7482
Acropolis Delicatessen Store	Asbury Park,NJ	(201) 988-3030
Acropolis Food Market	Washington,DC	(202) 829-1414
Acropolis Greek Restaurant	Hollywood,CA	(213) 463-8644
Acropolis Market	Detroit,MI	
Adelphia Delicatessen	Wilkes-Barre,PA	
Aditi Restaurant	Washington,DC	
Adnan	New York,NY	(718) 625-2115
Aegean Isles Restaurant	W. Los Angeles,CA	(213) 477-7991
Aesop's Tables	La Jolla,CA	(619) 455-1535
Afghan Bakery	Falls Church,VA	(703) 241-7855
Afghan Cuisine Restaurant	Hollywood,CA	(213) 483-8475
Afghan Grocery	Flushing,NY	(718) 461-7975
Afghan Kebab House # 1	New York,NY	(212) 307-1612
Afghan Kebab House # 2	New York,NY	(212) 517-2776
Afghan Market	Alexandria,VA	(703) 212-9529
Afghan Village Restaurant	New York,NY	(212) 979-6453
Agaty's Groceries	Pawtucket,RI	(401) 728-1660
Agop's Market	Glendale,CA	(818) 502-0924
Ahmad International	Sacramento,CA	(916) 451-2939
Ahwaz International Groceries	Anaheim,CA	(714) 772-4492
Aivazian Super Catering & Hall	Glendale,CA	(818) 241-8829
Akhtamar Armenian Restaurant	Sepulveda,CA	(818) 894-5656
Akhtamar Shish Kebab House	Cliffside Park,NJ	(201) 945-9850
Akoubian's Deli Grocery	Fountain Valley,CA	(714) 775-7977
Akropol Pastry Shop	Chicago,IL	
Akropolis Meat Market	New York,NY	(212) 728-1760
Al Hilal Halal Meat Shop	Houston,TX	(713) 988-4330
Al Nakheel	Vienna,VA	
Al's Italian American Deli	Montrose,CA	(818) 249-3031
Al-Ahram Supermarket	Anaheim,CA	(714) 527-9190
Al-Amir Lebanese Cuisine	New York,NY	(212) 737-1800
Al-Amir the Prince	Los Angeles,CA	(213) 931-8740
Al-Hilal Market	Los Angeles,CA	(213) 731-0868
Al-Khayam	N. Bergen,NJ	
Al-Madinah	Lomita,CA	(310) 325-4778
Al-Madinah	Garden Grove,CA	(714) 531-0321
Al-Manar Market	Daly City,CA	(415) 756-1133
Al-Manara Restaurant	Anaheim,CA	(714) 952-3239
Al-Maqha Restaurant	Washington,DC	(202) 342-6140
Al-Mimas Catering	Burbank,CA	(818) 845-5765
Al-Nogoom Grocery & Meat	Chicago,IL	(312) 918-1700
Al-Noor Market	Garden Grove,CA	(714) 839-5123
Al-Rasheed Grocery	Chicago,IL	(312) 925-4711
Al-Rawsha Restaurant	San Diego,CA	(619) 281-4259
Al-Salam Restaurant	Pomona,CA	(714) 593-5225
Al-Sham Restaurant	Anaheim,CA	(714) 220-0894
Al-Tayebat Market	Anaheim,CA	(714) 520-4723
Al-Wazir Restaurant	Hollywood,CA	(213) 856-0660
Al-Wazir	Glendale,CA	(818) 500-1578
Aladdin Kebob House	Duarte,CA	(818) 357-0512
Aladdin Restaurant	Glendora,CA	(818) 914-7755
Aladdin's Middle East Bakery	Cleveland,OH	(216) 861-0317
Aleksan Narliyan Grocery	Detroit,MI	
Aleman Meat & Grocery	Burbank,IL	(312) 425-2711
Alex Restaurant	Cliffside Park,NJ	(201) 945-4121
Alexander Bakery Corp	Miami,FL	(305) 858-4218
Alexander's Market	Malibu,CA	(310) 457-9776
Alexis Deli & Grocery	Montrose,CA	(818) 957-5687
Algiers Coffee House	Cambridge,MA	(617) 492-1557
Ali Baba Bakery	Minneapolis,MN	
Ali Baba Foods	West Covina,CA	(818) 810-5108
Ali Baba Market	Anaheim,CA	(714) 774-5064
Ali Baba Restaurant	Anaheim,CA	(714) 774-5632
Ali's Market	Redlands,CA	(714) 798-7454
Aljibani Halal Market	Diamond Bar,CA	(714) 861-3865
Almaden Bazar	San Jose,CA	(408) 268-6867
Aloonak Market	Los Angeles,CA	(310) 820-1844
Aloupis Company	Washington,DC	
Alpha Catering	Oxnard,CA	(805) 486-4554
Altira Wholesale, Inc.	Chicago,IL	(312) 476-0511
Alvand Market	Costa Mesa,CA	(714) 545-7177
Alvie's Restaurant	San Diego,CA	(619) 232-0529
Alvin's Scrumptious	San Francisco,CA	(415) 661-2888
Alwan Pastry Shop	Brooklyn,NY	
Amamchyan Market	Hollywood,CA	(213) 462-8675
American Armenian Grocery	Pasadena,CA	(818) 794-9220
American International Foods	Los Angeles,CA	(213) 225-4151
American Oriental Grocery	Southfield,MI	(313) 352-5733
American Pita Corporation	Houston,TX	(713) 776-3976
American Spice Trading Co.	Los Angeles,CA	(213) 664-2232
Amir Shish Kabob	New Hyde Park,NY	(516) 326-1010
Amir's Bakery	Paterson,NJ	(201) 345-5030
Amo's Produce & Grocery	Van Nuys,CA	(818) 904-9938
Amoretti	Chatsworth,CA	(818) 346-1454
Anahit Market	Sunland,CA	(818) 353-1968
Andre Market	Glendale,CA	(818) 548-5884
Andre Mini Kabob	Glendale,CA	(818) 247-1772
Andre' Market	Richardson,TX	(214) 644-7644
Andre's Cafe	Glendale,CA	(818) 549-9590
Andre's Restaurant	Fresno,CA	(209) 229-6353
Andrea's House of Pizza	Watertown,MA	(617) 924-1760

Ethnic Cookbooks

Business Names-115

Andrew's Delicatessen	Asbury Park, NJ	
Andros Dinner	Belmont, MA	(617) 484-7322
Andros Restaurant	Scottsdale, AZ	(602) 945-9573
Andy's Burgers	N. Hollywood, CA	(818) 985-9855
Angel Cafe	Los Angeles, CA	(213) 936-3708
Angel Candies, Inc.	City of Commerce, CA	(818) 961-4171
Angel's Catering	Glendale, CA	(818) 507-8518
Angel's Market	Tarpon Springs, FL	(813) 937-6731
Angelo Merlina & Sons	Seattle, WA	
Ani Grocery & Deli	Glendale, CA	(818) 241-7229
Ani Restaurant	Hollywood, CA	(213) 661-6393
Anoush Bakery	N. Hollywood, CA	(818) 766-2998
Anoush Deli & Grocery	Hollywood, CA	(213) 465-4062
Anoush Family Restaurant	Hollywood, CA	(213) 662-5234
Anthony Lazieh	Central Falls, RI	
Antoine's Pastry Shop	Newton, MA	
Antoine's Restaurant	La Jolla, CA	(619) 456-1144
Antone's Import Co.	Houston, TX	(713) 526-1046
Antonio Sofo & Son Import. Co.	Toledo, OH	
Antoyan Wholesale Produce	Santa Fe Springs, CA	(213) 693-6966
Apadana Market & Deli.	Westlake Village, CA	(818) 991-1268
Apadana Restaurant	Tempe, AZ	(602) 945-5900
Aphrodite Greek Imports	Falls Church, VA	(703) 931-5055
Apollo Greek Imports	Arlington, VA	
Apollo Market	Hawthorne, CA	(213) 644-8956
Ara Deli & Grocery	Glendale, CA	(818) 241-2390
Ara's Catering	Toronto,	(416) 495-9549
Ara's Pastry	Hollywood, CA	(213) 661-1116
Arabic Grocery & Bakery	Miami, FL	
Arabic Town	Highland Park, MI	
Ararat Armenian Restaurant	New York, NY	(212) 752-2828
Ararat Bakeries	Sanger, CA	(209) 875-7579
Ararat Bakery & Deli	Toronto,	(416) 782-5722
Ararat Bakery	Bayside, NY	(718) 225-3478
Ararat Catering	Glendale, CA	(818) 243-7468
Ararat Fruit Market	Hollywood, CA	
Ararat Middle Eastern Cuisine	Anaheim, CA	(714) 778-5657
Ararat Restaurant	Watertown, MA	(617) 924-4100
Ararat Sandwich	Los Angeles, CA	(213) 488-1499
Arax Deli	Montebello, CA	(213) 721-1986
Arax Market	Fresno, CA	(209) 237-5048
Arax Market	Watertown, MA	(617) 924-3399
Arax Restaurant	Scarborough,	(416) 288-1485
Araz Bakery	N. Hollywood, CA	(818) 753-0839
Araz International Grocery	Granada Hills, CA	(818) 368-8442
Araz Restaurant	Studio City, CA	(818) 766-1336
Ardem Grocery	Hollywood, CA	(213) 665-6984
Aremia Imported Foods	Grand Blanc, MI	
Aresh Grocery	Denver, CO	(303) 752-9272
Aresh Meat & Grocery	Burbank, CA	(818) 569-7405
Arian Del Mart	Sacramento, CA	(916) 363-6982
Arimes Market	Lexington, KY	
Arka Grocery & Record	Hollywood, CA	(213) 666-6949
Armand's Bake Shop, Inc.	Gaithersburg, MD	
Armani Bakery, Inc.	Glendale, CA	(213) 662-7479
Armen & Salpi M. East Cuisine	Tarzana, CA	(818) 343-1301
Armen Foods	New York, NY	(718) 729-3749
Armenia International Market	N. Hollywood, CA	(818) 760-4848
Armenian Bakery	Scarborough,	(416) 757-1559
Armenian Cuisine	Fresno, CA	(209) 435-4892
Armenian Delight	Broomall, PA	(215) 353-1981
Armenian Garden Cuisine	Garden Grove, CA	(714) 775-4499
Armenian Gourmet	Sunnyvale, CA	(408) 732-3910
Armenian Kitchen	Scarborough,	(416) 757-7722
Armenian Pizza	Philadelphia, PA	
Armenian Royal Hotel	Asbury Park, NJ	(201) 775-3475
Armitage Restaurant	Hollywood, CA	(213) 664-5467
Armtex	Pasadena, CA	(818) 797-0040
Arpa Best Food	Glendale, CA	(818) 507-1626
Arsen's Flaming Shish Kebab	Burlington, MA	(617) 273-3800
Arsen's Liquor and Deli	San Francisco, CA	(415) 673-4900
Arsham's Deli & Grocery	Hollywood, CA	(213) 660-7508
Artesia Market	Redondo Beach, CA	(310) 379-6995
Arthurs Fine Liquors	Albuquerque, NM	
Arto's Coffee Shop	Los Angeles, CA	(213) 627-1970
Arya Food Imports	Chicago, IL	(312) 878-2092
Arya International Market	San Diego, CA	(619) 274-9632
Arzan Market	Tustin, CA	(714) 544-6706
Asadur's Market	Rockville, MD	(301) 770-5558
Ashta Lebanese Ice Cream	Hollywood, CA	(213) 461-5070
Asia Center & Grocery	Falls Church, VA	(703) 533-2112
Assal Supermarket I	Vienna, VA	(703) 281-2248
Assal Supermarket II	Falls Church, VA	(703) 578-3232
Assan Caltex Foods	Canoga Park, CA	(818) 700-8657
Astoria Superette	Astoria, NY	(212) 728-8928
At Our Place	New York, NY	(212) 864-1410
Athenian Gardens Restaurants	San Diego, CA	(619) 295-0812
Athenian Gardens	Hollywood, CA	(213) 469-7038
Athenian Gyros	Glendale, CA	(818) 240-3631
Athenian Market	Northridge, CA	(818) 363-1160
Athens Bakery & Grocery Co.	Detroit, MI	
Athens Greek & Italian Deli	Dayton, OH	
Athens Grocery	Chicago, IL	(312) 454-0940
Athens Imported Food	Indianapolis, IN	(317) 632-0269
Athens Imported Foods & Wines	Cleveland, OH	(216) 861-8149
Athens Market	San Diego, CA	(619) 234-1955
Athens West	Anaheim, CA	(714) 826-2560
Athina Supermrche	Chomedey,	(514) 682-8010
Atilla's Restaurant	Arlington, VA	(703) 920-4900
Atlas Foods	Tampa, FL	(813) 933-5581
Atlas Market	Sherman Oaks, CA	(818) 784-2763
Atlas Oriental Pastry Shop	Buffalo, NY	
Attari Food- Deli and Spices	Sunnyvale, CA	(408) 773-0290
Attari	Los Angeles, CA	(310) 470-1003
Avakian's Grocery	Glendale, CA	(818) 242-3222
Avegerinos	New York, NY	(212) 688-8828
Avo's Bakery	Reseda, CA	(818) 774-1032
Ayoub's Fruits & Vegetable	Ottawa,	(613) 233-6417
Azar Kamarei Catering	San Jose, CA	(408) 245-6141
Aziz Import Co.	Dallas, TX	(214) 369-6982

B

B & E. Masion d'Aliments	N.D.G., Quebec,	(514) 482-0262
B.M.G. Restaurant	San Jose, CA	(408) 559-7330
Baba Aroush Nuts	Pasadena, CA	(818) 798-5338
Baba Kabob	Falls Church, VA	
Babouch Moroccan Restaurant	San Pedro, CA	(310) 831-0246
Babylon Bakery	Turlock, CA	(209) 634-8061
Babylon Bakery	Sun Valley, CA	(818) 767-6076
Baccarat Night Club	Sherman Oaks, CA	(818) 784-3300
Baccarat Restaurant	Sunnyvale, CA	(408) 261-1234
Bacchus Restaurant	Washington, DC	
Bacchus Restaurant	Bethesda, MD	(301) 657-1722
Badry's Catering	San Jose, CA	(408) 274-0738
Baggal Market	Rockville, MD	(301) 424-5522
Bagramian Hall	Montebello, CA	
Bahar Market	Toronto, Ontario,	(416) 256-1268
Bahar Market	Great Neck, NY	(516) 466-2222

116-Business Names

Ethnic Cookbooks

Bahar Restaurant	Vienna,VA	(703) 242-2427
Bahnan's Bakery & Market	Worcester,MA	(508) 791-8566
Bakery Afghan	Falls Church,VA	(703) 241-7855
Bakery Panos	Pasadena,CA	(818) 791-1311
Bakker Produce, Inc.	Griffith,IN	(219) 924-8950
Balboa Liquor	Sepulveda,CA	(818) 891-5985
Balian Ice Cream Co.	Los Angeles,CA	(213) 261-6111
Balian Markets	Los Angeles,CA	(213) 870-9219
Balian's Grocery	San Francisco,CA	(415) 664-1870
Balji's Deli	Costa Mesa,CA	(714) 631-0855
Balkan Armenian Restaurant	New York,NY	(212) 689-7925
Balkan Bakery	New York,NY	
Bamian Restaurant	Washington,DC	(202) 338-1896
Bamiyan Restaurant	Washington,DC	
Bamiyan Restaurant	Alexandria,VA	(703) 548-9006
Barmaki's Pastry Shop	Anaheim,CA	(714) 776-2621
Barmaky Restaurant	Glendale,CA	(818) 240-6133
Barsamian Grocery	Cambridge,MA	(617) 661-9300
Baruir's Oriental-American Gro	Sunnyside,NY	(212) 784-0842
Barzizza Brothers, Inc.	Memphis,TN	(901) 744-0054
Basmati Rice Imports, Inc.	Irvine,CA	(714) 474-4220
Basmati Rice of New York, Inc	Glendale,NY	(718) 628-1082
Bay Bistro	San Mateo,CA	(415) 347-8686
Bazaar Market	Whitestone,NY	(718) 762-4222
Bazaar Pars	San Jose,CA	(408) 985-8545
Bazaarak Persian/M.E. Grocer	Hayward,CA	(510) 581-7253
Bazar Market # 1	Los Angeles,CA	(213) 852-1981
Bazar Market # 2	Los Angeles,CA	(213) 274-9077
Bazar	Dallas,TX	(214) 702-9505
Bazarak (Victorian Liquor)	Hayward,CA	(415) 581-7253
Bazarcheh Restaurant	Beverly Hills,CA	(310) 273-7420
Beijing Islamic Restaurant	Montebello,CA	(213) 728-8021
Bel Age Restaurant	W. Hollywood,CA	(310) 854-6247
Bell-Bates Co.,Inc	New York,NY	(212) 267-4300
Ben Disalvo & Sons,	Madison,WI	
Ben's International	Tarzana,CA	(818) 705-2816
Bennie's	New York,NY	(212) 633-2044
Best Buy Market	Glendale,CA	(818) 244-3892
Best Chicken, the	Northridge,CA	(818) 772-7771
Betar's Market	Bridgeport,CT	
Better Life	Santa Ana,CA	(714) 547-0613
Betty's Place Restaurant	Northridge,CA	(818) 775-1281
Beverly Hills Kabab (Firouz)	Beverly Hills,CA	(310) 657-6257
Beverly Hills Meats	Beverly Hills,CA	
Beverly Hills Pita House	Beverly Hills,CA	(213) 659-8347
Beverly Market	Los Angeles,CA	(213) 278-6329
Bezjian's Grocery, Inc.	Hollywood,CA	(213) 663-1503
Bharat Bazar	La Puente,CA	(818) 912-2014
Bianca's Deli	Hollywood,CA	(213) 669-1829
Biblos International Foods	San Jose,CA	(408) 371-4829
Big Apple Market	La Puente,CA	(818) 918-2335
Big Bite Sandwiches	Glendale,CA	(818) 241-0687
Big Bite Sandwiches	Montrose,CA	(818) 957-5162
Bijan Bakery & Cafe	San Jose,CA	(408) 247-4888
Bijan Market	Santa Monica,CA	(213) 395-8979
Bijan Specialty Food	Ambleside, Vancouver,	(604) 925-1055
Bismillah Halal Meat Market	Langley Park,MD	(301) 434-0051
Bisoutoun Restaurant	Reseda,CA	(818) 434-5115
Bistro-Metro Restaurant	Forest Hills,NY	(718) 263-5444
Bit of Lebanon	San Carlos,CA	
Bitar's	Philadelphia,PA	
Black Orchid Restaurant	Annandale,VA	(703) 941-4400
Black Sea Restaurant	Los Angeles,CA	(213) 653-2090
Blikian Brothers Meat Co.	Hollywood,CA	(213) 665-4123
Blikian Brothers Meat Co.	N. Hollywood,CA	(818) 985-0201

Bob Corey's Flaming	Terre Haute,IN	
Bobby Kebobby	New York,NY	(212) 840-3700
Bobby Kebobby	Forest Hills,NY	(718) 263-3700
Bootleggers Liquor & Deli	Glendale,CA	(818) 240-6605
Boucouralas Brothers Super M.	Saco,ME	(207) 284-4314
Bourock	New York,NY	(718) 624-9614
Brashov Restaurant	Hollywood,CA	(213) 660-0309
Bread & Kabob	Falls Church,VA	(703) 845-2900
Bread & Pizz	Houston,TX	(713) 783-9898
Brentwood Village Market	Brentwood,CA	
Broadway Mart & Deli	Glendale,CA	(818) 243-3332
Broiler	Hollywood,CA	(213) 462-5101
Broiler	Los Angeles,CA	(310) 470-0525
Bruno Foods	Cincinnati,OH	
Bruno's Food Store	Birmingham,AL	
Bucharest Grocery	Hollywood,CA	(213) 462-8407
Buena Market	Buena Park,CA	
Burbank Bakery	Burbank,CA	(818) 841-7209
Burger Continental	Pasadena,CA	(818) 792-6634
Burger Time	Fresno,CA	(209) 432-4178
Buy Direct Food Warehouse	San Jose,CA	(408) 292-2211
Byblo's Bakery, Inc.	Jackson Heights,NY	(718) 779-6909
Byblos A Lebanese Cuisine	Los Angeles,CA	(213) 475-9558
Byblos Deli & Sandwiches	Orange,CA	(714) 538-7180
Byblos Middle Eastern Cuisine	Highland Park,MI	(313) 867-0923
Byblos Middle Eastern Cuisin	West Bloomfield,MI	(313) 932-3770
Byblos Restaurant	New York,NY	(212) 687-0808
Byblos on the Boardwalk	W. Bloomfield,MI	(313) 932-3770

C

C & K Importing Co.	Los Angeles,CA	(213) 737-2970
Cafe Al Dente	San Francisco,CA	(415) 772-8933
Cafe De Leon	San Francisco,CA	(415) 664-1050
Cafe Karnak	Orange,CA	(714) 997-8323
Cafe Markarian	Burbank,CA	(818) 567-0170
Cafe Mediterranean	Burbank,CA	(818) 769-0865
Cafe Paris	Glendale,CA	(818) 247-5787
Cafe Rose	Falls Church,VA	(703) 532-1700
Cafe de Jour (French Pastry)	Glendale,CA	(818) 247-9645
Cahalan Groceries	San Jose,CA	(408) 226-5992
Cake Castle	Cleveland,OH	(216) 381-5782
Calamata Groceries	Wilkes Barre,PA	(717) 823-7761
California Fruit and Produce	Watertown,MA	
California Market & Deli	Glendale,CA	(818) 244-9541
Calliope's	San Diego,CA	(619) 291-5588
Calvert Delicatessen	Washington,DC	
Campus Eastern Foods	Columbia,MO	
Canton Importing Co.	Canton,OH	
Capello's Import. & American	Dallas,TX	
Capitol Italian Grocery	Harrisburg,PA	
Caras Greek Product Co.	Columbia,SC	
Caravan Market	Gaithersburg,MD	(301) 258-8380
Caravan Restaurant	New York,NY	(212) 262-2021
Caravansary Gourmet	San Francisco,CA	(415) 362-4641
Caravansary Restaurant	San Francisco,CA	(415) 921-3466
Cardoos Int. Food Corp.	Providence,RI	(401) 272-9373
Cardoos Inter. Food Corp.	Hyannis,MA	(617) 775-7702
Cardullo's Gourmet Shop	Cambridge,MA	(617) 491-8888
Carlo Beverage Enterprises	Glendale,CA	
Carlo Washington Produce	Pasadena,CA	(818) 797-0017
Carmel Grocery	San Diego,CA	(619) 538-1069
Carmel Kohsher Market	Los Angeles,CA	(310) 479-4030
Carmen's Pastries	Glendale,CA	(818) 243-8761

Ethnic Cookbooks

Business Names-117

Carousel Restaurant	Hollywood,CA	(213) 660-8060
Carvel Ice Cream Store	Providence,RI	(401) 272-7412
Casa Blanca	Hollywood,CA	(213) 466-3353
Casa d'Mama	Annandale,VA	(703) 256-3780
Casablanca International	Hollywood,CA	(213) 467-8230
Casablanca Restaurant	Albany,CA	(510) 525-2000
Casablanca	Alexandria,VA	(703) 549-6464
Casbah Armenian Restaurant	Chicago,IL	(312) 935-7570
Cash Produce Co.	Birmingham,AL	
Caspian Catering Service	San Francisco,CA	(415) 581-7253
Caspian Meat Market	Orange,CA	(714) 998-8440
Caspian Persian Cuisine	Sunnyvale,CA	(408) 248-6332
Caspian Regional Cuisine	Sunnyvale,CA	(408) 248-6332
Caspian Restaurant	Irvine,CA	(714) 651-8454
Caspian Tea Room	Washington,DC	(202) 244-6363
Cater Craft Foods, Inc.	Montebello,CA	
Cater-Maid Bake Shop	Phoenix,AZ	
Catering By Arut	Hollywood,CA	(213) 668-9115
Catering by Herach & Ara	Montebello,CA	(213) 724-5622
Cazablanca Restaurant	New York,NY	(212) 599-0899
Cedar Foods	Downsview,	(416) 661-8999
Cedar Market	Royal Oak,MI	(313) 547-7856
Cedar's Bakery	Teaneck,NJ	(201) 837-4330
Cedars of Lebanon	New York,NY	(212) 725-9251
Central Deli	Fresno,CA	(209) 222-9327
Central Food Stores Inc.	Hackensack,NJ	
Central Grocery Company	New Orleans,LA	(504) 523-1620
Central Market	Glendale,CA	(818) 240-3450
Century Market	Los Angeles,CA	(310) 473-1568
Cerritos Produce	Anaheim,CA	(714) 995-1407
Chandelier Restaurant	Houston,TX	(713) 785-5855
Charleys Famous Hamburger	Lemon Grove,CA	(714) 460-2690
Charlie Kabob	Santa Monica,CA	(213) 393-5535
Charlie's Market	San Francisco,CA	(415) 681-9569
Chatanoga Restaurant	Santa Clara,CA	(408) 241-1200
Chayka Restaurant	Hollywood,CA	(213) 660-3739
Cheese Market, the	Knoxville,TN	(615) 525-3352
Cheese N Coffee	Albuquerque,NM	(505) 883-1226
Chef Bijan	Casselberry,FL	(407) 260-8855
Chef Diko Catering	Tujunga,CA	(818) 951-3799
Chef's Corner	La Crescenta,CA	(818) 249-3539
Chelokababi	Sunnyvale,CA	(408) 737-1222
Chelsea's Restaurant	Washington,DC	(202) 298-8222
Chelstoon Hall	Beverly Hills,CA	(213) 854-7272
Chez Ali Baba Restaurant	Montreal,	(514) 982-9393
Chez Momo	New York,NY	(212) 979-8588
Chez Nassons Restaurant	Montreal,	(514) 276-2719
Chicken City	Ridgefield Park,NJ	(201) 941-1772
Chicken Eatery	Sherman Oaks,CA	(818) 990-4445
Chicken Rotissary	Van Nuys,CA	(818) 781-0615
Choopan Kabab House	Flushing,NY	(718) 886-0786
Ciel International, Inc.	S. Hackensack,NJ	(201) 807-9329
Cio-Ce-Pol Restaurant	Los Angeles,CA	(310) 479-5160
City Lights Super Night Club	Hollywood,CA	(213) 489-7571
City Market	San Diego,CA	(619) 583-5811
Classy Catering	Sun Valley,CA	(213) 875-1030
Clover Leaf Market, Inc.	Southfield,MI	(313) 357-0400
Club 44 Night Club	Glendale,CA	(818) 241-0215
Club Cafe	Falls Church,VA	(703) 476-8737
Club Tehran	Studio City,CA	(818) 985-5800
Coffee Najjar, Inc.	Riverside,CA	(714) 276-4966
Colbeh Iran	Reseda,CA	(818) 344-2300
Colbeh Restaurant	Great Neck,NY	(516) 466-8181
Columbia Delicatessen	Washington,DC	
Commerce International	Miami,FL	(407) 678-6737

Connemara Food Mart	Latham,NY	(518) 785-7555
Constantine International	Montrose,CA	(818) 249-6574
Constantine's Delicatessen	Bayside,NY	
Consumer's Market	Youngstown,OH	
Continental Pastry Shop	Seattle,WA	
Cordoos International Food Cor	Dedham,MA	(617) 329-3230
Cottage Market	Watertown,MA	(617) 924-9718
Country Manor	N. Canton,OH	(216) 499-0070
Crest Delicatessen Ltd.	East Orange,NJ	
Crystal Restaurant	Van Nuys,CA	(818) 776-9191
Crown Market	Glendale,CA	(818) 956-0113
Crystal Palace	New York,NY	(718) 545-8402
Crystal Restaurant	Van Nuys,CA	(818) 776-9191
Cuisine on the Green	Duarte,CA	(818) 359-3388
Culinary Creations	,MA	(617) 893-6865
Culmore Restaurant	Falls Church,VA	(703) 820-7171

D

Da Giovanni Fruit Store	Montreal,	(514) 332-2550
Daglian's Grocery	Van Nuys,CA	(818) 786-5595
Daily Bread Bakery	Arlington,VA	(703) 920-2525
Dairy Fair Delicatessen	Hempstead,NY	
Damascus Bakery	Brooklyn,NY	(718) 855-1456
Damascus Imported Grocery	Hollywood,FL	(305) 962-4552
Damavand Market	Fremont,CA	(510) 793-2606
Dan's Super Subs	Woodland Hills,CA	(818) 702-8880
Dana Point Liquor & Deli	Dana Point,CA	(714) 861-6455
Danaian's Bakery	Hollywood,CA	(213) 664-8842
Daniel's Bakery	Brighton Center,MA	(617) 254-7718
Danielle's Bakery & Imported	El Cajon,CA	(619) 579-1999
Danny's Foods	Parkville,MD	
Danny's Fresh Meat & Produce	Van Nuys,CA	(818) 708-9775
Dar Es Salam	Georgetown,DC	(202) 342-1925
Dar Maghreb Restaurant	Hollywood,CA	(213) 876-7651
Darband Kabobi	Houston,TX	(713) 975-8350
Darband Restaurant	Beverly Hills,CA	(310) 859-8585
Darband Restaurant	Great Neck,NY	(516) 829-0030
Dariush Restaurant	Lawndale,CA	(310) 644-8672
Darvish Restaurant	Los Angeles,CA	(310) 659-1112
Darvish Restaurants	Toronto,	(416) 535-5530
Darvish	New York,NY	(212) 475-1600
Darya Restaurant	Santa Ana,CA	(714) 557-6600
Darya Restaurant	Orange,CA	(714) 921-2773
David Restaurant	Santa Clara,CA	(408) 986-1666
Day Mart Market	Tarzana,CA	(818) 996-8805
Ddroubi's Bakery & Imports	Houston,TX	(713) 988-5897
Del Mar & Co., Inc.	Detroit,MI	(313) 961-5504
Del-Pack Foods Abjad Corporat.	Chatsworth,CA	(818) 407-0887
Delaurenti's Italian Market	Seattle,WA	
Delicacies, Inc.	Cranston,RI	(401) 461-4774
Delphi Deli & Cheese Shop	Fort Lee,NJ	(201) 592-1697
Demmas Shish Kebob	St. Louis,MO	
Demoulas Super Market No.1	Andover,MA	
Demoulas Super Market No.10	Tweksbury,MA	
Demoulas Super Market No.11	Wilmington,MA	
Demoulas Super Market No.2	Chelmsford,MA	
Demoulas Super Market No.3	Haverhill,MA	
Demoulas Super Market No.4	Lawrence,MA	
Demoulas Super Market No.5	Lowell,MA	
Demoulas Super Market No.6	Lowell,MA	
Demoulas Super Market No.7	Methuen,MA	
Demoulas Super Market No.8	N. Andover,MA	
Demoulas Super Market No.9	Pinehurst,MA	

118-Business Names — Ethnic Cookbooks

Demoulas Super Market, Inc.	Salem, NH	(603) 898-5161
Derian Egg Co.	Los Angeles, CA	(213) 263-3447
Derian Foods	Los Angeles, CA	(213) 263-3447
Dick's Liquor & Deli.	La Jolla, CA	
Dimitri's Greek Cuisine	Solana Beach, CA	(619) 259-0733
Dimyan's Market	Danbury, CT	
Diran International Grocery	Van Nuys, CA	(818) 988-2882
Discount Produce Market	Reseda, CA	(818) 344-2959
Discount Produce Market	Sun Valley, CA	(818) 768-0091
Ditmars & 35th St. Market	Astoria, NY	
Do Do Inc.	Union City, NJ	(201) 863-3350
Dokan Market, Inc.	Bethesda, MD	(301) 657-2361
Domestic Foods	Ontario,	(613) 236-6421
Donikian's Market	Burlingame, CA	(415) 348-9297
Dorr's Liquor	Redondo Beach, CA	
Downtown Delicatessen	Portland, OR	
Downtown Kabab	Los Angeles, CA	(213) 612-0222
Droubi's Bakery & Grocery	Houston, TX	(713) 782-6160
Droubi's Bakery & Grocery	Houston, TX	(713) 790-0101
Droubi's Bakery & Grocery	Houston, TX	(713) 988-5897
Dudemaine Groceteria	Montreal,	(514) 334-8267
Dunes Motel Restaurant	Hollywood, CA	(213) 467-5171
Dvin Fresh Meat & Fish Market	Glendale, CA	(818) 547-4454
Dvin Market	Montebello, CA	(213) 725-7250
Dvin Market	Reseda, CA	(818) 344-0408

E

E & I International, Inc.	Rockville, MD	(301) 984-8287
E. Demakis & Co. Inc.	Lynn, MA	(617) 595-1557
Eaquire Souvlaki & Steak	Scarborough,	(416) 497-0618
East Trade Company	Charlotte, NC	
Eastern Lamejun Bakers	Belmont, MA	(617) 484-5239
Eastern Market	Modesto, CA	(209) 575-0344
Eastern Star Bakery	Miami, FL	(305) 854-6381
Easy Shop	New Britain, CT	(203) 225-7810
Economy Greek Market	Denver, CO	(303) 623-9682
Eden Market	San Leandro, CA	(510) 276-0212
Edna's Coffee & Grocery	Glendale, CA	(818) 243-0445
Eema's Market	Woodland Hills, CA	(818) 702-9272
Eilat Bakery # 1	Los Angeles, CA	(213) 653-5553
El Greco's Restaurant	Tucson, AZ	(601) 623-2398
El Morocco Restaurant	Worcester, MA	(508) 756-7117
El Morocco Restaurnat	Hollywood, CA	(213) 654-9550
El Nejme Armenian Restaurant	N. Hollywood, CA	(818) 505-8255
El-Ajami Restaurant	San Demas, CA	(714) 394-0681
El-Comedor	Hollywood, CA	(213) 661-5309
El-Manara	New York, NY	(718) 745-2284
Elat Market	Los Angeles, CA	(310) 659-0576
Elena's Greek Armenian Resta.	Glendale, CA	(818) 241-5730
Elias Kosher Market	Los Angeles, CA	(213) 278-7503
Ella Wendy	New York, NY	(212) 686-2349
Elliniki Agora Market	New York, NY	(212) 728-9122
Ellis Bakery	Akron, OH	
Elysee Pastry Shop	Los Angeles, CA	(310) 208-6505
Emil's Grocery	Saugus, CA	(805) 297-3184
Emir Grocery	Flushing, NY	
Empire Coffee and Tea Co.	New York, NY	(212) 564-1460
Encino Market	Encino, CA	(818) 343-7900
Epicurean International, Inc.	Rockville, MD	(301) 231-0700
Erebuni Grocery	Hollywood, CA	(213) 664-1700
Erivan Dairy	Oreland, PA	
Ernest Grocery Inc.	Baltimore, MD	
Estia	New York, NY	(212) 628-9100
Etoile French Bakery	Woodland Hills, CA	(818) 704-8461
Euclid Liquors	Upland, CA	
Euphrates Bakery Inc.	Watertown, MA	
Euphrates Grocery	Boston, MA	
European Deli Middle East	Concord, CA	(510) 689-1011
European Gourmet Deli	San Diego, CA	(619) 582-0444
European Grocery Store	Pittsburgh, PA	
European Importing Co.	Houston, TX	
European Sausages	N. Hollywood, CA	(818) 982-2325
Excel Market	Norfolk, VA	

F

Fairfax Family Market	Los Angeles, CA	(213) 852-1981
Fairouz Greek & Lebanese Cuis.	San Diego, CA	(619) 225-0308
Fairuz M.E. Grocery & Deli	Pomona, CA	(714) 596-2932
Faisal International Market	Riverside, CA	(714) 784-7111
Fakhr El Din	Los Angeles, CA	(213) 747-7839
Falafel Arax	Hollywood, CA	(213) 663-9687
Falafel Palace	Northridge, CA	(818) 993-0734
Falafel Roxy # 1	Los Angeles, CA	(818) 781-0805
Falafel Roxy # 2	Van Nuys, CA	(818) 781-0805
Falafel'N'Stuff	New York, NY	(212) 879-7023
Family Grocery	Pasadena, CA	(818) 791-1086
Family Market	Northridge, CA	(818) 349-2222
Family Meat Market & Produce	Chicago, IL	(312) 434-0095
Family Produce & Market	Anaheim, CA	(714) 821-7102
Famous Kabob	Sacramento, CA	(916) 483-1700
Fantazia Restaurant	Downey, CA	(310) 869-5733
Farah's Imported Foods	Jacksonville, FL	(904) 388-0691
Fard Candies	Torrance, CA	(310) 326-6012
Farhad Restaurant	Campbell, CA	(408) 866-1588
Farid Restaurant	Los Angeles, CA	(213) 622-0808
Farin Co.	Van Nuys, CA	(818) 376-0188
Farmer's Ranch	Montebello, CA	(213) 728-2615
Father Nature's Cafe	Tarzana, CA	(818) 344-7758
Fattal's Syrian Bakery	Paterson, NJ	(201) 742-7125
Fernando's Int. Food Mkt.	Miami, FL	(305) 566-3104
Fertitta's Delicatessens	Shreveport, LA	
Fettoosh	Washington, DC	(202) 342-1199
Fiddler's Coffee Shop	Los Angeles, CA	(213) 931-8167
Filippo's Italian Groc. & Liqu.	Phoenix, AZ	
Finney's Cafeteria	Los Angeles, CA	(213) 688-0995
Fish Town	Brooklyn, NY	
Five Star Food Distributor	Hayward, CA	(415) 782-4654
Five Stars Corp. Market	Falls Church, VA	(703) 256-6000
Five Ten Mini Market	Santa Clarita, CA	(805) 259-2680
Flames Shahrzad Restaurant	Los Angeles, CA	(213) 470-3242
Flaming Pit	Gaithersburg, MD	(301) 977-0700
Flamingo Grocery Inc.	Fort Lauderdale, FL	
Flor de Cafe Bakery	Glendale, CA	(818) 543-1401
Food Factory	Arlington, VA	
Food Mart	Orange, CA	(714) 538-9428
Food Stop Market	El Sobrante, CA	(510) 223-1111
Food of All Nations	Glendale, CA	(818) 956-5572
Foothill Market	Monrovia, CA	(818) 301-0089
Foothill Village Market	Glendale, CA	(818) 242-1257
Four Star Catering, Inc.	Montebello, CA	(213) 724-4162
Four Star Meat Co., Inc.	Wilmington, CA	(310) 549-2830
Foxies Delicatessen	Atlanta, GA	
Franklin Int. Grocery	Hollywood, CA	(213) 465-0214
Fred Bridge and Co.	New York, NY	
Freddie's Market	Niagara Falls, NY	(716) 285-8344
Freeport Italian American Deli	Freeport, NY	

Ethnic Cookbooks

Business Names-119

Freeway Market	La Crescenta,CA	(818) 249-6701
French Gourmet	La Jolla,CA	(619) 454-6113
Fresh " N" Green	La Puente,CA	(818) 917-6189
Fresh Market	Burbank,CA	(818) 848-4742
Fresno Deli	Fresno,CA	(209) 225-7906
Friendly Grocery Company	New York,NY	(212) 923-2654
Fruits and Things	New York,NY	

G

G & A Grocery	Hazlet,NJ	(201) 264-0176
G & M Deli	San Francisco,CA	
G.B. Ratto & Co.Int. Grocers	Oakland,CA	(415) 832-6503
Gabriel Importing Co.	Detroit,MI	(313) 961-2890
Galanides, Inc.	Norfolk,VA	
Galanides-Raleigh Inc.	Raleigh,NC	
Galil Importing Corp.	Glendale,NY	(718) 894-2030
Galina's Deli	Chicago,IL	
Galleon & Constandina's Cuisin	Los Angeles,CA	(213) 388-9478
Gambino Restaurant	Los Alisos,CA	(714) 458-2249
Garden Produce	Glendale,CA	(818) 240-4821
Garden of Delights	New York,NY	
Gardullo's Gourmet Shop	Cambridge,MA	
Garine Deli & Grocery	Van Nuys,CA	(818) 786-0946
Garni Bakery	Willowdale,	(416) 492-7200
Garny Fruits & Nuts	Glendale,CA	(818) 242-9240
Garny Grocery	Burbank,CA	(818) 841-7965
Garo's Basturma	Pasadena,CA	(818) 794-0460
Garo's Snack Bar	Los Angeles,CA	(213) 689-4832
Garson Restaurant	Houston,TX	(713) 781-0400
Gary's Submarine Sandwich	N. Hollywood,CA	(818) 763-0886
Geary Wholesale Company	Hayward,CA	(415) 887-6797
Genoosi's Imported Foods	Columbus,OH	
George A. Nassaur	Vicksburg,MS	(601) 636-4443
George A. Skaff & Sons	Sioux City,IA	
George Malko	Brooklyn,NY	
George's Delicatessen	Atlanta,GA	
George's Food Market	S. Milwaukee,WI	(414) 762-1232
George's Middle East Market	Paterson,NJ	(201) 278-1771
George's Shish Kebab # 2	Fresno,CA	(209) 264-9433
George's Shish Kebab	Fresno,CA	(209) 228-8556
George's Townhouse	Washington,DC	(202) 342-2278
Georgetown Cafe	Washington,DC	(202) 333-0215
Georgia's Greek Cuisine	San Diego,CA	(619) 284-1007
Georgig's Bakery, Inc.	Hollywood,CA	
Georgio's Calif. Pizza & Pasta	Studio City,CA	(818) 985-1072
Giavis Market	Lowell,MA	(617) 458-4721
Ginger Grocer	Montclair,NJ	(201) 744-1012
Gino's World Food Mart	Spokane,WA	
Gira Market Int. Grocery	Alexandria,VA	(703) 370-3632
Girazian Fruit Co.	Kingsburg,CA	(209) 888-2255
Glen Elk Market	Glendale,CA	(818) 545-0325
Glendale 1st Produce	Glendale,CA	(818) 247-3730
Glendale Bakery	Glendale,CA	(818) 247-2966
Glendale Farmer's Market	Glendale,CA	(818) 507-8041
Glendale Fish & Meat Market	Glendale,CA	(818) 502-1800
Glendale House of Liquore	Glendale,CA	(818) 243-5855
Glendale Market	Glendale,CA	(818) 243-2554
Glenoaks Deli & Grocery	Glendale,CA	(818) 247-4021
Glenoaks Market	Burbank,CA	(818) 559-7508
Global Bakeries, Inc.	Pacoima,CA	(818) 896-0525
Goglanian Bakeries Inc.	Costa Mesa,CA	(714) 642-3570
Golchin Overseas Corp.	Sylmar,CA	(818) 896-6127
Golden Dream	Pasadena,CA	(818) 798-7952
Golden French Bakers	Glendale,CA	(818) 507-0039
Golden French Bakers	Van Nuys,CA	(818) 785-1184
Golden State Bakery	Hollywood,CA	(213) 666-6713
Golden Steer Steak House	Las Vegas,NV	(702) 384-4470
Golestan Persian Cuisine	Woodland Hills,CA	(818) 347-0577
Golestan Restaurant	Los Angeles,CA	(213) 470-3867
Gondola Restaurant	Chicago,IL	(312) 737-0386
Gondole Restaurant	Anaheim,CA	(714) 952-1185
Good Earth Foods	New York,NY	
Good Fast Pizza	Glendale,CA	(818) 500-0006
Good Fellow Produce	Glendale,CA	(818) 243-3745
Good Foods Market	Pasadena,CA	(818) 794-5367
Gourmet Affair	Cleveland,OH	(216) 397-1414
Gourmet Basket	McLean,VA	
Gourmet Bazaar	Honolulu,HI	(808) 923-7658
Gourmet Food & Beverage	San Francisco,CA	(415) 626-1847
Gourmet International Market	Herndon,VA	(703) 478-6393
Gourmet Market, Inc.	Washington,DC	
Gower Gulch Grill	Hollywood,CA	(213) 463-5530
Grandia Palace	Hollywood,CA	(213) 462-8628
Grapeleaf Restaurant, The	San Francisco,CA	(415) 668-1515
Great Greek Restaurant	Sherman Oaks,CA	(818) 905-5250
Great Gyros, the	La Jolla,CA	(619) 696-0424
Grecian Cave	New York,NY	(718) 545-7373
Grecian Cuisine	Marina Del Rey,CA	(213) 822-6221
Grecian Paradise	Tarzana,CA	(818) 705-0633
Grecian Phoenix Pastries	Chicago,IL	
Grecian Village	Studio City,CA	(818) 508-0884
Greek Agora and Deli	Hollywood,CA	(213) 462-3766
Greek American Foods	San Francisco,CA	(415) 864-0978
Greek American Grocery Co.	Miami,FL	
Greek American Grocery Store	Miami,FL	
Greek American Importing Co.	Richmond,VA	
Greek Armenian Deli	Downey,CA	(310) 862-4566
Greek Connection, The	Los Angeles,CA	(310) 659-2271
Greek Corner Restaurant # 1	San Diego,CA	(619) 287-3303
Greek Corner Restaurant # 2	San Diego,CA	(619) 484-9197
Greek House Importing Co.	Doweny,CA	(310) 862-1220
Greek Island Delights	San Mateo,CA	(415) 341-3383
Greek Islands Restaurants	Phoenix,AZ	(602) 274-3515
Greek Market & Restaurants	Northridge,CA	(818) 349-9689
Greek Pastries by Despine's	Milwaukee,WI	
Greek Place	Orlando,FL	(407) 352-6930
Greek Store Liberty Market	Kennilworth,NJ	(201) 272-2550
Greek Town Restaurnat	San Diego,CA	(619) 232-0461
Greek Village	New York,NY	(212) 288-7378
Green Field Market	Azusa,CA	(818) 969-4232
Green Market # 1	Los Angeles,CA	(213) 470-3808
Green Market # 2	Los Angeles,CA	(310) 276-9336
Grocery House Market	N. Hollywood,CA	(818) 503-1222
Gugasian Hall	Santa Ana,CA	
Gyro Time Restaurant	Westchester,CA	(310) 337-1728

H

H. & H. Grocers	Baltimore,MD	(301) 728-0022
H. Roth & Son	New York,NY	
HHH Distributors	Takoma Park,MD	
Habib Restaurant	Las Vegas,NV	(702) 388-9119
Haddad Bakery	Downsview,	
Haddy's Food Market	Charleston,WV	
Haddy's Prime Meats	Charleston,WV	
Hagop Shish Kebab	Cliffside Park,NJ	(201) 943-9817
Hagop's Restaurant	Sherman Oaks,CA	(818) 995-8254

120-Business Names

Ethnic Cookbooks

Haig's Delicacies	San Francisco,CA	(415) 752-6283
Haji Baba Middle Eastern Food	Tempe,AZ	(602) 894-1905
Haji Baba Restaurant	Tempe,AZ	(602) 894-2442
Hajji Baba Night Club	San Diego,CA	(619) 298-2010
Hajji Baba Pasargad Restaurant	Miami,FL	(305) 221-7929
Hakeems's Bakery & Grocery	Albuquerque,NM	(505) 881-4019
Hakim Afghan Restaurant	Alexandria,VA	
Halal Meat Market	Alexandria,VA	
Halal Meats Deli & Grocery	San Jose,CA	(408) 865-1222
Halalco	Falls Church,VA	
Hanoian's Liquors	Fresno,CA	(209) 233-7304
Hanoian's Market	Fresno,CA	(209) 233-7301
Hansen's Cakes	Tarzana,CA	(818) 708-1208
Harbor Liquor	Harbor City,CA	(310) 326-9554
Harry's Deli	Cleveland Heights,OH	
Hassan's Restaurnats	Newport Beach,CA	(714) 675-4668
Hassey Grocery Store	Lawrence,MA	(617) 686-6096
Hatam Restaurant	San Rafael,CA	(415) 454-8888
Hatam Restaurant	Anaheim,CA	(714) 991-6262
Hawthorne Market	Torrance,CA	(310) 373-4448
Heidi's Around the World Food	St. Louis,MO	
Hellas Baking Co.	Somerville,MA	
Hellas Greek Imports	Washington,DC	
Hellas Grocery Store & Pastry	Chicago,IL	
Hellenic-American Import	San Francisco,CA	
Heller's Baking Co.	Pasadena,CA	(818) 794-5422
Henry's B.B.Q. Chicken	Glendale,CA	(818) 242-8222
Henry's Delicatessen Inc.	Cranston,RI	
Hi "Hye" Market	Pawtucket,RI	(401) 728-1596
Hi Ho Market	Orange,CA	(714) 637-9525
High Meat Co.	Delano,CA	(805) 725-1125
Hillside Lodge	Tannersville,NY	(518) 589-5544
Hilton Pastry Shop	New York,NY	(212) 274-6399
Hinkley Market	Hinkley,CA	(619) 253-2315
Hollywood Deli & Jr. Market	Hollywood,CA	(213) 460-4373
Hollywood Kabob Restaurant	Hollywood,CA	(213) 463-4363
Hollywood Mart	Hollywood,CA	(213) 464-3566
Hollywood Meat Market	Hollywood,CA	(213) 467-7640
Hollywood Restaurant	Forest Hills,NY	(718) 275-5200
Holy Land Bakery & Grocery	Chicago,IL	(312) 588-3306
Holy Land Mini Market	Westminster,CA	(714) 839-9865
Holy Land Restaurants	Scarborough,	(416) 755-0137
Homa International Market	Los Alamitos,CA	(213) 596-9999
Homs'y Groceries	Dedham,MA	(617) 326-9659
Honolulu Jr. Market and Deli	Montrose,CA	(818) 249-2532
Hons Market	Van Nuys,CA	(818) 996-5553
House of Kabab	Montebello,CA	(213) 721-8956
House of Shish Kebab	Fresno,CA	(209) 432-0700
House of Yemen	New York,NY	(212) 532-3430
Hun-I-Nut Co.	San Jose,CA	
Hy Mart Deli	N. Hollywood,CA	(818) 506-7264
Hye Bakery	Montebello,CA	(213) 722-8706
Hye Center Market	Reseda,CA	(818) 701-7784
Hye Deli	Fresno,CA	(209) 431-7798
Hye Land Motel & Hotel	Tannersville,NY	(518) 589-5700
Hye Market & Deli	Glendale,CA	(818) 566-9942
Hye Middle Eastern Food Shop	New York,NY	
Hye Neighbor Market	Panorama City,CA	(818) 994-4592
Hye Quality Bakery	Fresno,CA	(209) 445-1511

I

IZI Deli	Fresno,CA	(209) 251-6599
Ian Caterers, Inc.	Los Angeles,CA	(213) 721-0740
Ibis	New York,NY	(212) 753-3429
Imperial Gaz Co.	Santa Fe Springs,CA	(213) 693-8423
Impero Import Co.Inc	Waterbury,CT	
Import Liquor & Food Stores	Houston,TX	
Indo Pak Foods	Haywood,CA	(415) 782-4654
Indo-European Foods, Inc.	Glendale,CA	(818) 247-1000
International Bakery	Hollywood,CA	(213) 953-1724
International Bread and Crois.	Los Angeles,CA	
International Cuisine Caterer	Rockville,MD	
International Deli	San Jose,CA	(408) 286-2036
International Deli	Sherman Oaks,CA	(818) 990-4916
International Fine Foods	Detroit,MI	
International Food	Hollywood,CA	
International Food Bazar	San Jose,CA	(408) 365-1922
International Food Bazar	San Jose,CA	(408) 559-3397
International Food Bazar	Portland,OR	(503) 228-1960
International Food Center	Anaheim,CA	(714) 533-7730
International Food Market	Roslyn Heights,NY	(516) 625-5800
International Food Market	Davis,CA	(916) 756-4262
International Food Mart	Leonia,NJ	(201) 947-4449
International Food Mart	Nashville,TN	(615) 333-9651
International Foods	Chicago,IL	(312) 478-8643
International Foods	Rochester,NY	(716) 288-3686
International Gift Corner	Memphis,TN	
International Golden Foods,Inc	Niles,IL	(312) 764-3333
International Grocery Store	New York,NY	(212) 279-5514
International Grocery of S.D.	San Diego,CA	(619) 569-0362
International Grocery	Duarte,CA	(818) 301-0270
International House	Rockville,MD	(301) 279-2121
International Market	Washington,DC	
International Market & Deli	Washington,DC	(202) 293-0499
International Market Place	Dearborn,MI	(313) 274-6100
International Market	Livonia,MI	(313) 522-2220
International Market	La Jolla,CA	(619) 454-5835
International Market	Anaheim,CA	(714) 774-9191
International Market	San Gabriel,CA	(818) 286-4077
International Mini Market	Philadelphia,PA	
International Super Market	Denver,CO	(303) 934-3337
International Super Market	Hawthorne,CA	(310) 676-1482
Iran Market	Houston,TX	(713) 789-5943
Iran Market	Reseda,CA	(818) 342-9753
Iransara	San Jose,CA	(408) 241-3912
Islam Grocery International	Arlington,VA	
Islamic Food Mart	Los Angeles,CA	(213) 383-2583
Islamic Food Restaurant	Los Angeles,CA	(213) 386-5332
Israeli Accents	Rockville,MD	
Italian American Delicatessen	Freeport,NY	
Italian Deli & Produce	N. Hollywood,CA	(818) 982-5781
Italian Imported Super Market	Tampa,FL	
Italian Importing Co.	Des Moines,IA	
Italian Middle East Market	Sherman Oaks,CA	(818) 995-6944
Italo-American Importing	St. Louis,MO	(314) 645-9781

J

J & J International Import	San Jose,CA	(408) 428-9221
J & K Grocers	San Bernardino,CA	(714) 882-1700
J & M Liquor	Los Angeles,CA	
J & T Greek-Italian Deli	New York,NY	(212) 545-7920
J. B.'s Grocery	Glendale,CA	(818) 249-8224

Ethnic Cookbooks

J.M. Armelli Liquor Co.	Los Angeles,CA	
Jabourian's Grocery	Northridge,CA	(818) 349-5746
Jack's Cold Cuts	Cornwells,PA	(215) 639-2346
Jack's Deli & Ice Cream	Los Angeles,CA	(213) 627-9997
Jack's International Deli	Glendale,CA	(818) 242-3054
Jacob's Grocery & Deli	Van Nuys,CA	(818) 782-0536
Jaleh Catering	San Jose,CA	(408) 277-0506
Jamai Coffee Co.	Glendale,CA	(818) 241-8156
James Heonis Co.	Raleigh,NC	
Janet's Catering	Glendale,CA	(818) 248-8907
Javan Restaurant	Los Angeles,CA	(310) 207-5555
Jerry G. Bishop's Greek Island	San Diego,CA	(619) 239-5216
Jerusalem Bakery & Grocery	Irving,TX	(214) 257-0447
Jerusalem Restaurant	Falls Church,VA	(703) 845-1622
Jim Dandy Fried Chicken	Los Angeles,CA	(213) 666-8627
Jim's Family Catering & Bakery	Worcester,MA	(508) 752-1731
Jimmy's Deli	Fremont,CA	(415) 490-2056
Joelle's Kabobland Deli	Glendale,CA	(818) 500-3962
Joey Kay's Market	Paterson,NJ	(201) 523-9809
John's Delicatessen	Morristown,NJ	
John's Fruit Market	New York,NY	(718) 278-0705
John's Market	Elizabeth,NJ	
Johnny's Italian & Greek Deli	Santa Barbara,CA	
Jonelle's Restaurants & Cater.	Flushing,NY	(718) 699-0500
Jons Supermarket	Hollywood,CA	(213) 461-9382
Jons Supermarket	Glendale,CA	(818) 244-8206
Jons Supermarket	Van Nuys,CA	(818) 781-1772
Jonson's Market	Culver City,CA	(213) 390-9639
Jordan Halal Meat	Houston,TX	(713) 785-4455
Jose's Delicatessen	Palo Alto,CA	
Joseph Assi Bakery & Deli	Jacksonville,FL	(904) 398-5167
Joseph Baratta	Miami,FL	
Joseph's Brothers Market	Manchester,NH	(603) 623-0302
Joseph's Cafe & Restaurants	Hollywood,CA	(213) 462-8697
Joseph's Place	Downsview Ontario,	(416) 739-7221
Jovina's Chocolates	Glendale,CA	(818) 502-0549
Just Like Home Restaurant	San Francisco,CA	(415) 681-3337

K

K & M International	Hollywood,CA	(213) 465-6146
K & S Deli	Rosemead,CA	(818) 288-2333
K & S Quality Meat	Jackson Heights,NY	
K & T Meat Market	New York,NY	(212) 728-3810
K. Barishian	Providence,RI	
K.G. Apikoglu, Inc.	New York,NY	(212) 730-2500
Kabab House (KababKhouneh)	Glendale,CA	(818) 243-7001
Kabab Royal	Irvine,CA	(714) 476-9901
Kababi-e-Nader	New York,NY	(212) 683-4833
Kabob House	San Jose,CA	(408) 559-7330
Kabob House	Concord,CA	(510) 671-6969
Kabob No. 1	San Diego,CA	(619) 222-2656
Kabob's Palace	Azusa,CA	(818) 334-6759
Kaboby Restaurant #1	Los Angeles,CA	(310) 208-9208
Kaboby Restaurant #2	Sherman Oaks,CA	(818) 501-9830
Kabul Afghani Cuisine	Huntington,NY	(516) 549-5506
Kabul Caravan	Arlington,VA	(703) 522-8394
Kabul Kabab House	Flushing,NY	(718) 461-1919
Kabul West	Bethesda,MD	(301) 986-8566
Kachin's Place	Los Angeles,CA	(213) 622-5621
Kadouri Import Corp.	New York,NY	(212) 677-5441
Kafe Katz	Rockville,MD	
Kal's Market	Glendale,CA	(818) 507-7810
Kalamata Food Imports, Inc.	New York,NY	(718) 626-1250

Kalunian Grocery	Dorchester,MA	
Kam Shing Co.	Chicago,IL	
Kanani's Omar Khayyam Rest.	New York,NY	(212) 879-5353
Kandes Liquor & Imports	Victoria,TX	
Kandoo Grocery	Chicago,IL	(312) 275-0006
Karabagh Armenian Meat Market	Hollywood,CA	(213) 469-5787
Karo's Catering	N. Hollywood,CA	(818) 509-3952
Karo's Importing Deli	Hollywood,CA	(213) 465-6486
Karoon Restaurant	Orange,CA	(714) 997-8323
Karoun Armenian Restaurant	Newtonville,MA	(617) 964-3400
Karoun Market	Hollywood,CA	(213) 665-7237
Karoun Restaurant	San Jose,CA	(408) 947-1520
Kasra Restaurant	San Francisco,CA	(415) 752-1101
Kasra Skeweres	San Francisco,CA	(415) 433-4747
Kassos Brothers	New York,NY	(212) 932-5479
Katina Ice Gream & Bakery	Glendale,CA	(818) 247-4068
Katmandu	Washington,DC	
Katz Kosher Supermarket	Rockville,MD	
Kavar Restaurant	Hollywood,CA	(213) 669-1260
Kaysery Food Co.	Scarborough,	(416) 498-0547
Kazan Restaurant	McLean,VA	(703) 734-1960
Kebab Bakery & Delicatessen	Denver,CO	
Kebob House	Crystal City,VA	
Kehayan Importing Co.	New York,NY	
Keiv Restaurant	Montebello,CA	(213) 722-3321
Kelly's Food Mart	Rockford,IL	
Kermanig Bakery	Glendale,CA	(818) 246-2750
Key Club Restaurant	N. Hollywood,CA	(818) 765-6600
Khaledian Brothers Deli	Glendale,CA	(818) 246-5382
Khan Baba (House of Kabab)	Canoga Park,CA	(818) 887-5450
Kharobar Market	New York,NY	(212) 714-9666
Khatib Butcher Shop	Falls Church,VA	(703) 845-9388
Khayber International	Fremont,CA	(510) 795-9549
Khayyam International Market	Saint Louis,MO	(314) 727-8993
Khayyam's Chelo Kabab	Albany,CA	(510) 526-7200
Khazar Markets	Los Angeles,CA	(213) 655-8674
Khooban Foods Inc.	Gardena,CA	(310) 719-2390
Khorak Market	Toronto, Ontario,	(416) 221-7558
Khyber Halal Market	Arlington,VA	(703) 525-8323
Khyber Pass	Washington,DC	
Khyber Pass	New York,NY	(212) 473-0989
Khyber Pass	San Diego,CA	(619) 224-8200
Khyber Pass	San Diego,CA	(619) 571-3749
King Cheese & Deli	Pasadena,CA	(818) 791-2254
King Deli	Los Angeles,CA	(310) 204-1149
King Falafel	New York,NY	(718) 745-4188
King Market	Glendale,CA	(818) 246-4015
King of Pita Bakery, Inc.	Alexandria,VA	(703) 941-8999
Kiryakos Grocery	New York,NY	(718) 545-3931
Kismet Grocery	Burlingame,CA	(415) 343-8919
Kismet Oriental Pastries Co.	Astoria,NY	
Kizmet Fancy Grocery	Hempstead,NY	
Koko's Grocery	N. Hollywood,CA	(818) 763-6731
Kolbeh Restaurant	Washington,DC	(202) 342-2000
Kolbeh Restaurant	San Diego,CA	(619) 273-8171
Konanyan Meat Co., Inc.	Los Angeles,CA	(818) 242-5603
Koo Koo Roo Restaurant	Los Angeles,CA	(213) 383-6628
Koo Koo Roo Restaurant	Los Angeles,CA	(213) 655-9045
Kouche Restaurant	Laguna Hills,CA	(714) 588-8999
Koutoubia Restaurant	Los Angeles,CA	(310) 475-0729
Kozanian Grocery	Hollywood,CA	(213) 668-2514
Kozanian Grocery	Glendale,CA	(818) 502-1013
Kozanian Grocery	N. Hollywood,CA	(818) 952-9030
Kradjian Importing	Glendale,CA	(818) 502-1313
Krinos Foods, Inc.	Long Island City,NY	(718) 729-9000

122-Business Names

Ethnic Cookbooks

Krivaar Cafe	San Francisco,CA	(415) 781-0894
Kupelian Foods, Inc.	Ridgefield Park,NJ	(201) 440-8055

L

L & H Superette	Detroit,MI	
L. Paletta's	San Antonio,TX	
La Belle Epooue	Los Angeles,CA	(213) 669-7640
La Boheme Greenwich Village	New York,NY	(212) 473-6447
La Cresta Market & Liquor	La Crescenta,CA	(818) 248-0098
La Galette Pastry # 1	Sherman Oaks,CA	(818) 905-0726
La Galette Pastry # 2	Hollywood,CA	(213) 467-6606
La Marquise International	Los Angeles,CA	(213) 668-1030
La Mediterranee	San Rafael,CA	(415) 258-9123
La Mediterranee	San Francisco,CA	(415) 431-7210
La Mediterranee	Berkeley,CA	(415) 540-7730
La Mediterranee	San Francisco,CA	(415) 921-2956
La Mediterranee	Pasadena,CA	(818) 797-1558
La Mesa Market	La Mesa,CA	(619) 589-6789
La Miche	Cupertino,CA	(408) 725-1131
La Miche	Sunnyvale,CA	(408) 730-5518
La Miche	Fremont,CA	(415) 795-1105
La Strada Restaurant	Los Angeles,CA	(213) 664-2955
Laconia Grocery	Boston,MA	
Lahmajoon Kitchen	Fresno,CA	(209) 264-5454
Lake Forest Mini Market	Lake Forest,CA	(714) 859-9132
Lake Murray Liquor & Market	La Mesa,CA	(619) 464-8477
Lavash Corporation of America	Los Angeles,CA	(213) 663-5249
Lave Lee Restaurant	Studio City,CA	(818) 980-8158
Layalina Restaurant	N. Hollywood,CA	(818) 766-6575
Le Capitaine	Montreal,	(514) 489-2642
Le Gourmet Caterers	New York,NY	(718) 778-6666
Le Gourmet Elegance	Glendale,CA	(818) 956-5079
Le Palais Bakery	Los Angeles,CA	(213) 659-8345
Le Papillon Restaurant	Monrovia,CA	(818) 357-7211
Le Petit Gourmet	Douglaston,NY	(718) 224-9665
Lebanese Butcher	Falls Church,VA	(703) 533-2903
Lebanese Delicatessen	Dayton,OH	
Lebanese Grocery	Roslindale,MA	(617) 469-2900
Lebanese Taverna Restaurant	Arlington,VA	
Lebanese-Syrian Bakery	St. Louis,MO	
Lefferts Kosher Meat	Kew Gardens,NY	(718) 441-6887
Leo's Place	Cambridge,MA	(617) 354-9192
Leo's Sandwiches	Glendale,CA	(818) 247-2050
Leon's Food Mart	Lincoln,NB	
Leon's Grocery & Deli	Van Nuys,CA	(818) 787-8910
Leonardo's Italian Redondo Beach,CA		(310) 316-4433
Lev's Armenian Market	Montebello,CA	(213) 721-2391
Levant International Food	Bellflower,CA	(310) 920-0623
Liamos Market	Nashua,NH	
Lida's Food Center	Orange,CA	(714) 998-7760
Lignos Groceries	Mobile,AL	(205) 432-9870
Lingos Grocery	Salt Lake City,UT	
Little Rose Armenian Grocery	Pasadena,CA	(818) 797-9022
Little Russia	Glendale,CA	(818) 243-4787
Loft Catering	San Jose,CA	(408) 866-2200
Los Feliz European Deli	Hollywood,CA	(213) 660-9412
Lucky Boy Market	New York,NY	
Lucky's Restaurant	Glendale,CA	(818) 242-8415
Lucy's Mini Mart	Pasadena,CA	(818) 791-1177
Luxe Restaurant	Silver Spring,MD	(301) 565-2622

M

M & A Kebab King Catering	Montebello,CA	(213) 725-1395
M & J Market & Deli	N. Hollywood,CA	(818) 765-7671
M & M International Deli	N. Hollywood,CA	(818) 980-0608
M & M Liquor & Market	Glendale,CA	(818) 848-7470
M & M Market	Cypress,CA	(310) 220-2207
M & R International Cuisine	Tarzana,CA	(818) 705-6630
Mac's Deli	Monrovia,CA	(818) 303-3016
Madinah Restaurant Party Hall	Los Angeles,CA	(213) 383-9976
Magic Lamp	Pasadena,CA	(818) 795-8701
Maha Imports and Groceries	Santa Clara,CA	(408) 248-5025
Mahroukian Meat Market	Pasadena,CA	(818) 791-1223
Mahtab Market	Rancho Palos Verdes,CA	(310) 833-6026
Main Importing Grocery, Inc.	Montreal,	(514) 861-5681
Mainly Cheese Inc.	Glen Rock,NJ	(201) 447-4141
Majestic Market	Southfield,MI	(313) 352-8556
Makhoul Corner Store	Allentown,PA	
Mama Ayesha's	Washington,DC	
Mamoun's Middle East Food	West Covina,CA	(213) 339-3122
Mandik's Pastry Shop	Union City,NJ	(201) 866-3827
Manhattan Express	Van Nuys,CA	(818) 997-3663
Manigian Grocery	,NJ	(201) 531-6810
Manley Produce	San Francisco,CA	
Marash Bakery	Watertown,MA	(617) 924-0098
Marash Catering	Pasadena,CA	(213) 629-2802
Marash Coffee Shop	Los Angeles,CA	(213) 385-4302
Marathon Restaurant	Long Beach,CA	(310) 437-6346
Marcel's Bakery	N. Hollywood,CA	(818) 765-3844
Marche Adonis	Montreal,	(514) 382-8606
Margosian Beverage Co.	Fresno,CA	(209) 264-2823
Marhaba Market	Norwalk,CA	(310) 864-2665
Maria's Greek Corner	Vienna,VA	
Maria's Pizza Restaurants	Cranston,RI	(401) 785-1150
Market Express & Liquor	Van Nuys,CA	(818) 781-0325
Marko's Pizzeria	Van Nuys,CA	(818) 780-6114
Marouch Hollywood	Hollywood,CA	(213) 662-9325
Marrakesh Restaurant	Washington,DC	
Marrakesh Restaurant # 1	Studio City,CA	(818) 788-6354
Marrakesh Restaurant # 2	Newport Beach,CA	(714) 645-8384
Marrakesh Restaurant # 3	La Mesa,CA	(619) 462-3663
Marrakesh Restaurant # 4	La Jolla,CA	(619) 454-2500
Mary's Greek Grocery	Philadelphia,PA	(215) 722-2845
Mashti Ice Cream	Hollywood,CA	(213) 874-0144
Masis Bakery	Hollywood,CA	(213) 667-3001
Masis Grocery	Las Vegas,NV	(702) 369-0090
Masis Market	Fresno,CA	(209) 224-1228
Massis Armenian Food	Glendale,CA	(818) 242-2333
Massis Armenian Sandwich	Los Angeles,CA	(213) 623-8302
Massis Bakery	Watertown,MA	(617) 924-0537
Massis Grocery & Deli	Canoga Park,CA	(818) 888-6664
Massoud Restaurant	Los Angeles,CA	(213) 748-1768
Max's Market	New York,NY	
Maxim's Nutricare, Inc.	Salt Lake City,UT	(801) 262-6767
Maykadeh Restaurant	San Francisco,CA	(415) 362-8286
Mc Allister Grocery	San Francisco,CA	(415) 861-5315
Mediterranean Bakery	Weston,	(416) 743-2267
Mediterranean Bakery	Alexandria,VA	(703) 751-1702
Mediterranean Bakery	Richmond,VA	(804) 285-1488
Mediterranean Coffee	Houston,TX	(713) 827-7799
Mediterranean Deli	Washington,DC	
Mediterranean Feast	Tarzana,CA	(818) 705-7961
Mediterranean Food Store	Ellicott City,MD	(301) 465-8555
Mediterranean Gourmet	Williston Park,NY	(516) 741-3664

Ethnic Cookbooks

Business Names-123

Mediterranean Groceries & Deli	Laguna Hills,CA	(714) 770-2007
Mediterranean Imports	Oklahoma City,OK	
Mediterranean Imports	Waukegan,IL	(312) 244-4040
Mediterranean Imports	West Roxbury,MA	(617) 323-4341
Mediterranean Kabob Room	Monrovia,CA	(818) 358-7177
Mediterranean Kitchen	Bensalem,PA	(215) 245-5278
Mediterranean Marketplace	Worcester,MA	(508) 755-0258
Mediterranean Store	Arlington,VA	(703) 527-0423
Mediterranean	Fresno,CA	(209) 229-6347
Menora Market	Los Angeles,CA	(310) 854-0447
Mere Milia	Chomedey Laval,	(514) 681-8895
Mesopotamia Restaurant	Chicago,IL	(312) 348-0654
Metropolis Restaurant	Los Angeles,CA	(310) 659-3333
Metropolitan Coffee Co.	Akron,OH	
Miami Restaurant	Reseda,CA	(818) 705-3322
Michael Nafash & Sons	Union City,NJ	
Michael's Deli & Grocery	Hollywood,CA	(213) 662-6311
Michell's Grocery	Florence,SC	
Microcosmos	New York,NY	(718) 728-7093
Mid-Eastern Pastries & Grocery	San Diego,CA	(619) 295-2311
Middle East Bakery	Takoma Park,MD	
Middle East Bakery	Wilkes-Barre,PA	
Middle East Bakery	San Mateo,CA	
Middle East Baking Co.	Atlanta,GA	
Middle East Connection	Burbank,CA	(818) 843-8339
Middle East Foods	Cleveland,OH	
Middle East Foods	Santa Clara,CA	(408) 248-5112
Middle East Grocery	Denver,CO	(303) 756-4580
Middle East Lamejun	Fairview,NJ	(201) 941-5662
Middle East Market	Takoma Park,MD	
Middle East Market	Arcadia,CA	(818) 574-1971
Middle East Restaurant #2	Whittier,CA	(310) 696-2224
Middle East Restaurant	Cambridge,MA	(617) 492-9181
Middle East Restaurant	Anaheim,CA	(714) 826-8700
Middle East Restaurant	Alhambra,CA	(818) 576-1048
Middle East Restaurant	Altadena,CA	(818) 797-2576
Middle East Trading	Chicago,IL	(312) 262-2848
Middle Eastern & Armenian Cat.	Pasadena,CA	(818) 792-7663
Middle Eastern Bakery	Hollywood,CA	
Middle Eastern Bakery & Grocer	Chicago,IL	(312) 561-2224
Middle Eastern Bakery	Albuquerque,NM	(505) 255-2939
Middle Eastern Bazar	Las Vegas,NV	(702) 731-6030
Middle Eastern Groceries	Smyrna,GA	
Middle Eastern Grocery	Anaheim,CA	(714) 826-8700
Middle Eastern Market & Deli	Las Vegas,NV	(702) 736-8887
Middle Eastern Market	Berkeley,CA	(510) 548-2213
Middle Eastern Restaurant	Alhambra,CA	(818) 281-1006
Mideast Specialty	Bridgeport,CT	(203) 878-8337
Mignon Bakery	Glendale,CA	(818) 246-2217
Mihran's Restaurants	Tarzana,CA	(818) 342-2290
Mikaelyan Food Market	Glendale,CA	(818) 548-8045
Mikailian Meat Products	Valencia,CA	(805) 257-1055
Mike's Catering	Glendale,CA	(818) 241-1463
Milano Super Market Inc.	Hamden,CT	
Miller's Market	Reseda,CA	(818) 345-9222
Mini Kabob	Glendale,CA	(818) 244-1343
Minoo Khosher Restaurant	Los Angeles,CA	(310) 478-0072
Minoo Market	Huntington Beach,CA	(714) 962-0305
Mira International Foods, Inc.	Hoboken,NJ	(201) 963-8289
Mission Liquor	Pasadena,CA	(818) 794-7026
Mitaya Fine Cuisine	Markham, Ontario,	(416) 940-6296
Mixed Nuts	Santa Ana,CA	
Mixed Nuts	Hollywood,CA	(213) 663-3915
Mixed Nuts	Glendale,CA	(818) 240-9282
Moby Dick Cafe	Bethesda,MD	
Model Food Importers & Distri.	Portland,ME	(207) 774-3671
Molfetas Restaurants	South Hakensack,NJ	(201) 440-1771
Molfetas	New York,NY	(212) 840-9537
Mona Lisa Catering	Northridge,CA	(818) 887-2424
Moomjean Meat Co.	Montebello,CA	(213) 263-7856
Morae Restaurant	La Place Shopping,FL	(813) 977-6018
Morgan's Grocery	St. Paul,MN	
Moroccan Restaurant	Las Vegas,NV	(702) 736-7655
Moroccan Star	New York,NY	(718) 643-0800
Moscow Nights Restaurant	Reseda,CA	(818) 349-5300
Moshe Dragon	Rockville,MD	
Moulasadra Grocery	Los Angeles,CA	(213) 470-4646
Moun of Tunis Restaurant	Hollywood,CA	(213) 874-3333
Mount of Olives Market	Falls Church,VA	(703) 379-1156
Mourad Grocery	Highland Park,MI	
Moustache Cafe	Tysons Corner,VA	(703) 893-1100
Movses Golden Pastry	Burbank,CA	(818) 559-5200
Mr. Big Burger	Burbank,CA	(818) 846-1406
Mr. Chicken	Oxnard,CA	(805) 988-9645
Mr. Chicken	Van Nuys,CA	(818) 786-1055
Mr. Deli	La Crescenta,CA	(818) 957-7018
Mr. Lamb of California	S. El Monte,CA	(310) 697-6103
Mt. Ararat Coffee Traders	Los Banos,CA	(209) 826-1961
Mukuch Aintab Catering	Sun Valley,CA	(818) 768-4929
Mumms Restaurant	N. Hollywood,CA	(818) 763-7087
Mustang Cafe	Dallas,TX	(214) 306-4888

N

N & K Groceries & Deli	El Cajon,CA	(619) 447-9471
Nablus Grocery	Yonkers,NY	
Nader Grocery	New York,NY	(212) 686-5793
Nader International Foods	New York,NY	(212) 889-1752
Nader International	New York,NY	(212) 481-3117
Nafash & Sons	Union City,NJ	
Nagilah Market	Forest Hills,NY	(718) 268-2626
Nakeysa	Washington,DC	
Nasr Mini Market	Scarborough,	(416) 757-1611
Nassim Grocery	Pomona,CA	(714) 593-8244
Natalie Pastry Shop	Los Angeles,CA	(213) 470-4811
National Foods	Denver,CO	
Naz Market	Anaheim,CA	(714) 956-8926
Nazarian's Courtyard	Watervliet,NY	(518) 273-1104
Nea Hellas	New York,NY	(718) 278-7304
Near East Bakery	Miami,FL	
Near East Bakery	New York,NY	(718) 875-0016
Near East Baking Co.	West Roxbury,MA	(617) 327-0217
Near East Food Products, Inc.	Leominster,MA	
Near East Foods	San Diego,CA	(619) 284-6361
Near East Importing Co. Inc.	Glendale,NY	(212) 894-3600
Near East Market	Providence,RI	
Near East Market	Cranston,RI	(401) 941-9763
Neda's Market	Costa Mesa,CA	(714) 650-5424
Nemouneh (Unique Market)	Santa Ana,CA	(714) 836-8674
Nettuno Italian Delicacies	Cincinnati,OH	
New Deal Grocery	Chicago,IL	
New Parthenon Restaurant	Detroit,MI	(313) 963-8888
New Santa Clara Market	San Francisco,CA	
New World Market	San Francisco,CA	(415) 751-8810
New York Cafe	Falls Church,VA	
New York New York Restaurant	Santa Clara,CA	(408) 727-4420
New York Restaurant	Astoria,NY	(718) 726-3254
New Yorker Delicatessen	Roanoke,VA	
Next Door Deli	Burbank,CA	(818) 842-2383

124-Business Names — Ethnic Cookbooks

Nick's Importing Co.	Oklahoma City,OK	
Nick's Produce & Import. Co.	Richmond,VA	
Nick's Produce	Richmond,VA	(804) 644-0683
Nicol's	Encino,CA	(818) 881-3099
Nissan Market	N. Hollywood,CA	(818) 763-3424
Nite Rock Club Cafe	Tujunga,CA	(818) 352-1265
Nizam's	W. Vienna,VA	
Nob Hill Banquet Center	Panorama City,CA	(818) 989-2222
Nobakht Pastry Shop	Reseda,CA	(818) 708-2608
Noble Bakery	Hollywood,CA	(213) 656-7136
Norik Bakery	Toronto,	(416) 757-8314
Norooz Bazar	Berkeley,CA	(408) 295-2323
Norooz Grocery & Deli	Springfield,VA	(703) 866-4444
North Street Market	New Britain,CT	(203) 229-5481
Northridge Bakery	Northridge,CA	(818) 993-7469
Nory	Winnetka,CA	
Noura Restaurant	W. Hollywood,CA	(213) 651-4581
Nouri's Syrian Bakery & Grocer	Paterson,NJ	
Nur, Inc.	Raleigh,NC	
Nut Crackers	Glendale,CA	(818) 545-9730
Nuts Bazaar	Oakland,CA	(510) 601-1997

O

O'Neil's Department Store Food	Akron,OH	
O.K. Fairbank's Sugar Market	Keene,NH	
Oasis Date Gardens	Thermal,CA	(619) 399-5665
Oasis Mart Importing Co.	Royal Oak,MI	(313) 588-2210
Oasis Mart	Royal Oak,MI	(313) 549-0001
Ohanyan's Int. Delicatessen	Fresno,CA	(209) 225-4290
Old Fashion Deli	Glendale,CA	(818) 244-9300
Old Sasoun Bakery	Pasadena,CA	(818) 791-3280
Old Town Greek Cuisine	San Diego,CA	(619) 291-5770
Old Town's Chicken	Monrovia,CA	(818) 303-3393
Old World Market	Bethesda,MD	(301) 654-4880
Olive Paradis Restaurant	Falls Church,VA	(703) 534-4433
Olson's Grocery	Omaha,NB	
Olympia Food of all Nations	River Edge,NJ	(201) 261-3703
Olympia Grocery	Milwaukee,WI	
Olympia Market	Worcester,MA	
Olympic Produce Market	Pasadena,CA	(818) 797-7437
Omar Khayam Restaurant	Huntington Beach,CA	(714) 373-0810
Omar's Pastry	Garden Grove,CA	(714) 531-3551
Omid Market	Mission Viejo,CA	(714) 458-7343
One & One Pizza & Deli	Glendale,CA	(818) 246-9496
Orchard Market	Towson,MD	(301) 339-7700
Orchid Market	Granada Hills,CA	(818) 366-6969
Orchid Restaurant	Costa Mesa,CA	(714) 557-8070
Orient Export Trading Co.	New York,NY	(212) 685-3451
Orient Express	San Francisco,CA	(415) 957-1795
Oriental Import-Export Co.	Houston,TX	
Oriental Pastry & Grocery	Brooklyn,NY	(718) 875-7687
Oven Fresh Bakery	Glendale,CA	(818) 249-3587
Ozzies Restaurant	City of Commerce,CA	(213) 726-0944
Ozzies Restaurant	Orange,CA	(714) 633-3280

P

P & S Importing Co.	Waterbury,CT	
Paak International Gourmet	San Mateo,CA	(415) 574-3536
Pacific Food Bazar	Glendale,CA	(818) 956-1021
Pacific Food Mart	Glendale,CA	(818) 242-8352
Pak Dairy, Inc.	Glendale,CA	(818) 244-9435
Palestine Bakery	Chicago,IL	(312) 925-5978
Paletta's Imported Foods	San Antonio,TX	(512) 828-0678
Palette Restaurant	Hollywood,CA	(213) 654-8094
Palmer Market	Glendale,CA	(818) 243-4879
Pamchal Restaurant	Los Angeles,CA	(310) 473-0309
Pamir Cuisine of Afghanistan	Morristown,NJ	(201) 605-1095
Pamir Cuisine of Afghanistan	New York,NY	(212) 734-3791
Pamir Food Market	Fremont,CA	(510) 790-7015
Pan Hellenic Pastry Shop	Chicago,IL	(312) 454-1886
Panjoyan Produce	Costa Mesa,CA	(714) 646-5718
Panos Char Broiler	Van Nuys,CA	(818) 780-4041
Panos Pastry Shop # 1	Hollywood,CA	(213) 661-0335
Panos Pastry Shop # 2	Glendale,CA	(818) 502-0549
Papa Garo's	Redondo Beach,CA	(213) 540-7272
Papa Joe's Deli	Cypress,CA	(714) 527-2350
Papa Joe's Liqour Deli	Anaheim,CA	(714) 826-0981
Papa John's Restaurant	Rockville,MD	(301) 340-6970
Papa Pooche	Sun Valley,CA	(818) 504-9086
Papa's Restaurant	Berkeley,CA	(510) 841-0884
Papadakis Taverna Restaurant	San Pedro,CA	(310) 548-1186
Paparian's Food Market	Albany,NY	
Paradise Health Juice	Los Angeles,CA	(213) 628-4530
Paradise Pastry	Glendale,CA	(818) 545-4000
Paradise Restaurant	Bethesda,MD	
Paradise Restaurant	Mountain View,CA	(415) 968-5949
Paradiso Restaurant	Los Angeles,CA	(310) 475-1427
Pari's Deli	San Francisco,CA	(415) 771-2219
Paros Restaurant	Hollywood,CA	(213) 469-2610
Pars International Market	N. Vancouver,	(604) 988-3515
Pars Market	Bellevue,WA	(206) 641-5265
Pars Market	Los Angeles,CA	(310) 859-8125
Pars Market	Milwaukee,WI	(414) 278-7175
Pars Market	San Diego,CA	(619) 566-7277
Pars Restaurant	Miami,FL	(305) 551-1099
Pars Restaurant	Torrance,CA	(310) 370-4838
Pars Restaurant	San Bruno,CA	(415) 871-5151
Pars Restaurant	Irvine,CA	(714) 832-8324
Partamian Armenian Bakery	Los Angeles,CA	(213) 937-2870
Pasadena Kabob House	Pasadena,CA	(818) 795-3499
Pasha Restaurant	San Francisco,CA	(415) 885-4477
Pasha's Afghan Cuisine	La Jolla,CA	(619) 454-9229
Patchi	Los Angeles,CA	(213) 464-0862
Patchi	Glendale,CA	(818) 547-4317
Paterson Syrian Bakery	Paterson,NJ	(201) 279-2388
Patisserie Armenia	Montreal,	(516) 389-4696
Patrik's Quick Market	Glendale,CA	(818) 247-7329
Pavo Co., Inc.	Minneapolis,MN	(612) 533-4525
Pawinda Restaurnat	San Diego,CA	(619) 454-9229
Payton Kabob	Glendale,CA	(818) 242-8776
Periyali	New York,NY	(212) 463-7890
Persepolis Restaurant	Bethesda,MD	(301) 656-9339
Persian Center Bazaar	San Jose,CA	(408) 241-3700
Perspolis Restaurant	San Jose,CA	(408) 265-5090
Perspolis Restaurants	Anaheim,CA	(714) 991-7600
Peter Pan Superette	Arlington,MA	(617) 648-9771
Petit Cafe	San Francisco,CA	(415) 387-5266
Petrossian Restaurant	New York,NY	(212) 245-2214
Pharaoh's Market	Orange,CA	(714) 633-2360
Phoenicia Bakery & Deli	Austin,TX	(512) 447-4444
Phoenicia Imports & Deli	Houston,TX	(713) 558-0416
Phoenicia Restaurant	Glendale,CA	(818) 956-7800
Phoenician Imports	Glendale,CA	(818) 247-0500
Picasso's Restaurants	Arlington,MA	(617) 648-2800
Pick-A-Deli	Glendale,CA	(818) 244-4190
Pieri's Delicacies Inc	Portland,OR	
Piggly Wiggly	Charlestown,SC	

Ethnic Cookbooks

Pikapita	Washington,DC	
Pita Inn	Skokie,IL	(708) 677-0211
Pittsburgh Grocery Store	Pittsburgh,PA	
Pizza Boy	Glendale,CA	(818) 247-5748
Pizza Man	Burbank,CA	(818) 843-3341
Pizza and Chicken Colorado	Los Angeles,CA	(213) 254-0777
Pizzajoun	Montreal,	(514) 383-5588
Plaka	New York,NY	(212) 674-9709
Player's Liquor	Manhattan Beach,CA	(310) 545-5664
Pollo Clasico	Sacramento,CA	(916) 369-8445
Polsano's Deli	Oklahoma City,OK	
Pondfield Produce Market	Yonkers,NY	(914) 961-9566
Ponzo's Deli	Pasadena,CA	(818) 794-5682
Pop's Restaurant and Grocery	Vienna,VA	
Port of Athens Restaurant	N. Hollywood,CA	(818) 508-9486
Poseidon Greek Bakery	New York,NY	(212) 757-6173
Pouri Bakery	Glendale,CA	(818) 244-4064
Prime Produce	Van Nuys,CA	(818) 905-9538
Princess Meat and Deli	Toronto,	(416) 752-4692
Progress Grocery Co.	New Orleans,LA	
Purity Importing Co.	Dallas,TX	
Pyramid Bakery	New York,NY	(718) 392-2702
Pyramid Market	Oakland,CA	(415) 428-1833

Q

Quality Produce	La Puente,CA	(818) 918-1225
Quik Pik Market	Sherman Oaks,CA	(818) 501-6094
Quincy Syrian Baking Co.	Quincy,MA	

R

R. A. Medonic	Wheeling,WV	
R. H. Macy & Co.	Herald Square,NY	(212) 695-4400
Raffi's Place # 1	Glendale,CA	(818) 241-9960
Raffi's Place # 2	Glendale,CA	(818) 247-0575
Rahal & Sons, Inc.	Miami,FL	
Rainbow Produce & Grocery	San Francisco,CA	(415) 731-8715
Rainbow Stores	Los Angeles,CA	(310) 397-5090
Ramallah Market	Worth,IL	(708) 361-5665
Ramsar Maket	Los Angeles,CA	(213) 651-1601
Ramses Deli	Toronto,	(416) 755-0244
Rana Food Store	Arlington,TX	
Randy's M.E. Market & Catering	La Habra,CA	(714) 738-1337
Restaurant Asmar	Montreal,	
Restaurant Georges	Chomedey,	(514) 681-8189
Reza Restaurant	Anaheim,CA	(714) 778-2005
Rio Deli & Market	Woodland Hills,CA	(818) 999-9486
Rio's Market	Redondo Beach,CA	(310) 542-8616
Ritza Restaurant	Los Angeles,CA	(213) 934-2215
Riviera Restaurants	Glendale,CA	(818) 500-8700
Roastin' Chicken	La Habra,CA	(310) 690-4588
Roastin' Chicken	Tujunga,CA	(818) 249-7607
Robert's Catering Service	Burbank,CA	(818) 848-8337
Robert's Fresh Produce	Tujunga,CA	(818) 352-7787
Roberto's Restaurant	West Covina,CA	(818) 331-0606
Rodeo Deli & Grocery	Glendale,CA	(818) 244-6969
Roma Importing Co.	Latham,NY	(518) 785-7480
Ron's Market	Hollywood,CA	(213) 465-1164
Rooster Brand Products Corp.	Los Angeles,CA	(213) 582-5000
Rooz Market	Irvine,CA	(714) 559-8535
Rooz Supermarket & Deli	Seattle,WA	(206) 363-8639
Rose International Foods	Beaverton,OR	(503) 646-7673
Rose Enternational Market	Mt. View,CA	(415) 960-1900
Rose Market	Los Angeles,CA	(213) 470-2121
Rose Market	Mountain View,CA	(415) 960-1900
Rose's Restaurant	Canoga Park,CA	(818) 716-5222
Roses International Trade, Inc	Los Angeles,CA	
Rosicler Restaurant	Pasadena,CA	(818) 792-9700
Royal Coffee & Tea Co.	Oklahoma City,OK	(405) 848-2002
Royal Events	Hollywood,CA	(213) 667-9141
Royal George Grocery	Montreal,	(514) 277-4123
Royal Kabab	Irvine,CA	(714) 476-9901
Royal Morocco	Saratoga,CA	(408) 741-0224
Royal Perspolis Restaurant	Beverly Hills,CA	(310) 281-0777
Ruben's Market	Pico Rivera,CA	(310) 949-1322
Rubic's Bakery	Pacoima,CA	(818) 890-7299
Russian House	Woodland Hills,CA	(818) 348-5112
Russo's Imported Foods	Grand Rapids,MI	

S

S & D Caterers	Hewlett,NY	(516) 374-6300
S & J Importing	Long Beach,CA	(310) 599-1341
S.E.A. Catering	Montebello,CA	(213) 724-3782
Saadoun's Cuisine of Bagdad	Costa Mesa,CA	(714) 642-0800
Saam Middle East Restaurant	Pasadena,CA	(818) 793-8496
Saba Meat & Market	Chicago,IL	(312) 539-0080
Sabrina Middle East Restaurant	Culver City,CA	(310) 398-2308
Saghi Restaurant	Orange,CA	(714) 974-3353
Sahadi Importing Co. Inc.	Moonachie,NJ	
Sahadi Importing Co., Co.	Brooklyn,NY	(718) 624-4550
Sahag's Basturma	Hollywood,CA	(213) 661-5311
Sahar Meat & Grocery	Chicago,IL	(312) 583-7772
Sahar Mini Market	Azusa,CA	(818) 969-5010
Sahar Restaurant	Azusa,CA	(818) 969-9150
Sahara II	Tampa,FL	(813) 989-3612
Sahara Lebanese Cuisine	Redondo Beach,CA	(310) 371-1533
Sahara Natural Foods, Inc.	Berkeley,CA	
Sahara Restaurnat	Sherman Oaks,CA	(818) 995-4609
Sahara Room	San Diego,CA	(619) 427-8880
Saharex Imports, Inc.	City of Commerce,CA	(213) 722-0391
Sako's Bakery	Glendale,CA	(818) 247-3333
Sako's Mini-Mart	Boston,MA	(617) 782-8920
Sako's Sandwich Shop	Santa Fe Springs,CA	(310) 693-1138
Salam International Market	Winter Park,FL	(407) 657-5560
Salamat Market	Orange,CA	(714) 921-0153
Salar Restaurant	Glendale,CA	(818) 500-8661
Salim's Middle Eastern Food	Pittsburgh,PA	
Salimi Grocery	Forest Hills,NY	(718) 793-2984
Sally's Place	Brooklyn,NY	(718) 680-4615
Salt & Peper (Felfel Namakie)	Houston,TX	(713) 783-9996
Sam's Armenian Bakery	Glendale,CA	(818) 247-6281
Sam's Food Market	Culver City,CA	(310) 390-5705
Sam's International Deli	Hollywood,CA	(213) 935-7212
Sam's Liquor	Montebello,CA	(213) 722-1313
Sam's Market	Huntington Woods,MI	(313) 541-8990
Sam's Pastry	Glendale,CA	(818) 246-3811
Samadi Sweets Cafe	Falls Church,VA	(703) 578-0606
Saman Market	Woodland Hills,CA	(818) 347-8002
Samira's	New York,NY	(718) 745-2416
Samiramis Imports, Inc.	San Francisco,CA	(415) 824-6555
San Diego Importing Co.	San Diego,CA	
Sandpiper Inn, the	Desert Hot Springs,CA	(619) 329-6455
Sandwich Construction Co.	Burbank,CA	(818) 842-0715
Sandwich Shop	Valencia,CA	
Sandwiches By Connal	Pasadena,CA	(818) 798-0751
Santa Monica Food House	Santa Monica,CA	

126-Business Names

Ethnic Cookbooks

Santa Monica Khosher	Los Angeles,CA	(213) 473-4435
Santa Monica Market	Los Angeles,CA	(310) 207-5530
Santa Teresa Bakery	San Jose,CA	(408) 578-1520
Santos Agency, Inc.	San Leandro,CA	(510) 357-0277
Sara's Pastries	Anaheim,CA	(714) 776-4493
Saray-e Ghalandar	Reseda,CA	(818) 343-5115
Sarkis Aprozar Grocery	New York,NY	(212) 937-4682
Sasoon Meat Market	Glendale,CA	(818) 243-2484
Sasoon Restaurant	Tarzana,CA	(818) 708-8986
Sasoun Bakery	Hollywood,CA	(213) 661-1868
Sasoun Mini Market	Montebello,CA	(213) 724-6971
Sassoon Bakery & Grocery	Clovis,CA	(209) 323-1185
Sassoon Market	Watertown,MA	(617) 924-1560
Sassoon Restaurants	Fresno,CA	(209) 224-0577
Sassoon Supermarche	Montreal,	(514) 337-7923
Sawaya Delicatessen	Birmingham,AL	
Sayat Nova	Chicago,IL	(312) 644-9159
Sayat Nova	Des Plaines,IL	(708) 296-1776
Sayfy's Groceteria	Montreal,	(514) 277-1257
Sears Fine Food	San Francisco,CA	(415) 986-1160
Selin Market	Glendale,CA	(818) 502-0403
Sepahan Market	Van Nuys,CA	(818) 988-6278
Serge's Deli	N. Hollywood,CA	(818) 765-1200
Setareh Market	Los Angeles,CA	(310) 820-6513
Sevan Bakery & Grocery	Reseda,CA	(818) 343-0486
Sevan Bakery	Watertown,MA	(617) 924-9843
Sevan Deli & Imported Foods	Montebello,CA	(213) 721-3804
Sevan Falafel	Reseda,CA	(818) 881-3909
Sevan Grocery	Hollywood,CA	(213) 665-6406
Sevan Grocery	Santa Ana,CA	(714) 775-3776
Sevan Mini Market	Burbank,CA	(818) 845-3069
Sevan Restaurant	New York,NY	(212) 545-9538
Shad Zee Bakery	Los Angeles,CA	(213) 474-7907
Shahbaz Restaurant	Los Angeles,CA	(213) 936-3708
Shahrzad International Market	Atlanta,GA	(404) 843-0549
Shahrzad International Market	Santa Ana,CA	(714) 850-0808
Shahrzad Restaurant	Sherman Oaks,CA	(818) 905-6363
Shahrzad Restaurant	Encino,CA	(818) 906-1616
Shalak Market	Montclair,CA	(714) 946-7077
Shalimar Grocery	La Puente,CA	(818) 918-6227
Shalizar Restaurant	Montclair,CA	(714) 946-8481
Shalizeh Restaurant	Panorama City,CA	(818) 894-7557
Shallah's Middle Eastern Imp.	Danbury,CT	
Shalom Market & Bakery	Silver Spring,MD	
Shalom Meat Market	Encino,CA	(818) 345-8612
Shalton Restaurant	Los Angeles,CA	(213) 891-1984
Shammas Oriental Domestic Food	New York,NY	(212) 855-2455
Shammy's Market	Woodland Hills,CA	(818) 883-9811
Shamshiri Restaurant # 1	Los Angeles,CA	(310) 474-1410
Shamshiri Restaurant # 2	Hollywood,CA	(213) 469-8434
Shamshiri Restaurant # 3	Northridge,CA	(818) 885-7846
Shamshiri Restaurant # 4	Glendale,CA	(818) 246-9541
Shamshiri Restaurant	San Jose,CA	(408) 998-0122
Shandiz Restaurant	Bethesda,MD	(301) 961-8989
Shant's Imported Foods	Reseda,CA	(818) 708-0945
Shari Ghul-Ghula	Alexandria,VA	
Sharzad Grocery	Stamford,CT	(203) 323-5363
Shatila Sweet Trays	Dearborn,MI	(313) 582-1952
Shaul's & Hershel's Meatmarket	Wheaton,MD	
Sheik Cafe	San Diego,CA	(619) 234-5888
Shekarchi Kabab # 1	Los Angeles,CA	(213) 474-6911
Shekarchi Kabab # 2	Los Angeles,CA	(213) 746-4600
Shelled Nuts	Hanford,CA	(209) 584-1209
Shemiran Market	W. Los Angeles,CA	(213) 836-7286
Shemshad Food, Inc.	La Crescenta,CA	(818) 249-9066

Shepherd's Cove	Downey,CA	(310) 862-9441
Sherwood Grocery	Upper Derby,PA	
Shiekh Grocery Co.	Cleveland,OH	
Shirak Armenian Grocery	La Crescenta,CA	(818) 249-3314
Shirak Meat Product Ltd.	Scarborough,	(416) 266-7519
Shiraz Food Market	Miami,FL	(305) 264-8282
Shiraz Market	Reno,NV	(702) 829-1177
Shiraz Market	Carmichel,CA	(916) 486-1200
Shiraz Restaurant	Sherman Oaks,CA	(818) 789-7788
Shireen's Gourmet, Inc.	Hackensack,NJ	(201) 488-4907
Shirinian Grocery	Glendale,CA	(818) 243-0611
Shish Kabob Cafe	San Deigo,CA	(619) 265-7800
Shish Kabob Express	Van Nuys,CA	(818) 787-6718
Shish Kabob Grill	Los Angeles,CA	(213) 824-7739
Shish Kabob House	La Jolla,CA	(619) 459-4016
Shish Kabob Palace	Great Neck,NY	(516) 487-2228
Shish Kebab Restaurant	Port Washington,NY	(516) 883-9309
Shish Kebab at Blvd. Cafe	Fairview,NJ	(201) 945-8702
Shlomo's Meat & Fish Market	Baltimore,MD	
Sholeh Restaurant	Los Angeles,CA	(213) 470-9131
Shoosh International	San Francisco,CA	(415) 626-1847
Shop and Save	Trenton,NJ	
Shoppers Meat Market	Cleveland,OH	(216) 442-8440
Shoumine Restaurant	Houston,TX	(713) 266-6677
Shtoura Quality	Allentown,PA	(215) 435-9103
Si's BiRite Quality Meats	Strongsville,OH	(216) 238-8660
Sibian's Restaurants	Whittier,CA	(310) 698-6808
Sibo, Abu-Salim Restaurant	New York,NY	(212) 686-2031
Siham's Deli & Sandwiches	Fullerton,CA	(714) 871-0131
Silver Platter Catering	Monrovia,CA	(818) 791-8248
Simon X. Mandros	Lancaster,PA	
Simon's Kohser Restaurants	Los Angeles,CA	(310) 657-5552
Simon's Kosher Restaurants	Los Angeles,CA	(213) 627-6535
Sinbad Food Imports	Columbus,OH	
Sipan Deli & Grocery	Sunland,CA	(818) 352-3881
Skenderis Greek Imports	Washington,DC	(202) 265-9664
Skewer's	Washington,DC	
Sky Line Butcher Shop	Falls Church,VA	
Smiling Fruit	New York,NY	(212) 932-8006
Smorgasbord Restaurant & Cater	Montrose,CA	(818) 248-9536
Smyrna Lowell Confectionary Co	Lowell,MA	(617) 453-9573
Sneaky's Pizza	Glendale,CA	(818) 247-3399
Sofi Restaurant	Los Angeles,CA	(213) 651-0346
Sofian Market	Garden Grove,CA	(714) 530-7450
Soghomonian Farms	Sanger,CA	(209) 252-7848
Soofer Co., Inc. Sadaf	Los Angeles,CA	(213) 234-6666
Soojian, Inc.	Sanger,CA	(209) 875-7579
Soultany Restaurant	Hollywood,CA	(213) 876-3398
Souren & Voc's Friendly Hills	Whittier,CA	(213) 693-6116
South Gate Frozen Food	South Gate,CA	(213) 567-1359
Sparta Greek Deli	Los Angeles,CA	(213) 622-5950
Sparta Grocery	Chicago,IL	
Sphinx	Los Angeles,CA	(310) 477-2358
Spiro's House of Pizza	Providence,RI	(401) 273-7755
Spiro's Market	Dover,NJ	(201) 361-0884
Sports Grill	Irvine,CA	(714) 551-6142
Spring Market	Fullerton,CA	(714) 879-7139
Squire	Great Neck,NY	(516) 487-4032
St. Georges Bakery & Grocery	Winter Park,FL	(407) 647-1423
Stagecoach Restaurant	San Francisco,CA	(415) 956-4650
Stamatelos Grocery	Pensacola,FL	(904) 433-0963
Stamoolis Brotheres Co.	Pittsburgh,PA	
Stani	New York,NY	(718) 728-4966
Star Kabab	Long Beach,CA	(310) 434-4848
Star Market	Chicago,IL	

Ethnic Cookbooks

Business Names-127

Stark Liquor & Jr. Market	Van Nuys,CA	(818) 780-3041
Starr Liquor	Van Nuys,CA	(818) 780-1640
Steak in a Sack	Falls Church,VA	
Stella Foods Co.,Inc.	Baltimore,MD	
Stella's Pizza & Subs	Watertown,MA	(617) 924-5692
Stemma Confectionery	Detroit,MI	
Steve's Superette	Pensacola,FL	
Steve-Vin Bake-A-Deli, Inc.	Watertown,MA	(617) 924-3666
Steven's Steakhouse	City of Commerce,CA	(213) 723-9856
Stoukas Imports	Detroit,MI	
Stoyanof's	San Francisco,CA	(415) 664-3664
Subway Sandwiches	Glendale,CA	(818) 243-9692
Subway Sandwiches	Glendale,CA	(818) 244-0411
Sugar's Campus Store	Washington,DC	
Sultan's Delight, Inc.	Staten Island,NY	(718) 720-1557
Sultan's Kebabs Restaurant	Hollywood,FL	(305) 927-0002
Sultani Restaurant	Hollywood,CA	(213) 876-3389
Sun Beverage Co. (Abali)	Los Angeles,CA	(818) 409-0117
Sun-Ni Armenian String Cheese	Upper Darby,PA	(215) 853-3449
Sunflower Grocery & Deli	Covina,CA	(818) 339-1141
Sunflower Grocery	Rego Park,NY	(718) 275-0479
Sunland Produce	Sun Valley,CA	(818) 504-6629
Sunnyland Bulghur Co.	Fresno,CA	(209) 233-4983
Sunnyvale Market (Tajrish)	Walnut Creek,CA	(510) 932-8404
Sunrise Bakery	Turlock,CA	(209) 632-3228
Sunrise Deli	San Francisco,CA	(415) 664-8210
Sunrise Market & Deli	Washington,DC	(202) 333-1972
Sunset Grocery & Meats	Hollywood,CA	(213) 664-8455
Sunset House Restaurant	Hollywood,CA	(213) 464-6555
Sunshine Liquor Market, Inc.	Buena Park,CA	(714) 522-3670
Super California	Canoga Park,CA	(818) 703-1612
Super Doyar	Springfield,VA	(703) 866-0222
Super Hero's	Watertown,MA	(617) 924-9507
Super Jordan Market	Los Angeles,CA	(310) 478-1706
Super Sahel	Houston,TX	(713) 266-7360
Super Saver Market	Riverside,CA	(714) 684-8252
Super Shilan Market	Northridge,CA	(818) 993-7064
Super Vanak International Food	Chicago,IL	(312) 465-2424
Super Vanak International Food	Houston,TX	(713) 952-7676
Supreme International Foods	Forest Hills,NY	(718) 897-4700
Susan's Catering	,VA	(703) 369-1413
Swedish Inn	Woodland Hills,CA	(818) 884-7461
Sweet Stop	Washington,DC	(202) 342-2080
Sweety's Cafe	Great Neck,NY	(516) 466-6260
Sweis International Market	Van Nuys,CA	(818) 785-8193
Syria-Lebanon Baking Co.	Cleveland,OH	
Syrian Grocery Imp.Co.Inc.	Boston,MA	(617) 426-1458

T

Tabeer Restaurant	Langley Park,MD	
Tabrizi Bakery	Watertown,MA	(617) 926-0880
Tak Grocery Store	Centereach,NY	(516) 737-6244
Take-5	Studio City,CA	(818) 509-0084
Tampa Deli & Middle East.	Riverside,CA	(714) 688-6113
Tanouri Restaurant	Los Angeles,CA	(213) 470-7003
Tarabya	Great Neck,NY	(516) 482-0760
Tarikyan Grocery	Hollywood,CA	(213) 660-5229
Tarver's Delicacies	Sunnyvale,CA	
Tarzana Armenian Grocery	Tarzana,CA	(818) 881-6278
Tarzana Armenian Grocery	Woodland Hills,CA	(818) 703-7836
Tarzana Armenian Grocery	Santa Monica,CA	(310) 576-6473
Taslakian's Pastry	Hollywood,CA	(213) 662-5588
Taste It, House of Cookies	Pasadena,CA	(818) 794-4280
Tasty Hamburger	Los Angeles,CA	(213) 623-4798
Taverna Vraka	New York,NY	(718) 721-3007
Taverna	Roslyn,NY	(516) 484-8860
Tavilian Grocery	Hollywood,CA	(213) 665-3988
Tavous Restaurant	Annandale,VA	(703) 941-1451
Tea Room, Newport Beach	Newport Beach,CA	(714) 756-0121
Tea Sara Restaurant	San Jose,CA	(408) 265-5090
Tea Sara Restaurant	San Jose,CA	(408) 241-5115
Tehran Market	Santa Monica,CA	(213) 393-6719
Tehran Pars Market	Encino,CA	(818) 788-6950
Tehrani Restaurant	Redondo Beach,CA	(310) 214-2626
Temco, Inc.	Glendale,CA	(818) 241-2333
Temple Torah	Little Neck,NY	(718) 423-2100
Termeh Market & Deli	Laguna Niguel,CA	(714) 831-4000
Thanos Imported Groceries	Syracuse,NY	
Thomas Market	Wheaton,MD	(301) 942-0839
Thousand & One Nights	Van Nuys,CA	(818) 705-2666
Three Crown Gourmet	Encino,CA	(818) 774-1412
Three Sisters Delicatessen	Chicago,IL	
Tiffany's Bakery	Glendale,CA	(818) 242-3470
Tigran's Grocery	Glendale,CA	(818) 243-2323
Tilda Marketing, Inc.	Englewood Cliff,NJ	(201) 569-0909
Tip Top Cafe	Los Angeles,CA	(213) 653-6222
Tochal Market	Los Angeles,CA	(213) 470-6454
Tom's Ravioli Co.	Newark,NJ	
Tony's Grocery & Fresh Meat	Panorama City,CA	(818) 782-6195
Tony's Market	Providence,RI	(401) 421-4700
Top Star Co.	Willowdale,	(416) 477-1877
Topkapi Restaurant	Fairfax,VA	
Topping and Co.	Milwaukee,WI	(414) 383-8911
Toreeno Broasted Chicken	Manhattan Beach,CA	(310) 546-7775
Toufayan Bakery	North Bergen,NJ	(201) 861-4131
Towne House	Albuquerque,NM	(505) 255-0057
Tri EZ Foods	San Jose,CA	(408) 978-5612
Tripoli	New York,NY	(718) 596-5800
Tru-Valu Market	Sacramento,CA	(916) 443-4256
Tu-Tu Halal Meat Market	Falls Church,VA	(703) 998-5322
Turlock Bakery	Granada Hills,CA	(818) 360-7223
Tweeten's Liquor & Deli	Pleasant Hill,CA	(510) 825-2422

U

UN Market	San Francisco,CA	(415) 563-4726
Uncle Paulie's	Fresno,CA	(209) 233-1111
Union Market Station Rest.	Watertown,MA	(617) 923-0480
Unique Market	Glendale,CA	(818) 247-2633
United Food/Massis Food	Los Angeles,CA	(213) 627-3917
United Foods & Supply Corp.	Union City,CA	(510) 471-0984
United Supermarket	New York,NY	
University Market	Akron,OH	
University Market Place	Washington,DC	(202) 667-2206
University Pantry Deli	Charlotte,NC	(704) 549-9156
Up All Night	Sherman Oaks,CA	(818) 501-8661
Uptown Deli	Farmington Hills,MI	(313) 626-3715
Ureni Restaurant	Hollywood,CA	(213) 666-4686

V

V & K Distributing Co.	Burbank,CA	(818) 848-1926
V & K Distributing Co.	Van Nuys,CA	(818) 904-0479
V. J. Market	Burbank,CA	(818) 843-3613
Vahagen Armenian Cuisine	Glendale,CA	(818) 241-1496
Vahe's Armenian Cuisine	Watertown,MA	(617) 924-9463
Vahe's Grocery	Canoga Park,CA	(818) 702-9092

128-Business Names

Ethnic Cookbooks

Valley Bakery	Fresno,CA	(209) 485-2700
Valley Food Market	Reseda,CA	(818) 343-0337
Valley Hye Market	Van Nuys,CA	(818) 786-5271
Valley Ice Cream Distributing	Van Nuys,CA	(818) 780-0641
Van Nuys Cafe	Van Nuys,CA	(818) 994-9948
Van's Kabab	Tujunga,CA	(818) 353-1239
Vanak Kabob Restaurant	Yorba Linda,CA	(714) 993-0655
Vardashen Meat & Grocery	N. Hollywood,CA	(818) 765-5725
Variety Food Market	Stanton,CA	(714) 761-5571
Vatan Market	Los Angeles,CA	(310) 659-4000
Ventura Kosher Meat	Tarzana,CA	(818) 881-3777
Verdugo Market & Deli	Glendale,CA	(818) 241-5424
Vic & Ray's Liquor	Canoga Park,CA	(818) 348-9172
Vic's of San Carlos	San Carlos,CA	(415) 595-2606
Victor's Cheese Corp.	Palisades Park,NJ	(201) 947-3677
Victoria Importing Co.	New Britain,CT	
Victory Meat & Grocery	Van Nuys,CA	(818) 787-4081
Villa Market	Chevy Chase,MD	(301) 951-0062
Villa Market	Glendale,CA	(818) 500-9005
Village Deli	New Millford,NJ	(201) 261-3035
Village Market	Fontana,CA	(714) 822-5613
Village Pastry Shop	Glendale,CA	(818) 241-2521
Village Persian Restaurant	Orange,CA	(714) 282-1010
Village Super Market Inc.	South Orange,NJ	
Violet's	Eagle Rock,CA	(213) 255-4562
Virginia & Spanish Peanut Co.	Providence,RI	(401) 421-2543
Virginia's Mid-East Cafe	Sylvan Lake,MI	(313) 681-7170

W

Washington Dairy Product Co.	Chicago,IL	
Wayside Market	Silver Spring,MD	
West Meat Market	Chicago,IL	(312) 769-4956
Westwood Grocery	Los Angeles,CA	(213) 475-9804
Wheatly Bake Shop	Greenvale,NY	(516) 621-7575
Wiley's Hastings Liquors	Pasadena,CA	(818) 351-9786
Wine Gardern Restaurant	Oakland,CA	(415) 835-4433
Wine Room Restaurant	Hollywood,CA	(213) 462-7672
Wing Wing Imported Groceries	Boston,MA	
Wooden Shoe Pastry Shop	Silver Spring,MD	
Worldwide Foods	Dallas,TX	(214) 824-8860

Y

Yafa Restaurant	Los Angeles,CA	(213) 934-7255
Yaldzlar Restaurant	New York,NY	(212) 557-0055
Yaranush Middle Eastern	New Jersey,NJ	(914) 682-8449
Yas Bakery & Confectionery	Rockville,MD	(301) 762-5416
Yasaman Restaurant	Huntington Beach,CA	(714) 968-7333
Yasha's	N. Hollywood,CA	(818) 508-0905
Yassin Royal Bakery	Dearborn,MI	(313) 945-1550
Yazdi Pastry Shop	Seal Beach,CA	(213) 598-9880
Yekta Deli & Grocery	Elmhurst,NY	(718) 335-6828
Yekta Middle Eastern Grocery	Rockville,MD	(301) 984-1190
Yemeni Cafe	New York,NY	(718) 834-9533
Yepremian Hall	Glendale,CA	(818) 241-1463
Yeraz International Grocery	Sepulveda,CA	(818) 895-1838
Yerevan Bakery, Inc.	New York,NY	(718) 729-5400
Yerevan Deli & Bakery	N. Hollywood,CA	(818) 509-0243
Yerevan Lahmadjoun	Montreal,	(514) 270-1076
Yerevan Ranch Market	Montebello,CA	(213) 722-3780
Yes International Food Co.	New York,NY	(212) 227-4695
Yosh Bazaar	Burlingame,CA	(415) 343-5833
Youngsville Super Market	Manchester,NH	(603) 622-6353

Your Market	Los Angeles,CA	(310) 287-0815
Your Place # 1	Beverly Hills,CA	(310) 858-1977
Your Place # 2	Encino,CA	(818) 501-4646

Z

Z	New York,NY	(212) 254-0960
Zabar's	New York,NY	(212) 787-2000
Zahle Restaurant	Montreal,	(514) 336-3013
Zakarian Family Variety Store	Scarborough,	(416) 298-4118
Zand Market	Albany,CA	(510) 528-7027
Zand Market	Thousand Oaks,CA	(805) 494-3646
Zangezour Meat Market	Glendale,CA	(818) 545-9988
Zankou Chicken	Hollywood,CA	(213) 665-7842
Zankou Chicken	Glendale,CA	(818) 244-2237
Zaven's	Chicago,IL	(312) 787-8260
Zeitoon Grocery	Glendale,CA	(818) 247-7093
Zetlian Bakery	Los Angeles,CA	(213) 728-2839
Zeytun Restaurant	Hollywood,CA	(213) 664-3000
Zorba B.B.Q.	Fresno,CA	(209) 225-6774
Zorba's	Washington,DC	
Zov's Bistro	Tustin,CA	(714) 838-8855
Zvartnotz Grocery	Glendale,CA	(818) 956-0712
Zygos Taverna	New York,NY	(718) 728-7070

Ethnic Food Marketplace Georgraphical Listings for the U.S. and Canada

Canada

A & A Foods	Ottawa	(613) 737-2144
Ara's Catering	Toronto	(416) 495-9549
Ararat Bakery & Deli	Toronto	(416) 782-5722
Arax Restaurant	Scarborough	(416) 288-1485
Armenian Bakery	Scarborough	(416) 757-1559
Armenian Kitchen	Scarborough	(416) 757-7722
Athina Supermrche	Chomedey	(514) 682-8010
Ayoub's Fruits & Vegetable	Ottawa	(613) 233-6417
B & E. Masion d'Aliments	N.D.G., Quebec	(514) 482-0262
Bahar Market	Toranto, Ontario	(416) 256-1268
Bijan Specialty Food	Ambleside, Vancouver	(604) 925-1055
Cedar Foods	Downsview	(416) 661-8999
Chez Ali Baba Restaurant	Montreal	(514) 982-9393
Chez Nassons Restaurant	Montreal	(514) 276-2719
Da Giovanni Fruit Store	Montreal	(514) 332-2550
Darvish Restaurants	Toronto	(416) 535-5530
Domestic Foods	Ontario	(613) 236-6421
Dudemaine Groceteria	Montreal	(514) 334-8267
Eaquire Souvlaki & Steak	Scarborough	(416) 497-0618
Garni Bakery	Willowdale	(416) 492-7200
Haddad Bakery	Downsview	
Holy Land Restaurants	Scarborough	(416) 755-0137
Joseph's Place	Downsview Ontario	(416) 739-7221
Kaysery Food Co.	Scarborough	(416) 498-0547
Khorak Market	Toronto, Ontario	(416) 221-7558
Le Capitaine	Montreal	(514) 489-2642
Main Importing Grocery, Inc.	Montreal	(514) 861-5681
Marche Adonis	Montreal	(514) 382-8606
Mediterranean Bakery	Weston	(416) 743-2267
Mere Milia	Chomedey Laval	(514) 681-8895
Mitaya Fine Cuisine	Markham, Ontario	(416) 940-6296
Nasr Mini Market	Scarborough	(416) 757-1611
Norik Bakery	Toronto	(416) 757-8314
Pars International Market	N. Vancouver	(604) 988-3515
Patisserie Armenia	Montreal	(516) 389-4696
Pizzajoun	Montreal	(514) 383-5588
Princess Meat and Deli	Toronto	(416) 752-4692
Ramses Deli	Toronto	(416) 755-0244
Restaurant Asmar	Montreal	
Restaurant Georges	Chomedey	(514) 681-8189
Royal George Grocery	Montreal	(514) 277-4123
Sassoon Supermarche	Montreal	(514) 337-7923
Sayfy's Groceteria	Montreal	(514) 277-1257
Shirak Meat Product Ltd.	Scarborough	(416) 266-7519
Top Star Co.	Willowdale	(416) 477-1877
Yerevan Lahmadjoun	Montreal	(514) 270-1076
Zahle Restaurant	Montreal	(514) 336-3013
Zakarian Family Variety Store	Scarborough	(416) 298-4118

Alabama

Bruno's Food Store	Birmingham	
Cash Produce Co.	Birmingham	
Lignos Groceries	Mobile	(205) 432-9870
Sawaya Delicatessen	Birmingham	

Arizona

Andros Restaurant	Scottsdale	(602) 945-9573
Apadana Restaurant	Tempe	(602) 945-5900
Cater-Maid Bake Shop	Phoenix	
El Greco's Restaurant	Tucson	(601) 623-2398
Filippo's Italian Groc.& Liqu.	Phoenix	
Greek Islands Restaurants	Phoenix	(602) 274-3515
Haji Baba Middle Eastern Food	Tempe	(602) 894-1905
Haji Baba Restaurant	Tempe	(602) 894-2442

California

1 Stop Market	Canoga Park	(818) 713-9165
10 to 10 International Cuisine	Glendale	(818) 545-8506
4 Seasons Produce	Glendale	(818) 244-9698
4 Star General's Kebob	Los Angeles	(213) 482-5240
7 Star Deli & Market	Granada Hills	(818) 363-8577
7 to 7 Market	Torrance	(213) 370-5707
A & P Market	Glendale	(818) 243-2709
A-1 Liquor & Jr. Mart	Glendale	(818) 500-8471
Abadan Bazar	Reseda	(818) 345-7602
Abner's Broasted Chicken	Woodland Hills	(818) 340-9466
Abou Khodor Restaurant # 1	Glendale	(818) 241-5562
Abou Khodor Restaurant # 2	Hollywood	(213) 461-5070
Acacia Grocery	Glendale	(818) 956-5341
Acropolis Greek Restaurant	Hollywood	(213) 463-8644
Aegean Isles Restaurant	W. Los Angeles	(213) 477-7991
Aesop's Tables	La Jolla	(619) 455-1535
Afghan Cuisine Restaurant	Hollywood	(213) 483-8475
Agop's Market	Glendale	(818) 502-0924
Ahmad International	Sacramento	(916) 451-2939
Ahwaz International Groceries	Anaheim	(714) 772-4492
Aivazian Super Catering & Hall	Glendale	(818) 241-8829
Akhtamar Armenian Restaurant	Sepulveda	(818) 894-5656
Akoubian's Deli Grocery	Fountain Valley	(714) 775-7977
Al's Italian American Deli	Montrose	(818) 249-3031
Al-Ahram Supermarket	Anaheim	(714) 527-9190
Al-Amir the Prince	Los Angeles	(213) 931-8740
Al-Hilal Market	Los Angeles	(213) 731-0868
Al-Madinah	Lomita	(310) 325-4778
Al-Madinah	Garden Grove	(714) 531-0321
Al-Manar Market	Daly City	(415) 756-1133
Al-Manara Restaurant	Anaheim	(714) 952-3239
Al-Mimas Catering	Burbank	(818) 845-5765
Al-Noor Market	Garden Grove	(714) 839-5123
Al-Rawsha Restaurant	San Diego	(619) 281-4259
Al-Salam Restaurant	Pomona	(714) 593-5225
Al-Sham Restaurant	Anaheim	(714) 220-0894
Al-Tayebat Market	Anaheim	(714) 520-4723
Al-Wazir Restaurant	Hollywood	(213) 856-0660
Al-Wazir	Glendale	(818) 500-1578
Aladdin Kebob House	Duarte	(818) 357-0512
Aladdin Restaurant	Glendora	(818) 914-7755
Alexander's Market	Malibu	(310) 457-9776
Alexis Deli & Grocery	Montrose	(818) 957-5687
Ali Baba Foods	West Covina	(818) 810-5108
Ali Baba Market	Anaheim	(714) 774-5064

130-Geographical Listing — Ethnic Cookbooks

Ali Baba Restaurant	Anaheim	(714) 774-5632
Ali's Market	Redlands	(714) 798-7454
Aljibani Halal Market	Diamond Bar	(714) 861-3865
Almaden Bazar	San Jose	(408) 268-6867
Aloonak Market	Los Angeles	(310) 820-1844
Alpha Catering	Oxnard	(805) 486-4554
Alvand Market	Costa Mesa	(714) 545-7177
Alvie's Restaurant	San Diego	(619) 232-0529
Alvin's Scrumptious Coffee Tea	San Francisco	(415) 661-2888
Amamchyan Market	Hollywood	(213) 462-8675
American Armenian Grocery	Pasadena	(818) 794-9220
American International Foods	Los Angeles	(213) 225-4151
American Spice Trading Co.	Los Angeles	(213) 664-2232
Amo's Produce & Grocery	Van Nuys	(818) 904-9938
Amoretti	Chatsworth	(818) 346-1454
Anahit Market	Sunland	(818) 353-1968
Andre Market	Glendale	(818) 548-5884
Andre Mini Kabob	Glendale	(818) 247-1772
Andre's Cafe	Glendale	(818) 549-9590
Andre's Restaurant	Fresno	(209) 229-6353
Andy's Burgers	N. Hollywood	(818) 985-9855
Angel Cafe	Los Angeles	(213) 936-3708
Angel Candies, Inc.	City of Commerce	(818) 961-4171
Angel's Catering	Glendale	(818) 507-8518
Ani Grocery & Deli	Glendale	(818) 241-7229
Ani Restaurant	Hollywood	(213) 661-6393
Anoush Bakery	N. Hollywood	(818) 766-2998
Anoush Deli & Grocery	Hollywood	(213) 465-4062
Anoush Family Restaurant	Hollywood	(213) 662-5234
Antoine's Restaurant	La Jolla	(619) 456-1144
Antoyan Wholesale Produce	Santa Fe Springs	(213) 693-6966
Apadana Market & Deli.	Westlake Village	(818) 991-1268
Apollo Market	Hawthorne	(213) 644-8956
Ara Deli & Grocery	Glendale	(818) 241-2390
Ara's Pastry	Hollywood	(213) 661-1116
Ararat Bakeries	Sanger	(209) 875-7579
Ararat Catering	Glendale	(818) 243-7468
Ararat Deli & Grocery	Glendale	(818) 243-0918
Ararat Fruit Market	Hollywood	
Ararat International Grocery	Hawaiian Gardens	(310) 420-2022
Ararat Middle Eastern Cuisine	Anaheim	(714) 778-5657
Ararat Sandwich	Los Angeles	(213) 488-1499
Arax Bakery	Hollywood	(213) 666-7313
Arax Deli	Montebello	(213) 721-1986
Arax Groceries & Deli	Van Nuys	(818) 705-0395
Arax Market	Fresno	(209) 237-5048
Araz Bakery	N. Hollywood	(818) 753-0839
Araz International Grocery	Granada Hills	(818) 368-8442
Araz Restaurant	Studio City	(818) 766-1336
Ardem Grocery	Hollywood	(213) 665-6984
Aresh Meat & Grocery	Burbank	(818) 569-7405
Arian Del Mart	Sacramento	(916) 363-6982
Arka Grocery & Record	Hollywood	(213) 666-6949
Armani Bakery, Inc.	Glendale	(213) 662-7479
Armen & Salpi M. East Cuisine	Tarzana	(818) 343-1301
Armenia International Market	N. Hollywood	(818) 760-4848
Armenian Cuisine	Fresno	(209) 435-4892
Armenian Garden Cuisine	Garden Grove	(714) 775-4499
Armenian Gourmet	Sunnyvale	(408) 732-3910
Armitage Restaurant	Hollywood	(213) 664-5467
Armtex	Pasadena	(818) 797-0040
Arpa Best Food	Glendale	(818) 507-1626
Arsen's Liquor and Deli	San Francisco	(415) 673-4900
Arsham's Deli & Grocery	Hollywood	(213) 660-7508
Artesia Market	Redondo Beach	(310) 379-6995
Arto's Coffee Shop	Los Angeles	(213) 627-1970
Arya International Market	San Diego	(619) 274-9632
Arzan Market	Tustin	(714) 544-6706
Ashta Lebanese Ice Cream	Hollywood	(213) 461-5070
Assan Caltex Foods	Canoga Park	(818) 700-8657
Athenian Gardens Restaurants	San Diego	(619) 295-0812
Athenian Gardens	Hollywood	(213) 469-7038
Athenian Gyros	Glendale	(818) 240-3631
Athenian Market	Northridge	(818) 363-1160
Athens Market	San Diego	(619) 234-1955
Athens West	Anaheim	(714) 826-2560
Atlas Market	Sherman Oaks	(818) 784-2763
Attari Food- Deli and Spices	Sunnyvale	(408) 773-0290
Attari	Los Angeles	(310) 470-1003
Avakian's Grocery	Glendale	(818) 242-3222
Avo's Bakery	Reseda	(818) 774-1032
Azar Kamarei Catering	San Jose	(408) 245-6141
B.M.G. Restaurant	San Jose	(408) 559-7330
Baba Aroush Nuts	Pasadena	(818) 798-5338
Babouch Moroccan Restaurant	San Pedro	(310) 831-0246
Babylon Bakery	Turlock	(209) 634-8061
Babylon Bakery	Sun Valley	(818) 767-6076
Baccarat Night Club	Sherman Oaks	(818) 784-3300
Baccarat Restaurant	Sunnyvale	(408) 261-1234
Badry's Catering	San Jose	(408) 274-0738
Bagramian Hall	Montebello	
Bakery Panos	Pasadena	(818) 791-1311
Balboa Liquor	Sepulveda	(818) 891-5985
Balian Ice Cream Co.	Los Angeles	(213) 261-6111
Balian Markets	Los Angeles	(213) 870-9219
Balian's Grocery	San Francisco	(415) 664-1870
Balji's Deli	Costa Mesa	(714) 631-0855
Barmaki's Pastry Shop	Anaheim	(714) 776-2621
Barmaky Restaurant	Glendale	(818) 240-6133
Basmati Rice Imports, Inc.	Irvine	(714) 474-4220
Bay Bistro	San Mateo	(415) 347-8686
Bazaar Pars	San Jose	(408) 985-8545
Bazaarak Persian/M.E. Grocer	Hayward	(510) 581-7253
Bazar Market # 1	Los Angeles	(213) 852-1981
Bazar Market # 2	Los Angeles	(213) 274-9077
Bazarak (Victorian Liquor)	Hayward	(415) 581-7253
Bazarcheh Restaurant	Beverly Hills	(310) 273-7420
Beijing Islamic Restaurant	Montebello	(213) 728-8021
Bel Age Restaurant	W. Hollywood	(310) 854-6247
Ben's International	Tarzana	(818) 705-2816
Best Buy Market	Glendale	(818) 244-3892
Best Chicken, the	Northridge	(818) 772-7771
Better Life	Santa Ana	(714) 547-0613
Betty's Place Restaurant	Northridge	(818) 775-1281
Beverly Hills Kabab (Firouz)	Beverly Hills	(310) 657-6257
Beverly Hills Meats	Beverly Hills	
Beverly Hills Pita House	Beverly Hills	(213) 659-8347
Beverly Market	Los Angeles	(213) 278-6329
Bezjian's Grocery, Inc.	Hollywood	(213) 663-1503
Bharat Bazar	La Puente	(818) 912-2014
Bianca's Deli	Hollywood	(213) 669-1829
Biblos International Foods	San Jose	(408) 371-4829
Big Apple Market	La Puente	(818) 918-2335
Big Bite Sandwiches	Glendale	(818) 241-0687
Big Bite Sandwiches	Montrose	(818) 957-5162
Bijan Bakery & Cafe	San Jose	(408) 247-4888
Bijan Market	Santa Monica	(213) 395-8979
Bisoutoun Restaurant	Reseda	(818) 434-5115
Bit of Lebanon	San Carlos	
Black Sea Restaurant	Los Angeles	(213) 653-2090

Ethnic Cookbooks   Geographical Listing-131

Blikian Brothers Meat Co.	Hollywood	(213) 665-4123		Club 44 Night Club	Glendale	(818) 241-0215
Blikian Brothers Meat Co.	N. Hollywood	(818) 985-0201		Club Tehran	Studio City	(818) 985-5800
Bootleggers Liquor & Deli	Glendale	(818) 240-6605		Coffee Najjar, Inc.	Riverside	(714) 276-4966
Brashov Restaurant	Hollywood	(213) 660-0309		Colbeh Iran	Reseda	(818) 344-2300
Brentwood Village Market	Brentwood			Constantine International	Montrose	(818) 249-6574
Broadway Mart & Deli	Glendale	(818) 243-3332		Crown Market	Glendale	(818) 956-0113
Broiler	Hollywood	(213) 462-5101		Crystal Restaurant	Van Nuys	(818) 776-9191
Broiler	Los Angeles	(310) 470-0525		Cuisine on the Green	Duarte	(818) 359-3388
Bucharest Grocery	Hollywood	(213) 462-8407		Daglian's Grocery	Van Nuys	(818) 786-5595
Buena Market	Buena Park			Damavand Market	Fremont	(510) 793-2606
Burbank Bakery	Burbank	(818) 841-7209		Dan's Super Subs	Woodland Hills	(818) 702-8880
Burger Continental	Pasadena	(818) 792-6634		Dana Point Liquor & Deli	Dana Point	(714) 861-6455
Burger Time	Fresno	(209) 432-4178		Danaian's Bakery	Hollywood	(213) 664-6842
Buy Direct Food Warehouse	San Jose	(408) 292-2211		Danielle's Bakery & Imported	El Cajon	(619) 579-1999
Byblos A Lebanese Cuisine	Los Angeles	(213) 475-9558		Danny's Fresh Meat & Produce	Van Nuys	(818) 708-9775
Byblos Deli & Sandwiches	Orange	(714) 538-7180		Dar Maghreb Restaurant	Hollywood	(213) 876-7651
C & K Importing Co.	Los Angeles	(213) 737-2970		Darband Restaurant	Beverly Hills	(310) 859-8585
Cafe Al Dente	San Francisco	(415) 772-8933		Dariush Restaurant	Lawndale	(310) 644-8672
Cafe De Leon	San Francisco	(415) 664-1050		Darvish Restaurant	Los Angeles	(310) 659-1112
Cafe Karnak	Orange	(714) 997-8323		Darya Restaurant	Santa Ana	(714) 557-6600
Cafe Markarian	Burbank	(818) 567-0170		Darya Restaurant	Orange	(714) 921-2773
Cafe Mediterranean	Burbank	(818) 769-0865		David Restaurant	Santa Clara	(408) 986-1666
Cafe Paris	Glendale	(818) 247-5787		Day Mart Market	Tarzana	(818) 996-8805
Cafe de Jour (French Pastry)	Glendale	(818) 247-9645		Del-Pack Foods Abjad Corporat.	Chatsworth	(818) 407-0887
Cahalan Groceries	San Jose	(408) 226-5992		Derian Egg Co.	Los Angeles	(213) 263-3447
California Market & Deli	Glendale	(818) 244-9541		Derian Foods	Los Angeles	(213) 263-3447
Calliope's	San Diego	(619) 291-5588		Dick's Liquor & Deli.	La Jolla	
Caravansary Gourmet Shop & Res	San Francisco	(415) 362-4641		Dimitri's Greek Cuisine	Solana Beach	(619) 259-0733
Caravansary Restaurants & Deli	San Francisco	(415) 921-3466		Diran International Grocery	Van Nuys	(818) 988-2882
Carlo Beverage Enterprises	Glendale			Discount Produce Market	Reseda	(818) 344-2959
Carlo Washington Produce	Pasadena	(818) 797-0017		Discount Produce Market	Sun Valley	(818) 768-0091
Carmel Grocery	San Diego	(619) 538-1069		Donikian's Market	Burlingame	(415) 348-9297
Carmel Kohsher Market	Los Angeles	(310) 479-4030		Dorr's Liquor	Redondo Beach	
Carmen's Pastries	Glendale	(818) 243-8761		Downtown Kabab	Los Angeles	(213) 612-0222
Carousel Restaurant	Hollywood	(213) 660-8060		Dunes Motel Restaurant	Hollywood	(213) 467-5171
Casa Blanca	Hollywood	(213) 466-3353		Dvin Fresh Meat & Fish Market	Glendale	(818) 547-4454
Casablanca International	Hollywood	(213) 467-8230		Dvin Market	Montebello	(213) 725-7250
Casablanca Restaurant	Albany	(510) 525-2000		Dvin Market	Reseda	(818) 344-0408
Caspian Catering Service	San Francisco	(415) 581-7253		Eastern Market	Modesto	(209) 575-0344
Caspian Meat Market	Orange	(714) 998-8440		Eden Market	San Leandro	(510) 276-0212
Caspian Persian Cuisine	Sunnyvale	(408) 248-6332		Edna's Coffee & Grocery	Glendale	(818) 243-0445
Caspian Regional Cuisine	Sunnyvale	(408) 248-6332		Eema's Market	Woodland Hills	(818) 702-9272
Caspian Restaurant	Irvine	(714) 651-8454		Eilat Bakery # 1	Los Angeles	(213) 653-5553
Cater Craft Foods, Inc.	Montebello			El Morocco Restaurnat	Hollywood	(213) 654-9550
Catering By Arut	Hollywood	(213) 668-9115		El Nejme Armenian Restaurant	N. Hollywood	(818) 505-8255
Catering by Herach & Ara	Montebello	(213) 724-5622		El-Ajami Restaurant	San Demas	(714) 394-0681
Central Deli	Fresno	(209) 222-9327		El-Comedor	Hollywood	(213) 661-5309
Central Market	Glendale	(818) 240-3450		Elat Market	Los Angeles	(310) 659-0576
Century Market	Los Angeles	(310) 473-1568		Elena's Greek Armenian Resta.	Glendale	(818) 241-5730
Cerritos Produce	Anaheim	(714) 995-1407		Elias Kosher Market	Los Angeles	(213) 278-7503
Charleys Famous Hamburger	Lemon Grove	(714) 460-2690		Elysee Pastry Shop	Los Angeles	(310) 208-6505
Charlie Kabob	Santa Monica	(213) 393-5535		Emil's Grocery	Saugus	(805) 297-3184
Charlie's Market	San Francisco	(415) 681-9569		Encino Market	Encino	(818) 343-7900
Chatanoga Restaurant	Santa Clara	(408) 241-1200		Erebuni Grocery	Hollywood	(213) 664-1700
Chayka Restaurant	Hollywood	(213) 660-3739		Etoile French Bakery	Woodland Hills	(818) 704-8461
Chef Diko Catering	Tujunga	(818) 951-3799		Euclid Liquors	Upland	
Chef's Corner	La Crescenta	(818) 249-3539		European Deli Middle East	Concord	(510) 689-1011
Chelokababi	Sunnyvale	(408) 737-1222		European Gourmet Deli	San Diego	(619) 582-0444
Chelstoon Hall	Beverly Hills	(213) 854-7272		European Sausages	N. Hollywood	(818) 982-2325
Chicken Eatery	Sherman Oaks	(818) 990-4445		Fairfax Family Market	Los Angeles	(213) 852-1981
Chicken Rotissary	Van Nuys	(818) 781-0615		Fairouz Greek & Lebanese Cuis.	San Diego	(619) 225-0308
Cio-Ce-Pol Restaurant	Los Angeles	(310) 479-5160		Fairuz M.E. Grocery & Deli	Pomona	(714) 596-2932
City Lights Super Night Club	Hollywood	(213) 489-7571		Faisal International Market	Riverside	(714) 784-7111
City Market	San Diego	(619) 583-5811		Fakhr El Din	Los Angeles	(213) 747-7839
Classy Catering	Sun Valley	(213) 875-1030		Falafel Arax	Hollywood	(213) 663-9687

132-Geographical Listing — Ethnic Cookbooks

Falafel Palace	Northridge	(818) 993-0734
Falafel Roxy # 1	Los Angeles	(818) 781-0805
Falafel Roxy # 2	Van Nuys	(818) 781-0805
Family Grocery	Pasadena	(818) 791-1086
Family Market	Northridge	(818) 349-2222
Family Produce & Market	Anaheim	(714) 821-7102
Famous Kabob	Sacramento	(916) 483-1700
Fantazia Restaurant	Downey	(310) 869-5733
Fard Candies	Torrance	(310) 326-6012
Farhad Restaurant	Campbell	(408) 866-1588
Farid Restaurant	Los Angeles	(213) 622-0808
Farin Co.	Van Nuys	(818) 376-0188
Farmer's Ranch	Montebello	(213) 728-2615
Father Nature's Cafe	Tarzana	(818) 344-7758
Fiddler's Coffee Shop	Los Angeles	(213) 931-8167
Finney's Cafeteria	Los Angeles	(213) 688-0995
Five Star Food Distributor	Hayward	(415) 782-4654
Five Ten Mini Market	Santa Clarita	(805) 259-2680
Flames Shahrzad Restaurant	Los Angeles	(213) 470-3242
Flor de Cafe Bakery	Glendale	(818) 543-1401
Food Mart	Orange	(714) 538-9428
Food Stop Market	El Sobrante	(510) 223-1111
Food of All Nations	Glendale	(818) 956-5572
Foothill Market	Monrovia	(818) 301-0089
Foothill Village Market	Glendale	(818) 242-1257
Four Star Catering, Inc.	Montebello	(213) 724-4162
Four Star Meat Co., Inc.	Wilmington	(310) 549-2830
Franklin Int. Grocery	Hollywood	(213) 465-0214
Freeway Market	La Crescenta	(818) 249-6701
French Gourmet	La Jolla	(619) 454-6113
Fresh " N" Green	La Puente	(818) 917-6189
Fresh Market	Burbank	(818) 848-4742
Fresno Deli	Fresno	(209) 225-7906
G & M Deli	San Francisco	
G.B. Ratto & Co.Int. Grocers	Oakland	(415) 832-6503
Galleon & Constandina's Cuisin	Los Angeles	(213) 388-9478
Gambino Restaurant	Los Alisos	(714) 458-2249
Garden Produce	Glendale	(818) 240-4821
Garine Deli & Grocery	Van Nuys	(818) 786-0946
Garny Fruits & Nuts	Glendale	(818) 242-9240
Garny Grocery	Burbank	(818) 841-7965
Garo's Basturma	Pasadena	(818) 794-0460
Garo's Snack Bar	Los Angeles	(213) 689-4832
Gary's Submarine Sandwich	N. Hollywood	(818) 763-0886
Geary Wholesale Company	Hayward	(415) 887-6797
George's Shish Kebab # 2	Fresno	(209) 264-9433
George's Shish Kebab	Fresno	(209) 228-8556
Georgia's Greek Cuisine	San Diego	(619) 284-1007
Georgig's Bakery, Inc.	Hollywood	
Georgio's Calif. Pizza & Pasta	Studio City	(818) 985-1072
Girazian Fruit Co.	Kingsburg	(209) 888-2255
Glen Elk Market	Glendale	(818) 545-0325
Glendale 1st Produce	Glendale	(818) 247-3730
Glendale Bakery	Glendale	(818) 247-2966
Glendale Farmer's Market	Glendale	(818) 507-8041
Glendale Fish & Meat Market	Glendale	(818) 502-1800
Glendale House of Liquore	Glendale	(818) 243-5855
Glendale Market	Glendale	(818) 243-2554
Glenoaks Deli & Grocery	Glendale	(818) 247-4021
Glenoaks Market	Burbank	(818) 559-7508
Global Bakeries, Inc.	Pacoima	(818) 896-0525
Goglanian Bakeries Inc.	Costa Mesa	(714) 642-3570
Golchin Overseas Corp.	Sylmar	(818) 896-6127
Golden Dream	Pasadena	(818) 798-7952
Golden French Bakers	Glendale	(818) 507-0039
Golden French Bakers	Van Nuys	(818) 785-1184
Golden State Bakery	Hollywood	(213) 666-6713
Golestan Persian Cuisine	Woodland Hills	(818) 347-0577
Golestan Restaurant	Los Angeles	(213) 470-3867
Gondole Restaurant	Anaheim	(714) 952-1185
Good Fast Pizza	Glendale	(818) 500-0006
Good Fellow Produce	Glendale	(818) 243-3745
Good Foods Market	Pasadena	(818) 794-5367
Gorky's Restaurant	Los Angeles	(213) 627-4060
Gourmet Food & Beverage Dist.	San Francisco	(415) 626-1847
Gower Gulch Grill	Hollywood	(213) 463-5530
Grandia Palace	Hollywood	(213) 462-8628
Grapeleaf Restaurant, The	San Francisco	(415) 668-1515
Great Greek Restaurant	Sherman Oaks	(818) 905-5250
Great Gyros, the	La Jolla	(619) 696-0424
Grecian Cuisine	Marina Del Rey	(213) 822-6221
Grecian Paradise	Tarzana	(818) 705-0633
Grecian Village	Studio City	(818) 508-0884
Greek Agora and Deli	Hollywood	(213) 462-3766
Greek American Foods	San Francisco	(415) 864-0978
Greek Armenian Deli	Downey	(310) 862-4566
Greek Connection, The	Los Angeles	(310) 659-2271
Greek Corner Restaurant # 1	San Diego	(619) 287-3303
Greek Corner Restaurant # 2	San Diego	(619) 484-9197
Greek House Importing Co.	Doweny	(310) 862-1220
Greek Island Delights	San Mateo	(415) 341-3383
Greek Market & Restaurants	Northridge	(818) 349-9689
Greek Town Restaurnat	San Diego	(619) 232-0461
Green Field Market	Azusa	(818) 969-4232
Green Market # 1	Los Angeles	(213) 470-3808
Green Market # 2	Los Angeles	(310) 276-9336
Grocery House Market	N. Hollywood	(818) 503-1222
Gugasian Hall	Santa Ana	
Gyro Time Restaurant	Westchester	(310) 337-1728
Hagop's Restaurant	Sherman Oaks	(818) 995-8254
Haig's Delicacies	San Francisco	(415) 752-6283
Hajji Baba Night Club	San Diego	(619) 298-2010
Halal Meats Deli & Grocery	San Jose	(408) 865-1222
Hanoian's Liquors	Fresno	(209) 233-7304
Hanoian's Market	Fresno	(209) 233-7301
Hansen's Cakes	Tarzana	(818) 708-1208
Harbor Liquor	Harbor City	(310) 326-9554
Hassan's Restaurnats	Newport Beach	(714) 675-4668
Hatam Restaurant	San Rafael	(415) 454-8888
Hatam Restaurant	Anaheim	(714) 991-6262
Hawthorne Market	Torrance	(310) 373-4448
Hellenic-American Im.Fd.&Past.	San Francisco	
Heller's Baking Co.	Pasadena	(818) 794-5422
Henry's B.B.Q. Chicken	Glendale	(818) 242-8222
Hi Ho Market	Orange	(714) 637-9525
High Meat Co.	Delano	(805) 725-1125
Hinkley Market	Hinkley	(619) 253-2315
Hollywood Deli & Jr. Market	Hollywood	(213) 460-4373
Hollywood Kabob Restaurant	Hollywood	(213) 463-4363
Hollywood Mart	Hollywood	(213) 464-3566
Hollywood Meat Market	Hollywood	(213) 467-7640
Holy Land Mini Market	Westminster	(714) 839-9865
Homa International Market	Los Alamitos	(213) 596-9999
Honolulu Jr. Market and Deli	Montrose	(818) 249-2532
Hons Market	Van Nuys	(818) 996-5553
House of Kabab	Montebello	(213) 721-8956
House of Shish Kebab	Fresno	(209) 432-0700
Hun-I-Nut Co.	San Jose	
Hy Mart Deli	N. Hollywood	(818) 506-7264
Hye Bakery	Montebello	(213) 722-8706

Ethnic Cookbooks

Geographical Listing-133

Hye Center Market	Reseda	(818) 701-7784
Hye Deli	Fresno	(209) 431-7798
Hye Market & Deli	Glendale	(818) 566-9942
Hye Neighbor Market	Panorama City	(818) 994-4592
Hye Quality Bakery	Fresno	(209) 445-1511
IZI Deli	Fresno	(209) 251-6599
Ian Caterers, Inc.	Los Angeles	(213) 721-0740
Imperial Gaz Co.	Santa Fe Springs	(213) 693-8423
Indo Pak Foods	Haywood	(415) 782-4654
Indo-European Foods, Inc.	Glendale	(818) 247-1000
International Bakery	Hollywood	(213) 953-1724
International Bread and Crois.	Los Angeles	
International Deli	San Jose	(408) 286-2036
International Deli	Sherman Oaks	(818) 990-4916
International Food	Hollywood	
International Food Bazar	San Jose	(408) 365-1922
International Food Bazar	San Jose	(408) 559-3397
International Food Center	Anaheim	(714) 533-7730
International Food Market	Davis	(916) 756-4262
International Grocery of S.D.	San Diego	(619) 569-0362
International Grocery	Duarte	(818) 301-0270
International Market	La Jolla	(619) 454-5835
International Market	Anaheim	(714) 774-9191
International Market	San Gabriel	(818) 286-4077
International Super Market	Hawthorne	(310) 676-1482
Iran Market	Reseda	(818) 342-9753
Iransara	San Jose	(408) 241-3912
Islamic Food Mart	Los Angeles	(213) 383-2583
Islamic Food Restaurant	Los Angeles	(213) 386-5332
Italian Deli & Produce	N. Hollywood	(818) 982-5781
Italian Middle East Market	Sherman Oaks	(818) 995-6944
J & J International Import	San Jose	(408) 428-9221
J & K Grocers	San Bernardino	(714) 882-1700
J & M Liquor	Los Angeles	
J. B.'s Grocery	Glendale	(818) 249-8224
J.M. Armelli Liquor Co.	Los Angeles	
Jabourian's Grocery	Northridge	(818) 349-5746
Jack's Deli & Ice Cream	Los Angeles	(213) 627-9997
Jack's International Deli	Glendale	(818) 242-3054
Jacob's Grocery & Deli	Van Nuys	(818) 782-0536
Jaleh Catering	San Jose	(408) 277-0506
Jamai Coffee Co.	Glendale	(818) 241-8156
Janet's Catering	Glendale	(818) 248-8907
Javan Restaurant	Los Angeles	(310) 207-5555
Jerry G. Bishop's Greek Island	San Diego	(619) 239-5216
Jim Dandy Fried Chicken	Los Angeles	(213) 666-8627
Jimmy's Deli	Fremont	(415) 490-2056
Joelle's Kabobland Deli	Glendale	(818) 500-3962
Johnny's Italian & Greek Deli	Santa Barbara	
Jons Supermarket	Hollywood	(213) 461-9382
Jons Supermarket	Glendale	(818) 244-8206
Jons Supermarket	Van Nuys	(818) 781-1772
Jonson's Market	Culver City	(213) 390-9639
Jose's Delicatessen	Palo Alto	
Joseph's Cafe & Restaurants	Hollywood	(213) 462-8697
Jovina's Chocolates	Glendale	(818) 502-0549
Just Like Home Restaurant	San Francisco	(415) 681-3337
K & M International	Hollywood	(213) 465-6146
K & S Deli	Rosemead	(818) 288-2333
Kabab House (KababKhouneh)	Glendale	(818) 243-7001
Kabab Royal	Irvine	(714) 476-9901
Kabob House	San Jose	(408) 559-7330
Kabob House	Concord	(510) 671-6969
Kabob No. 1	San Diego	(619) 222-2656
Kabob's Palace	Azusa	(818) 334-6759
Kaboby Restaurant #1	Los Angeles	(310) 208-9208
Kaboby Restaurant #2	Sherman Oaks	(818) 501-9830
Kachin's Place	Los Angeles	(213) 622-5621
Kal's Market	Glendale	(818) 507-7810
Karabagh Armenian Meat Market	Hollywood	(213) 469-5787
Karo's Catering	N. Hollywood	(818) 509-3952
Karo's Importing Deli	Hollywood	(213) 465-6486
Karoon Restaurant	Orange	(714) 997-8323
Karoun Market	Hollywood	(213) 665-7237
Karoun Restaurant	San Jose	(408) 947-1520
Kasra Restaurant	San Francisco	(415) 752-1101
Kasra Skeweres	San Francisco	(415) 433-4747
Katina Ice Cream & Bakery	Glendale	(818) 247-4068
Kavar Restaurant	Hollywood	(213) 669-1260
Keiv Restaurant	Montebello	(213) 722-3321
Kermanig Bakery	Glendale	(818) 246-2750
Key Club Restaurant	N. Hollywood	(818) 765-6600
Khaledian Brothers Deli	Glendale	(818) 246-5382
Khan Baba (House of Kabab)	Canoga Park	(818) 887-5450
Khayber International	Fremont	(510) 795-9549
Khayyam's Chelo Kabab	Albany	(510) 526-7200
Khazar Markets	Los Angeles	(213) 655-8674
Khooban Foods Inc.	Gardena	(310) 719-2390
Khyber Pass	San Diego	(619) 224-8200
Khyber Pass	San Diego	(619) 571-3749
King Cheese & Deli	Pasadena	(818) 791-2254
King Deli	Los Angeles	(310) 204-1149
King Market	Glendale	(818) 246-4015
Kismet Grocery	Burlingame	(415) 343-8919
Koko's Grocery	N. Hollywood	(818) 763-6731
Kolbeh Restaurant	San Diego	(619) 273-8171
Konanyan Meat Co., Inc.	Los Angeles	(818) 242-5603
Koo Koo Roo Restaurant	Los Angeles	(213) 383-6628
Koo Koo Roo Restaurant	Los Angeles	(213) 655-9045
Kouche Restaurant	Laguna Hills	(714) 588-8999
Koutoubia Restaurant	Los Angeles	(310) 475-0729
Kozanian Grocery	Hollywood	(213) 668-2514
Kozanian Grocery	Glendale	(818) 502-1013
Kozanian Grocery	N. Hollywood	(818) 952-9030
Kradjian Importing	Glendale	(818) 502-1313
Krivaar Cafe	San Francisco	(415) 781-0894
La Belle Epoque	Los Angeles	(213) 669-7640
La Cresta Market & Liquor	La Crescenta	(818) 248-0098
La Galette Pastry # 1	Sherman Oaks	(818) 905-0726
La Galette Pastry # 2	Hollywood	(213) 467-6606
La Marquise International	Los Angeles	(213) 668-1030
La Mediterranee	San Rafael	(415) 258-9123
La Mediterranee	San Francisco	(415) 431-7210
La Mediterranee	Berkeley	(415) 540-7730
La Mediterranee	San Francisco	(415) 921-2956
La Mediterranee	Pasadena	(818) 797-1558
La Mesa Market	La Mesa	(619) 589-6789
La Miche	Cupertino	(408) 725-1131
La Miche	Sunnyvale	(408) 730-5518
La Miche	Fremont	(415) 795-1105
La Strada Restaurant	Los Angeles	(213) 664-2955
Lahmajoon Kitchen	Fresno	(209) 264-5454
Lake Forest Mini Market	Lake Forest	(714) 859-9132
Lake Murray Liquor & Market	La Mesa	(619) 464-8477
Lavash Corporation of America	Los Angeles	(213) 663-5249
Lave Lee Restaurant	Studio City	(818) 980-8158
Layalina Restaurant	N. Hollywood	(818) 766-6575
Le Gourmet Elegance	Glendale	(818) 956-5079
Le Palais Bakery	Los Angeles	(213) 659-8345
Le Papillon Restaurant	Monrovia	(818) 357-7211

134-Geographical Listing — Ethnic Cookbooks

Leo's Sandwiches	Glendale	(818) 247-2050
Leon's Grocery & Deli	Van Nuys	(818) 787-8910
Leonardo's Italian & Greek Del	Redondo Beach	(310) 316-4433
Lev's Armenian Market	Montebello	(213) 721-2391
Levant International Food	Bellflower	(310) 920-0623
Lida's Food Center	Orange	(714) 998-7760
Little Rose Armenian Grocery	Pasadena	(818) 797-9022
Little Russia	Glendale	(818) 243-4787
Loft Catering	San Jose	(408) 866-2200
Los Feliz European Deli	Hollywood	(213) 660-9412
Lucky's Restaurant	Glendale	(818) 242-8415
Lucy's Mini Mart	Pasadena	(818) 791-1177
M & A Kebab King Catering	Montebello	(213) 725-1395
M & J Market & Deli	N. Hollywood	(818) 765-7671
M & M International Deli	N. Hollywood	(818) 980-0608
M & M Liquor & Market	Glendale	(818) 848-7470
M & M Market	Cypress	(310) 220-2207
M & R International Cuisine	Tarzana	(818) 705-6630
Mac's Deli	Monrovia	(818) 303-3016
Madinah Restaurant Party Hall	Los Angeles	(213) 383-9976
Magic Lamp	Pasadena	(818) 795-8701
Maha Imports and Groceries	Santa Clara	(408) 248-5025
Mahroukian Meat Market	Pasadena	(818) 791-1223
Mahtab Market	Rancho Palos Verdes	(310) 833-6026
Mamoun's Middle East Food	West Covina	(213) 339-3122
Manhattan Express	Van Nuys	(818) 997-3663
Manley Produce	San Francisco	
Marash Catering	Pasadena	(213) 629-2802
Marash Coffee Shop	Los Angeles	(213) 385-4302
Marathon Restaurant	Long Beach	(310) 437-6346
Marcel's Bakery	N. Hollywood	(818) 765-3844
Margosian Beverage Co.	Fresno	(209) 264-2823
Marhaba Market	Norwalk	(310) 864-2665
Market Express & Liquor	Van Nuys	(818) 781-0325
Marko's Pizzeria	Van Nuys	(818) 780-6114
Marouch Hollywood	Hollywood	(213) 662-9325
Marrakesh Restaurant # 1	Studio City	(818) 788-6354
Marrakesh Restaurant # 2	Newport Beach	(714) 645-8384
Marrakesh Restaurant # 3	La Mesa	(619) 462-3663
Marrakesh Restaurant # 4	La Jolla	(619) 454-2500
Mashti Ice Cream	Hollywood	(213) 874-0144
Masis Bakery	Hollywood	(213) 667-3001
Masis Market	Fresno	(209) 224-1228
Massis Armenian Food	Glendale	(818) 242-2333
Massis Armenian Sandwich	Los Angeles	(213) 623-8302
Massis Grocery & Deli	Canoga Park	(818) 888-6664
Massoud Restaurant	Los Angeles	(213) 748-1768
Maykadeh Restaurant	San Francisco	(415) 362-8286
Mc Allister Grocery	San Francisco	(415) 861-5315
Mediterranean Feast	Tarzana	(818) 705-7961
Mediterranean Groceries & Deli	Laguna Hills	(714) 770-2007
Mediterranean Kabob Room	Monrovia	(818) 358-7177
Mediterranean	Fresno	(209) 229-6347
Menora Market	Los Angeles	(310) 854-0447
Metropolis Restaurant	Los Angeles	(310) 659-3333
Miami Restaurant	Reseda	(818) 705-3322
Michael's Deli & Grocery	Hollywood	(213) 662-6311
Mid-Eastern Pastries & Grocery	San Diego	(619) 295-2311
Middle East Bakery	San Mateo	
Middle East Connection	Burbank	(818) 843-8339
Middle East Foods	Santa Clara	(408) 248-5112
Middle East Market	Arcadia	(818) 574-1971
Middle East Restaurant #2	Whittier	(310) 696-2224
Middle East Restaurant	Anaheim	(714) 826-8700
Middle East Restaurant	Alhambra	(818) 576-1048
Middle East Restaurant	Altadena	(818) 797-2576
Middle Eastern & Armenian Cat.	Pasadena	(818) 792-7663
Middle Eastern Bakery	Hollywood	
Middle Eastern Grocery	Anaheim	(714) 826-8700
Middle Eastern Market	Berkeley	(510) 548-2213
Middle Eastern Restaurant	Alhambra	(818) 281-1006
Mignon Bakery	Glendale	(818) 246-2217
Mihran's Restaurants	Tarzana	(818) 342-2290
Mikaelyan Food Market	Glendale	(818) 548-8045
Mikailian Meat Products	Valencia	(805) 257-1055
Mike's Catering	Glendale	(818) 241-1463
Miller's Market	Reseda	(818) 345-9222
Mini Kabob	Glendale	(818) 244-1343
Minoo Khosher Restaurant	Los Angeles	(310) 478-0072
Minoo Market	Huntington Beach	(714) 962-0305
Mission Liquor	Pasadena	(818) 794-7026
Mixed Nuts	Santa Ana	
Mixed Nuts	Hollywood	(213) 663-3915
Mixed Nuts	Glendale	(818) 240-9282
Mona Lisa Catering	Northridge	(818) 887-2424
Moomjean Meat Co.	Montebello	(213) 263-7856
Moscow Nights Restaurant	Reseda	(818) 349-5300
Moulasadra Grocery	Los Angeles	(213) 470-4646
Moun of Tunis Restaurant	Hollywood	(213) 874-3333
Movses Golden Pastry	Burbank	(818) 559-5200
Mr. Big Burger	Burbank	(818) 846-1406
Mr. Chicken	Oxnard	(805) 988-9645
Mr. Chicken	Van Nuys	(818) 786-1055
Mr. Deli	La Crescenta	(818) 957-7018
Mr. Lamb of California	S. El Monte	(310) 697-6103
Mt. Ararat Coffee Traders	Los Banos	(209) 826-1961
Mukuch Aintab Catering	Sun Valley	(818) 768-4929
Mumms Restaurant	N. Hollywood	(818) 763-7087
N & K Groceries & Deli	El Cajon	(619) 447-9471
Nassim Grocery	Pomona	(714) 593-8244
Natalie Pastry Shop	Los Angeles	(213) 470-4811
Naz Market	Anaheim	(714) 956-8926
Near East Foods	San Diego	(619) 284-6361
Neda's Market	Costa Mesa	(714) 650-5424
Nemouneh (Unique Market)	Santa Ana	(714) 836-8674
New Santa Clara Market	San Francisco	
New World Market	San Francisco	(415) 751-8810
New York New York Restaurant	Santa Clara	(408) 727-4420
Next Door Deli	Burbank	(818) 842-2383
Nicol's	Encino	(818) 881-3099
Nissan Market	N. Hollywood	(818) 763-3424
Nite Rock Club Cafe	Tujunga	(818) 352-1265
Nob Hill Banquet Center	Panorama City	(818) 989-2222
Nobakht Pastry Shop	Reseda	(818) 708-2608
Noble Bakery	Hollywood	(213) 656-7136
Norooz Bazar	Berkeley	(408) 295-2323
Northridge Bakery	Northridge	(818) 993-7469
Nory	Winnetka	
Noura Restaurant	W. Hollywood	(213) 651-4581
Nut Crackers	Glendale	(818) 545-9730
Nuts Bazaar	Oakland	(510) 601-1997
Oasis Date Gardens	Thermal	(619) 399-5665
Ohanyan's Int. Delicatessen	Fresno	(209) 225-4290
Old Fashion Deli	Glendale	(818) 244-9300
Old Sasoun Bakery	Pasadena	(818) 791-3280
Old Town Greek Cuisine	San Diego	(619) 291-5770
Old Town's Chicken	Monrovia	(818) 303-3393
Olympic Produce Market	Pasadena	(818) 797-7437
Omar Khayam Restaurant	Huntington Beach	(714) 373-0810
Omar's Pastry	Garden Grove	(714) 531-3551

Ethnic Cookbooks

Geographical Listing-135

Omid Market	Mission Viejo	(714) 458-7343
One & One Pizza & Deli	Glendale	(818) 246-9496
Orchid Market	Granada Hills	(818) 366-6969
Orchid Restaurant	Costa Mesa	(714) 557-8070
Orient Express	San Francisco	(415) 957-1795
Oven Fresh Bakery	Glendale	(818) 249-3587
Ozzies Restaurant	City of Commerce	(213) 726-0944
Ozzies Restaurant	Orange	(714) 633-3280
Paak International Gourmet	San Mateo	(415) 574-3536
Pacific Food Bazar	Glendale	(818) 956-1021
Pacific Food Mart	Glendale	(818) 242-8352
Pak Dairy, Inc.	Glendale	(818) 244-9435
Palette Restaurant	Hollywood	(213) 654-8094
Palmer Market	Glendale	(818) 243-4879
Pamchal Restaurant	Los Angeles	(310) 473-0309
Pamir Food Market	Fremont	(510) 790-7015
Panjoyan Produce	Costa Mesa	(714) 646-5718
Panos Char Broiler	Van Nuys	(818) 780-4041
Panos Pastry Shop # 1	Hollywood	(213) 661-0335
Panos Pastry Shop # 2	Glendale	(818) 502-0549
Papa Garo's	Redondo Beach	(213) 540-7272
Papa Joe's Deli	Cypress	(714) 527-2350
Papa Joe's Liqour Deli	Anaheim	(714) 826-0981
Papa Pooche	Sun Valley	(818) 504-9086
Papa's Restaurant	Berkeley	(510) 841-0884
Papadakis Taverna Restaurant	San Pedro	(310) 548-1186
Paradise Health Juice	Los Angeles	(213) 628-4530
Paradise Pastry	Glendale	(818) 545-4000
Paradise Restaurant	Mountain View	(415) 968-5949
Paradiso Restaurant	Los Angeles	(310) 475-1427
Pari's Deli	San Francisco	(415) 771-2219
Paros Restaurant	Hollywood	(213) 469-2610
Pars Market	Los Angeles	(310) 859-8125
Pars Market	San Diego	(619) 566-7277
Pars Restaurant	Torrance	(310) 370-4838
Pars Restaurant	San Bruno	(415) 871-5151
Pars Restaurant	Irvine	(714) 832-8324
Partamian Armenian Bakery	Los Angeles	(213) 937-2870
Pasadena Kabob House	Pasadena	(818) 795-3499
Pasha Restaurant	San Francisco	(415) 885-4477
Pasha's Afghan Cuisine	La Jolla	(619) 454-9229
Patchi	Los Angeles	(213) 464-0862
Patchi	Glendale	(818) 547-4317
Patrik's Quick Market	Glendale	(818) 247-7329
Pawinda Restaurnat	San Diego	(619) 454-9229
Payton Kabob	Glendale	(818) 242-8776
Persian Center Bazaar	San Jose	(408) 241-3700
Perspolis Restaurant	San Jose	(408) 265-5090
Perspolis Restaurants	Anaheim	(714) 991-7600
Petit Cafe	San Francisco	(415) 387-5266
Pharaoh's Market	Orange	(714) 633-2360
Phoenicia Restaurant	Glendale	(818) 956-7800
Phoenician Imports	Glendale	(818) 247-0500
Pick-A-Deli	Glendale	(818) 244-4190
Pizza Boy	Glendale	(818) 247-5748
Pizza Man	Burbank	(818) 843-3341
Pizza and Chicken Colorado	Los Angeles	(213) 254-0777
Player's Liquor	Manhattan Beach	(310) 545-5664
Pollo Clasico	Sacramento	(916) 369-8445
Ponzo's Deli	Pasadena	(818) 794-5682
Port of Athens Restaurant	N. Hollywood	(818) 508-9486
Pouri Bakery	Glendale	(818) 244-4064
Prime Produce	Van Nuys	(818) 905-9538
Pyramid Market	Oakland	(415) 428-1833
Quality Produce	La Puente	(818) 918-1225
Quik Pik Market	Sherman Oaks	(818) 501-6094
Raffi's Place # 1	Glendale	(818) 241-9960
Raffi's Place # 2	Glendale	(818) 247-0575
Rainbow Produce & Grocery	San Francisco	(415) 731-8715
Rainbow Stores	Los Angeles	(310) 397-5090
Ramsar Maket	Los Angeles	(213) 651-1601
Randy's M.E. Market & Catering	La Habra	(714) 738-1337
Reza Restaurant	Anaheim	(714) 778-2005
Rio Deli & Market	Woodland Hills	(818) 999-9486
Rio's Market	Redondo Beach	(310) 542-8616
Ritza Restaurant	Los Angeles	(213) 934-2215
Riviera Restaurants	Glendale	(818) 500-8700
Roastin' Chicken	La Habra	(310) 690-4588
Roastin' Chicken	Tujunga	(818) 249-7607
Robert's Catering Service	Burbank	(818) 848-8337
Robert's Fresh Produce	Tujunga	(818) 352-7787
Roberto's Restaurant	West Covina	(818) 331-0606
Rodeo Deli & Grocery	Glendale	(818) 244-6969
Ron's Market	Hollywood	(213) 465-1164
Rooster Brand Products Corp.	Los Angeles	(213) 582-5000
Rooz Market	Irvine	(714) 559-8535
Rose International Market	Mt. View	(415) 960-1900
Rose Market	Los Angeles	(213) 470-2121
Rose Market	Mountain View	(415) 960-1900
Rose's Restaurant	Canoga Park	(818) 716-5222
Roses International Trade, Inc	Los Angeles	
Rosicler Restaurant	Pasadena	(818) 792-9700
Royal Events	Hollywood	(213) 667-9141
Royal Kabab	Irvine	(714) 476-9901
Royal Morocco	Saratoga	(408) 741-0224
Royal Perspolis Restaurant	Beverly Hills	(310) 281-0777
Ruben's Market	Pico Rivera	(310) 949-1322
Rubic's Bakery	Pacoima	(818) 890-7299
Russian House	Woodland Hills	(818) 348-5112
S & J Importing	Long Beach	(310) 599-1341
S.E.A. Catering	Montebello	(213) 724-3782
Saadoun's Cuisine of Bagdad	Costa Mesa	(714) 642-0800
Saam Middle East Restaurant	Pasadena	(818) 793-8496
Sabrina Middle East Restaurant	Culver City	(310) 398-2308
Saghi Restaurant	Orange	(714) 974-3353
Sahag's Basturma	Hollywood	(213) 661-5311
Sahar Mini Market	Azusa	(818) 969-5010
Sahar Restaurant	Azusa	(818) 969-9150
Sahara Lebanese Cuisine	Redondo Beach	(310) 371-1533
Sahara Natural Foods, Inc.	Berkeley	
Sahara Restaurnat	Sherman Oaks	(818) 995-4609
Sahara Room	San Diego	(619) 427-8880
Saharex Imports, Inc.	City of Commerce	(213) 722-0391
Sako's Bakery	Glendale	(818) 247-3333
Sako's Sandwich Shop	Santa Fe Springs	(310) 693-1138
Salamat Market	Orange	(714) 921-0153
Salar Restaurant	Glendale	(818) 500-8661
Sam's Armenian Bakery	Glendale	(818) 247-6281
Sam's Food Market	Culver City	(310) 390-5705
Sam's International Deli	Hollywood	(213) 935-7212
Sam's Liquor	Montebello	(213) 722-1313
Sam's Pastry	Glendale	(818) 246-3811
Saman Market	Woodland Hills	(818) 347-8002
Samiramis Imports, Inc.	San Francisco	(415) 824-6555
San Diego Importing Co.	San Diego	
Sandpiper Inn, the	Desert Hot Springs	(619) 329-6455
Sandwich Construction Co.	Burbank	(818) 842-0715
Sandwich Shop	Valencia	
Sandwiches By Connal	Pasadena	(818) 798-0751
Santa Monica Food House	Santa Monica	

136-Geographical Listing

Ethnic Cookbooks

Santa Monica Khosher	Los Angeles	(213) 473-4435
Santa Monica Market	Los Angeles	(310) 207-5530
Santa Teresa Bakery	San Jose	(408) 578-1520
Santos Agency, Inc.	San Leandro	(510) 357-0277
Sara's Pastries	Anaheim	(714) 776-4493
Saray-e Ghalandar	Reseda	(818) 343-5115
Sasoon Meat Market	Glendale	(818) 243-2484
Sasoon Restaurant	Tarzana	(818) 708-8986
Sasoun Bakery	Hollywood	(213) 661-1868
Sasoun Mini Market	Montebello	(213) 724-6971
Sassoon Bakery & Grocery	Clovis	(209) 323-1185
Sassoon Restaurants	Fresno	(209) 224-0577
Sears Fine Food	San Francisco	(415) 986-1160
Selin Market	Glendale	(818) 502-0403
Sepahan Market	Van Nuys	(818) 988-6278
Serge's Deli	N. Hollywood	(818) 765-1200
Setareh Market	Los Angeles	(310) 820-6513
Sevan Bakery & Grocery	Reseda	(818) 343-0486
Sevan Deli & Imported Foods	Montebello	(213) 721-3804
Sevan Falafel	Reseda	(818) 881-3909
Sevan Grocery	Hollywood	(213) 665-6406
Sevan Grocery	Santa Ana	(714) 775-3776
Sevan Mini Market	Burbank	(818) 845-3069
Shad Zee Bakery	Los Angeles	(213) 474-7907
Shahbaz Restaurant	Los Angeles	(213) 936-3708
Shahrzad International Market	Santa Ana	(714) 850-0808
Shahrzad Restaurant	Sherman Oaks	(818) 905-6363
Shahrzad Restaurant	Encino	(818) 906-1616
Shalak Market	Montclair	(714) 946-7077
Shalimar Grocery	La Puente	(818) 918-6227
Shalizar Restaurant	Montclair	(714) 946-8481
Shalizeh Restaurant	Panorama City	(818) 894-7557
Shalom Meat Market	Encino	(818) 345-8612
Shalton Restaurant	Los Angeles	(213) 891-1984
Shammy's Market	Woodland Hills	(818) 883-9811
Shamshiri Restaurant # 1	Los Angeles	(310) 474-1410
Shamshiri Restaurant # 2	Hollywood	(213) 469-8434
Shamshiri Restaurant # 3	Northridge	(818) 885-7846
Shamshiri Restaurant # 4	Glendale	(818) 246-9541
Shamshiri Restaurant	San Jose	(408) 998-0122
Shant's Imported Foods	Reseda	(818) 708-0945
Sheik Cafe	San Diego	(619) 234-5888
Shekarchi Kabab # 1	Los Angeles	(213) 474-6911
Shekarchi Kabab # 2	Los Angeles	(213) 746-4600
Shelled Nuts	Hanford	(209) 584-1209
Shemiran Market	W. Los Angeles	(213) 836-7286
Shemshad Food, Inc.	La Crescenta	(818) 249-9066
Shepherd's Cove	Downey	(310) 862-9441
Shirak Armenian Grocery	La Crescenta	(818) 249-3314
Shiraz Market	Carmichel	(916) 486-1200
Shiraz Restaurant	Sherman Oaks	(818) 789-7788
Shirinian Grocery	Glendale	(818) 243-0611
Shish Kabob Cafe	San Deigo	(619) 265-7800
Shish Kabob Express	Van Nuys	(818) 787-6718
Shish Kabob Grill	Los Angeles	(213) 824-7739
Shish Kabob House	La Jolla	(619) 459-4016
Sholeh Restaurant	Los Angeles	(213) 470-9131
Shoosh International	San Francisco	(415) 626-1847
Sibian's Restaurants	Whittier	(310) 698-6808
Siham's Deli & Sandwiches	Fullerton	(714) 871-0131
Silver Platter Catering	Monrovia	(818) 791-8248
Simon's Kohser Restaurants	Los Angeles	(310) 657-5552
Simon's Kosher Restaurants	Los Angeles	(213) 627-6535
Sipan Deli & Grocery	Sunland	(818) 352-3881
Smorgasbord Restaurant & Cater	Montrose	(818) 248-9536
Sneaky's Pizza	Glendale	(818) 247-3399
Sofi Restaurant	Los Angeles	(213) 651-0346
Sofian Market	Garden Grove	(714) 530-7450
Soghomonian Farms	Sanger	(209) 252-7848
Soofer Co., Inc. Sadaf	Los Angeles	(213) 234-6666
Soojian, Inc.	Sanger	(209) 875-7579
Soultany Restaurant	Hollywood	(213) 876-3398
Souren & Voc's Friendly Hills	Whittier	(213) 693-6116
South Gate Frozen Food	South Gate	(213) 567-1359
Sparta Greek Deli	Los Angeles	(213) 622-5950
Sphinx	Los Angeles	(310) 477-2358
Sports Grill	Irvine	(714) 551-6142
Spring Market	Fullerton	(714) 879-7139
Stagecoach Restaurant	San Francisco	(415) 956-4650
Star Kabab	Long Beach	(310) 434-4848
Stark Liquor & Jr. Market	Van Nuys	(818) 780-3041
Starr Liquor	Van Nuys	(818) 780-1640
Steven's Steakhouse	City of Commerce	(213) 723-9856
Stoyanof's	San Francisco	(415) 664-3664
Subway Sandwiches	Glendale	(818) 243-9692
Subway Sandwiches	Glendale	(818) 244-0411
Sultani Restaurant	Hollywood	(213) 876-3389
Sun Beverage Co. (Abali)	Los Angeles	(818) 409-0117
Sunflower Grocery & Deli	Covina	(818) 339-1141
Sunland Produce	Sun Valley	(818) 504-6629
Sunnyland Bulghur Co.	Fresno	(209) 233-4983
Sunnyvale Market (Tajrish)	Walnut Creek	(510) 932-8404
Sunrise Bakery	Turlock	(209) 632-3228
Sunrise Deli	San Francisco	(415) 664-8210
Sunset Grocery & Meats	Hollywood	(213) 664-8455
Sunset House Restaurant	Hollywood	(213) 464-6555
Sunshine Liquor Market, Inc.	Buena Park	(714) 522-3670
Super California	Canoga Park	(818) 703-1612
Super Jordan Market	Los Angeles	(310) 478-1706
Super Saver Market	Riverside	(714) 684-8252
Super Shilan Market	Northridge	(818) 993-7064
Swedish Inn	Woodland Hills	(818) 884-7461
Sweis International Market	Van Nuys	(818) 785-8193
Take-5	Studio City	(818) 509-0084
Tampa Deli & Middle East.	Riverside	(714) 688-6113
Tanouri Restaurant	Los Angeles	(213) 470-7003
Tarikyan Grocery	Hollywood	(213) 660-5229
Tarver's Delicacies	Sunnyvale	
Tarzana Armenian Grocery # 1	Tarzana	(818) 881-6278
Tarzana Armenian Grocery # 2	Woodland Hills	(818) 703-7836
Tarzana Armenian Grocery # 3	Santa Monica	(310) 576-6473
Taslakian's Pastry	Hollywood	(213) 662-5588
Taste It, House of Cookies	Pasadena	(818) 794-4280
Tasty Hamburger	Los Angeles	(213) 623-4798
Tavilian Grocery	Hollywood	(213) 665-3988
Tea Room, Newport Beach	Newport Beach	(714) 756-0121
Tea Sara # 2	San Jose	(408) 265-5090
Tea Sara Restaurant	San Jose	(408) 241-5115
Tehran Market	Santa Monica	(213) 393-6719
Tehran Pars Market	Encino	(818) 788-6950
Tehrani Restaurant	Redondo Beach	(310) 214-2626
Temco, Inc.	Glendale	(818) 241-2333
Termeh Market & Deli	Laguna Niguel	(714) 831-4000
Thousand & One Nights	Van Nuys	(818) 705-2666
Three Crown Gourmet	Encino	(818) 774-1412
Tiffany's Bakery	Glendale	(818) 242-3470
Tigran's Grocery	Glendale	(818) 243-2323
Tip-Top Deli	Los Angeles	(213) 653-6222
Tochal Market	Los Angeles	(213) 470-6454
Tony's Grocery & Fresh Meat	Panorama City	(818) 782-6195

Ethnic Cookbooks — Geographical Listing-137

Toreeno Broasted Chicken	Manhattan Beach	(310) 546-7775
Tri EZ Foods	San Jose	(408) 978-5612
Tru-Valu Market	Sacramento	(916) 443-4256
Turlock Bakery	Granada Hills	(818) 360-7223
Tweeten's Liquor & Deli	Pleasant Hill	(510) 825-2422
UN Market	San Francisco	(415) 563-4726
Uncle Paulie's	Fresno	(209) 233-1111
Unique Market	Glendale	(818) 247-2633
United Food/Massis Food Servic	Los Angeles	(213) 627-3917
United Foods & Supply Corp.	Union City	(510) 471-0984
Up All Night	Sherman Oaks	(818) 501-8661
Ureni Restaurant	Hollywood	(213) 666-4686
V & K Distributing Co.	Burbank	(818) 848-1926
V & K Distributing Co.	Van Nuys	(818) 904-0479
V. J. Market	Burbank	(818) 843-3613
Vahagen Armenian Cuisine	Glendale	(818) 241-1496
Vahe's Grocery	Canoga Park	(818) 702-9092
Valley Bakery	Fresno	(209) 485-2700
Valley Food Market	Reseda	(818) 343-0337
Valley Hye Market	Van Nuys	(818) 786-5271
Valley Ice Cream Distributing	Van Nuys	(818) 780-0641
Van Nuys Cafe	Van Nuys	(818) 994-9948
Van's Kabab	Tujunga	(818) 353-1239
Vanak Kabob Restaurant	Yorba Linda	(714) 993-0655
Vardashen Meat & Grocery	N. Hollywood	(818) 765-5725
Variety Food Market	Stanton	(714) 761-5571
Vatan Market	Los Angeles	(310) 659-4000
Ventura Kosher Meat	Tarzana	(818) 881-3777
Verdugo Market & Deli	Glendale	(818) 241-5424
Vic & Ray's Liquor	Canoga Park	(818) 348-9172
Vic's of San Carlos	San Carlos	(415) 595-2606
Victory Meat & Grocery	Van Nuys	(818) 787-4081
Villa Market	Glendale	(818) 500-9005
Village Market	Fontana	(714) 822-5613
Village Pastry Shop	Glendale	(818) 241-2521
Village Persian Restaurant	Orange	(714) 282-1010
Violet's	Eagle Rock	(213) 255-4562
Westwood Grocery	Los Angeles	(213) 475-9804
Wiley's Hastings Liquors	Pasadena	(818) 351-9786
Wine Gardern Restaurant	Oakland	(415) 835-4433
Wine Room Restaurant	Hollywood	(213) 462-7672
Yafa Restaurant	Los Angeles	(213) 934-7255
Yasaman Restaurant	Huntington Beach	(714) 968-7333
Yasha's	N. Hollywood	(818) 508-0905
Yazdi Pastry Shop	Seal Beach	(213) 598-9880
Yepremian Hall	Glendale	(818) 241-1463
Yeraz International Grocery	Sepulveda	(818) 895-1838
Yerevan Deli & Bakery	N. Hollywood	(818) 509-0243
Yerevan Ranch Market	Montebello	(213) 722-3780
Yosh Bazaar	Burlingame	(415) 343-5833
Your Market	Los Angeles	(310) 287-0815
Your Place # 1	Beverly Hills	(310) 858-1977
Your Place # 2	Encino	(818) 501-4646
Zand Market	Albany	(510) 528-7027
Zand Market	Thousand Oaks	(805) 494-3646
Zangezour Meat Market	Glendale	(818) 545-9988
Zankou Chicken	Hollywood	(213) 665-7842
Zankou Chicken	Glendale	(818) 244-2237
Zeitoon Grocery	Glendale	(818) 247-7093
Zetlian Bakery	Los Angeles	(213) 728-2839
Zeytun Restaurant	Hollywood	(213) 664-3000
Zorba B.B.Q.	Fresno	(209) 225-6774
Zov's Bistro	Tustin	(714) 838-8855
Zvartnotz Grocery	Glendale	(818) 956-0712

Colorado

Ace Baking Co.	Denver	(303) 296-7482
Aresh Grocery	Denver	(303) 752-9272
Economy Greek Market	Denver	(303) 623-9682
International Super Market	Denver	(303) 934-3337
Kebab Bakery & Delicatessen	Denver	
Middle East Grocery	Denver	(303) 756-4580
National Foods	Denver	

Connecticut

Betar's Market	Bridgeport	
Dimyan's Market	Danbury	
Easy Shop	New Britain	(203) 225-7810
Impero Import Co.Inc	Waterbury	
Mideast Specialty	Bridgeport	(203) 878-8337
Milano Super Market Inc.	Hamden	
North Street Market	New Britain	(203) 229-5481
P & S Importing Co.	Waterbury	
Shallah's Middle Eastern Imp.	Danbury	
Sharzad Grocery	Stamford	(203) 323-5363
Victoria Importing Co.	New Britain	

District of Columbia

Acropolis Food Market	Washington	(202) 829-1414
Aditi Restaurant	Washington	
Al-Maqha Restaurant	Washington	(202) 342-6140
Aloupis Company	Washington	
Bacchus Restaurant	Washington	
Bamian Restaurant	Washington	(202) 338-1896
Bamiyan Restaurant	Washington	
Calvert Delicatessen	Washington	
Caspian Tea Room	Washington	(202) 244-6363
Chelsea's Restaurant	Washington	(202) 298-8222
Columbia Delicatessen	Washington	
Dar Es Salam	Georgetown	(202) 342-1925
Fettoosh	Washington	(202) 342-1199
George's Townhouse	Washington	(202) 342-2278
Georgetown Cafe	Washington	(202) 333-0215
Gourmet Market, Inc.	Washington	
Hellas Greek Imports	Washington	
International Market	Washington	
International Market & Deli	Washington	(202) 293-0499
Katmandu	Washington	
Khyber Pass	Washington	
Kolbeh Restaurant	Washington	(202) 342-2000
Lebanese Taverna Restaurant	Washington	
Mama Ayesha's	Washington	
Marrakesh Restaurant	Washington	
Mediterranean Deli	Washington	
Nakeysa	Washington	
Pikapita	Washington	
Skenderis Greek Imports	Washington	(202) 265-9664
Skewer's	Washington	
Sugar's Campus Store	Washington	
Sunrise Market & Deli	Washington	(202) 333-1972
Sweet Stop	Washington	(202) 342-2080
University Market Place	Washington	(202) 667-2206
Zorba's	Washington	

138-Geographical Listing — Ethnic Cookbooks

Florida

Alexander Bakery Corp	Miami	(305) 858-4218
Angel's Market	Tarpon Springs	(813) 937-6731
Arabic Grocery & Bakery	Miami	
Atlas Foods	Tampa	(813) 933-5581
Chef Bijan	Casselberry	(407) 260-8855
Commerce International	Miami	(407) 678-6737
Damascus Imported Grocery	Hollywood	(305) 962-4552
Eastern Star Bakery	Miami	(305) 854-6381
Farah's Imported Foods	Jacksonville	(904) 388-0691
Fernando's Int. Food Mkt.	Miami	(305) 566-3104
Flamingo Grocery Inc.	Fort Lauderdale	
Greek American Grocery Co.	Miami	
Greek American Grocery Store	Miami	
Greek Place	Orlando	(407) 352-6930
Hajji Baba Pasargad Restaurant	Miami	(305) 221-7929
Italian Imported Super Market	Tampa	
Joseph Assi Bakery & Deli	Jacksonville	(904) 398-5167
Joseph Baratta	Miami	
Morae Restaurant	La Place Shopping	(813) 977-6018
Near East Bakery	Miami	
Pars Restaurant	Miami	(305) 551-1099
Rahal & Sons, Inc.	Miami	
Sahara II	Tampa	(813) 989-3612
Salam International Market	Winter Park	(407) 657-5560
Shiraz Food Market	Miami	(305) 264-8282
St. Georges Bakery & Grocery	Winter Park	(407) 647-1423
Stamatelos Grocery	Pensacola	(904) 433-0963
Steve's Superette	Pensacola	
Sultan's Kebabs Restaurant	Hollywood	(305) 927-0002

Georgia

1001 Night Restaurant	Atlanta	(404) 851-9566
Foxies Delicatessen	Atlanta	
George's Delicatessen	Atlanta	
Middle East Baking Co.	Atlanta	
Middle Eastern Groceries	Smyrna	
Shahrzad International Market	Atlanta	(404) 843-0549

Hawaii

Gourmet Bazaar	Honolulu	(808) 923-7658

Illinois

Akropol Pastry Shop	Chicago	
Al-Nogoom Grocery & Meat	Chicago	(312) 918-1700
Al-Rasheed Grocery	Chicago	(312) 925-4711
Aleman Meat & Grocery	Burbank	(312) 425-2711
Altira Wholesale, Inc.	Chicago	(312) 476-0511
Arya Food Imports	Chicago	(312) 878-2092
Athens Grocery	Chicago	(312) 454-0940
Casbah Armenian Restaurant	Chicago	(312) 935-7570
Family Meat Market & Produce	Chicago	(312) 434-0095
Galina's Deli	Chicago	
Gondola Restaurant	Chicago	(312) 737-0386
Grecian Phoenix Pastries	Chicago	
Hellas Grocery Store & Pastry	Chicago	
Holy Land Bakery & Grocery	Chicago	(312) 588-3306
International Foods	Chicago	(312) 478-8643
International Golden Foods, Inc	Niles	(312) 764-3333
Kam Shing Co.	Chicago	
Kandoo Grocery	Chicago	(312) 275-0006
Kelly's Food Mart	Rockford	
Mediterranean Imports	Waukegan	(312) 244-4040
Mesopotamia Restaurant	Chicago	(312) 348-0654
Middle East Trading	Chicago	(312) 262-2848
Middle Eastern Bakery & Grocer	Chicago	(312) 561-2224
New Deal Grocery	Chicago	
Palestine Bakery	Chicago	(312) 925-5978
Pan Hellenic Pastry Shop	Chicago	(312) 454-1886
Pita Inn	Skokie	(708) 677-0211
Ramallah Market	Worth	(708) 361-5665
Saba Meat & Market	Chicago	(312) 539-0080
Sahar Meat & Grocery	Chicago	(312) 583-7772
Sayat Nova	Chicago	(312) 644-9159
Sayat Nova	Des Plaines	(708) 296-1776
Sparta Grocery	Chicago	
Star Market	Chicago	
Super Vanak International Food	Chicago	(312) 465-2424
Three Sisters Delicatessen	Chicago	
Washington Dairy Product Co.	Chicago	
West Meat Market	Chicago	(312) 769-4956
Zaven's	Chicago	(312) 787-8260

Indiana

Athens Imported Food	Indianapolis	(317) 632-0269
Bakker Produce, Inc.	Griffith	(219) 924-8950
Bob Corey's Flaming	Terre Haute	

Iowa

George A. Skaff & Sons	Sioux City	
Italian Importing Co.	Des Moines	

Kentucky

A. Thomas Wholesale Meat Co.	Louisville	(502) 587-6947
Arimes Market	Lexington	

Louisiana

Central Grocery Company	New Orleans	(504) 523-1620
Fertitta's Delicatessens	Shreveport	
Progress Grocery Co.	New Orleans	

Maine

Boucouralas Brothers Super M.	Saco	(207) 284-4314
Model Food Importers & Distri.	Portland	(207) 774-3671

Maryland

Armand's Bake Shop, Inc.	Gaithersburg	
Asadur's Market	Rockville	(301) 770-5558
Bacchus Restaurant	Bethesda	(301) 657-1722
Baggal Market	Rockville	(301) 424-5522
Bismillah Halal Meat Market	Langley Park	(301) 434-0051
Caravan Market	Gaithersburg	(301) 258-8380
Danny's Foods	Parkville	
Dokan Market, Inc.	Bethesda	(301) 657-2361
E & I International, Inc.	Rockville	(301) 984-8287

Ethnic Cookbooks

Geographical Listing-139

Epicurean International, Inc.	Rockville	(301) 231-0700
Ernest Grocery Inc.	Baltimore	
Flaming Pit	Gaithersburg	(301) 977-0700
H. & H. Grocers	Baltimore	(301) 728-0022
HHH Distributors	Takoma Park	
International Cuisine Caterer	Rockville	
International House	Rockville	(301) 279-2121
Israeli Accents	Rockville	
Kabul West	Bethesda	(301) 986-8566
Kafe Katz	Rockville	
Katz Kosher Supermarket	Rockville	
Luxe Restaurant	Silver Spring	(301) 565-2622
Mediterranean Food Store	Ellicott City	(301) 465-8555
Middle East Bakery	Takoma Park	
Middle East Market	Takoma Park	
Moby Dick Cafe	Bethesda	
Moshe Dragon	Rockville	
Old World Market	Bethesda	(301) 654-4880
Orchard Market	Towson	(301) 339-7700
Papa John's Restaurant	Rockville	(301) 340-6970
Paradise Restaurant	Bethesda	
Persepolis Restaurant	Bethesda	(301) 656-9339
Shalom Market & Bakery	Silver Spring	
Shandiz Restaurant	Bethesda	(301) 961-8989
Shaul's & Hershel's Meatmarket	Wheaton	
Shlomo's Meat & Fish Market	Baltimore	
Stella Foods Co.,Inc.	Baltimore	
Tabeer Restaurant	Langley Park	
Thomas Market	Wheaton	(301) 942-0839
Villa Market	Chevy Chase	(301) 951-0062
Wayside Market	Silver Spring	
Wooden Shoe Pastry Shop	Silver Spring	
Yas Bakery & Confectionery	Rockville	(301) 762-5416
Yekta Middle Eastern Grocery	Rockville	(301) 984-1190

Massachusetts

A & A Food Market Inc.	Cambridge	
Algiers Coffee House	Cambridge	(617) 492-1557
Andrea's House of Pizza	Watertown	(617) 924-1760
Andros Dinner	Belmont	(617) 484-7322
Antoine's Pastry Shop	Newton	
Ararat Restaurant	Watertown	(617) 924-4100
Arax Market	Watertown	(617) 924-3399
Arsen's Flaming Shish Kebab	Burlington	(617) 273-3800
Bahnan's Bakery & Market	Worcester	(508) 791-8566
Barsamian Grocery	Cambridge	(617) 661-9300
California Fruit and Produce	Watertown	
Cardoos Inter. Food Corp.	Hyannis	(617) 775-7702
Cardullo's Gourmet Shop	Cambridge	(617) 491-8888
Cordoos International Food Cor	Dedham	(617) 329-3230
Cottage Market	Watertown	(617) 924-9718
Culinary Creations		(617) 893-6865
Daniel's Bakery	Brighton Center	(617) 254-7718
Demoulas Super Market No.1	Andover	
Demoulas Super Market No.10	Tweksbury	
Demoulas Super Market No.11	Wilmington	
Demoulas Super Market No.2	Chelmsford	
Demoulas Super Market No.3	Haverhill	
Demoulas Super Market No.4	Lawrence	
Demoulas Super Market No.5	Lowell	
Demoulas Super Market No.6	Lowell	
Demoulas Super Market No.7	Methuen	
Demoulas Super Market No.8	N. Andover	
Demoulas Super Market No.9	Pinehurst	
E. Demakis & Co. Inc.	Lynn	(617) 595-1557
Eastern Lamejun Bakers	Belmont	(617) 484-5239
El Morocco Restaurant	Worcester	(508) 756-7117
Euphrates Bakery Inc.	Watertown	
Euphrates Grocery	Boston	
Gardullo's Gourmet Shop	Cambridge	
Giavis Market	Lowell	(617) 458-4721
Hassey Grocery Store	Lawrence	(617) 686-6096
Hellas Baking Co.	Somerville	
Homs'y Groceries	Dedham	(617) 326-9659
Jim's Family Catering & Bakery	Worcester	(508) 752-1731
Kalunian Grocery	Dorchester	
Karoun Armenian Restaurant	Newtonville	(617) 964-3400
Laconia Grocery	Boston	
Lebanese Grocery	Roslindale	(617) 469-2900
Leo's Place	Cambridge	(617) 354-9192
Marash Bakery	Watertown	(617) 924-0098
Massis Bakery	Watertown	(617) 924-0537
Mediterranean Imports	West Roxbury	(617) 323-4341
Mediterranean Marketplace	Worcester	(508) 755-0258
Middle East Restaurant	Cambridge	(617) 492-9181
Near East Baking Co.	West Roxbury	(617) 327-0217
Near East Food Products, Inc.	Leominster	
Olympia Market	Worcester	
Peter Pan Superette	Arlington	(617) 648-9771
Picasso's Restaurants	Arlington	(617) 648-2800
Quincy Syrian Baking Co.	Quincy	
Sako's Mini-Mart	Boston	(617) 782-8920
Sassoon Market	Watertown	(617) 924-1560
Sevan Bakery	Watertown	(617) 924-9843
Smyrna Lowell Confectionary Co	Lowell	(617) 453-9573
Stella's Pizza & Subs	Watertown	(617) 924-5692
Steve-Vin Bake-A-Deli, Inc.	Watertown	(617) 924-3666
Super Hero's	Watertown	(617) 924-9507
Syrian Grocery Imp.Co.Inc.	Boston	(617) 426-1458
Tabrizi Bakery	Watertown	(617) 926-0880
Union Market Station Rest.	Watertown	(617) 923-0480
Vahe's Armenian Cuisine	Watertown	(617) 924-9463
Wing Wing Imported Groceries	Boston	

Michigan

Acropolis Market	Detroit	
Aleksan Narliyan Grocery	Detroit	
American Oriental Grocery	Southfield	(313) 352-5733
Arabic Town	Highland Park	
Aremia Imported Foods	Grand Blanc	
Athens Bakery & Grocery Co.	Detroit	
Byblos Middle Eastern Cuisine	Highland Park	(313) 867-0923
Byblos Middle Eastern Cuisine	West Bloomfield	(313) 932-3770
Cedar Market	Royal Oak	(313) 547-7856
Clover Leaf Market, Inc.	Southfield	(313) 357-0400
Del Mar & Co., Inc.	Detroit	(313) 961-5504
Gabriel Importing Co.	Detroit	(313) 961-2890
International Fine Foods	Detroit	
International Market Place	Dearborn	(313) 274-6100
International Market	Livonia	(313) 522-2220
L & H Superette	Detroit	
Majestic Market	Southfield	(313) 352-8556
Mourad Grocery	Highland Park	
New Parthenon Restaurant	Detroit	(313) 963-8888
Oasis Mart Importing Co.	Royal Oak	(313) 588-2210
Oasis Mart	Royal Oak	(313) 549-0001

140-Geographical Listing — Ethnic Cookbooks

Russo's Imported Foods	Grand Rapids	
Sam's Market	Huntington Woods	(313) 541-8990
Shatila Sweet Trays	Dearborn	(313) 582-1952
Stemma Confectionery	Detroit	
Stoukas Imports	Detroit	
Uptown Deli	Farmington Hills	(313) 626-3715
Virginia's Mid-East Cafe	Sylvan Lake	(313) 681-7170
Yassin Royal Bakery	Dearborn	(313) 945-1550

Minnesota

Ali Baba Bakery	Minneapolis	
Morgan's Grocery	St. Paul	
Pavo Co., Inc.	Minneapolis	(612) 533-4525

Mississippi

George A. Nassaur	Vicksburg	(601) 636-4443

Missouri

Campus Eastern Foods	Columbia	
Demmas Shish Kebob	St. Louis	
Heidi's Around the World Food	St. Louis	
Italo-American Importing	St. Louis	(314) 645-9781
Khayyam International Market	Saint Louis	(314) 727-8993
Lebanese-Syrian Bakery	St. Louis	

Nevada

Golden Steer Steak House	Las Vegas	(702) 384-4470
Habib Restaurant	Las Vegas	(702) 388-9119
Masis Grocery	Las Vegas	(702) 369-0090
Middle Eastern Bazar	Las Vegas	(702) 731-6030
Middle Eastern Market & Deli	Las Vegas	(702) 736-8887
Moroccan Restaurant	Las Vegas	(702) 736-7655
Shiraz Market	Reno	(702) 829-1177

New Hampshire

Demoulas Super Market, Inc.	Salem	(603) 898-5161
Joseph's Brothers Market	Manchester	(603) 623-0302
Liamos Market	Nashua	
O.K. Fairbank's Sugar Market	Keene	
Youngsville Super Market	Manchester	(603) 622-6353

New Jersey

Acropolis Delicatessen Store	Asbury Park	(201) 988-3030
Akhtamar Shish Kebab House	Cliffside Park	(201) 945-9850
Al-Khayam	N. Bergen	
Alex Restaurant	Cliffside Park	(201) 945-4121
Amir's Bakery	Paterson	(201) 345-5030
Andrew's Delicatessen	Asbury Park	
Armenian Royal Hotel	Asbury Park	(201) 775-3475
Cedar's Bakery	Teaneck	(201) 837-4330
Central Food Stores Inc.	Hackensack	
Chicken City	Ridgefield Park	(201) 941-1772
Ciel International, Inc.	S. Hackensack	(201) 807-9329
Crest Delicatessen Ltd.	East Orange	
Delphi Deli & Cheese Shop	Fort Lee	(201) 592-1697
Do Do Inc.	Union City	(201) 863-3350
Fattal's Syrian Bakery	Paterson	(201) 742-7125
G & A Grocery	Hazlet	(201) 264-0176
George's Middle East Market	Paterson	(201) 278-1771
Ginger Grocer	Montclair	(201) 744-1012
Greek Store Liberty Market	Kennilworth	(201) 272-2550
Hagop Shish Kebab	Cliffside Park	(201) 943-9817
International Food Mart	Leonia	(201) 947-4449
Joey Kay's Market	Paterson	(201) 523-9809
John's Delicatessen	Morristown	
John's Market	Elizabeth	
Kupelian Foods, Inc.	Ridgefield Park	(201) 440-8055
Mainly Cheese Inc.	Glen Rock	(201) 447-4141
Mandik's Pastry Shop	Union City	(201) 866-3827
Manigian Grocery		(201) 531-6810
Michael Nafash & Sons	Union City	
Middle East Lamejun	Fairview	(201) 941-5662
Mira International Foods, Inc.	Hoboken	(201) 963-8289
Molfetas Restaurants	South Hakensack	(201) 440-1771
Nafash & Sons	Union City	
Nouri's Syrian Bakery & Grocer	Paterson	
Olympia Food of all Nations	River Edge	(201) 261-3703
Pamir Cuisine of Afghanistan	Morristown	(201) 605-1095
Paterson Syrian Bakery	Paterson	(201) 279-2388
Sahadi Importing Co. Inc.	Moonachie	
Shireen's Gourmet, Inc.	Hackensack	(201) 488-4907
Shish Kebab at Blvd. Cafe	Fairview	(201) 945-8702
Shop and Save	Trenton	
Spiro's Market	Dover	(201) 361-0884
Tilda Marketing, Inc.	Englewood Cliff	(201) 569-0909
Tom's Ravioli Co.	Newark	
Toufayan Bakery	North Bergen	(201) 861-4131
Victor's Cheese Corp.	Palisades Park	(201) 947-3677
Village Deli	New Millford	(201) 261-3035
Village Super Market Inc.	South Orange	
Yaranush Middle Eastern Gourme	New Jersey	(914) 682-8449

New Mexico

Arthurs Fine Liquors	Albuquerque	
Cheese N Coffee	Albuquerque	(505) 883-1226
Hakeems's Bakery & Grocery	Albuquerque	(505) 881-4019
Middle Eastern Bakery	Albuquerque	(505) 255-2939
Towne House	Albuquerque	(505) 255-0057

New York

A-Z Food Market	Great Neck	(516) 829-3525
Adnan	New York	(718) 625-2115
Afghan Grocery	Flushing	(718) 461-7975
Afghan Kebab House # 1	New York	(212) 307-1612
Afghan Kebab House # 2	New York	(212) 517-2776
Afghan Village Restaurant	New York	(212) 979-6453
Akropolis Meat Market	New York	(212) 728-1760
Al-Amir Lebanese Cuisine	New York	(212) 737-1800
Alwan Pastry Shop	Brooklyn	
Amir Shish Kabob	New Hyde Park	(516) 326-1010
Ararat Armenian Restaurant	New York	(212) 752-2828
Ararat Bakery	Bayside	(718) 225-3478
Armen Foods	New York	(718) 729-3749
Astoria Superette	Astoria	(212) 728-8928
At Our Place	New York	(212) 864-1410
Atlas Oriental Pastry Shop	Buffalo	
Avegerinos	New York	(212) 688-8828
Bahar Market	Great Neck	(516) 466-2222

Ethnic Cookbooks

Geographical Listing-141

Balkan Armenian Restaurant	New York	(212) 689-7925
Balkan Bakery	New York	
Baruir's Oriental-American Gro	Sunnyside	(212) 784-0842
Basmati Rice of New York, Inc	Glendale	(718) 628-1082
Bazaar Market	Whitestone	(718) 762-4222
Bell-Bates Co.,Inc	New York	(212) 267-4300
Bennie's	New York	(212) 633-2044
Bistro-Metro Restaurant	Forest Hills	(718) 263-5444
Bobby Kebobby	New York	(212) 840-3700
Bobby Kebobby	Forest Hills	(718) 263-3700
Bourock	New York	(718) 624-9614
Byblo's Bakery, Inc.	Jackson Heights	(718) 779-6909
Byblos Restaurant	New York	(212) 687-0808
Caravan Restaurant	New York	(212) 262-2021
Cazablanca Restaurant	New York	(212) 599-0899
Cedars of Lebanon	New York	(212) 725-9251
Chez Momo	New York	(212) 979-8588
Choopan Kabab House	Flushing	(718) 886-0786
Colbeh Restaurant	Great Neck	(516) 466-8181
Connemara Food Mart	Latham	(518) 785-7555
Constantine's Delicatessen	Bayside	
Crystal Palace	New York	(718) 545-8402
Dairy Fair Delicatessen	Hempstead	
Damascus Bakery	Brooklyn	(718) 855-1456
Darband Restaurant	Great Neck	(516) 829-0030
Darvish	New York	(212) 475-1600
Ditmars & 35th St. Market	Astoria	
El-Manara	New York	(718) 745-2284
Ella Wendy	New York	(212) 686-2349
Elliniki Agora Market	New York	(212) 728-9122
Emir Grocery	Flushing	
Empire Coffee and Tea Co.	New York	(212) 564-1460
Estia	New York	(212) 628-9100
Falafel'N'Stuff	New York	(212) 879-7023
Fish Town	Brooklyn	
Fred Bridge and Co.	New York	
Freddie's Market	Niagara Falls	(716) 285-8344
Freeport Italian American Deli	Freeport	
Friendly Grocery Company	New York	(212) 923-2654
Fruits and Things	New York	
Galil Importing Corp.	Glendale	(718) 894-2030
Garden of Delights	New York	
George Malko	Brooklyn	
Good Earth Foods	New York	
Grecian Cave	New York	(718) 545-7373
Greek Village	New York	(212) 288-7378
H. Roth & Son	New York	
Hillside Lodge	Tannersville	(518) 589-5544
Hilton Pastry Shop	New York	(212) 274-6399
Hollywood Restaurant	Forest Hills	(718) 275-5200
House of Yemen	New York	(212) 532-3430
Hye Land Motel & Hotel	Tannersville	(518) 589-5700
Ibis	New York	(212) 753-3429
International Food Market	Roslyn Heights	(516) 625-5800
International Foods	Rochester	(716) 288-3686
International Grocery Store	New York	(212) 279-5514
Italian American Delicatessen	Freeport	
J & T Greek-Italian Deli	New York	(212) 545-7920
John's Fruit Market	New York	(718) 278-0705
Jonelle's Restaurants & Cater.	Flushing	(718) 699-0500
K & S Quality Meat	Jackson Heights	
K & T Meat Market	New York	(212) 728-3810
K.G. Apikoglu, Inc.	New York	(212) 730-2500
Kababi-e-Nader	New York	(212) 683-4833
Kabul Afghani Cuisine	Huntington	(516) 549-5506
Kabul Kabab House	Flushing	(718) 461-1919
Kadouri Import Corp.	New York	(212) 677-5441
Kalamata Food Imports, Inc.	New York	(718) 626-1250
Kanani's Omar Khayyam Rest.	New York	(212) 879-5353
Kassos Brothers	New York	(212) 932-5479
Kehayan Importing Co.	New York	
Kharobar Market	New York	(212) 714-9666
Khyber Pass	New York	(212) 473-0989
King Falafel	New York	(718) 745-4188
Kiryakos Grocery	New York	(718) 545-3931
Kismet Oriental Pastries Co.	Astoria	
Kizmet Fancy Grocery	Hempstead	
Krinos Foods, Inc.	Long Island City	(718) 729-9000
La Boheme Greenwich Village	New York	(212) 473-6447
Le Gourmet Caterers	New York	(718) 778-6666
Le Petit Gourmet	Douglaston	(718) 224-9665
Lefferts Kosher Meat	Kew Gardens	(718) 441-6887
Lucky Boy Market	New York	
Max's Market	New York	
Mediterranean Gourmet	Williston Park	(516) 741-3664
Microcosmos	New York	(718) 728-7093
Molfetas	New York	(212) 840-9537
Moroccan Star	New York	(718) 643-0800
Nablus Grocery	Yonkers	
Nader Grocery	New York	(212) 686-5793
Nader International Foods	New York	(212) 889-1752
Nader International	New York	(212) 481-3117
Nagilah Market	Forest Hills	(718) 268-2626
Nazarian's Courtyard	Watervliet	(518) 273-1104
Nea Hellas	New York	(718) 278-7304
Near East Bakery	New York	(718) 875-0016
Near East Importing Co. Inc.	Glendale	(212) 894-3600
New York Restaurant	Astoria	(718) 726-3254
Orient Export Trading Co.	New York	(212) 685-3451
Oriental Pastry & Grocery	Brooklyn	(718) 875-7687
Pamir Cuisine of Afghanistan	New York	(212) 734-3791
Paparian's Food Market	Albany	
Periyali	New York	(212) 463-7890
Petrossian Restaurant	New York	(212) 245-2214
Plaka	New York	(212) 674-9709
Pondfield Produce Market	Yonkers	(914) 961-9566
Poseidon Greek Bakery	New York	(212) 757-6173
Pyramid Bakery	New York	(718) 392-2702
R. H. Macy & Co.	Herald Square	(212) 695-4400
Roma Importing Co.	Latham	(518) 785-7480
S & D Caterers	Hewlett	(516) 374-6300
Sahadl Importing Co., Co.	Brooklyn	(718) 624-4550
Salimi Grocery	Forest Hills	(718) 793-2984
Sally's Place	Brooklyn	(718) 680-4615
Samira's	New York	(718) 745-2416
Sarkis Aprozar Grocery	New York	(212) 937-4682
Sevan Restaurant	New York	(212) 545-9538
Shammas Oriental Domestic Food	New York	(212) 855-2455
Shish Kabob Palace	Great Neck	(516) 487-2228
Shish Kebab Restaurant	Port Washington	(516) 883-9309
Sibo, Abu-Salim Restaurant	New York	(212) 686-2031
Smiling Fruit	New York	(212) 932-8006
Squire	Great Neck	(516) 487-4032
Stani	New York	(718) 728-4966
Sultan's Delight, Inc.	Staten Island	(718) 720-1557
Sunflower Grocery	Rego Park	(718) 275-0479
Supreme International Foods	Forest Hills	(718) 897-4700
Sweety's Cafe	Great Neck	(516) 466-6260
Tak Grocery Store	Centereach	(516) 737-6244
Tarabya	Great Neck	(516) 482-0760

142-Geographical Listing

Ethnic Cookbooks

Taverna Vraka	New York	(718) 721-3007
Taverna	Roslyn	(516) 484-8860
Temple Torah	Little Neck	(718) 423-2100
Thanos Imported Groceries	Syracuse	
Tripoli	New York	(718) 596-5800
United Supermarket	New York	
Wheatly Bake Shop	Greenvale	(516) 621-7575
Yaldzlar Restaurant	New York	(212) 557-0055
Yekta Deli & Grocery	Elmhurst	(718) 335-6828
Yemeni Cafe	New York	(718) 834-9533
Yerevan Bakery, Inc.	New York	(718) 729-5400
Yes International Food Co.	New York	(212) 227-4695
Z	New York	(212) 254-0960
Zabar's	New York	(212) 787-2000
Zygos Taverna	New York	(718) 728-7070

North Carolina

East Trade Company	Charlotte	
Galanides-Raleigh Inc.	Raleigh	
James Heonis Co.	Raleigh	
Nur, Inc.	Raleigh	
University Pantry Deli	Charlotte	(704) 549-9156

Ohio

Aladdin's Middle East Bakery	Cleveland	(216) 861-0317
Antonio Sofo & Son Import. Co.	Toledo	
Athens Greek & Italian Deli	Dayton	
Athens Imported Foods & Wines	Cleveland	(216) 861-8149
Bruno Foods	Cincinnati	
Cake Castle	Cleveland	(216) 381-5782
Canton Importing Co.	Canton	
Consumer's Market	Youngstown	
Country Manor	N. Canton	(216) 499-0070
Ellis Bakery	Akron	
Genoosi's Imported Foods	Columbus	
Gourmet Affair	Cleveland	(216) 397-1414
Harry's Deli	Cleveland Heights	
Lebanese Delicatessen	Dayton	
Metropolitan Coffee Co.	Akron	
Middle East Foods	Cleveland	
Nettuno Italian Delicacies	Cincinnati	
O'Neil's Department Store Food	Akron	
Shiekh Grocery Co.	Cleveland	
Shoppers Meat Market	Cleveland	(216) 442-8440
Si's BiRite Quality Meats	Strongsville	(216) 238-8660
Sinbad Food Imports	Columbus	
Syria-Lebanon Baking Co.	Cleveland	
University Market	Akron	

Oklahoma

Mediterranean Imports	Oklahoma City	
Nick's Importing Co.	Oklahoma City	
Polsano's Deli & Gourmet Food	Oklahoma City	
Royal Coffee & Tea Co.	Oklahoma City	(405) 848-2002

Oregon

Downtown Delicatessen	Portland	
International Food Bazar	Portland	(503) 228-1960
Pieri's Delicacies Inc	Portland	
Rose International Foods	Beaverton	(503) 646-7673

Wisconsin

Ben Disalvo & Sons,	Madison	
George's Food Market	S. Milwaukee	(414) 762-1232
Greek Pastries by Despine's	Milwaukee	
Olympia Grocery	Milwaukee	
Pars Market	Milwaukee	(414) 278-7175
Topping and Co.	Milwaukee	(414) 383-8911

Pennsylvania

Adelphia Delicatessen	Wilkes-Barre	
Armenian Delight	Broomall	(215) 353-1981
Armenian Pizza	Philadelphia	
Bitar's	Philadelphia	
Calamata Groceries	Wilkes Barre	(717) 823-7761
Capitol Italian Grocery	Harrisburg	
Erivan Dairy	Oreland	
European Grocery Store	Pittsburgh	
International Mini Market	Philadelphia	
Jack's Cold Cuts	Cornwells	(215) 639-2346
Makhoul Corner Store	Allentown	
Mary's Greek Grocery	Philadelphia	(215) 722-2845
Mediterranean Kitchen	Bensalem	(215) 245-5278
Middle East Bakery	Wilkes-Barre	
Pittsburgh Grocery Store	Pittsburgh	
Salim's Middle Eastern Food	Pittsburgh	
Sherwood Grocery	Upper Derby	
Shtoura Quality	Allentown	(215) 435-9103
Simon X. Mandros	Lancaster	
Stamoolis Brotheres Co.	Pittsburgh	
Sun-Ni Armenian String Cheese	Upper Darby	(215) 853-3449

Rhode Island

Agaty's Groceries	Pawtucket	(401) 728-1660
Anthony Lazieh	Central Falls	
Cardoos Int. Food Corp.	Providence	(401) 272-9373
Carvel Ice Cream Store	Providence	(401) 272-7412
Delicacies, Inc.	Cranston	(401) 461-4774
Henry's Delicatessen Inc.	Cranston	
Hi "Hye" Market	Pawtucket	(401) 728-1596
K. Barishian	Providence	
Maria's Pizza Restaurants	Cranston	(401) 785-1150
Near East Market	Providence	
Near East Market	Cranston	(401) 941-9763
Spiro's House of Pizza	Providence	(401) 273-7755
Tony's Market	Providence	(401) 421-4700
Virginia & Spanish Peanut Co.	Providence	(401) 421-2543

South Carolina

Caras Greek Product Co.	Columbia	
Michell's Grocery	Florence	
Piggly Wiggly	Charlestown	

Tennessee

Barzizza Brothers, Inc.	Memphis	(901) 744-0054
Cheese Market, the	Knoxville	(615) 525-3352
International Food Mart	Nashville	(615) 333-9651

Ethnic Cookbooks

Geographical Listing-143

International Gift Corner	Memphis	

Texas

Al Hilal Halal Meat Shop	Houston	(713) 988-4330
American Pita Corporation	Houston	(713) 776-3976
Andre' Market	Richardson	(214) 644-7644
Antone's Import Co.	Houston	(713) 526-1046
Aziz Import Co.	Dallas	(214) 369-6982
Bazar	Dallas	(214) 702-9505
Bread & Pizz	Houston	(713) 783-9898
Capello's Import. & American	Dallas	
Chandelier Restaurant	Houston	(713) 785-5855
Darband Kabobi	Houston	(713) 975-8350
Ddroubi's Bakery & Imports	Houston	(713) 988-5897
Droubi's Bakery & Grocery	Houston	(713) 782-6160
Droubi's Bakery & Grocery	Houston	(713) 790-0101
Droubi's Bakery & Grocery	Houston	(713) 988-5897
European Importing Co.	Houston	
Garson Restaurant	Houston	(713) 781-0400
Import Liquor & Food Stores	Houston	
Iran Market	Houston	(713) 789-5943
Jerusalem Bakery & Grocery	Irving	(214) 257-0447
Jordan Halal Meat	Houston	(713) 785-4455
Kandes Liquor & Imports	Victoria	
L. Paletta's	San Antonio	
Mediterranean Coffee	Houston	(713) 827-7799
Mustang Cafe	Dallas	(214) 306-4888
Oriental Import-Export Co.	Houston	
Paletta's Imported Foods	San Antonio	(512) 828-0678
Phoenicia Bakery & Deli	Austin	(512) 447-4444
Phoenicia Imports & Deli	Houston	(713) 558-0416
Purity Importing Co.	Dallas	
Rana Food Store	Arlington	
Salt & Peper (Felfel Namakie)	Houston	(713) 783-9996
Shoumine Restaurant	Houston	(713) 266-6677
Super Sahel	Houston	(713) 266-7360
Super Vanak International Food	Houston	(713) 952-7676
Worldwide Foods	Dallas	(214) 824-8860

West Virginia

Haddy's Food Market	Charleston	
Haddy's Prime Meats	Charleston	
R. A. Medonic	Wheeling	

Utah

Lingos Grocery	Salt Lake City	
Maxim's Nutricare, Inc.	Salt Lake City	(801) 262-6767

Virginia

A La Mode Ice Cream & Pastry	Springfield	(703) 455-1055
Afghan Bakery	Falls Church	(703) 241-7855
Afghan Market	Alexandria	(703) 212-9529
Al Nakheel	Vienna	
Aphrodite Greek Imports	Falls Church	(703) 931-5055
Apollo Greek Imports	Arlington	
Asia Center & Grocery	Falls Church	(703) 533-2112
Assal Market I	Vienna	(703) 281-2248
Assal Market II	Falls Church	(703) 578-3232
Atilla's Restaurant	Arlington	(703) 920-4900
Baba Kabob	Falls Church	
Bahar Restaurant	Vienna	(703) 242-2427
Bakery Afghan	Falls Church	(703) 241-7855
Bamiyan Restaurant	Alexandria	(703) 548-9006
Black Orchid Restaurant	Annandale	(703) 941-4400
Bread & Kabob	Falls Church	(703) 845-2900
Cafe Rose	Falls Church	(703) 532-1700
Casa d'Mama	Annandale	(703) 256-3780
Casablanca	Alexandria	(703) 549-6464
Club Cafe	Falls Church	(703) 476-8737
Culmore Restaurant	Falls Church	(703) 820-7171
Daily Bread Bakery	Arlington	(703) 920-2525
Excel Market	Norfolk	
Five Stars Corp. Market	Falls Church	(703) 256-6000
Food Factory	Arlington	
Galanides, Inc.	Norfolk	
Gira Market Int. Grocery	Alexandria	(703) 370-3632
Gourmet Basket	McLean	
Gourmet International Market	Herndon	(703) 478-6393
Greek American Importing Co.	Richmond	
Hakim Afghan Restaurant	Alexandria	
Halal Meat Market	Alexandria	
Halalco	Falls Church	
Islam Grocery International	Arlington	
Jerusalem Restaurant	Falls Church	(703) 845-1622
Kabul Caravan	Arlington	(703) 522-8394
Kazan Restaurant	McLean	(703) 734-1960
Kebob House	Crystal City	
Khatib Butcher Shop	Falls Church	(703) 845-9388
Khyber Halal Market	Arlington	(703) 525-8323
King of Pita Bakery, Inc.	Alexandria	(703) 941-8999
Lebanese Butcher	Falls Church	(703) 533-2903
Lebanese Taverna Restaurant	Arlington	
Maria's Greek Corner	Vienna	
Mediterranean Bakery	Alexandria	(703) 751-1702
Mediterranean Bakery	Richmond	(804) 285-1488
Mediterranean Deli	Arlington	
Mediterranean Store	Arlington	(703) 527-0423
Mount of Olives Market	Falls Church	(703) 379-1156
Moustache Cafe	Tysons Corner	(703) 893-1100
New York Cafe	Falls Church	
New Yorker Delicatessen	Roanoke	
Nick's Produce	Richmond	(804) 644-0683
Nizam's	W. Vienna	
Norooz Grocery & Deli	Springfield	(703) 866-4444
Olive Paradis Restaurant	Falls Church	(703) 534-4433
Pop's Restaurant and Grocery	Vienna	
Samadi Sweets Cafe	Falls Church	(703) 578-0606
Shari Ghul-Ghula	Alexandria	
Sky Line Butcher Shop	Falls Church	
Steak in a Sack	Falls Church	
Super Doyar	Springfield	(703) 866-0222
Susan's Catering		(703) 369-1413
Tavous Restaurant	Annandale	(703) 941-1451
Topkapi Restaurant	Fairfax	
Tu-Tu Halal Meat Market	Falls Church	(703) 998-5322

Washington

Continental Pastry Shop	Seattle	
Delaurenti's Italian Market	Seattle	
Gino's World Food Mart	Spokane	
Pars Market	Bellevue	(206) 641-5265
Rooz Supermarket & Deli	Seattle	(206) 363-8639

Ethnic Cookbooks

Order Form

8 1/2 X 11, 144 pages, perfect binding, $ 29.95. 1992.

3rd Edition   ISBN: 0-931539-06-4

A key reference tool for Middle Eastern & Greek food industry

Please send me _____ copy(ies) of **Ethnic Cookbooks and Food Marketplace**
Second edition @ 29.95 per copy, plus $2.00 per copy for shipping. (California residents please add $2.48 for sales tax.

Enclosed is my check or money order for $ _____ (U.S. currency).

Name: _____

Business Name: _____

Address: _____

City: _____ State: _____ Zip: _____

Telephone: _____ Telephone : _____

____ I am also interested in **Mailing list of Food Marketplace** on pressure sensitive labels, @ $295.00. (Over 2000 businesses).

Please clip and mail with check or money order to:

Armenian Reference Books Co.
P.O. Box 231
Glendale, CA 91209   (818) 504-2550

If you need complete mailing list of Middle Eastern Food Marketplace in the U.S.A. & Canada, or cookbooks in English language, just call (818) 504-2550 for more information.